A MOMENT OF GRACE

A MOMENT OF GRACE

John Cardinal O'Connor

on the

Catechism of the Catholic Church

IGNATIUS PRESS   SAN FRANCISCO

Cover by Riz Boncan Marcella

© 1995 Ignatius Press, San Francisco
ISBN 0–89870–554–1
Library of Congress catalogue number 95–76621
Printed in the United States of America

CONTENTS

PREFACE

As will be obvious to any reader, I suspect, the catechetical homilies presented here were recorded at the time of delivery each Sunday, then transcribed. They were not written in advance and read from the pulpit. They were preached, all of them, in St. Patrick's Cathedral during the course of my Sunday Masses.

The style, therefore, is informal, except where I quote directly from the text of the *Catechism*. Since no official version existed in English when I began preaching the series, I had to translate from the French, Spanish, or Italian texts in print. Hence, my translations do not pretend to be authoritative.

Otherwise, and particularly after the official English text appeared, I tried to be faithful to the precise wording for the most part, but I admit to taking a preacher's liberty when ordinary language seemed more readily understandable to listeners than the exact wording of the text might have been. I do not believe I have been guilty of any substantive errors.

—J. O'C.

I

"Now Is a Moment of Grace"

FIRST SUNDAY OF ADVENT
NOVEMBER 28, 1993

On this First Sunday of Advent, the beginning of a New Year for the Church, I am launching a series of homilies on the new *Catechism of the Catholic Church*. Every Sunday for one full year, with the exception of summer months, I will read to you and comment on selected passages from the *Catechism*, from the beginning of the book until the end. The *Catechism* is approximately six hundred pages, but don't be alarmed. The passages I select will add up to approximately one hundred fifty pages, or one-fourth of the original, and I will spread them over the course of forty-one Sundays, which means only a few pages each Sunday.

However, I cannot neglect the Sacred Scriptures read in the Mass each Sunday. So I will be trying to mesh paragraphs of the *Catechism* with readings from the Sacred Scriptures, hoping that I don't confuse both in the bargain.

Before I begin reading selected passages, I want to tell you of something that happened to me the other day. I went to confession to a wonderful elderly priest, older even than I am. This is what he said to me—I wrote it down when I got home:

> Now is a moment of grace. Something big is about to happen; something very big. And it's going to happen to *you*. We are about to begin Advent. God has become incarnate in the human condition, for *you*, personally for *you*. God has become a little baby right in the middle of the sins you have just told me about. You have reason for new and wonderful hope.

I'll tell you, I left that confessional feeling highly excited over the coming of Advent—a very personal excitement over the fact that Christ came to us almost two thousand years ago as one of us, and that He is still coming, each day, in each Mass, and in a thousand different ways. And that He *would* have come if I—if you—were the only person in the world.

I had already read the Sacred Scriptures for today, in preparation for this homily, and I began thinking about them again as I left the confessional.

Isaiah, the great prophet some seven hundred years and more before

Christ, and those who followed in his footsteps, prophesying in his name, gave us today's first reading (Is 63:16–17, 19; 64:2–7). It's essentially the story of the Israelites awaiting the return of the Lord, Who seemed to have abandoned them to their own sins. In other words, it's an Advent prayer, pleading for the Advent, the arrival of the Messiah and Redeemer.

But most touching, perhaps, is the humble submission of the words: "Yet, O Lord, you are our father; we are the clay and you are the potter: we are all the work of your hands."

The Responsorial Psalm furthers the Advent theme: "Rouse your power and come to save us" (Ps 80:2–3, 15–16, 18–19). St. Paul, then, in his letter to the Corinthians, prays that the Messiah, the Lord Jesus, will strengthen us and prepare us for the day of *His* final Advent as our Judge (1 Cor 1:3–9).

The Gospel lovingly warns us that this final Advent can come for any one of us at any moment and pleads with us to be ready for judgment (Mk 13:33–37).

As I pondered all this, I thought of a homily given by our Holy Father, Pope John Paul II, on the first Sunday of Advent in 1992. He said: "I truly hope that Advent, a time of waiting, listening, and hoping, will be a favorable time for all believers to strengthen their faith and confirm their commitment to give a consistent witness of their Christian life." Then he went on to say: "In this context of spiritual renewal we can also see the publication of the new *Catechism of the Catholic Church*" (John Paul II, Nov. 29, 1992, Rome).

I believe the same: that Advent is the perfect season to begin a series of presentations of the teachings of the new *Catechism*. The completion of the *Catechism* is itself an advent. It's the arrival in modern form, to meet the complex needs of our day, of this extraordinary synthesis of our age-old faith, stretching back to the dawn of time. From the call of Abraham to the call of John the Baptist the whole world awaited the Advent of the Messiah. From the prophecy of Isaiah read to us today, asking God to save us from our own sins, to the words of Christ of the Gospel, sent by God precisely for that purpose, it is clear that we are a pilgrim people en route to our final Advent, our ultimate destiny.

The *Catechism of the Catholic Church* is given us to help light the way of our pilgrimage, to illuminate the path to eternal happiness. As my father-confessor said, "Something big is about to happen; something very big. This is, indeed, a moment of grace."

Let us turn now to Pope John Paul II's introduction to the *Catechism*, then to the Prologue.

In the introduction, our Holy Father tells us how the *Catechism* came into being and where he hopes it will lead us. This introduction, called an

Apostolic Constitution, is entitled *The Deposit of Faith* (*Fidei Depositum*) and begins:

> Guarding the deposit of faith is the mission which the Lord has entrusted to his Church and which she fulfills in every age. [The Lord has entrusted this mission to His Church, and all the Church must try to teach what the *Lord* has entrusted to us, not something we make up ourselves.] The Second Vatican Ecumenical Council . . . had as its intention and purpose to highlight the Church's apostolic and pastoral mission, and by making the truth of the Gospel shine forth, to lead all people to seek and receive Christ's love, which surpasses all knowledge (cf. Eph 3:19).

You will recall that the Second Vatican Council began in 1962 and concluded in 1965. There were almost three thousand bishops from all over the world in Rome participating in the Council. There were observers, theologians, catechists, and others, both Protestant and Catholic.

> The principal task entrusted to the Council by Pope John XXIII was to guard and present better the precious deposit of Christian doctrine in order to make it more accessible to the Christian faithful and to all people of good will. [The Council was saying that the Church has nothing to hide. "Open the windows and let the fresh air in! Let everyone see what we do and hear what we have to say."] For this reason the Council was not first of all to condemn the errors of time, but above all to strive calmly to show the strength and beauty of the doctrine of the faith. . . .

This is important. This *Catechism*, despite advance criticism by those who haven't yet seen it, is not a list of condemnations. This *Catechism* is to "strive calmly to show the strength and beauty of the doctrine of the faith". Having gone through the *Catechism* from cover to cover I can tell you it is serene reading. Our Holy Father continues:

> In this spirit, on January 25, 1985, I convoked an Extraordinary Assembly of the Synod of Bishops for the twentieth anniversary of the close of the Council. . . .
> On that occasion the Synod Fathers stated: "Very many have expressed the desire that a catechism or compendium of all Catholic doctrine regarding both faith and morals be composed. . . . The presentation of doctrine must be biblical and liturgical. It must be sound doctrine suited to the present life of Christians."

The Pope then goes on in his introduction to say that the bishops of the world recognized that not because of the Second Vatican Council but because of *misinterpretations* of the Second Vatican Council, because people failed to read and study the documents of the Council, there was a great deal of confusion. The teaching of the faith was so badly twisted and distorted in so many instances that the bishops of the world asked, "Can we have another look at the Second Vatican Council and everything that the Church has taught from the beginning synthesized in one new book—old teaching freshly worded in one document so we can end the confusion?"

Our Holy Father says:

> For this reason we thank the Lord wholeheartedly on this day when we can offer the entire Church this "reference text" entitled the *Catechism of the Catholic Church*, for a catechesis renewed at the living sources of the faith! . . .
>
> The *Catechism of the Catholic Church* is the result of very extensive collaboration: it was prepared over six years of intense work done in a spirit of complete openness and fervent zeal. . . .
>
> The project was the object of extensive consultation among all Catholic Bishops, their Episcopal Conferences or Synods, and of theological and catechetical institutes. . . .

In addition to bishops, many people all over the world were consulted. Laypersons who teach Christian doctrine were consulted, for example. There was *huge* collaboration. Our Holy Father tells us:

> A catechism should faithfully and systematically present the teaching of Sacred Scripture, the living Tradition of the Church and the authentic Magisterium, as well as the spiritual heritage of the Fathers and the Church's saints, to allow for a better knowledge of the Christian mystery and for enlivening the faith of the People of God. It should take into account the doctrinal statements which down the centuries the Holy Spirit has intimated to his Church. It should also help illumine with the light of faith the new situations and problems which had not yet emerged in the past.

The Pope is calling for a complete expression of the Church's doctrine and spiritual heritage, including, for example, the wisdom of St. Augustine and St. Thérèse, the Little Flower, among many others. This is what is meant by the "deposit of Faith"—the Scriptures, the tradition, all the councils, the teachings of the popes and the bishops, the teachings of the saints. All of this is the deposit of Faith handed on to us. And so, as Pope John Paul II reminds us,

> The *Catechism* will thus contain the new and the old (cf. Mt. 12:52), because the faith is always the same yet the source of ever new light. . . .

Thus St. Augustine speaks of "beauty—ever ancient, ever new". G. K. Chesterton said, "The wonderful thing about our Catholic Faith is not simply that it is nineteen hundred years old, but that it is nineteen hundred years *new*!"

The Apostolic Constitution continues:

In reading the *Catechism of the Catholic Church* we can perceive the wondrous unity of the mystery of God, his saving will, as well as the central place of Jesus Christ, the only-begotten Son of God, sent by the Father, made man in the womb of the Blessed Virgin Mary by the power of the Holy Spirit, to be our Savior. Having died and risen, Christ is always present in his Church, especially in the sacraments; he is the source of our faith, the model of Christian conduct and the Teacher of our prayer.

This is so important. Christ is *always* present. He will be here present in this Mass and is present in each one of us. We are temples of the Holy Spirit. Our Divine Lord said to His Apostles, "Don't worry. I will be with you all days, even to the end of the world" (Mt 28:19–20).

Finally, the Pope says in his introduction:

The *Catechism of the Catholic Church* . . . is a statement of the Church's faith and of Catholic doctrine, attested to or illumined by Sacred Scripture, Apostolic Tradition and the Church's Magisterium. *I declare it to be a valid and legitimate instrument for ecclesial communion and a sure norm for teaching the faith* . . . [emphasis added].

. . . The *Catechism of the Catholic Church*, lastly, is offered to every individual who asks us to give an account of the hope that is in us (cf. 1 Pet 3:15) and who wants to know what the Catholic Church believes. . . .

How different from what I heard on television out in Denver, when our Holy Father was there in August of 1993. Some commentator was saying, "I listen to this Pope and he gives us what he calls the Catholic Church, but I'm a Catholic and that's not what I believe." The Pope tells us the *Catechism* is a "valid and legitimate instrument" for teaching the teachings of the Catholic Church.

Let us turn now to the Prologue of the *Catechism*. The Prologue begins with a section entitled "To Live Is to Know and Love God". It's as simple as that—to live is to know and love God. If we don't know and love God we are not really alive, we are not fully human persons. The Prologue continues:

Infinitely perfect and happy in himself, God, in a plan of pure goodness, has freely created man to share in his happy life. That is why, at all times and in every place, he is close by man. He calls us and helps us seek him, know him and love him with all our own strength. [That's the purpose of the *Catechism*: that we will seek God, come to know Him better, and serve Him and love Him with all our strength.]

   Christ sent forth his chosen apostles, commanding them to proclaim the gospel: "Go therefore and make disciples of all nations, baptizing them in the name of the Father and of the Son and of the Holy Spirit, and teaching them to obey everything that I have commanded you. And remember, I am with you all days, to the end of the world" [Mt 28:19–20]. Strengthened by this mission, the apostles "went out and proclaimed the good news everywhere, while the Lord worked with them and confirmed the message by the signs that accompanied it" [Mk 10:20].

This treasure received by the apostles and guarded faithfully by them and their successors, all the faithful of Christ are called upon to transmit from generation to generation by professing the faith, living it in fraternal communion and celebrating it in liturgy and prayer.

Very early, the name catechesis was given to the whole of the Church's effort to make disciples, to help people believe that Jesus is the Son of God, so that believing they might have life in his name, and to educate and instruct them in this life, and so build up the Body of Christ.

We are called not simply to keep the Faith, but to *spread* the Faith.

The next caption in the Prologue is "The Aim and Intended Audience of the *Catechism*".

This *Catechism* aims at presenting an organic exposition and synthesis of the foundations and essential content of Catholic doctrine, as regards both faith and morals, in light of the Second Vatican Council and the whole of the Church's Tradition. Its principal sources are the sacred Scriptures, the Fathers of the Church, the Liturgy, and the Church's Magisterium.

An "organic . . . synthesis" means that you can't just pick pieces of it and use those that you might like. You must take it in its *totality*. It is like the elements of a body. If you pull pieces off, you do not have a whole body. And none of the pieces individually is a body.

How is the *Catechism* structured? Although it is only one volume, it is in four parts.

The plan of this *Catechism* is inspired by the great tradition of catechisms which are built on four pillars: the baptismal profession of faith (the creed), the sacraments of the faith, the life of faith (the commandments), and the prayer of believers (the Lord's Prayer).

Book One is called "The Profession of Faith". It says:

Those who belong to Christ through faith and baptism must confess their baptismal faith before others.

You cannot just keep it inside. That's what martyrdom was all about. If you were willing to give up your faith or deny your faith you would not be put to death. That is what many things are all about. It is easy to get along in this world if your faith is a very, very private thing. To live it publicly—that's very different.

The first book presents the revelation by which God first addresses and gives himself to man; it then explains the faith by which man responds to God. [This is a kind of simple definition of religion: to bring God to human beings and human beings to God.] The profession of faith recalls the gifts given to man by God as the Author of all that is good . . . and confesses our baptismal faith in the one God: the almighty *Father*, the Creator, his *Son* Jesus Christ, our Lord and Savior; and the *Holy Spirit*, the Sanctifier, in the holy Church. [In other words, the Sign of the Cross: "In the name of the Father, and of the Son, and of the Holy Spirit." That's what this teaches us.]

The second book is called "The Celebration of the Christian Mystery".

The catechism's second book explains how God's salvation, accomplished once for all through Christ Jesus in the Holy Spirit, is made present in the sacred actions of the Church's liturgy, especially in the seven sacraments. [The *Catechism* goes on to explain each of these sacraments.]

The third book ["Life of Faith"] discusses the ultimate goal of the human race created in God's image—happiness . . . [The *Catechism* is talking about happiness now and eternal happiness. We do everything that we think will make us happy. Even if we make sacrifices for others we feel there is some self-fulfillment in this. But there is a right way to try to achieve happiness and a wrong way. The *Catechism* spells it out for us, talking about happiness] and the ways of reaching it: through right conduct freely chosen with the help of God's law and grace, and through a life that fulfills Christ's twofold commandment of love already outlined in God's Ten Commandments. [In other words, love God with your whole heart and love your neighbor as yourself.]

The Prologue continues by describing book four on "Christian Prayer".

The last book treats the meaning and importance of prayer in the life of believers. It concludes with a brief commentary on the Lord's Prayer, whose seven petitions sum up the blessings for which we ought to hope, blessings our heavenly Father wants to give.

This is the shortest of the four books. I think it is one of the best. It takes us right into the heart of communication with God. It quotes, for example, the Little Flower and her famous "prayer is conversation with God" in which we listen and we talk. It's a very beautiful book.

Finally, the Prologue reminds us of our diversity, our uniqueness. Everybody is different. Everyone has a different educational background. Some speak different languages. The *Catechism* reminds us of this. It says:

Teachers must not imagine that a single kind of soul has been entrusted to them, and that consequently it is lawful to teach and form equally all the faithful in true piety with one and the same method! Let them realize that some are in Jesus Christ as new-born children [That's not an insult; it is certainly the case], others as adolescents and still others as adults in full command of their powers. Those who are called to the ministry of preaching must suit their words to the maturity and understanding of their hearers, as they hand on the teaching of the mysteries of faith and the rules of moral conduct.

The Prologue, which is part of the *Catechism* itself, concludes with this beautiful, absolutely indispensable passage. It gives us a new orientation and a reason for spiritual renewal. It says:

> To conclude this Prologue, it is fitting to recall this pastoral principle stated by the *Roman Catechism*:
> The whole aim of doctrine and teaching must be put in the context of the love that never ends. No matter how clearly we may explain what we must believe, hope or do, we must first and always make the love of our Lord so apparent that all may understand that every act of perfectly Christian virtue has no other origin and no other end than love.

In the first three centuries of the Church there were huge numbers of converts to the Catholic Faith, and one of the primary reasons for this was said to be that the pagans looked at the Christians and were astonished. They said, "Look how these Christians love one another!" The whole *Catechism* begins and ends in love.

2

The Key to the Universe

SECOND SUNDAY OF ADVENT
DECEMBER 5, 1993
PONTIFICAL MASS

Today we begin the first book of the *Catechism*, called "The Profession of Faith". This book takes the Creed and every article of the Faith and explains them in detail. The purpose of the *Catechism*, remember, is not to prove things; it is simply to tell us what the Church teaches, to give us a clear summary of what we call the "Deposit of Faith". Before actually going through the Articles of Faith, the *Catechism* prepares us with kind of a preamble. We will begin with this preamble today.

St. Ambrose, teacher of the famous St. Augustine, called faith "the firm foundation of all the virtues". We can't talk about Catholicism without talking about faith. But faith can't be merely lifeless and academic, nor does it mean anything without love. St. Ignatius of Antioch, a saint of the second century who died around the year 100, let himself be torn to pieces by the jaws of lions in the Roman arena rather than reject his faith. St. Ignatius said: ". . . faith is the beginning and the end is love, and God is the two of them brought into unity. After these comes whatever else makes up a Christian . . ." (Letter to Ephesians, 14). Or, as Cardinal Newman put it: "No one is a martyr for a conclusion, no one is a martyr for an opinion; it is faith that makes us martyrs" (Discourses to Mixed Congregations). Thomas Merton put it well in *Seeds of Contemplation*: "Ultimately faith is the only key to the universe. The final meaning of human existence, and the answers to the questions on which all our happiness depends, cannot be found in any other way." Faith is the key.

Let us now turn to the *Catechism*.

In the very first book, "The Profession of Faith", the *Catechism* raises a basic question, a question absolutely crucial if we are going to discern the meaning of life itself. It asks, What does it mean to believe? What is life's ultimate meaning? What does your life mean, what does mine mean? Are we, in fact, only specks in the universe, whirling about meaninglessly, not really going anywhere, doomed to die forever or to go on whirling about in some other form? Is this our destiny? If so, then why are we not all perfectly content? Why the restlessness within us? What is there about us that searches for "meaning" beyond everyday events? How do we differ, or *do* we differ, from the beasts of the field, birds of the air, fish in the waters, even from the plant life around us?

The *Catechism* answers these questions in speaking of man's "capacity" for God.

> The desire for God is written in the human heart, for man was created by God and for God who never ceases to draw us to himself. Only in God can we find the truth and happiness we constantly seek [27].

This capacity for God is deep within us. We are *made* that way. Nothing, no one, can completely fulfill us except God Himself. Only in total communion with God do we really find ourselves. St. Augustine, after searching among the intellectuals of the world of his day and indulging his passions, particularly for women, took himself a mistress and had a son out of wedlock. Finally, still unfulfilled, he gave up. What did he say? "My heart was made for you, O Lord, and it will not rest until it rests in You." St. Paul tells us, "In Him we live and move and have our being" (Acts 17:27–28).

The *Catechism* points out that all peoples of the earth, everywhere, through all ages, have had this desire deep within to try to find God, whatever they call God, however they represented God. There was always this inner restlessness. This is so much the case that we can rightly say that to be a *human* being is to be a *religious* being by nature. Obviously, this does not mean that everyone *is* religious in belief and practice. The *Catechism* recognizes this fact of life, but nonetheless points out:

> Although man can forget or reject God, God himself does not cease to call *everyone* to seek him, in order to live and find happiness. But this search requires of man the full effort of his intellect, a rectitude of will, "an upright heart," and finally the witness of others who teach us to seek God [30].

The search is one thing. How do we actually come to know and to love God, the *Catechism* asks, the God in whose image we are made? Apart from divine revelation, which we will explore in just a few minutes, how naturally can we look for God? The answer we get is that we can find God by way of the material world around us and its laws, and we can find Him within our own hearts, within the nature of human beings.

St. Thomas spoke of the five ways to prove the existence of God, and the *Catechism* includes these. There can be no effect that has not been caused; nothing can move that has not been moved by another; there can be no order in the universe unless there is an orderer; beauty would not exist without the ideal beauty existing somewhere that all beauty reflects. Finally, there is the somewhat complex argument from "contingency", or "becoming", which time hardly permits us to explore. Indeed, all five of these "arguments" are interrelated, and all require much lengthier study.

The *Catechism* quotes a very beautiful expression on this subject from St. Augustine. He says:

Question the beauty of the earth, question the beauty of the sea, question the beauty of the air, distending and diffusing itself, question the beauty of the sky, . . . question all these realities. All respond: See, we are beautiful. Their beauty is a profession. These beauties are subject to change. Who made them if not the Beautiful One who is not subject to change? [32].

St. Augustine's words were echoed very beautifully in a favorite book of mine by Dr. Viktor Frankl, a psychiatrist at the University of Vienna, who was a victim of the Holocaust. Dr. Frankl was a long time in Auschwitz and other Nazi prisons. When he was released by the Allies, after his whole family had been obliterated, he wrote this beautiful book, *Man's Search For Meaning*. I cite just one passage.

One day, a few days after the liberation, I walked through the country past flowering meadows, for miles and miles, toward the market town near the camp. Larks rose to the sky and I could hear their joyous song. There was no one to be seen for miles around; there was nothing but the wide earth and sky and the larks' jubilation and the freedom of space. I stopped, looked around, up to the sky—and then I went down on my knees. At that moment there was very little I knew of myself or of the world—I had but one sentence in mind—always the same: "I called to the Lord from my narrow prison and He answered me in the freedom of space."

How long I knelt there and repeated this sentence memory can no longer recall. But I know that on that day, in that hour, my new life started. Step for step I progressed, until I again became a human being [(New York: Pocket Books, 1959), pp. 141-42].

Dr. Frankl had found faith. His inspiring words reveal how faith and reason are so closely united and how we can see God in the material world around us and deeply within our own hearts.

The *Catechism* puts it this way:

Man's openness to truth and beauty, his sense of moral goodness, of freedom, the voice of his conscience and longing for the infinite and for happiness provoke him to ask himself about God's existence. Through all of this he can not help sensing his own spiritual soul. The soul, the "seed of eternity that we bear in ourselves, irreducible to the merely material" can originate only in God [33].

The *Catechism* points out that "in different ways, people can come to know the existence of a reality which is the first cause and ultimate goal of all things, a reality 'that everyone calls "God"' " [34].

These so-called "natural" means for coming to know God can tell us a great deal, then, but they *could* leave us very cold and unfeeling. It is fine to know there is a God, but does He care about me? What does God mean to us, to you personally, to me personally? For this we need something more. The *Catechism* tells us what it is:

> Our human faculties enable us to know that a personal God exists, but in order for us to be able to enter into real intimacy with God, our Creator willed both to reveal himself and to give us the grace that empowers us to accept this revelation in faith [35].

That's the key, *revelation*. The *Catechism* talks about not simply the "natural" means for coming to know about God, but revelation, God's revealing Himself. Of course, there are many obstacles to using reason effectively to arrive at truth, especially truth about God, religion, and morality. We are busy people. We don't take time to think, perhaps. We don't take time to pray, perhaps. The world is against us. It is in a conspiracy against purity. Some television programs, movies, and various other sorts of entertainment are hostile to the very notion of God. We need what we call "divine revelation". In this human condition, reason simply is not enough.

The *Catechism* says:

> Although by natural reason we can know God with certainty through his works, there is another order of knowledge, that of divine revelation, which man cannot attain at all by his own powers . . . [50].

> God who "dwells in inaccessible light," wants to share his own divine life with the people he freely created, in order to adopt them as sons and daughters in his only-begotten Son. God's self-revelation enables us to respond to him, and to know and love him far beyond our human capacity [52].

The *Catechism* goes on for several paragraphs to describe the various *stages* of revelation. God did not reveal Himself fully all at once. First He created Adam and Eve, and He revealed Himself to them, our first parents. Then we know what happened—they gave away Paradise. They and we could have been happy forever. They would have come to know God very intimately, but, through this mysterious thing called original sin, they rejected Him; so they were ejected from Paradise. Everything evil came into the world: killing, wars, diseases, poverty, suffering of every description, ignorance, sin.

Then there was this mysterious thing called a flood, to purify the world, as it were, and Noah was singled out by God. What does the ark represent? That God wanted Noah to preserve for the future everything living. God hadn't made what He made to destroy it. We are told He made a pact, a covenant, with Noah and with those who would follow Noah in awaiting the Messiah Who had been promised to Adam and Eve.

Advent is the preparation for the celebration of the coming of the Redeemer. It marks the long period of waiting through thousands of years until finally, in the fullness of revelation, Christ would be born a man. In between there are Adam and Eve, Noah, and the calling of Abraham from among the pagans. Abraham, you recall, was chosen to be the Father of all of those who would be believers, most immediately of the chosen race, the Israelites.

We are told about the vicissitudes of the Israelites. They are taken into slavery under the Egyptians, and then God selects Moses to lead them out of slavery to the Promised Land. Moses is clearly the forerunner of Christ, Who one day is going to lead all people out of the slavery of sin to heaven. God makes a covenant with Moses. Then a whole series of prophets, men and women, talk about what has happened and about the fact that the Messiah, the Redeemer, will come one day to save us. This is all part of revelation until we get, finally, to John the Baptist. He is always spoken of as standing between the Old Testament and the New Testament.

This takes us, of course, to today's Gospel.

> Here begins the Gospel of Jesus Christ, the Son of God. In Isaiah the prophet, it is written: "I send my messenger before you to prepare your way: a herald's voice in the desert, crying, 'Make ready the way of the Lord, clear him a straight path'" (Mk 1:1-3).

We said earlier that there are so many obstacles to coming to know God. John the Baptist tells the people, in essence, "Get rid of the baggage. Give up your sins. Make time to think and to pray. Come and be baptized as an external symbol of the fact that you want to convert your lives." He preached repentance. It is not easy to purify our minds and hearts. It is not easy to come to know God in this world of ours. So John the Baptist was saying, "Look! God is ready. God is about to send His Son. He's already here on this earth, and you are about to meet Him face to face. But you have to get ready for Him, or otherwise you will not even recognize Him, much less become associated with Him."

The *Catechism* tell us that, finally, after centuries of waiting for the Messiah, God was to reveal Himself in all His fullness by way of His Son, Jesus the Lord, called in the *Catechism* "Mediator and Fullness of All Revelation". God is revealing Himself fully now in His Son. The *Catechism* says:

> "Long ago God spoke to our ancestors in many and various ways by the prophets, but in these last days he has spoken to us through his Son" (Heb 1:1-2). The Christ, the Son of God made man, is the Father's unique, per-

fect and unsurpassable Word. God says everything in him; there will be no other word except for this Word [65].

Christ is the fullness of revelation.

The Second Vatican Council talks about this, and the *Catechism* quotes the Second Vatican Council:

> The Christian economy is the new and definitive Covenant, [a covenant with Adam and Eve, a covenant with Noah, a covenant with Moses carried out through the prophets, and with the coming of Christ the new and definitive Covenant], it will never pass away; and we are to await no new public revelation before the glorious manifestation of our Lord Jesus Christ. Yet even if revelation is already complete, it is not yet completely clarified; it remains for Christian faith gradually to explore and grasp more fully, over the course of centuries, its total significance [66].

This is why we have a pope, why we have bishops, why we have Councils of the Church, why we have catechisms—to explore revelation. We have to think about it. We have to pray about it. It gradually becomes clear through the days, through the years, through the centuries.

This section of the *Catechism*, introducing the meaning of faith, concludes with a mention of *private* revelations of faith, which, in some cases, have been recognized by the Church. (One might think of the revelations of the Sacred Heart of Jesus to Margaret Mary Alacoque or the appearance of the Virgin Mary to Bernadette at Lourdes as examples.) All of these are working out of the revelation of Christ. These are intended to help us "live out more fully" the revelation given us through Christ Himself. These are not new revelations; revelation is complete in the coming of Christ. These are further explanations, if you will, further clarifications.

The *Catechism* warns us of revelations proclaimed by certain religious sects and other bodies and individuals "that pretend to surpass or correct the revelation of which Christ is the fulfillment" [67]. It warns us there cannot be any such additions.

One of the most colorful ways of describing the relationship between faith and reason, and particularly the meaning of faith in our own lives, is found in what is one of my favorite books of all time. It was first published in 1928, and I think it has gone through some thirty-five printings—the book by Myles Connolly called *Mr. Blue*. Many of you may have read it at some point in your lives. The book is a fantasy about this fellow called "Blue", who lives out in his own unique way this revelation of faith through Jesus Christ. He is not a kook. He is not crazy. He is different. He takes the gospel seriously. I cite one scene from Myles Connolly's book. It was a cold, clear night, and Mr. Blue threw his hands up toward the stars and said:

My hands, my feet, my poor little brain, my eyes, my ears, all matter more than the whole sweep of these constellations! . . . God Himself, the God to Whom this whole universe-specked display is as nothing, God Himself had hands like mine and feet like mine, and eyes, and brain, and ears! . . . Without Christ we would be little more than bacteria breeding on a pebble in space, or glints of ideas in a whirling void of abstractions. Because of Him, I can stand here out under this cold immensity and know that my infinitesimal pulse-beats and my acts and thoughts are of more importance than this whole show of a universe. Only for Him, I would be crushed beneath the weight of all these worlds. Only for Him I would tumble dazed into the gasping chasms of space and time. Only for Him, I would be confounded before the awful fertility and intricacy of all life. Only for Him, I would be the merest of animalcules crawling on the merest of motes in a frigid Infinity. . . . But behold, behold! God wept and laughed and dined and wined and suffered and died even as you and I. Blah!—for the immensity of space! Blah!—for those who would have me a microcosm in the meaningless tangle of an endless evolution! I'm no microcosm. I, too, am a Son of God! [(New York: Doubleday, Image Books, 1954), pp. 40-41].

And so are you, and a daughter, thanks to your faith.

3

Handing on the Deposit of Faith

THIRD SUNDAY OF ADVENT
DECEMBER 12, 1993
PONTIFICAL MASS

Anyone who has spent a significant amount of time at sea knows how comforting is the light of a lighthouse. Despite all of the modern technical navigational instruments available—radar, sonar, and so on—if you're out in a storm, or if it's a dark or foggy night, there's nothing quite so comforting as seeing that light from somewhere on shore. The wonderful thing about a lighthouse is that its light is for everybody. It doesn't matter what nation you're from, what your color or your background, what language you speak, or whatever. If you're at sea, particularly if you're lost, that light is for you. Each lighthouse has its own specific "character", as it is technically called. For example, its light flashes at specific intervals and in different ways from other lighthouses, and so on. As a result, if you know the character of the lighthouse, you know exactly where you are. Mistaking the location of a lighthouse could create serious problems.

I speak of this because of today's Gospel, in which John the Baptist wants to make very clear that he is *not* the light (Jn 1:6–8; 19–28). To all of the people who are gathered around out in the desert to whom he is appealing to make straight the way of the Lord, be converted, be ready for His coming, he's saying, "I am not He. I am not the Word. I am here only as a *witness* to the Light, the Light Who will shine in the darkness, the Light that cannot be overcome by the darkness." Christ the Word has come to call all, without exception.

The new *Catechism of the Catholic Church* that we are examining makes very clear that the Church is *not* the light. The Church is more than a lighthouse; it's the living, breathing, dynamic Body of Christ. But the light of truth doesn't come *from* the Church, it comes *through* the Church. It is *Christ* who enlightens the Church with the Holy Spirit. It is *Christ* who speaks to us through Church teaching. It is *Christ* who speaks to all, again regardless of who we are, what our backgrounds may be, what sins we have committed, whether we're rich or poor, or whatever. *Christ* is speaking to each of us, is calling each of us safely in out of the darkness, in out of the storm. It's the *character* of the Church that serves as the living lighthouse. It is open to all. It preaches the same truth to all. It sheds the same light on all.

This takes us to the next section of the *Catechism*. For those of you who have not been here on these Sundays of Advent, let me note that we have begun a very difficult task. I find this the hardest thing I've ever done, and I may have bitten off more than I can chew. We are trying to cover the six hundred pages of the new *Catechism* over the course of the forty-two Sundays of the Church year, quoting directly from the *Catechism* and commenting on it. This is the summary of the teaching of the Church. This is what we call the "deposit of faith". This includes the Vatican Council and all its documents, and all of the other councils that have gone before, and everything back to John the Baptist, and all of the books of the Old Testament, as well as the books of the New Testament. I must warn you that the section we will be citing from today will be difficult for some people. It's very straightforward. It tells us what the Church thinks about itself. It tells us what the Church believes to be its own authority—authority given by our Divine Lord. It's going to be difficult for those people who have retained the name "Catholic" but reject the authority of the Church for all practical purposes.

The portion of the *Catechism* we will cover today talks about Divine Revelation and the Scriptures. Last week we talked about the fact that we can all get to know God through natural means, through the material world around us, and from examining our own hearts. As Immanuel Kant, the philosopher, put it, "The starry skies above me, the moral law within me. These tell me of the reality of God." But there has to be more than this. We come to know God most importantly through God's revelation of Himself.

We noted that the summation of God's telling us about Himself is in His sending His Word, the Word that became flesh, the Word that we call Jesus. That's where we begin today.

> God "desires everyone to be saved and to come to the knowledge of the truth" (1 Tim 2:4): that is to say, the knowledge of Christ Jesus. Christ must be proclaimed to all peoples and to all men so that his revelation may reach to the ends of the earth [74].

In the reading of Isaiah today we are told:

> He has sent me to bring glad tidings to the lowly,
>   to heal the brokenhearted,
> To proclaim liberty to the captives
>   and release to the prisoners,
> To announce a year of favor from the Lord
>   and a day of vindication by our God (Is 61:1–2; 10–11).

That is said to all of us. We are sinners, many of us lost in the darkness, many of us suffering, many of us poor, many of us imprisoned by sin or by other problems. Christ comes for *all* of us and the fullness of Revelation is in Him.

The *Catechism* says:

> Christ the Lord, in whom the whole Revelation of God Most High is summed up, commanded the apostles to preach the Gospel, promised beforehand by the prophets, fulfilled in his own person and promulgated by his own mouth [75].

There are some people who are still looking elsewhere. It was very faddish a few years ago to look to Zen Buddha to try to find the Lord, through the lotus blossom position, and so on. But everything we seek, everything we need, is in Christ.

The *Catechism* says:

> In keeping with the Lord's command, the Gospel was handed on both orally and in writing:
> — *orally* "by the apostles, who handed on, by the word of their preaching, their example, and the institutions they established . . ." [76].

The *Catechism* is making a point here. There are still some people who will say, "I accept Christ and His teaching but not the institutional Church. Don't give me all that nonsense about popes and bishops and what not." The *Catechism* reminds us that the apostles established the *institution* in accordance with the mandate of Christ to Peter: "You are Peter and on you I will build My Church." He said also that it must perdure until the end of time. Hence, there had to be appointed those who, after Christ had ascended into heaven and the apostles had died, would still carry on to the end of time.

In addition to the oral teaching of Christ handed on by the apostles, the Gospel was handed on "*in writing* by the apostles and others associated with them, who committed the message of salvation to writing under the inspiration of the Holy Spirit" [76].

The *Catechism* tells us that:

> "In order that the whole living gospel should always be kept intact and living in the Church, the apostles left bishops as their successors, giving them 'their own teaching authority'" [77].

Our Divine Lord said, "All authority is given Me in heaven and on earth. As the Father has sent Me, so also I send you. . . . Who hears you, hears Me. Who hears Me, hears Him who sent Me. Who despises you, despises Me" (Mt 28:18; Lk 10:16). And so the apostles rightly passed on their authority to the bishops.

The living transmission of the word, brought about by the Holy Spirit, is called Tradition, distinct from sacred Scripture though closely connected to it. Through Tradition, "the Church, in her teaching, life, and worship, perpetuates and transmits to every generation all that she is and all that she believes" [78].

A very important element of tradition includes the writings of the first three centuries, when people were still close to the oral word, to what was passed along before it could be diluted. We are told:

"*Sacred Scripture* is the word of God as it is put down in writing under the inspiration of the Holy Spirit."

"*Sacred Tradition* hands on God's word, once entrusted to the apostles by Christ the Lord and the Holy Spirit, and transmitted in its integrity to the apostles' successors, so that, enlightened by the Spirit of truth, they may faithfully keep, and spread it by their preaching" [81].

Now I quote what is one of the difficult things for some in the *Catechism*:

The result is that the Church, to which the transmission and interpretation of revelation is entrusted, "does not derive her certainty about all truths of Revelation from the holy Scriptures alone. That is why both Scripture and Tradition must be accepted and honored with equal sentiments of love and respect" [82].

This concept is difficult not only for those who won't accept the authority of the so-called institutional Church but also for those whom we call "fundamentalists", who see in the Bible and *only* in the Bible the fullness of Revelation and will not accept anything else. That's not what the Church teaches.

"The task of authentically interpreting God's Word, whether written or handed down orally, was entrusted solely to the teaching office of the Church, which exercises this authority in the name of Jesus Christ", namely, to the bishops in communion with the successor of Peter, the bishop of Rome [85]. [That's the formal title of the Pope—the Bishop of Rome.]

All the faithful share in the understanding and handing on of revealed truth. They have received the anointing of the Holy Spirit, who instructs them and guides them into all truth [91].

So *all* of us receive the Revelation. In all of us there's a certain kind of "passive infallibility" as long as we are in union with the bishops and the pope, who in turn must be in union with the teaching Christ and the apostles.

The *Catechism* goes on: "With the assistance of the Holy Spirit the Church's understanding of both the realities and the words of the heritage of faith can grow throughout her life . . ." [94]. The Church can't be static, she must be dynamic. She has to live for all ages. Her truth must be expressed in ways meaningful to all ages. The Church continues to grow, the Church continues to learn.

Every morning I say the 7:30 Mass, which is televised to many thousands of people. I preach for maybe four minutes at most, believe it or not. Most of the people who attend that Mass have to get to work. But I prepare very carefully for those few minutes, and it's absolutely astonishing that each day I get something new out of the Scriptures. I'm a priest for forty-eight years, and I have been preaching all my life, but every day I find new things in the Scriptures.

The *Catechism* tells us:

". . . the contemplation and study of believers who ponder these things in their hearts, and theological research in particular, deepen our knowledge of revealed truth [94].

"It is therefore clear that, by God's supremely wise provision, sacred Tradition, Sacred Scripture, and the Church's teaching authority, called the Magisterium, are so interconnected that none of these can stand without the others" [95].

That's, again, difficult for many people.

The *Catechism* says:

For this reason, the Church has always venerated the Sacred Scriptures as she venerates also the Lord's Body. She does not cease to present to the faithful the Bread of life, taken from the Table of God's Word [the Scriptures] and Christ's Body [103].

So we have received the Word in the Scriptures today. We will receive that Word made flesh in Holy Communion, the Word of God.

God is the author of Sacred Scripture. "The divinely revealed truth which the books of Sacred Scripture contain and present were recorded under the inspiration of the Holy Spirit" [105].

That's where the Church finds her nourishment.

God inspired the human authors of the sacred books. "God chose and employed certain men to compose these sacred books, making full use of their faculties and powers, so that, working in and through them, they should commit to writing, as true authors, all that conformed to his desire and only that" [106].

Not anybody could write a book and call it a book of the Bible. As Isaiah says, for instance, "The spirit of the Lord is upon me because He has anointed me." He could speak in the name of the Lord and write in the name of the Lord because the Lord chose him.

> In the Bible, God speaks to man in a human way. To interpret the Scripture correctly, it is necessary then to be attentive to what the human authors truly wanted to affirm and to what God wishes to reveal to us by their words [109].

> To discover *the sacred authors' intention*, it is necessary to take into account the conditions of their time and culture, the literary styles in use at the time, and the conventions of feeling, speaking, and narrating then current [110].

That's why we have ever new translations of the Bible. It's very difficult, however, to remain faithful to the essence of what was said and to put it in the style that would be meaningful to us today.

> According to an ancient tradition, we can distinguish between two overall senses of Scripture: the literal and the spiritual [115].

At the Last Supper, our Lord said over a piece of bread, "This is My Body." Over a cup of wine He said, "This is My Blood." We have to interpret that literally. Our Lord wasn't saying "This looks like My Body. This is a memorial of My Blood." He said, "This *is* My Body, this *is* My Blood." We interpret literally those words of Scripture. They mean exactly what they say. When you go to something like the Book of Jonah, however, you have what may be a spiritual or symbolic interpretation. Was Jonah swallowed by a whale? Did he live in the belly of the whale and then get thrown up on the shore? It could be, but we don't know the literal meaning of that text. We do know that it is a spiritual representation of the Resurrection of Christ that is to come. Our Divine Lord Himself, for instance, told people He was going to suffer, die, and rise again. They said, "Give us a sign." He responded, "You shall have no sign but the sign of Jonah the prophet."

When we're reading the Scriptures, this distinction between what is literally intended there and what is spiritual or symbolic is very important. St. Augustine says, however, "I should not have believed the gospel had not the authority of the Catholic Church already moved me." This, again, is very difficult for people. It was the Church who brought the Scriptures together into one meaningful whole, and therefore the Church, in accordance with apostolic tradition, the authority of the apostles, is able to say, "This constitutes the true Bible. These books are divinely inspired." There may be very beautiful writings that are not divinely inspired.

In that sense the Church comes before the New Testament. For example, our Divine Lord had lived, died, risen again, and ascended into heaven, and the Holy Spirit had come, before a single book of the New

Testament was written. Who wrote those books? Who preserved them? The Church.

The *Catechism* says:

Guided by the apostolic Tradition, the Church discerned which writings ought to be included in the list of Sacred Books. This entire list is called the *Canon* of the Scriptures. It includes 45 or 46 books for the Old Testament [sometimes called the Jewish writings], depending on how you count them, and then 27 for the New Testament, of which primary are the Gospels.

The Old Testament: Genesis, Exodus, Leviticus, Numbers, Deuteronomy, Joshua, Judges, Ruth, 1 and 2 Samuel, 1 and 2 Kings, 1 and 2 Chronicles, Ezra and Nehemiah, Tobit, Judith, Esther, 1 and 2 Maccabees, Job, Psalms, Proverbs, Ecclesiastes, the Song of Songs, the Wisdom of Solomon, Sirach (Ecclesiasticus), Isaiah, Jeremiah, Lamentations, Baruch, Ezekiel, Daniel, Hosea, Joel, Amos, Obadiah, Jonah, Micah, Nahum, Habakkuk, Zephaniah, Haggai, Zachariah, and Malachi.

The New Testament: The Gospels according to Matthew, Mark, Luke, and John, the Acts of the Apostles, the Letters of St. Paul to the Romans, 1 and 2 Corinthians, Galatians, Ephesians, Philippians, Colossians, 1 and 2 Thessalonians, 1 and 2 Timothy, Titus, Philemon, the Letter to the Hebrews, the Letters of James, 1 and 2 Peter, 1, 2, and 3 John, Jude, and Revelation (the Apocalypse) [120].

The *Catechism* says: "The Old Testament is an indispensable part of Sacred Scripture. Its books are divinely inspired and retain a permanent value, for the Old Covenant has never been revoked" [121].

There was a priest named Marcion in the fifth century who started a terrible heresy that the God of the Old Testament and the God of the New Testament must be two different people, because the God of the Old Testament was an angry judge and the God of the New Testament was kind, compassionate, and gentle. That's foolishness. Our Lord Himself said, "I have come not to destroy the law but to preserve it." Everything in those books of the Jewish Scriptures is very sacred, and the New Testament is rooted in them. It is hard to understand the New Testament without knowing the Old Testament.

"The principal purpose of the Old Testament was to prepare for the coming of Christ, the Savior of the world" [122].

Christians honor the Old Testament as God's word. The Church has always vigorously opposed the idea of rejecting the Old Testament under the pretext that the New has rendered it void [123].

The Divine Office that priests and religious pray every day has as its heart, for example, the 150 Psalms of the Old Testament. The Old Testament is very much part of the life of the Church. How enriched we could be if we read only a passage of it each day. St. Augustine sums up the relationship between the Old Testament and the New: "The New Testament lies hidden in the Old, the Old Testament is unveiled in the New."

"God's Word, a divine power for salvation to everyone who has faith, is set forth and displays its matchless power in the writings of the New Testament." These writings hand on to us the ultimate truth of divine Revelation. Their central object is Jesus Christ, God's incarnate Son: His acts, teachings, Passion and glorification, and his Church's beginnings under the action of the Holy Spirit [124].

For instance, in the Acts of the Apostles we are told the story of the beginnings of the Church.

The *Catechism* points out that there are three stages in the formation of the Gospels.

1. *The life and teaching of Jesus.* The Church holds firmly that the four Gospels . . . faithfully hand on what Jesus, the Son of God, during his life said and what he did.

2. *Word of mouth tradition.* "What the Lord said and did, the apostles communicated to their hearers after his ascension, . . . enlightened by the Spirit of truth on Pentecost."

3. *The written Gospels.* "The sacred authors therefore composed the four Gospels, choosing certain of the numerous elements handed down, either orally or already in writing, editing a synthesis of others, or explaining them in terms of the Church's current situation, and finally keeping the form of preaching, in such a way as always to deliver the honest truth about Jesus to us" [126].

The apostles talked together about what Jesus said and did. They didn't write everything. The Gospel of St. John says, "These and many other things Jesus did. If they were recorded here the world itself wouldn't be able to hold all the books in which they would be recorded" (Jn 21:25). The apostles had the advantage of living after Christ, seeing how people accepted or rejected the teaching, and especially seeing Christ's prophesies come true. For example, He said that the temple was going to be destroyed. By the time St. Luke was writing his Gospel, he had seen the destruction of the temple of Jerusalem in the year 70 A.D.

The Scriptures are intended for our spiritual welfare, for the salvation of our souls, not just for factual data. So St. Thérèse, the Little Flower, says: "But above all it is the Gospel that occupies my mind when I'm at prayer; in it I find all that is necessary for my poor soul. I'm always finding new lights there, hidden mysterious meanings."

Here, now, are the concluding words in this section of the *Catechism*:

> The Vatican Council decreed: "Access to the Sacred Scriptures ought to be opened wide to the Christian faithful" [131].

> "The 'study of the Sacred Scripture' should be the very soul of sacred theology. The ministry of the Word, too, whether in pastoral preaching, catechetics, or any form of Christian instruction, is nourished in health and thrives in holiness through this same Word of Scripture" [132].

> The Church "strongly and specifically exhorts all Christians . . . to learn 'the surpassing knowledge of Jesus Christ', by frequent reading of the divine Scriptures. 'Indeed, to ignore the Scriptures is to ignore Christ'" [133].

You often hear the nonsensical statement that the Church kept the Bible from the people. That's foolish! In medieval days, the Bible had to be written very tediously by hand, because there were no printing presses. A copy of the Bible was very precious. In order that it wouldn't be lost, it would be chained to a wall near a window in a monastery, and then even the poorest of the people could come and read it by the light coming in from the window. It was not the intention to keep the Bible from the people, but to make it available in a way that it wouldn't be stolen or given out to someone and lost, because it would take several years to transcribe another copy.

I began by talking about lighthouses. One of the Seven Wonders of the Ancient World, as you know, is the Lighthouse of Pharos on an island near Alexandria, Egypt. It was truly a wonder of the ancient world, because it was five hundred feet high and its light radiated for forty-two miles. It was phenomenal! How many lives it saved. But the light of a lighthouse is in no way comparable to the Light Who is Christ, radiating through His Church, making possible every day your salvation and mine.

4

God Wants You

FOURTH SUNDAY OF ADVENT
DECEMBER 19, 1993
PONTIFICAL MASS

When I was a young boy in Philadelphia, my father would take me to the parish mission at St. Clement's Parish. I remember so well this particular missionary priest who told us the story of the man he called the "famous atheist", Robert Ingersoll. It wasn't until I grew up that I learned that Mr. Ingersoll called himself not an atheist but an agnostic, and that he died in Dobbs Ferry, New York.

Well, atheist or agnostic, when Ingersoll lectured he would take out a pocket watch and, looking at it, say, "If there's a God, I dare him to strike me dead within five minutes." After five minutes had passed, Ingersoll would say triumphantly, "See, I'm still alive. There is no God."

The mission priest thereupon told us with equal triumph, "What Mr. Ingersoll really proved is that God is too kind and merciful to strike him dead!"

Since growing up, I've heard stronger arguments for both atheism and faith, but the reality is that arguments are infinitely less important than one burning reality, namely, that faith is a pure gift from God. We are talking about something completely beyond any argumentation. The missionary priest had it. Apparently Ingersoll didn't have it. That's fundamental.

In recent weeks our catechetical homilies have focused on how God reveals Himself to us. He reveals Himself naturally, through the world around us and from within our own hearts; supernaturally He reveals Himself through the Sacred Scripture, both Old and New Testaments, and apostolic tradition.

Today we begin the section of the *Catechism* that describes how we human beings respond to God and to His revelation. The *Catechism* says:

> By Revelation, the invisible God in his great love speaks to us "as friends and dwells among us, so that he may invite and receive us into communion with himself." The adequate response to this invitation is faith [142].

This invitation of a loving God is terribly important. The *Catechism* says:

33

With faith, man submits his own intelligence and his own will and with his whole being gives his assent to God the Revealer. Sacred Scripture calls this response of man to the revealing God "the obedience of faith" [143].

The Latin word for obedience is *ob-audire*, "to listen to". Obedience to faith involves an act of listening. Indeed, St. James tells us that "faith comes through hearing". The *Catechism* says:

> Obedience in the faith is to submit freely to the heard word of God because its truth is guaranteed by God, who is truth itself. Sacred Scripture proposes to us Abraham as the model of such obedience and the Virgin Mary as its perfect realization [144].

> The *Letter to the Hebrews*, in its great praise of the faith of Israel's ancestors, lays special emphasis on Abraham's faith: "By faith, Abraham obeyed the call to depart toward a country which he was to receive as an inheritance, and he set out not knowing where he was going" (Heb 11:8). By faith, he lived as a stranger and pilgrim in the Promised Land [145].

What a spectacular story we have in Abraham! He was reared in idolatry and paganism. He had no faith in the one true God. Then, out of nowhere, God appeared to him. This is what we read in Genesis:

> The Lord said to Abraham:
> Leave your country, your kinsfolk and your father's house,
> for the land which I will show you;
> I will bless you, and make your name great,
> In you shall all the nations of the earth be blessed.
>
> (Gen 12:1–3)

Why did God choose Abraham and choose his seed, the Israelites, to be the Chosen People? We have no answer except that given in the Book of Deuteronomy, the fifth book of the Old Testament. We read: "It was not because you are the largest of all nations that the Lord set his heart on you and chose you . . . it was because the Lord loved you (Dt 7:7ff.).

Faith is not only a gift from God, it is a gift of *love* from God. God has chosen us, or we wouldn't be here. Why us? Why not millions and millions and millions of others who don't have our faith? Because of God's love for us, and love is a mystery.

Abraham's response to God's call, says the *Catechism*, his willingness to go off into the unknown, was a tremendous act of faith, as was Abraham's belief in God's word that his barren wife, Sarah, would become the mother of countless millions. But Abraham's faith was a sheer gift of God, a gift of love. Without it he would have, he could have, believed nothing.

The *Catechism* gives us a beautiful definition of faith: "Abraham realized the definition of faith given by the letter to the Hebrews 11:1: 'Faith is the guarantee of good things that we hope for, the proof of realities which we cannot see' " [146].

This takes us to Mary. What a miracle of faith is Mary. Here is what the *Catechism* says, which is a direct reflection of what we just heard in the Gospel of St. Luke (Lk 1:26–38).

> The Virgin Mary realized in the most perfect manner obedience of faith. By faith Mary welcomed the annunciation and the promise brought by the angel Gabriel, believing that "nothing is impossible to God" and so giving her assent [to God's invitation to become the mother of His Son, Jesus]: "I am the servant of the Lord; may it be done to me according to your word" (Lk 1:37–38). Elizabeth greeted her: "Blessed is she who has believed in the fulfillment of that which has been said to her on the part of the Lord" (Lk 1:45). It is for this faith that all generations will proclaim her blessed [148].

Look at the impact of Mary's act of faith on her life. First, look at her relationship with Joseph. Poor Joseph! Suddenly, this woman he loves is pregnant, and he knows it is not by him. It had reached the point, we're told, that Joseph was minded to put Mary away in a home for unwed mothers. Otherwise, she could have been subjected to the law, in accordance with which she could be stoned to death for adultery.

Then we're told an angel appeared and said to Joseph, "Don't be afraid to take this woman for your wife, for that which is conceived in her is conceived by the Holy Spirit" (Mt 1:20). What an extraordinary act of faith on the part of Joseph to believe this! He accepted this as he accepted the fact that, at the time the Christ Child was to be born, the king was to demand that everyone go to his own city of origin to be counted. Joseph had to take his pregnant wife on a donkey over the rough roads of Galilee to Bethlehem. He gets to Bethlehem and cannot find a place for his wife to get warm or for the baby to be born, except in a stable. How difficult for his pride, but what a tremendous act of faith he made!

It has often been said that God saves his choicest suffering for his closest friends. Mary took a tremendous risk when she said to the angel, "Behold the handmaid of the Lord, be it done to me according to Thy word" (Lk 1:38). Was she then instantly rewarded with light, happiness, and peace? Not at all. She and Joseph were thrust into confusion and sorrow. They were totally dependent on *faith*.

The *Catechism* tells us:

> Throughout her life and until her last ordeal when Jesus, her son, died on the cross, her faith never wavered. Mary never ceased to believe in the fulfillment of the word of God. And so the Church venerates in Mary the realization of the most pure faith [149].

The *Catechism* continues:

Faith is personal adherence on the part of man to God; it is at the same time, and inseparably, free assent to the whole truth that God has revealed. [We cannot pick and choose what to believe.] Christian faith differs from our faith in a human person. It is just and good to entrust oneself totally to God and believe absolutely. It would be vain and mistaken to place such faith in a creature [150].

If we see a bus with a sign "Pelham", we have faith that that's where the bus is going. We do so on the authority of the people who sent that bus. They would lose money if that didn't regularly happen. But we don't *know* when we get on that bus that we are going to Pelham. We have human faith in human beings. The bus may break down or even get lost. With God we have *absolute* faith.

The *Catechism* says:

For the Christian, to believe in God is inseparably to believe in the one whom he sent, his "beloved Son," in whom the Father is "well pleased" (Mk 1:11). We can believe in Jesus Christ because he is God himself, the Word made flesh: "No one has ever seen God; it is God the only Son, who is close to the Father's heart, who has made him known" (Jn 1:18).

Christ tells us many things in the Scriptures about God His Father. We take these on faith.

The *Catechism* says:

No one can believe in Jesus Christ without sharing in his Spirit. It is the Holy Spirit who reveals to us who Jesus is. . . .

The Church does not cease to confess her faith in only one God: Father, Son and Holy Spirit [152].

There are only certain teachings of the Church that we consider to be absolutely, indispensably necessary for salvation. Belief in the Trinity is one.

The *Catechism* reminds us that faith is a *grace*, a free gift of God.

When St. Peter confesses that Jesus is the Christ, the Son of the living God, Jesus says to him that this revelation does not come "from flesh and blood" [in other words, no human being could have told you this, Peter], but "it comes from my Father in heaven" (Mt 16:17). Faith is a gift from God, a supernatural virtue [a power] infused by him [153].

It is not possible to believe except by grace and the internal help of the Holy Spirit. But it is no less true that to believe is an authentically *human* act. It is not contrary either to the freedom or the intelligence of a man to put his trust in God and to adhere to the truths revealed by God. Even in human relations, it does not contradict our own dignity to believe what other persons tell us about themselves and their intentions, or to trust their promises (for example, when a man and a woman marry). Still less does it contradict our dignity to "yield by faith the full submission of our intellect and will to God the revealer," and to enter into intimate union with him [154].

The *Catechism* continues:

Our motive for believing is not the fact that revealed truths appear as true and intelligible in the light of our natural reason. We believe "because of the authority of God himself who reveals them, who can neither deceive nor be deceived" [156].

We could use a microscope, chemical analysis, or anything else we want. There's no way that we can come to believe in the Trinity by reason alone; that takes faith. That is revealed by God.

Thus the miracles of Christ and the saints, the growth and the holiness of the Church . . . "are the most certain signs of divine revelation, adapted to the intelligence of all"; they are "motives of credibility," which show that faith is not just a blind impulse [156].

If we are holy—if priests are holy, if bishops are holy, if all of God's people are holy—a lot more people will come to believe. But this also works in reverse, sadly. Credibility is lost when we are not a holy people.

The *Catechism* says:

Faith is certain. It is more certain than all human knowledge because it is founded on the Word of God who cannot lie. While revealed truths can seem obscure to our reason and experience, "the certainty that the divine light gives is greater than that which the light of natural reason gives." As Cardinal Newman observes, "Ten thousand difficulties do not make one doubt" [157].

The *Catechism* cites an interesting expression of St. Anselm's in the eleventh century: "Faith seeks understanding." That's natural. We believe, but then we want to know more and more about the one in whom we believe, as a husband and wife want to come to know more and more about each other. This is what happens when we study the *Catechism*, when we study the Scriptures. It gives us a thirst to know more and more.

On the subject of faith and science the *Catechism* says:

"Though faith is above reason, there can never be any real discrepancy between faith and reason, since the same God who reveals mysteries and communicates faith has also bestowed the light of reason on the human spirit; God cannot deny himself nor can truth ever contradict truth." . . . Those "who strive in humility and perseverance to penetrate the secrets of things are being led, even if they are not aware of it, by the hand of God who sustains all things and makes them what they are" [159].

The *Catechism* says:

> To be human, the "response of faith given by man to God must be volun-
> tary [We are creatures of free will]; no person must be forced to embrace
> the faith unwillingly, for the act of faith is voluntary by its very nature." In-
> deed, Christ *invited* to faith and to conversion, he never constrained [160].

Jesus said to the apostles, "Come, follow Me." That was an invitation.
When they said, "Where do you live?" He said, "Come and see." That
was an invitation. The apostles were not forced to believe.

Next, the *Catechism* gives a very straightforward and simple statement:
"To believe in Jesus Christ and in the one who sent Him to save us is necessary for salvation" [161].

Then the *Catechism* answers the important question of perseverance in
faith.

> Faith is God's entirely free gift; but we can lose this precious gift, as St. Paul
> indicated to St. Timothy: "Fight the good fight, having faith and a good
> conscience. By rejecting conscience, certain persons have suffered ship-
> wreck in the faith" (1 Tim 1:18–19) [162].

It's frightening to realize that we don't really lose our faith. We throw it
away through negligence and through contempt.

The *Catechism* says:

> To live, grow, and persevere in faith until the end, we must nourish it with
> the word of God and beg the Lord to increase our faith [162].

> Faith enables us to enjoy in advance the light of the beatific vision, the goal
> of our pilgrimage here in this world. We shall see God "face to face," "as he
> is" (1 Cor 13:12) [163].

Faith really is the beginning of divine life. Here, however, the *Catechism*
reminds us:

> "We walk by faith, not by sight" (1 Cor 5:7); we know God as "in a mir-
> ror, in a confused fashion" (1 Cor 13:12). The faith is often lived out in
> darkness. Faith is able to be put to the test. The world in which we live of-
> ten seems very far from that which the faith promises us; the experiences of
> evil and of suffering, injustices, and death, seem to contradict the good
> news; they can shake our faith and may even become a temptation against it
> [164].

I find great consolation in what St. Thérèse, the Little Flower, says
about her own temptation against faith. She was suffering terribly from tuberculosis. She was racked with fever and with pain. She says:

> When my heart, weary of the enveloping darkness, tries to find some rest
> and strength in the thought of an everlasting life to come, my anguish only

increases. It seems to me that the darkness itself, borrowing the voice of the unbeliever, cries mockingly: "You dream of a land of light and fragrance, you believe that the Creator of these wonders will be yours forever, you think to escape one day from the mists in which you now languish. Hope on! Hope on! Look forward to death! It will give you, not what you hope, but a night darker still, the night of utter nothingness!"

What a terrible temptation against faith. She goes on:

> May God forgive me! He knows how I try to live my faith, even though it affords me no consolation. I have made more acts of faith during the past year than in all the rest of my life [Dorothy Day, *Thérèse* (Springfield, Ill.: Templegate, 1985), p. 160].

The *Catechism* continues:

> Faith is a personal act—the free response of man to the initiative of the God who reveals Himself. But faith is not an isolated act. No one can believe alone, as no one is able to live alone. No one has given faith to himself, as no one has given life to himself. Believers have received faith from others and ought to hand it on to others. Our love for Jesus and for others impels us to speak to others about our faith. Each believer is thus a link in the great chain of believers. I cannot believe without being supported by the faith of others, and by my faith I help support others in the faith [166].

This is a reminder of John Donne's "No Man Is an Island", in which he says: "No man is an island entire unto himself. Every man is a piece of the continent. Every man's death diminishes me because I am involved in mankind." And, of course, this is the teaching of the Mystical Body of Christ.

The *Catechism* goes on:

> "I believe": this is the faith of the Church professed personally by each believer, principally during Baptism. "We believe": this is the faith of the Church confessed by the bishops assembled in council or more generally by the liturgical assembly of believers. The Church, our mother, responding to God by faith, teaches us to say both "I believe" and "we believe" [167].

> It is at the same time the Church which believes and therefore bears, nourishes, and sustains my faith. . . . Through the Church we receive faith and new life in Baptism [168].

> Salvation comes from God alone; but because we receive the life of faith through the Church, she is our mother. "We believe the Church as the mother of our new birth, and not *in* the Church as if she were the author of our salvation" [169].

> We do not believe in formulas, but in those realities that they express, which faith allows us to reach out and "touch." St. Thomas Aquinas says,

"The believer's act of faith does not stop at the expression, but at the *reality* expressed." However, we do approach these realities with the help of formulas, which permit us to express and hand on the faith, to celebrate it in community, to assimilate and live it out ever more [170].

It is so unfortunate that on some mystical day they stopped teaching children prayers. Even today many adults come into confession, and they don't know the Act of Contrition, the Our Father, or the Hail Mary. I remember one child came in, however, who had a pretty good sense of it. When I said, "Please say the Act of Contrition", which includes the words "because I dread the loss of heaven and the pains of hell", he said, and this is true, "because I dread the loss of heaven, and it hurts like hell." He got the essence of it!

These are the concluding paragraphs of this section of the *Catechism*.

Through the centuries, in so many languages, cultures, peoples, and nations, the Church does not cease to confess her unique faith, received from only one Lord, transmitted by only one Baptism, and rooted in the conviction that all humanity has only one God and Father [172].

Then the *Catechism* gives this beautiful quotation from St. Irenaeus of Lyon, who lived around 250. He said:

Indeed, the Church, though scattered throughout the whole world, even to the ends of the earth, having received the faith from the apostles and their disciples . . . guards this preaching and faith with care, as dwelling in but a single house, and similarly believes as if having but one soul and a single heart, and preaches, teaches, and hands on this faith with a unanimous voice, as if possessing only one mouth [173].

For though languages differ throughout the world, the content of the Tradition is one and the same [174].

This faith which we have received from the Church let us conserve with care [175].

And certainly we say "Amen" to that.

5

God Tells Us Something about Himself

On the Trinity

FEAST OF THE HOLY FAMILY
DECEMBER 26, 1993
PONTIFICAL MASS

Despite the Christmas fatigue that many of us are undoubtedly experiencing, we must continue today our catechetical homilies on another section of the new *Catechism of the Catholic Church*. Today is the fifth of forty-one sessions. Unfortunately, it is one of the most complex and difficult, because much of this particular section of the *Catechism* deals with the Holy Trinity, one of the most profound of all mysteries. It's consoling, however, that we are not expected to understand the mystery itself. By the conclusion of today's session, neither you nor I will understand the mystery *itself* any better than we do at this moment. It is to be hoped, however, that we *will* understand more of what the Church *teaches* about the Trinity, more of what we *believe* about the Trinity.

Again, it's consoling that there's an old story concerning St. Augustine's pondering the mystery of the Trinity, in the hope of writing about it with some lucidity. It is said that he was walking along the seashore and saw a little youngster who had dug a hole in the sand. The youngster had a shell and would go to the ocean, fill the shell, come back, and pour the water into the hole. He went back and forth repeatedly, doing the same. St. Augustine asked, "What are you trying to do?" The child said, "I'm trying to put the ocean into this hole in the sand." St. Augustine said, "That's foolish. It's impossible." The child said, supposedly, "No more foolish and no more impossible than your trying to understand the Trinity." So don't expect too much of my explanation!

It is a good day to reflect on the Holy Trinity, however, since it is the Feast of the Holy Family. There is an intimate relationship between the Holy Family—indeed, between all family life—and the Trinity. But in a day in which our culture is so hostile to the family, in which divorce is so prevalent, in which family life has been so badly shattered in so many in-

41

stances, it is particularly important that we note this relationship. We are *social* beings, we human beings. We are not isolated individualists.

A man and a woman marry out of an expression of love and then to reproduce that love in what we call the family. We are social human beings because we are fashioned after the Trinity—one God in three Divine Persons, each of the Persons distinct from the other, each intensely loving the other, in no way separate from or separable from one another, and yet distinct and each God. God is a Social Being, and so are we who are made in His image.

The *Catechism* now takes us to the Profession of Faith. We usually think of two different creeds. There have been many creeds in the development of theology in the history of the Church, in accordance with the times and circumstances—this had to be stressed, or this had to be stressed. But today we use basically two different creeds, essentially the same—the Apostles' Creed and the Nicene Creed. The Apostles' Creed begins "I believe in God." The Nicene Creed that we use in every Mass begins "We believe in one God." The truths expressed are the same in each. The Apostles' Creed is shorter and represents explicitly what the apostles themselves believed and taught, intended for all peoples. The Nicene Creed came into existence later.

Early Christianity, as we know, was very severely punished. One could be exiled. Everything could be taken. One could be put to death. After Constantine won what was called the Battle of the Milvian Bridge, in 312, Christianity was granted a significant degree of freedom. So in 321 the bishops gathered together in Nicaea in Turkey and summarized in the Nicene Creed all of the truths of the faith expressed at that particular time. The Nicene Creed is the one we use in the Mass.

Such syntheses of faith are called creeds because the first word in Latin is *credo*, "I believe", or *credimus*, "we believe". They are also called symbols. We have all seen or read spy stories in which one person has a broken portion of a token or a symbol that fits together with a portion someone else has. So a creed is called a symbol because what each one of us believes fits together with what we all believe. We are One Church for all peoples everywhere.

The *Catechism* says: "The believer's 'first profession of faith' is made during Baptism. The symbol of faith is first and foremost the *baptismal* creed" [189].

Since baptism is given "in the name of the Father and of the Son and of the Holy Spirit" (Mt 28:19), so, when baptizing, we ask, usually the parents and godparents, since it's normally an infant, "Do you believe in one God?" "I do believe." "Do you believe in God the Father Almighty?" "I do believe." "Do you believe in God the Son?" "I do believe." "Do you believe in the Holy Spirit, one God?" "I do believe."

The Trinity is absolutely basic. Not often do we preach about it, perhaps because it is so difficult to preach about. We take it for granted, however, as a mystery. Again, when we make the Sign of the Cross, we are expressing our belief in the mystery of the Trinity. But it is important that we *think* about what we are doing.

The *Catechism* says:

> Our profession of faith begins with God, for God is the First and the Last, the beginning and end of everything. The Creed begins with God the Father, for the Father is the first Divine Person of the Most Holy Trinity; and with the creation of heaven and earth, for creation is the beginning and foundation of all the works of God [198].

The first article of the Creed is "I believe in God" or "We believe in one God." The entire Creed then speaks of God, and when it also speaks of humanity and of the world, it does so in relation to God. All of the articles of the Creed depend on this first one, God.

So with the commandments. All depend on the first commandment. "I am the LORD, your God, you shall have no strange gods before me." That first commandment was and is basic. The pagan peoples had created many gods. The Israelites were given the responsibility and the privilege of knowing that there is only one God.

> God revealed himself as the Unique One to the Chosen People, Israel. "Hear, O Israel! The LORD is our God, the LORD alone. You shall love the LORD your God with your whole heart, your whole mind, and your whole strength (Dt 6:4–5) [201].

Jesus repeated those words. The first and greatest of all commandments is "You shall love the Lord your God with your whole heart, your whole strength, your whole mind, your whole soul." In other words, there is no room for any other gods. Indeed, there is no room for anything that is hostile to God, that separates us from God.

Now the *Catechism* talks about the *name* of God. This is important and interesting. We find in the Book of Genesis a description of Adam and the creation of the world by God. God gives to Adam the right to name everything—the sun, the moon, the stars, all the beasts, the fishes, the birds of the air, the grass, the foliage, the fruits—because to be able to give a name was to indicate one's ownership. Adam was to "own" everything with Eve. They had complete possession of the world. But they could not name God; only God could name God.

The *Catechism* says:

> God revealed himself to his people, Israel, in making known his name to them. A name expresses our essence and identity and the meaning of our life. God has a name; he is not an anonymous force [203].

Israel moved far ahead of all the Greek and the ancient philosophies that thought of God simply as the first mover, the first cause, some primitive force in the universe. God is a person. God has a name, an identity.

The *Catechism* says: "By divulging this name, God makes known and in a way gives himself to others by becoming accessible, capable of being known more intimately and invoked in a personal way" [203].

Then the *Catechism* reminds us of a beautiful story in the Book of Exodus, the second book of the Old Testament. Moses, before he is the leader of the Israelites, is tending a flock of sheep. He suddenly sees a bush on fire at the foot of Mount Sinai. He goes over to see what this is. Then the voice of God comes from the bush, saying, "Stop where you are, Moses. Take off your sandals, for the ground on which you stand is holy ground. I am the God of your ancestors, the God of Abraham, of Isaac and Jacob" (Ex 3:6). This, then, was a God beyond space and time, the God who would save the Israelites and would save all of us. He will work out His saving plan for the rest of time.

God then told Moses to go to the Pharaoh and tell him that he, Moses, was to lead God's Chosen People from slavery to freedom. Moses asked, "Who shall I say sent me? If I go to the Israelites and say to them the God of my ancestors has sent me, they'll ask, 'What is his name?' What shall I say to them?" God said to Moses, in profoundly mysterious language, "You shall say to the Israelites: 'I AM WHO AM'. You shall say to the Israelites, 'I AM has sent me to you.' This is my name forever, my title for all generations."

What does it mean? As simply as we can express it: you exist, I exist, but we don't exist by our own power. God does. God is Being. Without using a lot of philosophical language, we can only say, "God is, always will be, always was." You and I came into being at a particular point. Everything that we think or say or do is dependent on God. Only God is self-dependent. Only God can say, "I AM" in the unique sense of that term. That's the way He defined Himself.

The *Catechism* moves on: "Over the centuries, Israel's faith reflected more clearly the riches contained in the revelation of the divine name. God is unique; there are no other gods beside Yahweh" [212].Though God is Creator of heaven and earth, the *Catechism* reminds us that He is above the world and history; that everything else will perish, but God will endure. Everything else will wear out like a garment. Everything else is changed like clothing. Everything else passes away; God is always the same and his years have no end (Ps 102:26–27). The revelation of the sublime name "I Am He Who Is" contains the truth that God alone *is*. God is all being. God is all perfection, without origin, without end [213].

The *Catechism* then talks about God's truth. It says: God is truth itself.

"God's truth is his wisdom, which commands the whole created order and governs the world" [216]. "When he sends his Son into the world it will be 'to testify to the truth' " (Jn 18:37) [217].

In the course of their history, the people of Israel discovered something else about God, infinitely important—that God had only one reason to reveal Himself to them, to create them, to create us, a single motive—to give them the free gift of his love.

But St. John in his Gospel goes beyond saying that God gives love and says, "God *is* love": God's very being is love. It is so hard for us to grasp these concepts, and, without grace, without faith, we couldn't at all. By sending his only Son and the Spirit of Love in the fullness of time, God has revealed to us his most intimate secret: God *is* an eternal exchange of love, God the Father, to God the Son, to God the Holy Spirit, to God the Son, to God the Father, to God the Holy Spirit in an endless circle of love.

Next, we are reminded in the *Catechism*: "To believe in one God and to love him with all our being will have enormous consequences on our whole life" [222].

Of course. What's the difference between those of us here today and those who are not here because they don't believe at all? How poor are those people who don't believe at all, and who don't know that God is love and loves us.

> To believe is to live in thanksgiving [the one God is the source of everything we are and have] (1 Cor 4:7) [224].

> To believe is to know the unity and true dignity of all people: Everyone is made "in the image and likeness of God" (Gen 1:26) [225].

> To believe is to make good use of created things [because they come from God] [226].

> To believe is to trust God in every circumstance, even in adversity [227].

> As St. Teresa of Avila put it:

> May nothing trouble you and nothing frighten you.
> Everything passes, but God never changes.
> Patience obtains all. Whoever has God
> Shall not want, for God alone is enough [227].

Now the *Catechism* goes deeply into the heart of the mystery of the Trinity, beginning with the very words "In the Name of the Father and of the Son and of the Holy Spirit". It notes: "Christians are baptized 'in the name of the Father and of the Son and of the Holy Spirit' (Mt 28:19)" [232]. But they are baptized in the *name*, not in the *names*, in the *name* of the Father and of the Son and of the Holy Spirit, because there is only one God.

> The mystery of the Holy Trinity is the central mystery of the faith and of the Christian life . . . the source of all other mysteries of the faith . . . [234].

In the Old Testament there are only shadows of the Trinity, not clear teaching of the Trinity—that had to come with Christ.

In today's Gospel, for example, we are reminded that when Mary and Joseph brought the Christ Child to the temple in accordance with the Jewish custom, there was this old, old prophet Simeon, who had spent his entire life in the temple, waiting. Waiting for what? Waiting for this. When they placed the Baby in his hands, the Gospel says, Simeon looked at the Baby and said, "Now, O Lord, you can dismiss your servant in peace, because my eyes have seen the glory of Your people, Israel, a light to enlighten the Gentiles." This was the revelation to Simeon—that God the Son had come. How was this revealed in him? Just as Jesus was conceived in the womb of Mary by God the Holy Spirit. Thus we see the Holy Trinity being revealed in the coming of Christ.

We are told in the *Catechism*:

> When the language of faith calls God "Father," it indicates two main things [now the *Catechism* forthrightly goes into the question of gender]: that God is the first origin and authority of everything and that he is, at the same time, goodness and kindness for all his children. God's parental tenderness can also be expressed by the image of motherhood, which indicates . . . the intimacy between Creator and creature [as the intimacy between a mother and an infant in her womb]. The language of faith builds on the human experience of parents, who are in a way the first representatives of God for man [239].

How fortunate then is the "intact family", with a good and kind and generous and loving father and mother. That's our introduction into the Trinity.

The *Catechism* continues:

> But experience also tells us that human parents are fallible and can disfigure the face of fatherhood and motherhood. It is fitting to recall that God is above all of this and above the human distinction between sexes. God is neither man nor woman. He is God. He transcends also human fatherhood and motherhood, although he is their origin and standard [239].

The *Catechism* then tell us that Jesus revealed that God is "Father" in a previously unheard-of sense. He is not only Father as Creator but Father eternally in relation to His Son, Jesus. We would not know this unless Jesus revealed it to us. Jesus Himself said:

"No one knows the Son except the Father, and no one knows the Father except the Son and anyone to whom the Son chooses to reveal him" (Mt 11:27) [240].

This is why the Apostles confessed Jesus as "the Word who in the beginning" was with God and is God, "the visible image of the invisible God" [241].

Those of you who came to the midday Mass on Christmas heard the Gospel from John: "In the beginning was the Word, the Word was with God, the Word was God." Of course, that Word was Jesus.

Before Jesus' suffering and death He was to announce the sending of the Holy Spirit. He said, "I will send you the Spirit of truth." Only after the Spirit of truth came did the apostles have the courage to go forth and teach and preach.

The Council of Constantinople, in the fourth century, had this to say:

We believe in the Holy Spirit, the Lord, the giver of life, who proceeds from the Father. . . . The Holy Spirit, who is the third person in the Trinity, is God, one and equal with God the Father and the Son, of the same substance and of the same nature . . . [245].

Human words. The only way we can describe these things, the only way we can get at all this mystery so far above us. In human terminology, however, when we speak of three persons, we're speaking of three different things altogether, three *separate* things altogether. Not so in God, in whom there are three persons, each himself God. So the *Catechism* says:

The Trinity is One. We do not confess three Gods, but only one God in three persons . . . . The divine persons do not divide the one divinity but each of them is God wholly and entirely: "The Father is that which the Son is, the Son is that which the Father is, the Father and the Son that which the Holy Spirit is, that is, one God by nature" [253].

Many parallels have been used through the years to "explain" the Trinity, but none is adequate. For instance, St. Patrick compared the Trinity to a shamrock, one stem with three leaves. The example fails. Each leaf is not a shamrock, only a leaf of a shamrock, which can be torn from the stem. Each Person of the Trinity is God and is inseparable from the other two Persons. The Trinity has been described as vapor, water, and ice, all the same substance in different forms or "modalities". Again, the example fails. Any one of those three is only a form of the same thing. Not so with the Trinity. The Father is not simply the Son or the Holy Spirit in a different form. God the Father is God the Father; God the Son is God the Son; God the Holy Spirit is God the Holy Spirit. Do we understand? Of course we don't. We *believe*. We believe because God has revealed Himself to us as a Trinity who is yet but one God.

The *Catechism* goes on to say about the Holy Trinity at work in creation and in carrying out the divine plan:

> . . . "one is the God and Father *from* whom all things are, and one is the Lord Jesus Christ *through* whom all things are [that's the way John puts it in his Gospel], and one is the Holy Spirit *in* whom all things are" [258].

> The ultimate goal of the whole divine plan is the entry of creatures into the perfect unity of the Blessed Trinity. Even now we are called to be dwellings for the Most Holy Trinity. "If anyone loves me," says the Lord, "he will keep my word, and my Father will love him and we will come to him, and make our home in him" (Jn 14:23) [260].

So this whole concept of the Trinity, all of this teaching is to remind us that this is what we are destined for—to be caught up in the Trinity because we are fashioned after the Trinity. If we were living our lives perfectly here on earth, then we would be living out the purpose of our creation. If everything that we thought and said and did was in perfect harmony with the will of God, then we would be truly living in the Trinity. Above all, the Trinity reminds us of the way we are supposed to live in our individual families and in the entire human family—in perfect harmony with one another, indeed loving one another unconditionally, regardless of our differences, recognizing that we are all one in the Holy Trinity—the Father, the Son, and the Holy Spirit—the Trinity after whom each one of us is fashioned.

A beautiful truth and the bedrock of our faith, but infinitely beyond our human reason. The child who advised St. Augustine (Was he the Christ Child?) certainly had it right.

6

The Truth about Creation

Last Sunday we continued our sessions on the new *Catechism* with the Creed, the profession of faith that we pray together immediately after the homily. The *Catechism* studies this profession of faith word by word. Last Sunday the opening words were "We believe in one God." There is only one God, but there are three Divine Persons in God, so we began with the Holy Trinity, the basic and most profound mystery of our faith.

We move now to the next section of the *Catechism*, treated in great detail: "We believe in one God, the Father Almighty, maker of heaven and earth and of all things visible and invisible." This section of the *Catechism* stresses most particularly the concept of the almighty power of God, because it is obviously so important in our lives, and everything else depends on it.

There was a political scientist at University of Yale, Harold Lasswell, who talked about politics in terms of who gets what, when, and how. His theory was that a political leader's power depends on what he has to distribute, who will receive the resources at his control, when these will be doled out, and how.

King Herod, just read about in today's Gospel, had some of this kind of power. Indeed, he had the awesome power over life and death. Fearing that the newly born Child would be a rival, he sent his soldiers to kill the Child. Lest there be a case of mistaken identity, he ordered his soldiers to kill all of the male children born recently in Bethlehem. This they did in what we call the "slaughter of the innocents".

The wise men recognized that the almighty power of God is infinitely different from that of Herod or of any other ruler. God gives freely of His goodness. God gives us life, He doesn't take it away from us. Because God is secure in His almighty power, He could send His Son to redeem us, even though He knew His Son was going to be crucified. God also could send Him in the weak, helpless form of a child, conceived of and through Mary, a virgin, because "nothing is impossible with God". He was born in a manger and yet attracted the whole world, that world symbolized by the wise men. This is God's sense of security in His own mighty power. The Creed appropriately begins "We believe in one God, the Father, the Almighty."

The *Catechism* tells us: "Of all the divine attributes, only God's omnipotence [His almighty power] is named in the Creed. God who created everything also rules everything and can do everything" [268]. "Nothing is impossible with God" [269].

When the angel came and invited Mary to be the Mother of the Son of God, Mary asked the obvious question, "How can this be? I am a virgin." The angel said, in essence, "God the Holy Spirit will come upon you. That which will be born of you, conceived within you, will be conceived and born by the power of God, for whom nothing is impossible."

The *Catechism* goes on:

> God is the Father Almighty. His fatherhood and almighty power complement each other. God reveals his almighty and fatherly power through the way he takes care of our needs; "I will be your father, and you shall be my sons and daughters, says the Lord God Almighty" (2 Cor 6:18) [270].

We pray constantly the prayer our Lord Himself taught us, "Our Father . . . give us this day our daily bread." We know You are all powerful. We know you could crush us, but you will not. You will take care of our needs. "God displays his power most clearly by freely forgiving our sins" [271].

We are told in the Gospel that our Divine Lord was presented with a paralytic. He said to him, "Your sins are forgiven." Those standing around said, "This is blasphemous. Who does He think He is, that He has the power to do this? God is the only one who can forgive sins." Then our Lord asked, "Is it easier to say, 'Your sins are forgiven', or to say, 'Get up and walk'? I will prove to you that the Son of Man has power on earth to forgive sins." So He said to the paralyzed man, "I tell you, pick up your bed and go home" (Lk 5:17–26). Our Lord made clear that to forgive sins was even a greater power than to heal a paralytic, because serious sin cuts us off completely from Almighty God, and only God can restore us to intimacy with Him.

The *Catechism* says:

> Faith in God the Father Almighty can be tried by the experience of evil and suffering. God can sometimes seem absent and incapable of stopping evil. But in a most mysterious way, God the Father has revealed his almighty power in the voluntary self-emptying and Resurrection of his Son, by which he conquered evil [272].

How often have we said, "How could such terrible things happen to such wonderful people? This is a fine family, and their son was killed in an automobile accident. This is a wonderful family, and their daughter has wandered off on drugs. How could God let this happen to good people?" This is a profound mystery.

We are told in the *Catechism*:

Only faith can fathom the mysterious ways of God's almighty power. This faith glories in its weaknesses in order to draw to itself Christ's power [273].

Nothing is then more apt to affirm our faith and our hope than the conviction deeply etched in our souls that nothing is impossible with God [274].

If we believe that, if that burns within our hearts, then we are prepared for anything.

The *Catechism* says that the teaching on creation

. . . concerns the very foundations of human and Christian life; for it makes explicit the response of the Christian faith to the elementary question that men of all times have asked themselves, the question "Where do we come from? Where are we going?" "What is our origin? What is our end?" "Where does everything that exists come from and where is it going?" [282].

The question of the origins of the world and of the human race has been the object of numerous scientific studies which have magnificently enriched our knowledge of the age and dimensions of the cosmos, the development of living forms and the appearance of man [283].

But we know at the same time that, valuable as many of these discoveries are, science cannot accurately determine the age of the world, the age of the human race. It seems that every few years we learn that another human fossil has been discovered, hundreds of thousands of years older than the one that was considered to be the oldest that had ever existed. Science is always groping; it never has absolute certitude about such things.

These [scientific] discoveries invite us to admire even more the grandeur of the Creator, prompting us to give him thanks for all his works and for the understanding and wisdom he gives to researchers and the learned [283].

The Church is glad of this. The Church has nothing to fear from the scientific world, if the scientific world follows logical principles and truly searches for truth.

A question of another order . . . goes beyond the proper domain of the natural sciences. It is not only a question of knowing when and how the universe arose materially, or when man appeared, but rather of discovering the *meaning* of such an origin: is it governed by chance, blind fate, anonymous necessity, or by a Being . . . intelligent and good, a being called "God"? And if the world does come from God's wisdom and goodness, why is there evil? Where does it come from? Who is responsible for it? Is there any liberation from it? [284]

In reflecting on other chapters of the *Catechism*, we have quoted from Dr. Viktor Frankl's book, *Man's Search for Meaning*. Dr. Frankl was a Jewish psychiatrist in a concentration camp under the Nazis. He became a Catholic and wrote this beautiful work about the essential search for meaning by human beings. Frederick Nietzsche, the philosopher, sometimes thought to be an atheist, said, "He who has a *why* to live can bear with almost any *how*."

The *Catechism* says:

> One finds in ancient religions and cultures numerous myths concerning origins. Certain philosophers have said that everything is God, that the world is God, or that the development of the world is the becoming of God (Pantheism). . . . Others have affirmed the existence of two eternal principles, Good and Evil, Light and Darkness, locked in a permanent struggle (Dualism, Manichaeism). Some admit that the world was made by God, but as by a watch-maker who, once he had made a watch, abandons it to itself (Deism). Finally, others do not accept any origin of the world, but see it as merely the interplay of material elements which have always existed (Materialism) [285].

You know also of Darwin's theory of "evolutionism", that higher forms have evolved from lower forms in a battle called "the survival of the fittest".

The *Catechism* says:

> Human intelligence has the capacity, certainly, to find a response to the question of origins. In fact, the existence of God the Creator can be known with certainty through his works in the light of human reason, even if this knowledge is often obscured and disfigured by error [286].

St. Paul describes this beautifully in the first chapter of his Letter to the People of Rome. Immanuel Kant, the philosopher, whom we have quoted before, says, "I can know God by the starry sky above me and the moral law within me."

The *Catechism* says, however:

> The truth about creation is so important for all human life that . . . beyond the natural knowledge that everyone can have of the Creator, God progressively revealed the mystery of creation to Israel [287].

He called Abram, who was practicing paganism, who saw human sacrifice all around, who lived among people who worshipped the sun and moon and the stars and various pagan gods. Abram didn't know any better himself. Suddenly, God seems to come from nowhere and calls Abram out of paganism and gives him the Truth, gives him the faith of the Chosen People, the Israelites. It starts with Abram, and it has never been lost. That was by God's revelation, a revelation not unlike what we call the Feast of the Epiphany.

We are told in the *Catechism*:

> Among all the words of Sacred Scripture about creation, the first three chapters of Genesis occupy a unique place. . . . The inspired authors have placed them at the beginning of Scripture to express, in their solemn language, the truths of creation, its origin and its end in God, its order and its goodness, the vocation of man, and finally the drama of sin and the hope of salvation [289].

The Book of Genesis is the book of beginnings, more accurately, the book of begetting, the book of conceiving the world. The story is told in poetic form; indeed, it is told in three different ways. The way best known is that God created the world in six days and rested on the seventh. We have no need to believe that these are six days of twenty-four hours. They could have been millions of years, but God in successive phases apparently created the world and all things. The *Catechism* reminds us of the words of Genesis: "In the beginning, God created the heaven and the earth" [out of nothing]. . . . All that exists depends on God who gives it being [290].

There are many theories, such as the one that taught that there are four elements—air, fire, earth, and water—and that somehow these all are reformulated into different forms. On the contrary, we believe that God created everything out of nothing.

The Gospel of St. John says:

> In the beginning was the Word . . . and the Word was God. . . . all was made by him, and without him nothing was made (Jn 1:1–3). The New Testament reveals that God created everything by the eternal Word, his beloved Son [291].

Christ was the blueprint. It was through Christ, fashioning everything after Christ, that God the Father made the world. But we are told in mysterious language that "God breathed across the waters and brought order out of chaos." Is this an early hint of the Holy Spirit?

The *Catechism* says:

> The Church's faith likewise affirms the creative action of the Holy Spirit, the "giver of life," the "Spirit Creator," . . . the "source of all good" [291].

> Scripture and Tradition constantly teach and celebrate this fundamental truth: "The world was created for the glory of God." [But] St. Bonaventure

explains that God created all things "not to *increase* his glory, but to show forth and *communicate* this glory," for God has no other reason for creating than his love and goodness . . . [293].

The *Catechism* says: "Creation's ultimate purpose is that God, 'the Creator of all beings, may become "all in all" and so fulfill both his glory and our happiness'" [294].

I am presently giving a retreat to a group of women considering the possibility of a religious vocation. I began by talking about God's sharing His being with us and that as a result of this we are infinitely valuable just because we *are*. We share God's glory by *being*. The world judges us by what we do, by what we produce, but we are of inestimable value simply because we *are*. Many of the women on this retreat have come to me and said they found this so comforting, because they work in a world that demands so much of them, where their status is measured by the kind of job they have, the money they make, where they live, and so on. But just to *be*, created by God, sharing in God's *being*, makes us of inestimable importance.

I read from the *Catechism* about the mother of those who are called the seven sons of Maccabee. King Antiochus was demanding that all the Jewish people abandon their practices, insisting, for instance, that they eat pork, when, at that time, it was forbidden. The sons in the Maccabee family said, "Why are you doing this? We would rather die then abandon the tradition of our ancestors." So the king cuts off their tongues, hands, and legs, and he throws them into boiling oil. Yet their mother, a woman of great faith, says to them:

> I do not know how you came into being in my womb. It was not I who gave you life and breath, nor I who set in order the elements within each of you. Therefore the Creator of the world, who shaped the human race and who is at the origin of all things, will in his mercy give life and breath back to you again, since you now forget yourselves for love of his laws. . . . My child, look at the heaven and the earth and see all that is in them, and recognize that God did not make them out of anything that existed. And in the same way the human race came into being (2 Macc 7:22–23, 28) [297].

Can you imagine that kind of faith, after seeing her own seven sons put to death rather than deny their faith? She encourages them, saying God is almighty. God brought you into existence. Don't fear this king and don't fear death.

We are told in the *Catechism*: "Because creation comes forth from God's goodness, it shares in that goodness—after each day of creation, 'God looked at the work of his hands and saw that it was good' . . ." (Gen 1:4) [299].

The Church teaches that this is not an evil world. On the contrary, it is made by Almighty God in His goodness. "He is present to his creatures at the most intimate level: 'In him we live and move and have our being'" (Acts 17:28) [300].

The *Catechism* says:

> After he has created it, God does not abandon his creation to itself. He not only gives it being and existence, but also and at every moment upholds and sustains it in being, gives us the power to act and brings us to our final end [301].

God holds us in the palm of His hand. If He withdrew His hand, we would simply cease to exist. But He loves us too much.

The *Catechism* continues:

> Jesus asks childlike abandon to the providence of our heavenly Father, who takes care of his children's smallest needs: "Do not worry, saying 'What will we eat?' or 'What will we drink?' . . . Your heavenly Father knows that you need all these things. But strive first for his kingdom and his justice, and all these things will be given to you as well" (Mt 6:31–33) [305].

That's what He meant by saying, "Become as little children." Does the tiny little child ask his father, "Are you going to bring home enough money from work to feed me, to clothe me, to put a roof over my head?" No, a child takes that for granted in the father. So, too, we have to take for granted trusting in God as our Father.

The magi made themselves as little children. They weren't fooled. They weren't frightened by King Herod and all his power and his soldiers. They weren't all puffed up with their own power, with their own wealth. They came as children to the crib of a Child.

> God is the sovereign master of his plan. But he also makes use of his creatures' cooperation for its fulfillment. . . . God grants us his creatures not only our existence, but also the dignity of acting in and of ourselves, of being causes and sources of one another and thus of cooperating in the accomplishment of his plan [306].

I met Mother Teresa on the day I was ordained a bishop, and the first words she said to me were "Give God permission." In other words, God wants to work through you, to use your hands, to use your feet, to look at the world through your eyes, to speak to people through your tongue. Give Him permission to do so. He can use every single one of us in His goodness.

The *Catechism* then talks to us about the terrible mystery of evil, doesn't pretend that we can understand it, but asks us to recognize the tremendous potential in suffering, suffering that comes from evil. We can unite this suffering with the suffering, crucifixion, and death of our Divine Lord and bring about untold good in the world. We don't understand this, but, instead of wasting our pain just because we don't understand it, we can unite it with the sufferings of our Lord and bring about incalculable good.

Finally, the *Catechism* quotes St. Thomas More, reminding us of the words of St. Paul:

> We know that all things work together for good for those who love God (Rom 8:28) [313].

> St. Thomas More, shortly before his martyrdom [he was killed by King Henry VIII], consoled his daughter, saying, "Nothing can come but what God wills. All that he wills, however bad it may seem to us, is in the long run better for us" [313].

It is so difficult for us to understand or accept, but so many things that we think are going to be bad are what we call "blessings in disguise". The *Catechism* concludes this section with this paragraph that I quote:

> We firmly believe that God is master of the world and of history. But the ways of divine providence are often unknown to us. It is only at the end, when our partial knowledge will cease, when we shall see God "face to face," that his ways will be known to us in full. Then God will have guided his creation, even through the dramas of evil and sin, to that endless sabbath rest for which he created the heavens and the earth [314].

As the Book of Revelation tells us, "There mourning and sorrow will be no more, nor weeping, for the former things will all be wiped away in the beauty of heaven." The *Catechism* is another set of guidelines on this pilgrimage to our eternal home.

7

Creation and the Fall

BAPTISM OF THE LORD
JANUARY 9, 1994
PONTIFICAL MASS

The final issue of *Time* magazine for 1993 has as a cover story what it calls "The New Age of Angels" (Dec. 27, 1993). It says that 69 percent of Americans believe angels exist, which will comfort the angels! It also says in this rather lengthy story that there are "angels-only boutiques, angel newsletters, angel seminars", and angel books. Indeed, it says that of religious books five of the ten on the paperback best-seller list are about angels. (Someone sent me at Christmas *Angel Voices*, by Karen Goldman.) The article gives its own answer to the question of why this rush on angels: "In their modern incarnation, these mighty messengers and fearless soldiers have been reduced to bite-size beings, easily digested. . . . For those who choke too easily on God and His rules, theologians observe, angels are the handy compromise, all fluff and meringue, kind, nonjudgmental. And they are available to everyone, like aspirin" (p. 56).

That's not quite a scriptural and theological explanation of angels! It is interesting, however, that angels are in the air, not to make a pun. One hears a lot about them these days, and we will be talking about them in this catechetical homily, the seventh in our series of homilies on the new *Catechism of the Catholic Church*.

Before this, however, we have to turn to the feast of the day and the Gospel, the important feast of the Baptism of our Lord. Our Lord did not enter the waters of the Jordan to be purified of sin. As you know, John the Baptist was teaching conversion and repentance to prepare for the coming of Christ. John the Baptist was not able to purify people of sin. But water is always a symbol of purification, and the Jewish people, by going through this purification ceremony, wanted to show that they wanted to be rid of their sins. It didn't affect them "objectively", but it showed that they wanted a change of heart. It was therefore very important. It is said that when our Lord entered the waters of baptism—with John resisting, incidentally—it was to show His approval of what was happening and to show that He would be consecrating these waters by

His presence, foreshadowing the sacrament of Baptism, essential for purification from original sin, which is very much part of today's session on the *Catechism*.

This is a major feast. We tend to settle for the Feast of the Epiphany, when our Lord is revealed to the wise men as the Son of God as an infant, but there are many other revelations. In the Eastern Church, particularly, this is a major feast. Perhaps close to a thousand years ago in Russia, for instance, in what was then St. Petersburg, the river would be frozen, and they would build a little temporary chapel on it. There they would have the sacred liturgy of the Mass. They would dig a hole in the ice right within the chapel. The ruler would be there. At a particular point the priest would reach down into the waters and bless everyone with the waters of the river, and the soldiers would all bow in adoration. They recognized this was a very important thing; it was symbolic of the waters of the River Jordan. Indeed, there are some countries in which people bury their dead by the ocean, because they say that Christ sanctified all waters, and that the sun lifts the waters of the Jordan, scatters it in clouds throughout the world, and then rains it down in different places. In a mysterious way, then, the bodies of the dead are brought in touch with the waters of the Jordan.

The baptism of Christ is a reminder of the water that sprang up miraculously by God's power in the desert to quench the thirst of the Israelites. It is a reminder, as well, that God parted the waters so the Israelites could escape slavery. But the importance of this feast is intimately connected with original sin. John the Baptist would not have been out there preaching, Christ would not have come, had it not been for original sin.

The section of the *Catechism* we will focus on today begins:

> The [Creeds] profess that God is "Creator of heaven and earth, . . . of the visible and invisible universe" [325].

> The Scriptural expression "heaven and earth" means everything that exists, creation in its entirety. . . . [T]he earth is the world of man. [Heaven is the world of the invisible.] Heaven can designate both the firmament and also the "place" proper for God—"our Father in heaven" [326].

God is a pure Spirit and, of course, doesn't need a place. But we think of the heavens—we tend to think of the sun and the moon and the stars and then whatever is above these—as the dwelling place of God.

The *Catechism* says:

> . . . God "from the beginning of time simultaneously created from nothing both orders of creatures, the spiritual and the bodily, that is, the angelic and the earthly; then the human person, who . . . shares in both orders, being composed of spirit and body" [327].

The existence of the spiritual, non-bodily beings that the sacred Scriptures usually call "angels" is a truth of faith [328].

Angels are servants and messengers of God [329].

The term "angel" means messenger.

The *Catechism* goes on to say: "From his Incarnation to his Ascension, the life of the Word incarnate was surrounded by the worship and service of angels" [333].

It was an angel who came to Mary and told her that God was inviting her to become the mother of His Son, Jesus.

The angels' song of praise at the birth of Christ [which we just sang in the Gloria] has not ceased to resound in the Church's praise: "Glory to God in the highest!" (Lk 2:14) [333].

Immediately after the story in today's Gospel of Jesus' baptism, we are told Jesus went into the desert and fasted for forty days and forty nights prior to beginning His public life, and angels ministered to Him in the desert. The *Catechism* says:

In its liturgy, the Church joins with the angels to worship . . . God; invokes their assistance, as in the beautiful words of the funeral Mass, "May the angels lead you into Paradise . . ." [335].

Angels are always at the service of God.

From infancy to death, human life is surrounded by angels' watchfulness and intercession. [Here the *Catechism* quotes St. Basil:] "Beside each believer stands an angel as protector and shepherd to conduct him through life" [336]. [This is clearly contrary to those who believe guardian angels are a myth.]

Now we leave the invisible world for a moment and go to the visible world. We are told:

God himself created the visible world in all its richness, diversity and order [337].

Nothing that exists does not owe its existence to God the Creator [338].

Each creature possesses its own goodness and perfection [339].

In the story of creation, remember, we are told at the end of each phase of creation, God looked at the work of His hands "and saw that it was good".

The *Catechism* says:

. . . For this reason man must respect the proper goodness of every creature, to avoid any disordered use of things, thereby scorning the Creator and bringing disastrous consequences on human beings and their environment [339].

All the problems with the environment are brought about by human beings who fail to reverence God's creation. The destruction of human beings in the womb is brought about by those who fail to recognize the sacredness of God's creation.

The order and harmony of the created world result from the diversity of beings and from the relations which exist among them. [All different but all sacred to God.] . . . The beauty of creation reflects the infinite beauty of the Creator . . . [341].

The *Catechism* goes on:

God loves all his creatures and takes care of each one, even the lowly sparrow. Nevertheless, Jesus said: "You are of more value than many sparrows," or again: "How much more valuable is a man than a sheep!" (Lk 12:6–7) [342].

Man is the summit of the work of creation, as the inspired account expresses by clearly distinguishing the creation of man from that of the other creatures [343].

After God finished the work of creation, we are told, very poetically, God "rested". God doesn't need rest in the sense that we understand rest. This phrase means God didn't create on that day. The Jewish world kept Saturday as the Sabbath, beginning on Friday evening. But Christ rose from the dead on Sunday. The *Catechism* calls this *the eighth day*, a very, very special day. The human person, the summit of God's creation, was supposed to worship Him on this special day of Sunday, the day that begins the "new creation" [349].

The *Catechism* goes on to talk about the nature of the human race and makes very clear that:

God created man "in his own image, in the image of God he created him, male and female he created them" (Gen 1:27). Man therefore occupies a unique place in creation . . . [355].

Of all visible creatures, only men are "capable of knowing and of loving their Creator." . . . They alone are called to share, by knowledge and love, in God's own life. They have been created for this end, and this is the fundamental reason for their dignity . . . [356].

We live in a world filled with contempt for the human person. We live in a world that brutalizes the human person. We live in a world that makes us no higher than beasts. As a matter of fact, there are people far more concerned about whales and snails than about human beings. The

Catechism reminds us that the human person is at the top of it all, at the summit. God placed Adam in charge of all things.

"Because he is in the image of God, every human individual possesses the dignity of a person: he is not only something, but someone" [357]. You are very special just because you *are*, because you're made in the image and likeness of God.

> God created everything for man, but men are created to serve and love God and to offer him all of creation . . . [358].

The *Catechism* says: "Graced by a common origin, *the human race forms a unity*. For God has made to spring from only one source all the descendants of man" (Acts 17:26) [360]. In other words, we are all brothers and sisters. If this fundamental teaching of the *Catechism* were observed, it would be the end of wars, it would be the end of hatred, the end of division in families, and so on.

> The human person, created in the image of God, is both a bodily and a spiritual being. In symbolic language Scripture tells us "the LORD God formed man from the dust of the earth, and then breathed into his nostrils the breath of life; and man became a living being" (Gen 2:7) [362].

> The human *body* shares in the dignity of God's image: it is a *human* body precisely because it is animated by a spiritual soul. The whole human person is intended to become, in the body of Christ, a temple of the Spirit:

> "Body and soul, but truly one, man, in his corporeal condition, brings together in himself the elements of the material world which culminate in him and freely praise their Creator. It is therefore forbidden for man to despise his bodily life. But, on the contrary, he must esteem and respect his body, which has been created by God and is destined to be raised on the last day" (*Gaudium et Spes*, no. 14) [364].

The *Catechism* goes on to tell us that all material creation is reflected in the human body. The human person also has a unique element: "The Church teaches that every spiritual soul is created immediately by God. The soul is not 'produced' by the parents . . ." [366]. Parents produce the elements that will become the human person, but God breathes into the womb of the woman the soul of this newly formed entity. The soul, which comes from God, does not perish when separated from the body at death but will be reunited with the body in the final resurrection.

The *Catechism* goes on to face clearly the question of man and woman.

> God *created* and *willed* man and woman in perfect equality as human persons. "Being man" or "being woman" is a good, a reality willed by God; man and woman have an inalienable dignity which comes immediately from

God their Creator. Man and woman are both in the image of God with equal dignity . . . [369].

Neither man nor woman, God himself is pure spirit in which there is no place for a difference of sexes. God is mother; God is father [370].

God can be considered a spouse. We human beings like to attribute our attributes to God, instead of recognizing that we are a reflection of God. Men and women are equally reflections of God.

God created man and woman *together* and willed each *for* the other. . . . "It is not good that the man should be alone. I will make him a helper as his partner" (Gen 2:18). None of the animals can be man's partner (Gen 2:19–20) [371].

God made man and woman "each for the other" . . . to be a communion of persons in which each can be "helper" for the other, for both are equal as persons . . . and complementary as masculine and feminine. In marriage, God unites them in such a way that, by forming "one flesh" (Gen 2:24), they might be able to transmit human life. . . . By transmitting human life to their descendants, man and woman, as spouses and parents, cooperate in a unique way in the Creator's work [372].

Childbirth and conception are not curses. These make a man and a woman co-creators with Almighty God.

We go on to this mystery of original sin.

The Church . . . teaches that our first parents, Adam and Eve, were created in a state of original holiness and justice [375].

. . . As long as he remained intimate with God, man would neither suffer nor die [376].

This entire harmony called original justice, foreseen for man in God's plan, would be lost by the sin of our first parents [379].

God is infinitely good and all his works are good. Yet no one can escape the experience of suffering or the evils in nature . . . . Where does evil come from? [385].

To try to understand what sin is, we must first recognize the deep bond between man and God, for only in this relationship is the evil of sin unmasked . . . [386].

We were all supposed to be in wonderful harmony with God, to live in Paradise and then to be taken even to a higher level, into heaven itself, face to face with God.

The true identity of sin is revealed as refusal of God and our opposition to him, which continue to burden the life of man and history [386].

Here is a very important passage from the *Catechism*:

> Without the knowledge Revelation gives us of God, we cannot recognize
> sin clearly and are tempted to explain it only as a developmental flaw, a psy-
> chological weakness, a mistake, or the necessary consequences of an inade-
> quate social structure, and so forth. Only in the knowledge of God's plan
> for humanity can we understand that sin is an abuse of the freedom that
> God gives to persons created with the potential to love God and one an-
> other [387].

Social plans, welfare plans, that ignore the reality of original sin are simply doomed to failure. We cannot build a utopia here. We are weak, fallen
human beings, and we sin. That destroys all of the most beautiful social
plans.

> The account of the "fall," original sin, uses figurative language, but affirms a
> fundamental event, a deed that took place at the beginning of the history of
> human beings. . . . All human history is marked by the original fault freely
> committed by our first parents [390].

> Behind the disobedient choice of our first parents there is a seductive voice
> opposed to God, which, out of envy, makes them fall into death. Scripture
> and the Church's Tradition see in this being a fallen angel, called "Satan" or
> the "devil". The Church teaches that he was at first a good angel, created
> by God . . . [391].

> Scripture speaks of a sin on the part of these angels. This "fall" consisted in
> the free choice of these created spirits, who radically and irrevocably re-
> jected God and his Kingdom . . . [392].

> God created man in his image and established him in his friendship. A spiri-
> tual creature, man can live out this friendship only in free obedience to
> God. It is this that expresses the prohibition made for man against eating of
> the tree of the knowledge of good and evil: God said, "From the day that
> you eat of this, you will die" (Gen 2:17) [396].

This was symbolic. God said, "You can have everything, but you may
not eat of this one tree that grows in the center of the Garden of Paradise,
called the 'tree of the knowledge of good and evil'." Did Adam and Eve
eat an apple or a pear or a plum? We don't know that. We know only that
they determined that they were going to eat of this particular tree, the one
that God said that they shouldn't eat of. The devil tempted them to do
this. What did they think they were going to accomplish? They would become like God Himself. If they ate of the fruit of the "tree of knowledge
of good and evil", *they* would determine what is right and what is wrong.
They wouldn't need God, they wouldn't need commandments, they

wouldn't be told any longer what to do or what not to do. *They* would determine what would be right and what would be wrong. That was the original sin.

Then we are told in the *Catechism*, "In this sin man preferred himself to God and by the same sin he scorned God" [398].

> Scripture portrays the dramatic consequences of this first disobedience. Adam and Eve immediately lost the grace of original holiness [399].

What happened after the first sin was committed? Adam blamed Eve. God said, "Why did you do this? How did you know that you are naked? Why are you ashamed now?" Adam said, "She made me do it." It's a very interesting thing. The first result of original sin was to divide a husband and wife, then came all of the things that have happened since.

> The harmony of original justice in which God had established them was then destroyed; the control of the soul's spiritual faculties over the body was shattered; and the union of man and woman was made subject to tensions; their relations were henceforth to be characterized by lust and domination. Harmony with creation was broken: visible creation became alien and hostile toward humanity. . . . Death entered human history [400].

Death in every form entered human history: crime, murder, drugs, abortion, euthanasia, disease. All these entered through original sin.

> Since this first sin, a veritable invasion of sin floods the world: the murder of Abel by his brother Cain; the universal corruption that followed in the wake of sin . . . [401].

In this extraordinary mystery that we don't pretend to understand, we find that Adam and Eve transmitted this sin through human nature. We receive human nature and receive the corruption, the destruction, the devastation of original sin. When we are baptized, it becomes possible for us to get back into heaven because Christ came and suffered and died for us and gave us the sacrament of Baptism to open the gates of heaven. Unfortunately, we're still left with all of the other faults that accrued because of original sin. We've lost what are called the "preternatural" gifts of God: freedom from death, from suffering, from temptation, and so on. We will be talking about that in a later session.

> The doctrine of original sin, connected with that of the redemption by Christ, illuminates the human condition and human activity in the world. . . . Ignoring the fact that humanity has a wounded nature inclined to evil gives rise to serious errors in the areas of education, politics, social action, and morals [407].

We think we're going to create a perfect world, but we forget about original sin.

The final paragraph in this section says:

> After the fall, man was not abandoned by God. On the contrary, God called him and in a mysterious way heralded his victory over evil and the recovery from his fall—the first announcement of the coming of the Messiah and Redeemer, that of a struggle between the serpent and the Woman, Mary, and of the final victory of the one descending from her [Jesus] (Gen 3:15) [410].

This was the announcement about Jesus, the One who humiliated Himself by having Himself baptized in the Jordan to show that one day, through His humiliation, through His suffering, through His death, and through the sacrament of Baptism, He would restore to us the possibility of heaven, perfect union with Almighty God for all eternity.

8

Jesus Came to Give Life, Not Death

COMMEMORATION OF *ROE V. WADE*
SECOND SUNDAY OF THE YEAR
JANUARY 16, 1994
PONTIFICAL MASS

We are grateful to the Knights of Columbus and the Columbiettes for arranging this Mass marking the anniversary of the *Roe v. Wade* decision. We dedicate this Mass to the sacred cause of human life and ask that everyone pray during this Mass and each day that we will recover in this land a sense of the sacredness of human life and put aside the contempt for human life demonstrated by the violence each day.

Even so, just as the mail must go through, and the show must go on, so we must have our weekly session on the new *Catechism*. However, even though there might not seem initially to be a direct relationship between this section of the *Catechism* and the cause of the sacredness of human life, we will find, I think, before we finish, that the basic reason for the respect of the human person is found in this section of the *Catechism*.

We have been reflecting in these past weeks on the Creed, both the Apostles' Creed and the Nicene Creed used at Mass. We have already talked about the words "I believe in one God, the Father Almighty, Maker of heaven and earth and of all things visible and invisible." Now we go to the next line in the Creed, "I believe in Jesus Christ, the only Son of God."

The *Catechism* says:

> We believe and confess that Jesus of Nazareth is the eternal Son of God made man. He was born a Jew of a daughter of Israel at Bethlehem when Herod the Great was king under the Roman emperor Caesar Augustus, a carpenter by trade, crucified in Jerusalem under the procurator Pontius Pilate during the reign of the emperor Tiberius. We believe and confess that Jesus came from God, descended from heaven and became flesh [423].

We believe this is true of *every* human person. Every one of us comes from God—not in the same way in which Jesus comes from God—but all human life comes from God.

66

The *Catechism* goes on: "From the beginning, the first disciples burned with the desire to proclaim Christ: 'We cannot keep from speaking about what we have seen and heard' " (Acts 4:20) [425].

This is true of those who have captured a sense of the sacredness of human life. So many people who give their own lives to this cause do so because they have come to recognize that every human person is made in the image and likeness of God. Many thought that the apostles were mad; many think that pro-life people are mad, and yet pro-life people recognize what we must all recognize and shout from the housetops: that every human life comes from God and belongs to God.

The *Catechism* continues:

At the heart of catechesis we find essentially a person, that of Jesus of Nazareth, the only Son of the Father, who suffered and died for us and who, now risen, lives with us forever. To catechize is to set forth, in Christ's person, the fullness of God's eternal plan. It is to seek understanding of the meaning of Christ's actions, words, and signs. The objective of catechesis is to put us . . . in communion with Jesus Christ, who alone can lead us in the Spirit to the Father's love and enable us to share in the life of the Holy Trinity [426].

We're not doing these sessions on the *Catechism* simply that we'll come to know more about our faith but that we'll come to know God more. We'll feel a closer communion with our Divine Lord, a more intimate contact with Jesus.

Next the *Catechism* talks about the name "Jesus".

In Hebrew, the name *Jesus* means "God saves." . . . Since God alone can forgive sins, it is he who, in Jesus, his eternal Son made man, "will save his people from their sins" (Mt 1:11). In Jesus, God sums up the entire history of salvation on behalf of men [430].

. . . "There is no other name under heaven given to men by which we can be saved [except the name of Jesus]" (Acts 4:12) [432].

The *Catechism* continues:

Jesus' name is at the heart of Christian prayer. All liturgical prayers conclude with the words "through our Lord Jesus Christ . . ." or "through Christ our Lord." The *Hail Mary* reaches its summit in the words "blessed is the fruit of your womb, Jesus." . . . Many Christians, such as St. Joan of Arc, have died with the name "Jesus" on their lips [435].

Many pro-life people have prayed the name of Jesus in the Hail Mary before abortion clinics and have suffered a great deal for doing so.

Next, the *Catechism* reflects on the name, "Christ", the "second half" of Jesus' name: "The word 'Christ' comes from the Greek translation of the Hebrew *Messiah*, which means 'anointed'" [436]. You and I were anointed in Baptism. We were set aside for Christ.

> To the shepherds, the angel announced Jesus' birth as the Messiah promised to Israel: "To you is born this day in the city of David a Savior, who is Christ, the Lord" (Lk 2:11). . . . God called Joseph to "take Mary as his wife, for the child in her is from the Holy Spirit," so that Jesus, "who is called Christ," should be born of Joseph's spouse into the messianic lineage of David (Mt 1:20) [437].

Peter confessed Jesus as "the Christ, the Son of the living God." You remember that awesome scene when Jesus asked the apostles, "Who do people say that I am?" The apostles probably shuffled their feet a bit when they said, "Well, some say you're John the Baptist; others say you're Elijah, risen from the dead." Then our Lord asked Peter, on whom the Church was to be built, and Peter cried out, "Thou art the Christ, the Son of the living God."

The *Catechism* says:

> . . . This would be, from the beginning, the center of the apostolic faith, first professed by Peter as the Church's foundation [442].

> The Gospels report that at two solemn moments, Christ's Baptism and Transfiguration, the Father's voice designated Jesus as his beloved Son. Jesus also called himself the only Son of God, and by this title affirmed his eternal preexistence (Jn 3:16). . . . The centurion exclaimed before the crucified Christ, "Truly this man was God's Son" (Mk 15:39) . . . [444].

The *Catechism* continues:

> From the beginning of Christian history, the affirmation of the lordship of Jesus over the world and over history also signifies the recognition that man should not submit his personal freedom absolutely to any earthly power but only to God the Father and the Lord Jesus Christ [450].

This is why we question and will continue to question that any president of the United States, any congressman, any congressional body, any governmental authority, while it may have the legal power, we question that it has the *moral* authority to demand that we pay to have infants killed in their mother's wombs. Only the Lord has authority over life and death.

The *Catechism* asks the question, "Why was the Word made flesh?"

> With the Creed, we respond by confessing: "For us men and for our salvation he came down from heaven; by the power of the Holy Spirit, he took flesh of the Virgin Mary, and became man" [456].

The *Catechism* gives four reasons for this:

The Word became flesh for us in order to save us by reconciling us with God, who "loved us and sent his Son to be the atoning sacrifice for our sins" [457].

Secondly:

The Word became flesh so that thus we might know God's love . . . . For "God so loved the world that he gave his only Son so that everyone who believes in him may not perish, but may have eternal life" (Jn 3:16) [458].

Thirdly:

The Word became flesh to be our model of holiness. . . . "I am the way, and the truth, and the life. No one comes to the Father except through me" (Jn 14:6). . . . Jesus is . . . the norm of the new law: "Love one another as I have loved you" (Jn 15:12) [459].

What did the first catechism in this country say? Why did God make me? "To know Him, to love Him, to serve Him in this life, and to be happy with Him forever in heaven."

Finally, we are told in the *Catechism*: "The Word became flesh to make us participants of the divine nature . . . " [460].

Think of that! St. Athanasius thought of it, and he came out with these bold words: "For the Son of God became man to make us God" [460]. Can we understand, then, why every person is sacred?

The *Catechism* goes on:

. . . [T]he Church calls the fact that God's Son assumed a human nature in order to accomplish our salvation through it "Incarnation" [461]. [This is from the Latin, which means "in the flesh".]

The unique and altogether singular event of the Incarnation of the Son of God does not mean that Jesus Christ is partly God and partly man, nor does it imply that he is the result of a confused mixture of the divine and the human. He became truly man while remaining truly God. Jesus Christ is true God and true man. During the first centuries, the Church had to defend and clarify this truth of faith against the heresies that falsified it [464].

The *Catechism* names a number of heresies:

The first heresies denied not so much Christ's divinity as his true humanity (Gnostic Docetism) [465].

The Monophysites affirmed that the human nature had ceased to exist as such in Christ when the divine person of God's Son assumed it [467].

But, the *Catechism* tells us: ". . . Jesus is inseparably true God and true man. He is truly the Son of God who, without ceasing to be God and Lord, became a man and our brother . . ." [469].

We might say that today's heresy is not so much whether Christ was human but whether unborn babies are human. To question that, it seems to me, certainly borders on the heretical.

> "The Son of God worked with the hands of a man, thought with the mind of a man, acted with the will of a man, and loved with the heart of a man. Born of the Virgin Mary, he truly became one of us, like unto us in all things except sin" (*Gaudium et Spes*, no. 22) [470].

The *Catechism* goes on:

> Jesus knew and loved each and every one of us during his life, his agony, and his Passion, and gave himself up for each of us . . . . He has loved us all with a human heart. For this reason, the Sacred Heart of Jesus, pierced by our sins and for our salvation, "is considered the chief sign and symbol of the . . . love with which the divine Redeemer continually loves the eternal Father" and all men without exception (Pius XII) [478].

So Jesus appeared to Margaret Mary Alacoque, that nun in the Visitation convent in France, revealing his heart with the words "Behold this heart that has so loved men and been loved so little in return."

The *Catechism* goes on:

> The Virgin Mary was invited to conceive him in whom the "whole fullness of divinity" would dwell "bodily" (Col 2:9). The divine response to her question "How can this be, since I know not man?" was given by the Spirit's power: "The Holy Spirit will come upon you" (Lk 1:34–35) [484].

We must remember that Mary was *invited* to become the Mother of the Son of God. She was a virgin. She could have said, "I can't do this. It's going to be terribly inconvenient. What will Joseph say? What will my parents say?" She was *invited*. What would have happened if Mary had said "no" to the angel? Would there have been a Christmas, a crucifixion? Would we be here today? Doesn't the Holy Spirit say the same to every woman, to every couple whom He invites to bear the child whose life can come only from God? "The Holy Spirit will come upon you. Do not be afraid."

The *Catechism* goes on:

> The Father's only-begotten Son, conceived as man in the womb of the Virgin Mary, is "Christ," that is to say, anointed by the Holy Spirit from the beginning of his human existence, though its manifestation took place only progressively: first to the shepherds, to the magi, to John the Baptist, and to Jesus' own disciples. The entire life of Jesus would manifest, then, "how God had anointed him in Spirit and in power" (Acts 10:38) [486].

But was Jesus not Jesus from the first instant of His conception? Is not every infant truly human from the first instant of conception, even though day by day that humanity is progressively manifested?

... [F]rom all eternity, God chose as his Son's mother a daughter of Israel, a young Jewish woman of Nazareth in Galilee, "a virgin engaged to a man whose name was Joseph, of the house of David. The virgin's name was Mary" (Lk 1:26–27) ... [488].

Through the centuries, the Church has become ever more aware that Mary, filled with grace by God, was redeemed from the moment of her conception [491].

This is why Pope Pius IX proclaimed in 1854 that Mary was conceived without original sin. The Church often speaks of Mary as the "Second Eve", but, whereas Eve helped usher death into the world, Mary ushered life into the world. All death—death from wars, death from crime, death from abortion, death from euthanasia, death from assisted suicide—all of these are related to original sin.

The *Catechism* talks about Mary's virginity:

From the first formulations of the faith, the Church has confessed that Jesus was conceived by the power of the Holy Spirit alone, in the womb of the Virgin Mary, and has also affirmed the bodily aspect of this event: Jesus was conceived "by the Holy Spirit without human seed" (Council of the Lateran) [496].

Jesus was conceived by the Holy Spirit, without a human father. And the Church has continued to teach and to preach that Mary was a virgin before the conception of Jesus and after she delivered Jesus. She was perpetually a virgin.

The *Catechism* says:

[T]he objection is sometimes raised that the Bible mentions "brothers and sisters of Jesus." The Church has always understood these passages as not designating other children of the Virgin Mary. In fact James and Joseph, though called "brothers of Jesus," are the sons of another Mary, a disciple of Christ, who is designated in a significant way as "the other Mary." It treats of close relatives of Jesus according to an expression common in the Old Testament [500].

Jesus is Mary's only son, but her spiritual motherhood extends to all men whom he came to save ... [501].

This concludes this portion of the *Catechism*, but it takes us to today's second reading, the letter of St. Paul to the people of Corinth, in which he reminds them, "You are the temples of the Holy Spirit. You are not your own. You have been purchased, and at what a price! So glorify God in your body" (1 Cor 6:13–15; 17–20). How, then, can anyone say, "This is *my* body. I can do whatever I want with it"? Moreover, since Mary is the spiritual mother of every human being, she is the mother of every baby in every mother's womb.

Remember, Jesus looked down at John at the foot of the Cross and said, "John, behold your mother." He looked at Mary and said, "Behold your son." In other words, Jesus was saying, "I'm giving you motherhood of the entire human race." So Mary is spiritually the mother of every unborn infant and of all of us.

Today's Gospel tells us that as soon as John the Baptist saw Jesus he said, "Behold the Lamb of God." That Lamb was to be crucified, was to be sacrificed on an altar for us. Certainly, Jesus hoped that His being sacrificed as the Lamb of God would mean that infants would not be sacrificed on the altar of a mother's womb; that sick people would not be sacrificed in a clinic, in a hospital. Jesus came to give life, not death.

I want to conclude by reading brief portions of a letter that I received shortly after Christmas. I do so because, in my mind at least, it ties together this section of the *Catechism* with the cause of the sacredness of human life. This woman wrote to me:

> . . . Father, if I forget to remember Jesus' example, my own spiritual deflation and following defeat remind me. I don't know how the world lives without God, but I have learned that I cannot. I have no peace without Him. No true joy, no sense of myself or where I fit in. In fact, the mere process of living stops making sense if God isn't in the equation. I think the hardest part is turning to Him *in my errors.*
>
> . . . I remember a teacher I had in high school saying, "If God can do anything, can He make a rock so heavy even He can't lift it?" And now, ten years later, the answer woke me up one night. Yes. He made us. He cannot lift us. It is we who must turn freely to His light. He can stand there shining and shining, but we must draw the shades on the darkness within ourselves. *Turn to Him in our errors. Seek His grace to heal. Fall, if we must fall, into His arms.*
>
> . . . I hope, rather than think of me in your prayers, if you have time, would you think of my children? Would you pray for them? That they get to play. That some angel in heaven hugs them. I am tortured by grief these past few months. . . . I hope, with God they forgive me as well. What a terrible thing for a soul to go through. Pray for their peace—James, William, Angela, and John. (One was miscarried, perhaps spared the pain of abortion?) Will I ever stop hurting? But if it meant forgetting that their hearts beat within me, I hope I don't. Better I should hurt forever.

It is because of lovely young women like her that on the fifteenth of October in 1984, when I first came to the Archdiocese, I announced what

I have announced again and again, and I announce it again today: any woman, of any color, of any religion, of any ethnic background, from anywhere, who is pregnant and in need, can come to the Archdiocese of New York, can come to me personally. We will provide hospitalization, medical care, legal care. If she wishes to keep her baby, we will help her do so; if she wishes to have her baby adopted, we will help her do so.

Nor do we condemn any woman who has ever had an abortion. Rather, we try to help her pick up the pieces of life and put them back together again. Why? Because of everything said in the *Catechism*, because of the basic reason that we are here, that we believe that every human being is sacred. We believe that just as firmly as we believe what we profess in the Creed, that Jesus Christ is true God and true man.

9

Peace Begins with the Family

WORLD DAY OF PEACE
THIRD SUNDAY OF THE YEAR
PONTIFICAL MASS

Even though today we will be addressing primarily our Holy Father's World Day of Peace Message, we will also address a section of the *Catechism of the Catholic Church*. We will find that the two are quite complementary. Rather than go in sequence, as we have been doing, we will move ahead to a portion of the *Catechism* that relates to our Holy Father's World Day of Peace Message.

At 9:30 this morning, Rome time, Pope John Paul II presided in St. Peter's at a Mass for Peace in the Balkans and especially in Bosnia-Herzegovina—precisely as we, today, reflect on his World Day of Peace Message. Just a few days ago, the Holy Father gave a brilliant analysis of the world situation, region by region, in some instances country by country. He concluded his roundup in these words:

> A FINAL WISH. Having begun the year which the United Nations Organization has dedicated to the Family, let us act in such a way that humanity will more and more resemble a genuine family in which each individual knows he is listened to, appreciated and loved, in which each is ready to sacrifice self for the benefit of the other, and no one hesitates to help the weaker one.

These words give us the key to this year's World Day of Peace Message, "The Family Creates the Peace of the Human Family", which is based on the Pope's conviction that unless and until we value and support the family and try to maintain the integrity of the family, there cannot be peace in the world. The *family* is the fundamental unit that contributes to peace. This particular World Day of Peace Message is addressed not simply to organizations such as the United Nations, involved formally, globally, in the quest for peace. It is addressed to each of us, members of a family.

I will quote the text only in part, though I strongly recommend that it be read in its entirety. The Pope says:

> The world longs for peace and has a desperate need of peace. Yet wars, conflicts, increasing violence and situations of social unrest and endemic

poverty continue to reap innocent victims and to cause divisions between individuals and peoples. *At times peace appears a truly unattainable goal!*

We must not lose heart. We know that, in spite of everything, peace is possible, because it is part of the original divine plan.

God wished humanity to live in harmony and peace, and laid the foundations for this in the very nature of the human being, created "in his image". The divine image develops not only in the individual but also in that *unique communion of persons* formed by a man and a woman so united in love that they become "one flesh" (Gen 2:24). It is written: "in the image of God he created them; male and female he created them" (Gen 1:27). This specific community of persons has been entrusted by the Lord with the mission of giving life and of nurturing it by the formation of a family. It thus . . . provides for the very future of humanity.

The initial harmony was disrupted by sin, but *God's original plan continues.* The family therefore remains the true foundation of society, constituting, in the words of the Universal Declaration of Human Rights, its "natural and fundamental nucleus".

The contribution which the family can offer to preserving and promoting peace is so important that I would like, on the occasion of the International Year of the Family, to devote this World Day of Peace Message to a reflection on the *close relationship between the family and peace* (no. 1).

The Pope continues:

Founded on love and open to the gift of life, *the family contains in itself the very future of society;* its most special task is to contribute effectively to a future of peace (no. 2).

[I]n many parts of the world, whole nations are caught in the spiral of bloody conflicts, of which *families are often the first victims:* either they are deprived of the main if not the only breadwinner, or they are forced to abandon home, land and property and flee into the unknown; in any event they are subjected to painful misfortunes which threaten all security. How can we fail to recall, in this regard, the bloody conflict between ethnic groups which is still going on in Bosnia-Herzegovina? And this is only one case, amid so many situations of war throughout the world!

In the face of such distressing situations, society often appears incapable of offering effective help, or even culpably indifferent (no. 3).

Nor can one forget that war and violence not only constitute divisive forces which weaken and destroy family structures; they also exercise a pernicious influence on people's minds, suggesting and practically imposing *models of behavior diametrically opposed to peace.* In this regard, one must deplore a very sad fact: these days, unfortunately, a growing number of boys and girls and even small children are playing a direct part in armed conflicts. They are forced to join armed militias and have to fight for causes they do not always understand. In other cases, they become involved in a real culture of violence in which life counts for very little and killing does not seem wrong (no. 4).

When our Holy Father talked about children this morning in Rome, he actually broke down and cried. This is how painful this situation is to him. He goes on:

> In other cases the family simply does not exist: thus there are thousands of children who have no home but the street and who can count on no resources except themselves. Some of these street children die tragically. Others are led into the use and even the sale of drugs and into prostitution, and not infrequently they end up in criminal organizations. Such scandalous and widespread situations cannot be ignored! The very future of society is at stake. A community which rejects children, or marginalizes them, or reduces them to hopeless situations, can never know peace (no. 4).

I'm sure many of you in the United Nations have visited countries where children roam the streets in the thousands. There can't be a scintilla of peace as long as that perdures! I've seen such all over the world, and I've seen it in Bosnia and Herzegovina and places similarly caught up in these tragedies. The Holy Father continues:

> *Children are the future already present among us*; they need to experience what peace means, so that they will be able to create a future of peace (no. 4).

> An enduring peaceful order needs *institutions which express and consolidate the values of peace*. The institution which most immediately responds to the nature of the human being is *the family*. It alone ensures the continuity and the future of society. . . .
> As the fundamental nucleus of society, *the family has a right to the full support of the State* in order to carry out fully its particular mission. State laws, therefore, must be directed to promoting its well-being, helping it to fulfill its proper duties. (no. 5).

Too often, tragically right here in the United States, legislation is quite the contrary of this—it is hostile to the integrity of the family. The Holy Father states:

> [I]t is the duty of the State to encourage and protect the authentic institution of the family, respecting its natural structure and its innate and inalienable rights. Among these, the fundamental one is *the right of parents* to decide, freely and responsibly, on the basis of their moral and religious convictions and with a properly formed conscience, *when to have a child*, and then to educate that child in accordance with those convictions (no. 5).

No state can tell families when they may or may not have children.

The Pope continues:

The State also has an important role in creating the conditions in which families can provide for their primary needs in a way befitting human dignity. Poverty, indeed destitution—a perennial threat to social stability, to the development of people and to peace—in our day affects too many families. . . .

In effect, no one can be at ease until an adequate solution has been found to the problem of poverty, which strikes families and individuals. Poverty is always a threat to social stability, to economic development and ultimately, therefore, to peace. Peace will always be at risk so long as individuals and families are forced to fight for their very survival (no. 5).

The Pope has much more to say about the relationship between the family and world peace, and his entire message should be studied carefully.

We must turn now, however, to the document to which he, himself, refers in his message, the new *Catechism of the Catholic Church*, and specifically to the section that is basic to Church teaching on the family and even basic to *all* Church social teaching, that is, the *fourth* of the Ten Commandments—"Honor your father and your mother, so that you will have a long life in the land that the Lord your God is giving you" (Ex 20:12). I quote from the *Catechism*:

This commandment constitutes one of the foundations of the Church's social teaching [2198].

The fourth commandment is addressed expressly to children in their relationships with their father and mother, because this relationship is the most universal. It also concerns relationships among family members. It calls for honor, affection, and gratitude toward the elderly and our forebears. [The business of euthanasia and assisted suicide is horribly opposed to the fourth commandment.] It extends to the duties of pupils to teachers, employees to employers, subordinates to their leaders, citizens to their nation and those who govern it.

This commandment implies and presupposes the duties of parents, instructors, teachers, leaders, magistrates, those who govern, and all those who exercise authority over others or over a community of persons [2199].

The fourth commandment demands reciprocal respect.

A man and a woman united in marriage, together with their children, form a family. This institution precedes any recognition of it by public authority, which is obliged to give such recognition, and is the norm in terms of which other forms of relationships are to be evaluated [2202].

If the *Catechism* were written in the language of political science, it would make the point that the family is the fundamental *mediating agency* in society. Mediating agencies are tremendously important. Unions represented here, independent educational systems, churches, the media—these are mediating agencies between the individual and the government. One of the primary purposes of the leaders of the French Revolution was to destroy mediating agencies so that the individual would be naked before government. And if we destroy the family, in this country or in any other, that is precisely what happens.

The *Catechism* says:

> The family is the original cell of social life. It is the natural society in which man and woman are called to give themselves to each other in love and in the gift of life. The authority, stability, and life of relationships within the family constitute the foundations of freedom, security, and fraternity within society. The family is the community in which, from infancy, we can learn moral values, begin to honor God, and make good use of our freedom. Family life is an initiation to life in society [2207].

Hitler knew this; Stalin knew this. They tried to turn children against their parents because they knew that, if you destroy the integrity of the family, the individual becomes completely vulnerable.

The *Catechism* continues:

> The family should be assisted and defended by appropriate social measures. . . . Larger communities should take care not to usurp the family's powers or meddle in its life [2209].

> The family's importance for society's life and well being impose on society a particular responsibility to support and strengthen marriage and the family [2210].

I wish those would read this who are responsible for the television, bus, and subway ads on condoms and lifestyles in contradiction to family values. We seem to be passionately engaged in *destroying* the family by way of hostile legislation, entertainment, and so on.

The *Catechism* goes on:

> The political community has a duty to honor the family, to assist it, and to assure it of the following:
>
> — the freedom to found a home, have children and bring them up in keeping with the parents' own moral and religious convictions;
>
> — the protection of the stability of the marriage bond and the institution of the family;
>
> — the freedom to profess their faith, to hand it on, and to raise their children in it, with the necessary means and institutions;

— the right to private property, freedom of enterprise, freedom to obtain work, lodging, the right to emigrate;

— according to the country's institutions, the right to medical care, assistance for the aged, and family benefits;

— the protection of security and public health, especially with regard to such dangers as dangerous drugs, pornography, alcoholism, etc.;

— the freedom to form associations with other families and so to be represented before civil authority.

If these were observed, peace in the world would follow as night follows day.

On the education of children, the *Catechism* states:

The fruitfulness of married love cannot be reduced to the procreation of children, but must extend to their moral education and spiritual formation. The parents' role in education is of such importance that it is almost impossible to replace them. "For parents the right and duty of education are fundamental and inalienable" [2221].

Parents are the first ones responsible for the education of their children. . . . The home is the appropriate place for education in the virtues. Such education requires an apprenticeship in self-denial, sound judgment, and self-control—the conditions for all true freedom [2223].

Schools are supposed to be supporting the values that should be taught at home, in the heart of the family. Governments at every level are supposed to be supportive of these as well.

The *Catechism* continues:

The home constitutes a natural environment for initiating the human being into mutual cooperation and community responsibilities . . . [2224].

As those primarily responsible for the education of their children, parents have the fundamental right to choose a school for them according to their own convictions. . . . Public authorities have the duty to guarantee this parental right and to assure that the conditions for its exercise actually exist [2229].

God's fourth commandment also enjoins us to honor all who, for our well-being, have received authority in society from God. The commandment clarifies the duties of those who exercise authority and those it benefits [2234].

The exercise of authority is measured morally by its divine origin, reasonable nature, and specific object. No one can command or institute what is contrary to the dignity of persons and the natural law [2235].

Political authorities are obliged to respect the fundamental rights of the human person [and the family] [2237].

The political rights attached to citizenship can and should be granted according to the requirements of the common good. They cannot be suspended by public authorities without legitimate and proportionate reasons. Political rights are meant to be exercised for the common good of the nation and the human community [2237].

Maintain that and one maintains peace in the world. The *Catechism* goes on to comment on the duties of citizens:

Those subject to authority should regard their superiors as representatives of God, who has instituted them as ministers of his gifts. . . . Loyal collaboration carries with it the right and at times the duty to engage in just protest against what may appear harmful to the dignity of persons and the good of community [2238].

Those who peacefully protest, with or without a rosary, before abortion clinics or in the vicinity of abortion clinics are loyal collaborators, trying to do what is right. They should not be branded as treasonable or un-American. They should not have incredible punishment imposed on them.

This morning, in front of my residence attached to the Cathedral, a group of those who are said to work for the Archdiocese protested that the Archdiocese of New York apparently does not yet have a contract with them. They have that right, *peacefully* to protest in front of my residence as the Archbishop of New York. I would never dream of depriving them of that right, and I resent it when government attempts to deprive people of the right to protest peacefully in front of an abortion clinic.

The *Catechism* continues:

Obedience to authority and co-responsibility for the common good generates a moral obligation to pay taxes, exercise the right to vote, and share in the defense of the country [2240].

The more prosperous nations are obliged, as far as possible, to welcome immigrants in search of security and the means of livelihood which they are unable to find in their country of origin. Public authorities should be vigilant in respecting the natural law that places guests under the protection of their hosts [2241].

The citizen is obliged in conscience not to follow commands of civil authorities that contradict the demands of the moral order, the fundamental rights of persons or the teachings of the Gospel. The justification for refusing obedience to civil authorities, when their demands are contrary to those of right conscience, can be found in the distinction between the service of

God and that of the political community. "Give therefore to Caesar the things that are Caesar's, and to God the things that are God's" (Mt 22:21) [2242].

This is the way we feel about a proposed health care program that violates the moral order and fundamental human rights by including abortion as a "health benefit" and a right and requiring the funding of such by taxpayers.

The *Catechism* states:

Resort to force of arms in resisting oppressive political power is not justified, except when the following conditions are met: (1) in the case of certain, serious, and prolonged violations of fundamental rights; (2) after all other means of redress have been exhausted; (3) without provoking worse disorders; (4) that there is a well-founded hope of success; (5) if it is impossible reasonably to foresee better solutions [2243].

Every institution is inspired, even if only implicitly, by a vision of man and his destiny, from which it derives its standards of judgment, its hierarchy of values, and rules of conduct. Most societies base their institutions on a certain supremacy of man over things. Only divinely revealed religion has clearly recognized in God, the Creator and Redeemer, the origin and destiny of man. The Church invites political authorities to measure their judgments and decisions by this inspired truth about God and man:

"Societies which ignore this standard or reject it in the name of their independence from God are brought to seek in themselves or to borrow from some ideology their criteria and purpose, and, not tolerating an objective criterion of good and evil, assert an explicit or implicit totalitarian power over man and his destiny, as history shows" [2244].

It belongs to the Church's mission to "pass moral judgment even on matters pertaining to politics, when required by the fundamental rights of persons or the salvation of souls, using all and only those means in keeping with the Gospel and the good of all according to the diversity of times and conditions" [2246].

Some would say to us, "Church—stay out of politics", by which they mean, of course, "Don't criticize politicians, however immoral their proposals may be. Don't' criticize immoral political programs. Mind your own business. Teach religion"—whatever their definition of religion is.

We turn to this morning's Scripture reading, the well-known story of Jonah, which I think is remarkably applicable. Practically everyone knows the story of Jonah's refusing to carry out the divine command to go preach to Nineveh. He is thrown overboard from his ship, and he is running away from God. He is swallowed by a whale—whether this is figuratively the case, symbolically, literally, we really don't know. But we do know that, finally, Jonah, perhaps out of fear, did what God told him. That is the essence of today's first reading. We are told:

> So Jonah made ready and went to Nineveh according to the Lord's bidding. Now Nineveh was an enormously large city; it took three days to go through it. Jonah began his journey through the city and had gone but a single day's walk announcing, "Forty days more and Nineveh shall be destroyed," when the people of Nineveh believed God; they proclaimed a fast and all of them, great and small, put on sackcloth.

> When God saw by their actions how they turned from their evil ways, he repented of the evil that he had threatened to do to them; he did not carry it out (Jonah 3:1–5; 10).

Who Jonah was, what he represented, again, whether he was figurative or literal, is not important. The lesson is very, very clear: God used Jonah as an instrument to bring about prevention of the destruction of this enormous city, Nineveh. First Jonah turned his back, then he went, and the people of Nineveh were saved.

The Holy Father has pleaded with the United Nations and other world organizations and with us as individuals, on behalf of so many places in the world, to be instruments of peace in Bosnia and Herzegovina and elsewhere, as Jonah was an instrument of peace in Nineveh. We cannot turn our backs on this plea. You of the United Nations: *you cannot run that risk.* We know it is difficult. We know that the very nature of your lives is difficult—many of you are separated from your families for long periods of time; many of you are running great risks; many of you are suffering many hardships. This includes not only those who are formal delegates from their country, but all who staff the United Nations, those related to the United Nations in various organizations. We know it is difficult, but you of all people must believe that *peace is possible!* You have accomplished a great deal on behalf of peace for virtually half a century. You must believe that peace is possible in the full sense of the term, true peace for all everywhere, not merely a cessation of armed conflict.

We salute you for all that you have done, for all that you have tried to do, and we plead with you, never lose hope, never give up. I ask this entire congregation in St. Patrick's Cathedral to thank you for your efforts. We could not do without you. God bless you.

10

Why Did Jesus Come?

Today we continue with our series on the new *Catechism of the Catholic Church.* This is our tenth session of forty-one in the series.

I spent a few days on Church business in Iceland this past week. It is a fascinating country from a religious perspective, because perhaps 90 to 95 percent of the people are Lutheran. Lutheranism is the state religion. Only three thousand Catholics live there. Yet the relationship is very fine, and the Lutherans treat the Catholics very amiably.

In speaking to a number of groups there, I found the value of the *Catechism* to be inestimable and the need for it to be critical. With the exception of last Sunday, when we had to move ahead in the *Catechism* to the social gospel of the Church because we were reflecting on the Holy Father's World Day of Peace Message, we have been basically following the Apostles' Creed or the Nicene Creed word by word. The portion of the *Catechism* we will focus on today begins with the words of the Creed "He was born of the Virgin Mary and became man." This section of the *Catechism* gives a kind of general description of the life of Jesus, somewhat different from what we have been doing to date.

The *Catechism* itself makes note of the fact that only certain incidents and events in the life of Christ are illustrated in the Creed. But the *entirety* of Christ's life is a mystery, and the *entirety* of His life brought us to our redemption. The *Catechism* says:

Many things about Jesus of interest to human curiosity [are not listed in the Creed and] do not figure in the Gospels [514].

At the end of the Gospel of St. John, we read the words, "These and many other things Jesus did which are not written here. If they were written down, I suppose that the whole world could not hold the books that would be written" (Jn 21:23). So, even in the Gospels we see only major incidents in the life of Christ.

The *Catechism* says:

The Gospels were written by men who were among the first to have the faith and who wished to make the faith known to others. Having known by faith who Jesus is, they could see and express the traces of his mystery throughout his earthly life [515].

The entire life of Christ—his words and deeds, his silences and suffering, his manner of being and speaking—is a revelation of the Father. Jesus can say: "Whoever sees me see the Father". . . . Our Lord became man in order to do his Father's will, even the least characteristics of his mysteries reveal God's love for us [516].

The next point the *Catechism* makes is crucial:

Christ's whole life is a mystery of *redemption*. Redemption comes to us above all through the blood of his cross, but this mystery is at work throughout Christ's entire life . . . [517].

Everything that Jesus did, said, and suffered aimed at restoring fallen humanity to its original vocation [518].

While in Iceland I was asked to give a lecture at the State University of Iceland, specifically to the theology department there. I was asked to speak to the faculty and the young students preparing to be Lutheran ministers, concerning the Lutheran–Catholic dialogue here in the United States. Key to this dialogue is a technical term of critical meaning to Lutheranism, what is called "justification by faith". This means, in part, that "there is only one name under heaven by which we can be saved", and that is the name of our Lord Jesus Christ. We can't get to heaven without faith in Him. They were somewhat surprised, I think, when I made the same point out of the *Catechism*. It is through the Blood of Jesus Christ, the Blood of the Cross, through the entirety of His life that redemption was worked out, and only in this can we reach eternal happiness.

The *Catechism* says:

In his entire life, Jesus reveals himself as our model, "the perfect man," who invites us to become his disciples and follow him. In his self-emptying, he has given us an example to imitate, through his prayer he draws us to pray, and by his poverty he calls us to accept deprivation and persecutions . . . [520].

Christ did what He did as a model for us. The *Catechism* continues:

All that Christ lived he makes possible for us to live in him and for him to live in us [521].

Jesus was born in the lowliness of a stable, into a poor family. Simple shepherds are the first witnesses to this event. It is in this poverty that the glory of heaven manifests itself [525].

To become a child in relation to God is the condition for entering the kingdom. For this, it is necessary to humble oneself, to become little, to be born
of God, and to become children of God . . . [526].

We have seen this before in these *Catechism* lessons. Our Divine Lord
Himself said, "Unless you become as little children, you cannot enter into
the kingdom of heaven" (Mk 10:15). It seems strange to us, but when Nicodemus, a high ranking Jew, went to Jesus by night, ashamed to be seen
during the day, and asked Him about salvation, Jesus said, "Unless you are
born again of water and the Holy Spirit, you cannot enter into the kingdom of heaven." Nicodemus asked, "How can I be born again? How can
I go back into my mother's womb?" Jesus meant that we humble ourselves, we enter into Baptism, we accept God's teaching.
      The *Catechism* continues:

The Epiphany is the manifestation of Jesus as Messiah of Israel, Son of God
and Savior of the World. [There are three major manifestations in Jesus' life
that we can call the Epiphany.] The great feast of Epiphany celebrates the
adoration of Jesus by the wise men [the so-called magi] from the East, together with his baptism in the Jordan and the wedding feast at Cana in Galilee. [The coming of the magi, moreover,] means that pagans can discover
Jesus and worship him as Son of God and Savior of the world but only by
turning toward the Jews and receiving from them the messianic promise
contained in the Old Testament [528].

Last week, after the Mass for the United Nations and the World Day of
Peace Message, a large number of the delegates in the United Nations
came into my residence for coffee. The Israeli Ambassador said to me, "I
was amazed at how many of your prayers are like Jewish prayers and how
many of the actions of the Mass are like the Jewish ritual." Of course this
is so, because Christianity is rooted in Judaism.
      The *Catechism* continues:

The presentation of Jesus in the temple shows him to be the firstborn Son
who belongs to the Lord. . . . Jesus is recognized [by Simeon] as the long-
expected Messiah, "the light of the nations" and the "glory of Israel," but
also "a sign of contradiction." The sword of sorrow predicted for Mary announced Christ's perfect and unique oblation on the cross that would im-
part the salvation God had "prepared in the presence of all peoples" [529].

When we read the Gospels we have to remember this. You cannot separate incidents in the life of Christ and say, "This is important. This is unimportant." The *totality* of His life is a mystery leading to redemption, the
ultimate is His crucifixion and death on the Cross and the Resurrection.
      The *Catechism* continues:

The flight into Egypt and the massacre of the innocents reveal the opposition of darkness to the light of Christ. . . . Christ's whole life was lived under the sign of persecution [530].

During the greater part of his life, Jesus shared the condition of the vast majority of men: a daily life spent without apparent greatness, a life filled with manual labor. His was the religious life of a Jew obedient to the law of God, life in the community [531].

After His birth and presentation in the temple, we learn nothing about his life until He is twelve years of age and is taken to the temple. Mary and Joseph think they have lost Him.

The finding of Jesus in the temple is the only event that breaks the silence of the Gospels about the hidden years of Jesus. Here Jesus permits us to catch a glimpse of the mystery of his total consecration to the mission that flows from his divine sonship: [he asks his parents when they come looking] "Did you not know that I must be about my Father's business?" Though Mary and Joseph did not understand these words, they accepted them in faith [534].

This had to have been terribly difficult! Mary and Joseph loved Jesus so, and they thought they had lost Him. Then when they find Him, after three days and nights, He asked, "Didn't you know I had to be about my Father's business?"

The *Catechism* continues:

Jesus' public life began with his baptism by John in the Jordan. . . . The Holy Spirit, in the form of a dove, came upon Jesus and a voice from heaven proclaimed, "This is my Son, the beloved" (Mt 3:13–17). Jesus' baptism is the manifestation [Epiphany] of Jesus as Messiah of Israel and Son of God [535].

In his baptism in the Jordan, Jesus anticipated the baptism of his death. . . . Jesus submitted entirely to his Father's will, accepting with love his baptism of death for the forgiveness of our sins. . . . At Christ's baptism, "the heavens were opened" (Mt 3:16)—the descent of Jesus and the Spirit, a prelude to the new creation [536].

This is important for us and our own baptism.

Through baptism, the Christian is sacramentally made like Jesus, who anticipates in his own baptism his death and Resurrection; it is necessary to enter into this mystery of humble self-emptying and repentance, go down into the water with Jesus, rise with him, be reborn of water and the Spirit, become the Father's beloved children in the only-begotten Son and "walk in newness of life" (Rom 6:4) . . . [537].

Today we usually sprinkle water to baptize, although we can still baptize by having people go into a pool of water, which is the way it was done originally and which is symbolic of entering into death, drowning as it were, so that we can rise to new life.

The *Catechism* continues:

The Gospels speak of a time of solitude for Jesus in the desert immediately after his baptism by John. . . . Jesus remained there for forty days without eating; he lived among savage beasts and angels waited on him. At the end of this period, Satan tempted Jesus three times. . . . Jesus warded off these attacks, which echo the temptations of Adam in Paradise [but Adam didn't succeed in overcoming temptation] . . . [538].

. . . Jesus is the new Adam who remained faithful, whereas the first Adam had given in to temptation [539].

The temptation of Jesus reveals the way in which the Son of God is Messiah, as opposed to the way proposed to him by Satan and the way men desire to attribute to him. . . . [People couldn't believe that the Messiah would be crucified—"If you're the Son of God, prove it and come down from the Cross." That was God's way, not man's way.] By the forty days of Lent, the Church unites herself each year to the mystery of Jesus in the desert [540].

By his word, through signs that reveal the reign of God, and by sending out his disciples, Christ called all people to come together around him. But above all, in his great Paschal mystery [We use that word "paschal" often. It is taken from the word *pasqua*, meaning "a lamb"—the sacrifice of the lamb, which was symbolic of the sacrifice of Jesus. When we speak of the "Paschal mystery", we're speaking of the sacrifice of Jesus on the Cross.]—his death on the cross and his Resurrection from the dead—he would accomplish in these the coming of his kingdom. "And I, when I am lifted up from the earth, will draw all men to myself" [542].

Jesus was sent to "bring good news to the poor" (Lk 4:18). . . . Jesus shared the life of the poor, from the manger to the cross; he experienced the hunger, thirst, and homelessness. Christ so identified himself with poor people of all kinds that he made an active love toward them the condition for entering his kingdom [544].

Jesus also invites sinners to the table of the kingdom [not only those materially poor]: "I have not come to call the righteous, but sinners" (Mk 2:17). He invites them to that conversion without which one cannot enter the kingdom, but in so doing showed them in word and deed his Father's boundless mercy for them and the vast "joy in heaven over one sinner who repents" (Lk 15:7) . . . [545].

. . . to gain the kingdom, it is necessary to give away everything else. Words are not enough; there must also be acts [546].

We are told in the *Catechism*:

Jesus accompanies his words with numerous miracles, wonders, and signs, which reveal that the kingdom is present in him. They attest that Jesus is the announced Messiah [547].

Despite his evident miracles, some people rejected Jesus and some even accused him of acting by the power of demons [548].

In freeing certain ones from the earthly evils of hunger, injustice, illness, and death . . . he did not come to abolish all evils here below, but to free us from the gravest slavery, sin, which . . . reduces us to a state of bondage [549].

The kingdom of God would be definitively established only through the cross of Christ [550].

Here's the key to this section of the *Catechism* and key to the teaching of Catholicism:

From the beginning of his public life, Jesus chose certain men, twelve in number, to be with him and to participate in his mission. He gave them a share in his authority and "sent them out to proclaim the kingdom of God and to heal" (Lk 9:2). . . . Through them he continues to guide the Church . . . [551].

Simon Peter occupied first place in the college of the Twelve Apostles. Jesus entrusted a unique mission to him. Through a revelation from the Father, Simon had confessed: "You are the Christ, the Son of the living God." In turn, our Lord had declared to him: "You are Peter, and on this rock I will build my Church, and the gates of Hell will not prevail against it" (Mt 16:18). . . . Peter's mission was to guard this faith from every error and to strengthen his brother apostles in it [552].

The *Catechism* goes on:

Jesus entrusted a specific authority to Peter: "I will give you the keys of the kingdom of heaven: whatever you bind on earth will be bound in heaven, whatever you loose on earth will be loosed in heaven" (Mt 16:19). The "power of the keys" designates the authority to govern the house of God, which is the Church. . . . The power to "bind and loose" designates the authority to forgive sins, pronounce doctrinal judgments, and make disciplinary decisions in the Church. Jesus has entrusted this authority to the Church, in general through the ministry of the apostles and in particular through the ministry of Peter, the only one of the Twelve to whom he explicitly gave the keys to the kingdom [553].

I want to go back to my few days in Iceland, but by way of today's Gospel, which is a fascinating one (Mt 1:21–28). We are told that Jesus entered the synagogue, and there He continued teaching. The synagogue was pre-cisely that, a place to teach. (There was only one temple in those days, the temple in Jerusalem. If they were fortunate, Jews could get there once a year.) Wherever there were ten or more Jews, there had to be a synagogue. The synagogue was the place for teaching and the place where the copy of the Torah, the first five books in the Old Testament, was kept.

One who was learned in the law could get up in the synagogue, if thirty years of age or older, and teach the law. The primary teachers of the law were called the scribes, those who had studied the law. They were called scribes because they transcribed the law from the ancient text. They got to know the law very, very well. The most illustrious of the scribes became rabbis. The scribes could teach, but they didn't teach on their own authority. They taught what those before them had taught of the first five books of the Old Testament. They applied these five books to practi-cally every activity in life, so that there were thousands of regulations taught by the scribes. But they did not teach on their own authority. This is what astonished the people in the Gospel. We are told, "The people were spellbound by Jesus' teaching, because He taught with authority and not like the scribes." Jesus said, "This is what I say to you. This is what Moses said." He didn't confer with any other authorities, and they were astonished by this. Jesus spoke on His own authority, and He did some-thing even beyond that: He backed up what He had to say.

We are told, "There was a man with an unclean spirit who shrieked: 'Jesus, Jesus of Nazareth, have you come here to destroy us? I know who you are—the Holy One of God!'" We are told Jesus rebuked him and said, "Get out of him, unclean spirit!" And the spirit did so.

The people were even further astonished. They said, "What does this mean? A completely new teaching in a spirit of authority! He gives orders to unclean spirits and they obey him!" They were amazed at this.

Recently, when I was in Iceland talking to a very amiable and very in-telligent group of Lutherans preparing for the ministry and their teachers, I talked not only about what we call the "dialogue", discussing together what each Church teaches, but "biologue"—that we have to live with one another in peace, in harmony, and in love. Even more important, each of us has to live out a "biologue" with Jesus and with one another in accord with the teachings of Jesus—we have to live out the model that Jesus gave us, or our words become as nothing. Jesus was believed not simply be-cause of what He said but of how He lived. Periodically, He would back up what He said with a miracle. But the miracles were not nearly so im-portant as the very nature of His life.

Then came the question from the Lutheran group: "But where do we get the authority and determination of what Jesus meant, of what the

Scriptures tell us? Of the early days of Christianity?" Then I had to express the basic teaching of the Catholic Church that we believe was transmitted to Peter and to the apostles, that is, the primacy of Peter. Someone asked, "In an attempt at unity, where does this put the Pope?" I didn't want to deceive regarding our teaching, so I said, "It was to Peter that our Lord said, 'You are Peter and on this rock I will build My Church.' We must, therefore, have this teaching authority."

I suggested to that group that the greatest obstacle to our practice of the faith is ignorance. This is, again, a reminder to me of the importance of the *Catechism*, of bringing into one place once more the basic teachings of the Church through all of the centuries.

After I had talked to this particular class of Lutherans, I talked to a group of Catholics. I talked to them about the *Catechism*. I found them hungry. It may be a long time before a *Catechism* is translated into Icelandic, an enormously difficult language that is spoken only in Iceland. But the people want it so very, very much. They are tired of confusion and ambiguity.

Let us conclude with these final passages from the *Catechism*:

> From the day Peter confessed that Jesus is the Christ, the Son of the living God, the Master "began to show his disciples that he must go to Jerusalem and suffer . . . and be put to death, and on the third day to rise" (Mt 16:21) [554].

This was Jesus' ultimate proof. He would actually *die* out of love for us, not only for the people of His day but for any one of us here, and then He would show that He was God by rising from the dead.

> Peter rejected this announcement, nor did the others understand it any better than he did. [They said, "That's foolish talk."] In this context, the mysterious episode of Jesus' Transfiguration on a high mountain took place, before three chosen witnesses: Peter, James, and John. Jesus' face and clothes became bright with light, and Moses and Elijah appeared, "speaking to him . . ." (Lk 9:31). A cloud covered him and a voice from heaven said: "This is my Son, my Chosen One; listen to him" (Lk 9:35) [554].

The *Catechism* says:

> On the threshold of his public life, Christ's baptism took place; on the threshold of his Passover, his Transfiguration. . . . From now on we share in the Lord's Resurrection through the Spirit who acts in the sacraments of Christ's Body [that is, the Church]. . . . The Transfiguration gives us a foretaste of Christ's glorious coming. . . . But it also recalls that "it is necessary to undergo many tribulations in order to enter into the kingdom of God" (Acts 14:22) . . . [556].

Although Jesus had always escaped popular attempts to make him king, he chose the time and prepared the details for his messianic entry into the city of "David, his father" (Lk 1:32). Acclaimed as son of David, as the one who brings salvation (*Hosanna* means "Save!"), the "King of Glory" entered into his City "riding on a donkey" (Ps 24:7–10). . . . And so the subjects of his kingdom, on that day, are the children and God's poor, who acclaim him as had the angels when they proclaimed him to the shepherds. Their acclamation, "Blessed is he who comes in the name of the Lord," is taken up by the Church in the Holy, Holy, Holy of the Eucharistic liturgy to begin the memorial of the Lord's Paschal mystery [559].

How beautiful is this teaching summarized for us in the *Catechism*! If each of us could but read the life of Christ in the Scriptures—the Old Testament giving us all of the background, and then the Gospels filled with love and mercy and compassion—we would get a deeper, clearer understanding of the love that Christ has for each one of us: a love that truly could convert our lives.

United with the Sufferings of Jesus

FIFTH SUNDAY OF THE YEAR
BLACK HISTORY SUNDAY
FEBRUARY 6, 1994
PONTIFICAL MASS

Today we continue our discussion of the *Catechism of the Catholic Church* with a session on the words from the Creed "He suffered under Pontius Pilate, was crucified, died and was buried." Today is Black History Sunday, so we will weave these two critical themes together.

On February 1, 1994, the *New York Post* carried an article called "The Man Who Invented Black History". He was Arthur Schomburg. The article is less about his life than about the Schomburg Center for Research of Black Culture, in the heart of Harlem. The Center, the article states, "was established in the New York Public Library building on 135th Street in 1926 with Schomburg's personal collection of 10,000 books, manuscripts and artifacts. Today, it houses a collection of more than 5 million items. Each year, 70,000 scholars visit to conduct research."

So those who think that the concept of Black History is fraudulent or is just something that has arisen in this era of "political correctness" have another thought coming. I would strongly recommend a visit to the Schomburg Research Center. Right now they are displaying an exhibition that traces the religious history of Ethiopia, to launch Black History Month. Ethiopian religious art is truly spectacular, the colors are magnificent. It is a very fine reminder of the depth and the roots of African-American and other Black History. Ethiopian religious art is very, very old, going back thousands of years.

We could talk about many achievements in Black History. But there is one today that I want to focus on because it stands out as a cause of great joy. Many of you know that since I have been here I have been actively pursuing the cause of sainthood of one Pierre Toussaint, who was a Haitian slave but who lived out most of his life here in New York. He amassed a good bit of money and gave it all to the poor. More than his money he gave *himself*, day after day. When he was not working, he would go around visiting the sick. Even during a plague, when so many others fled New York, he stayed. He died in the early part of the nineteenth century.

We have presented Pierre Toussaint's cause to Rome. There are two further things needed before the possibility of beatification and canonization. One is what we call the "deposition", a carefully constructed analysis of his life, historically and in terms of his behavior. The good news is that we have this—this huge tome, which is itself some six hundred pages, matching the length of the *Catechism*. This has been just completed under the direction of authorities in Rome by one of our New York priests, Father William Elder. It's magnificent! With that part done, all that remains is to have what we perceive to have been possible miracles through his intercession proved to be such, scientifically and medically.

I thought we'd spend time this morning reading of some favors received. These are things that people have written about that perhaps will be approved as miracles. Some of them are startling; all of them give us cause for great joy and great hope.

I read from the deposition:

> In 1967, Father Joseph Saget, a parish priest in St. Marc, Haiti, met Jesmer Lamothe, then twenty-five years old. Mr. Lamothe was a soccer coach, but with the priest's help he eventually opened a primary school. In 1973 he started noticeably losing weight. At the Albert Schweitzer Hospital . . . he was diagnosed with two cancers, one in the stomach and one in the lungs. The doctors told him to visit his family, because he had at most three months to live. He went for a second opinion at the Center for the Treatment of Cancer . . . where his cancer was also diagnosed as very advanced and without hope of cure. . . .
>
> Father Saget began to pray to Pierre Toussaint, and he encouraged Mr. Lamothe to do the same. . . . [The doctor] was utterly perplexed by the new set of X rays. No trace of the cancer, not even a scar, could be found in his abdomen or in his lungs. He was pronounced cured, went home, and resumed his duties as a school principal.

Our own Ellen Tarry, a leading black woman in New York, was present when this priest gave his testimony. She was there with two witnesses. This is one of the very important potential miracles. Unfortunately, the situation in Haiti has made it difficult to examine the records appropriately, but we are working on it.

Again from the deposition:

> On Dec. 11, 1964, Larone Ferranolo, age twelve, of Cliffside Park, New Jersey, her brother Andrew, age six, her sister, Maria, age four, were struck by an automobile. All three were unconscious when admitted to Englewood Hospital, and hospital records indicate that there was little hope for their recovery. . . . They were visited by Father Charles McTague, who

urged the family to invoke the intercession of Pierre Toussaint. The mother . . . writes: ". . . As a sign of the heroic sanctity of Pierre Toussaint, our prayers were answered and all three children recovered. . . . We have to attribute this to God through Pierre Toussaint's intercession."

Englewood hospital was the scene of yet another healing. John McBride . . . found that his son was unconscious, had turned the "bluest shade", and was making a sound like a "death rattle". At the hospital the admitting doctor said, "This boy is dead—clinically speaking." He was placed in intensive care and the father prayed to Pierre Toussaint. Joseph recovered and was discharged from the hospital. Mr. McBride writes, "I am convinced that it was the prayers and interest of Pierre Toussaint that woke me and saved my boy's life."

There are so many testimonies included in the deposition that we can't read them all. Permit me to cite just one more.

In April 1991 a woman from Flushing, New York, wrote about a cancerous tumor that had spread from her breast to her neck and clavicle. Radiation therapy was given to diminish the symptoms, but without any expectation of a cure. The radiation had to be terminated, due to complications that it caused. The patient went with a friend to St. Patrick's Cathedral to pray at the remains of Pierre Toussaint [which are beneath the high altar with all the previous archbishops of New York]. The following week an X ray showed no evidence of any tumor.

What are we to believe? It would *appear* that God is at work. If this can be demonstrated, I think the cause of Pierre Toussaint will be advanced and within the foreseeable future he could be beatified and then canonized. (Obviously, that is for the Holy See to determine, and I do not want to be seeming to preempt the judgment of the Holy See.) I see Pierre Toussaint as a perfect bridge between races in this race-torn, this terribly conflicted city. He was a black man who walked among blacks and whites indiscriminately, during the plague and at other difficult times, to care for blacks and whites indiscriminately. What a wonderful thing it will be if he is canonized!

What must be remembered about Pierre Toussaint is that much of his sanctity was in his acceptance of terrible sufferings. He was frequently rejected by those for whom he sacrificed most. He virtually rebuilt the burned-down Church of St. Peter and then was initially refused a pew there, because he was black. Wealthy white Catholics passed him in their carriages on their way to church on freezing, snowy, rainy days. They wouldn't pick him up, because he was black. But every day he went to Mass. He suffered severe illness. He suffered the death of those he loved most, his wife and adopted daughter, yet he never gave up. He was never embittered. That's the kind of acceptance of suffering that makes saints.

This takes us to Christ's suffering under Pontius Pilate, His crucifixion, His death and burial. We turn to the *Catechism*.

The Paschal mystery of Christ's cross and Resurrection stands at the heart of the good news that the apostles, and the Church following in their steps, must proclaim to the world. God's saving plan was fulfilled "once for all" (Heb 9:26) by the redemptive death of his Son Jesus Christ [571].

From the beginning of the public ministry of Jesus, certain Pharisees and partisans of Herod, with some priests and scribes, agreed to destroy him. Because of some of his acts—expelling demons, forgiving sins, healing on the sabbath day . . . his familiarity with sinners—some ill-intentioned people suspected Jesus of demonic possession. They accused him of blasphemy and false prophecy, religious crimes which the law punished with death by stoning [574].

This should make the poor of New York—blacks and whites—and everyone else who has been treated as an outcast recognize that Christ is their Savior.

The *Catechism* continues:

At the beginning of his Sermon on the Mount, Jesus solemnly warned: "Do not think that I have come to abolish the law or the prophets: I have come not to abolish but to fulfill. For truly I tell you, until heaven and earth pass away, not one letter, not one stroke of a letter will pass from the law, until all is accomplished. Therefore, whoever breaks one of the least of these commandments will be called least in the kingdom of heaven; whoever keeps them and teaches them will be called great in the kingdom of heaven" (Mt 5:17-19) [577].

This puts to rest once and for all the notion that it doesn't matter how we live, that God is so merciful and compassionate that what we do does not matter. That is not what Christ said.

The *Catechism* tells us:

Like the prophets, Jesus expressed the deepest respect for the Jerusalem temple. It was there that Joseph and Mary presented him forty days after his birth. At the age of twelve he decided to remain in the temple to remind his parents that he must be about his Father's business. Jesus went there each year during his hidden life at least for Passover. His public ministry was punctuated by pilgrimages to Jerusalem for the great Jewish feasts [583].

Jesus was a Jew, and He kept the Jewish law. This has to be remembered among those who still harbor anti-Semitism in their hearts. There is no room in the Catholic heart for racism or for anti-Semitism, and we must get this through our hearts once and for all.

The *Catechism* continues:

On the threshold of his Passion, Jesus announced the coming destruction of this wonderful building, of which not one stone would rest upon another [585].

Jesus identified himself with the temple by presenting himself as God's definitive dwelling-place among men. Therefore his being put to death bodily announced the destruction of the temple, which would reveal the dawning of a new age in the history of salvation: "The hour is coming when you will worship the Father neither on this mountain nor in Jerusalem" (Jn 4:21) [586].

Remember when Jesus was talking to the Samaritan woman? She was trying to make a game of it. She said, in effect, "You say we should worship in Jerusalem. Our fathers say we should worship here in Samaria. Who is right?" Jesus said, in essence, "The time will come when people will worship the Father neither here nor in Jerusalem, but will worship the Father as he really is. God is Spirit."

The *Catechism* continues:

Jesus scandalized the Pharisees by eating with tax collectors and sinners as familiarly as with themselves. Against those among them "who flattered themselves that they were righteous and regarded the others with contempt," Jesus affirmed: "I have come not to call the righteous but sinners to repentance" (Lk 5:32). He went further by proclaiming in the face of the Pharisees that, since sin is universal, those who pretend not to need salvation are blind to themselves [588].

Whether we are white or black, if we think we are so righteous that we don't need salvation, then we are as blind in ourselves as are those who are engaged in so-called "ethnic purification" in Bosnia-Herzegovina right now.

The *Catechism* continues:

Jesus scandalized all around especially when he identified his merciful conduct toward sinners with God's own attitude toward them. He went so far as to reveal that, by sharing the table of sinners, he was admitting them to the messianic banquet. Above all, Jesus placed the authorities on the horns of a dilemma by forgiving sins. By forgiving sins, Jesus either blasphemed as a man who made himself God's equal or spoke the truth, and his person really did make present and reveal God's name [589].

Among the religious authorities of Jerusalem, not only were the Pharisee Nicodemus and the influential Joseph of Arimathea both secret disciples of Jesus . . . but other religious authorities. On the eve of Christ's Passion, "many of them believed in him" (Jn 12:42) . . . [595].

Nicodemus, you will recall, was a high-ranking Pharisee who came to Jesus at night, because he didn't want to be seen by day, and asked how he could reach salvation. Jesus told him. Joseph of Arimathea owned the tomb in which Jesus was to be buried. Both Nicodemus and Joseph of Arimathea took Him down from the Cross.

The *Catechism* states:

> The religious authorities were not unanimous about what stance to take toward Jesus. The Pharisees threatened to excommunicate his followers; the high priest Caiaphas proposed and prophesied . . . it would be "better to have one man die for the people than to have the whole nation destroyed" (Jn 11:48–50); . . . [They] handed Jesus over to the Romans, accusing him of political revolt, a charge that put him in the same category as Barabbas, who had been accused of sedition. The high priests also threatened Pilate politically so that he would condemn Jesus to death [596].

> The historical complexity of Jesus' trial is revealed in the Gospel accounts. The personal sin of the participants . . . is known to God alone. . . . The Church declared in the Second Vatican Council:
> "What was perpetrated during the Passion cannot be imputed indiscriminately to all Jews living at that time or to the Jews of today. . . . Jews must not be portrayed as rejected or accursed by God, as if it followed from Sacred Scripture" [597].

We have corrected our catechetical textbooks. We have gotten rid of the notion that the Jews in general were responsible for the crucifixion and death of Christ. We have even changed the prayers that we use on Good Friday, to remind ourselves that it is the sins of all of us that are responsible.

The *Catechism* goes on:

> The Church, in its official teaching and in the witness of its saints, has never forgotten that "sinners themselves were all the authors and, as it were, the instruments of all the pains that the divine Redeemer endured" (*Roman Catechism*). Taking into account the fact that our sins affect Christ himself, the Church does not hesitate to impute to Christians the gravest responsibility in Jesus' Passion, a responsibility that has all too often been laid only on Jews:
> "We must regard as guilty of this horrible offense those who continue to relapse into their sins. Since our crimes made our Lord Jesus Christ suffer the torment of the cross, those who plunge themselves into disorders and evil crucify the Son of God anew in their hearts, for he is in them, and hold him up to contempt by their sins" [598].

> The violent death of Jesus . . . was part of the mystery of God's plan, as St. Peter explained to the Jews of Jerusalem in his first sermon on Pentecost:

"He was handed over according to the definite plan and foreknowledge of God" (Acts 2:23) [599].

. . . Jesus took on our guilt, in the state of sinful separation that characterizes our relationship with God, to the point that he could say in our name from the cross: "My God, my God, why have you forsaken me?" (Mk 15:34) [603].

By giving up his own Son for our sins, God revealed his plan of loving kindness for us, preceding any merit of ours: "In this is love: not that we loved God but that he loved us and sent his Son to be the atoning sacrifice for our sins" (1 Jn 4:10). God "proves his love for us in that while we were still sinners Christ died for us" (Rom 5:8) [604].

At the end of the parable of the lost sheep, Jesus recalled that God's love excludes no one: "So it is not the will of your Father in heaven that one of these little ones should be lost" (Mt 18:14). . . . The Church, following the apostles, teaches that Christ died for all men without exception: "There is not, never has been, and never will be a single person for whom Christ did not suffer" (Council of Quiercy) [605].

The *Catechism* says:

From the first moment of his Incarnation, the Son embraced the divine plan of salvation in his redemptive mission: "My food is to do the will of him who sent me and to complete his work" (Jn 4:34) [606].

That could have been written or said by Pierre Toussaint. He repeated things like that over and over again. "Whatever suffering comes my way, however I'm reviled, however I'm scorned, 'My food is to do the will of him who sent me and to complete his work.' "

. . . John the Baptist . . . both saw and revealed in Jesus the "Lamb of God who takes away the sins of the world" (Jn 1:19). He revealed also that Jesus is at the same time the suffering servant who, in silence, permits himself to be led to the slaughter bearing the sin of the multitudes, and the Paschal Lamb, the symbol of the redemption of Israel at the time of the first Passover [608].

Again, the same could be said of Pierre Toussaint, and I say that very seriously.

By embracing in his human heart the Father's love for men, Jesus "loved them to the end," for "no one has greater love than this, to lay down his life for his friends" (Jn 13:1). . . . Jesus said, "No one takes my life from me, but I lay it down of my own accord" (Jn 10:18). Such was the sovereign freedom of God's Son as he approached his death [609].

When they said to Pierre Toussaint "But you're only a slave", he said, "No one can make me a slave in my heart. In my heart, in my soul, I am a completely free man."

The *Catechism* goes on to tell us:

On the eve of his Passion, while still free, Jesus transformed his Last Supper into the memorial of his voluntary offering to the Father for the salvation of men: "This is my body, which is *given* for you" and "This is my blood of the covenant, which is *poured out* for many for the forgiveness of sins" (Lk 22:19) [610].

The *Catechism* goes on to note that on that very night, in the Garden of Gethsemane, He said, "Father, let this chalice of suffering pass from me. Nevertheless, not my will but thine be done." And He drank this chalice of His death (see 612).

No man, not even the greatest saint, was ever able to take on the sins of all and to offer himself in sacrifice for all. The existence in Christ of the divine person of the Son, who surpasses and at the same time embraces all human persons and who constitutes himself the head of all mankind, makes possible his redemptive sacrifice for all [616].

That is what Pierre Toussaint did. He took upon himself the suffering, the needs of all, in the image of Christ.

Finally, the *Catechism* tells us: "The cross is the unique sacrifice of Christ, 'sole mediator between God and men' (1 Tim 2:5). . . . He calls his disciples to 'take up their cross and follow him' (Mt 16:24) . . ." [618].

If one thing unites all of us here, everyone in the world, it is the phenomenon of suffering. It is inescapable. If we take that suffering and unite it with the sufferings of Christ on the Cross, then it can do untold good; it can work the kind of miracles that it would appear Pierre Toussaint worked through his suffering. That is what unites us—that suffering that we share with Christ.

The *Catechism* notes that even his mother was not spared; indeed, Mary was the one who was caused to suffer the most [see 618].

In the first reading, Job says:

> Is not man's life on earth a drudgery?
>> Are not his days those of a hireling?
> He is a slave who longs for the shade,
>> a hireling who waits for his wages.
> So I have been assigned months of misery,
>> and troubled nights have been told off for me (Job 7:1–4).

How many times have we heard that repeated in the sadness, the suffering, of Negro spirituals? Again, it's a phenomenon that we all share—the weariness, the tediousness, the sorrows of life.

St. Paul said to the people of Corinth: "Although I am not bound to anyone, I made myself the slave of all so as to win over as many as possible" (1 Cor 9:19). This is exactly what Pierre Toussaint did. It wasn't that he did not deplore the horrible institution of slavery; he accepted his slavery as a way of saving *all*. "I've made myself the slave of all," as St. Paul said, "so as to win over as many as possible."

We are told in the Gospel that our Divine Lord had gone off "to a lonely place in the desert; there He was absorbed in prayer. Simon and his companions managed to track Him down; and when they found Him, they told Him, "Everybody is looking for You!" Did Jesus say, "I'm busy praying"? No. He said, "Let us move on to the neighboring villages, so that I may proclaim the good news there also" (Mk 1:35–38).

I don't want to stretch the analogy too far, but Pierre Toussaint was a man of deep, daily prayer, and never did he refuse the needs of those who called to him. No matter how tired he was, how weary after a day's work, always he would go off to lay down his life for others—the sign of Christ, the sign of the saint.

12

What Difference
Does Christ's Resurrection Make?

SIXTH SUNDAY OF THE YEAR
FEBRUARY 13, 1994
PONTIFICAL MASS

Last Sunday we celebrated Black History Sunday and talked about Pierre Toussaint, the black servant of God, buried beneath this high altar, to whom are being imputed what may or may not be miracles, various medical cures that are not explainable by medical answers alone.

There is a great deal of difference between magic and miracles. When we go to a magic show and see an elephant disappear, we know that it really doesn't disappear. In some tricky way, it's hidden from our eyes. The laws of nature haven't been reversed. When we see a woman sawed in half, however realistic it appears, we know she's not being sawed in half. We are legitimately deceived by a trick; that's not a miracle.

The purpose of a miracle, which is workable only by the power of Almighty God and which actually suspends the laws of nature, is quite different. First, a miracle is worked out of God's goodness, compassion, and pity. Secondly, it is worked for the purpose of intensifying faith for the individual receiving the miracle or for those around. Our Lord did not work a miracle for Herod, for instance. Herod was a non-believer, and he was demanding magic. Thirdly, miracles are signs of what will come.

In today's Gospel we are told the miracle of the cleansing of the leper (Mk 1:40–45).

> A leper approached Jesus with a request, kneeling down as he addressed him: "If you will to do so, you can cure me." Moved with pity, Jesus stretched out his hand, touched him, and said: "I do will it. Be cured." The leprosy left him then and there, and he was cured.

All illness is, indirectly at least, related to original sin. Some illness, of course, is directly related to sin. We may drink too much and find ourselves with a bad liver. That's directly related to our own gluttony. All sin, however, is related to original sin. If it hadn't been for the original sin of Adam, there would be no sin on our part. When Jesus brings about a cure,

He is showing that He has power not only over a "medical situation", to call it such, but over sin, because in some way the illness is indirectly related with sin. This is especially true in the case of raising Lazarus from the dead.

Death itself came into the world through the original sin of Adam and Eve. When Jesus raises Lazarus from the dead, He is showing that He has the power over death, because He has the power over original sin. Why does Jesus have the power over it? The fundamental reason is that He is going to die to compensate for original sin.

Each miracle is a sign of what will come. The purification of this leper is a sign that all of us, if we die in grace, one day will be purified through the suffering, death, and Resurrection of Christ. The raising of Lazarus from the dead is a sign that one day we will be raised from the dead.

This brings us to today's section of the *Catechism*. We are told in this section that Jesus, after He suffered on the Cross, died, was buried, descended into hell, and on the third day rose again from the dead. He ascended into heaven, is seated at the right hand of the Father; He shall come to judge the living and the dead. The *Catechism* tells us:

> . . . In his plan of salvation, God ordained that his Son should not only "die for our sins" (1 Cor 15:3) but should also "taste death," that is to say that he should experience the state of death, the state of separation between his soul and his body, between the time he expired on the cross and the time he was raised from the dead [624].

That is the meaning of death for any one of us; our souls are separated from our bodies. This is why, incidentally, a priest normally will anoint a person even if the person seems to have been dead for an hour or so, because we define death as separation of the soul from the body, and we don't know exactly when the soul has left the body.

The *Catechism* continues:

> The death of Christ was a true death in that it put an end to his earthly human existence. But because of the union his body retained with the divine person of the Son, his did not become a mortal corpse like others . . . [627].

> Baptism, whose original and full sign is immersion, signifies effectively the descent into the tomb of the Christian who dies to sin with Christ for the sake of a new life: "We have been buried with Christ by baptism into death, so that, just as Christ was raised from the dead by the glory of the Father, so too we might live in newness of life" (Rom 6:4) [628].

> . . . The Apostles' Creed confesses in the same article of faith the descent of Christ into hell and his Resurrection from the dead on the third day . . . [631].

The Bible calls the realm of the dead, to which the dead Christ descended, "hell"—*Sheol* in Hebrew or *Hades* in Greek—because those who are there are deprived of the vision of God. . . . Jesus did not go down to hell to deliver the damned from hell, nor to destroy the hell of damnation, but to free the just who had preceded him in death [633].

I want to read portions of a very beautiful poem called "Limbo", written by Sister Mary Ida.

> The Ancient Greyness shifted
> Suddenly and thinned
> Like mist upon the moors
> Before a wind.
> An old, old prophet lifted
> A shining face and said:
> "He will be coming soon.
> The Son of God is dead;
> He died this afternoon."
>
> A murmurous excitement stirred
> All souls.
> They wondered if they dreamed—
> Save one old man who seemed
> Not even to have heard.
>
> And Moses standing,
> Hushed them all to ask
> If any had a welcome song prepared.
> If not, would David take the task?
>   .   .   .
>
> A breath of spring surprised them,
> Stilling Moses' words.
>   .   .   .
>
> And there He was
> Splendid as the morning sun and fair
> As only God is fair.
> And they, confused with joy,
> Knelt to adore
> Seeing that He wore
> Five crimson stars
> He never had before.

No canticle was sung.
None toned a psalm, or raised a greeting song.
A silent man alone
Of all that throng
Found tongue—
Not any other.

Close to His heart
When the embrace was done,
Old Joseph said,
"How is Your Mother,
How is Your Mother, Son?"

Joseph, the foster father of Jesus, was one of those wonderful souls waiting for the death of Christ so that the gates of heaven would be reopened.
We are told in the *Catechism*:

> The resurrection of Jesus is the culminating truth of our faith in Christ.
> [This is the ultimate miracle!] The first Christian community believed in
> and lived his Resurrection as its central truth, which its Tradition commu-
> nicated as fundamental and its New Testament writings established and
> preached, together with the cross, as the essential aspect of the Paschal mys-
> tery . . . [638].

> The mystery of the Resurrection of Christ is a real event, to whose histori-
> cal circumstances the New Testament bears witness [639].

> The first element we encounter in the structure of the Easter events is the
> empty tomb. In itself it is not a direct proof. The absence of Christ's body
> in the tomb could be explained otherwise [640].

Remember that the High Priest asked Pilate to post guards before the
tomb so that the body couldn't be stolen, thus giving His apostles the opportunity to say that Jesus had risen from the dead. It wasn't possible that
the body could have been stolen. Even so, there were theories that His
body had been thrown into a ditch and was never found, and so on.
The *Catechism* continues:

> Despite [the fact that the absence of Christ's body in the tomb could be ex-
> plained otherwise], the empty tomb constituted for all an essential sign. Its
> discovery by the disciples was their first step toward recognizing the fact it-
> self [640].

Christ's is the only empty tomb in the world that is honored. Lenin's
tomb was honored when the body of Lenin was in it. Christ's tomb is
honored because the body rose. We even have an order called the Knights

and Ladies of the Holy Sepulchre, who honor the sepulchre, the tomb, of Christ.

We return to the *Catechism*:

> Mary Magdalene and the holy women who came to complete the embalming of the body of Jesus, buried in haste because the sabbath began at sundown on Good Friday, were the first to encounter the Risen One. [To read the Gospels and to see the role of women in the life of Christ is marvelous indeed.] They were also the first messengers of the Resurrection of Christ to the apostles themselves. It was to the apostles that Jesus appeared later, first to Peter, then to the Twelve. Peter, called to confirm the faith of his brothers, sees the Resurrection before them, and it is on his witness that the community cries: "It is true that the Lord is risen and he has appeared to Simon [Peter]" (Lk 24:34) [641].

> Everything that happened during those Paschal days involved each of the apostles—and Peter in particular—in the building of the new era begun on Easter morning. As the Risen One's witnesses, they remain the foundation stones of his Church. The faith of the first community of believers was based on the witness of specific men known to the Christians and, for the most part, still living among them [642]. [And so is ours today. That's why we're called an "apostolic Church". We trace our beliefs back to the apostles, who saw the risen Christ.]

> Even when faced with the reality of the risen Christ, the disciples still doubted, so impossible did resurrection seem that they thought they had seen a ghost [644].

You remember the experience of Thomas, for instance. When the other apostles told him that Christ had risen from the dead, Thomas said, "I won't believe unless I put my hand into His side, my fingers into the holes in His hands and His feet." They still needed the Pentecost, when the Holy Spirit would come upon them fifty days later, to give them the strength, courage, and intensity of faith that they needed to live and to preach the faith.

The *Catechism* continues:

> By means of touch and the sharing of a meal, the risen Jesus established direct contact with his disciples and invited them to recognize that he was not a ghost and above all to report that the risen body in which he appeared to them was the same body that had been martyred and crucified, for it still bore the traces of his Passion. ["Come Thomas, put your hands into My side."] Yet at the same time this authentic, real body possessed the new properties of a glorious body, not limited by space and time but able to be present how and when he wills [645].

Next the *Catechism* talks about the work of the Holy Trinity in the Resurrection. It is a profound mystery.

> The three divine persons acted together in the Resurrection yet revealed their own proper roles. The Father's power raised Christ his Son . . . St. Paul emphasizes the manifestation of God's power by the working of the Holy Spirit . . . [648].

> Yet the Son brings about his own Resurrection by virtue of his divine power. Jesus announces that the Son of Man will have to suffer many things, die, and then rise. Elsewhere he affirms explicitly: "I lay down my life in order to take it up again. . . . I have power to lay it down and power to take it up again" (Jn 10:17–18) [649].

The *Catechism* tells us about the meaning and saving significance of the Resurrection.

> "If Christ has not been raised, then our preaching is in vain and your faith is in vain" (1 Cor 15:14). The Resurrection constitutes before all else the confirmation of all that Christ himself did and taught [651].

> His Resurrection is the fulfillment of the promises of both the Old Testament and of Jesus himself during his life on earth [652].

> The Resurrection confirms the truth of Jesus' divinity. He had said: "When you have lifted up the Son of Man, then you will realize that I AM" (Jn 8:28) [653].

This is the strange language that we saw in the Book of Exodus, the second book of the Old Testament. When God was sending Moses to the Pharaoh to set God's people free, Moses asked, "Who will I say sent me?" God said, "Tell them, 'I AM WHO AM.' Tell them, 'HE WHO IS' sent you." Jesus identifies Himself with this when He calls Himself "I AM."

In the words of the *Catechism*:

> The Paschal mystery has two aspects: by his death, Christ sets us free from sin; by his Resurrection, he opens for us the way to new life, and he brings about our adoption as God's children because we become brothers and sisters of Christ [654].

That's why we can pray the prayer "Our Father", the prayer that Christ taught. He makes us His brothers and sisters, therefore adopted children of His Father.

The *Catechism* continues:

> Finally, Christ's Resurrection—and the risen Christ himself—is the principle and source of our future resurrection: ". . . [F]or as all die in Adam, so all will be made alive in Christ" (1 Cor 15:20–22) [655].

"So then the Lord Jesus, after he had spoken to his apostles, was taken up into heaven and sat down at the right hand of God" (Mk 16:19). . . . Jesus' final appearance ended with the irreversible entry of his humanity into God's glory, symbolized by the cloud and heaven, where he has been seated from that time forward at God's right hand [659].

Only the one who came from the Father can go to the Father. "No one has ascended into heaven except the one who descended from heaven, the Son of Man" (Jn 3:13) [661]. [We couldn't ascend into heaven except that we follow the Christ who has prepared the way before us.]

The *Catechism* quotes our Divine Lord:

"And I, when I have been lifted up from the earth, will draw all men to myself" (Jn 12:32). . . . In heaven Christ permanently exercises his priesthood, for he "always lives to make intercession" for "those who approach God through him" (Heb 7:25) [662].

Christ . . . sits at the right hand of the Father: "By 'the Father's right hand' we understand the glory and honor of divinity . . . [663].

The right hand is always a place of honor. Even today, at a formal dinner, the host or hostess will usually have the senior guest at his or her right hand.

We are told in the Creed, "He will come again in glory to judge the living and the dead." The *Catechism* elucidates:

As Lord, Christ is also the head of the Church, his Body. Taken up to heaven and glorified after he had accomplished his mission, he continues to dwell on earth in his Church [669].

According to the Lord, the present time is the time of the Spirit and witness, but it is also a time still marked by "impending crisis" and the temptation of evil which does not spare the Church. This time of waiting and watching ushers in the struggles of the last days [672].

Before the coming of Christ, the Church must pass through a final trial that will shake the faith of many believers. The persecution that accompanies her pilgrimage on earth will reveal the mystery of wickedness in the form of a religious deception offering us an apparent solution to our problems at the price of apostasy from the truth. [This is what the devil did with Adam and Eve. He tried to separate them from the truth, telling them he could give them so much.] The supreme religious deception is that of the Antichrist, a pseudo-messianism by which the human race glorifies itself in place of God and his incarnate Messiah [675].

This "supreme religious deception" can be found in a world that is completely secular, where there is no room for God, a world that tries to create a utopia without God here on this earth.

The *Catechism* explains:

> The Church will enter the glory of the kingdom only through its final Pass-over, when it will follow its Lord in his death and Resurrection. [We can't get excited about persecutions of the Church. We are told that the disciple cannot be greater than the master. We are going to suffer and we are going to die before we rise.] . . . The triumph of God over the revolt of evil will take the form of the final judgment, after this passing world has been shaken to its foundation [677].

The *Catechism* then comments on the section of the Creed addressing the judgment of the living and the dead.

> Following in the steps of the prophets and John the Baptist, Jesus pro-claimed the judgment of the last day. . . . On the last day Christ will say: "Whatever you have done to the least of my brothers, that you have done unto me" (Mt 25:40) [678].

You remember that scene that our Lord describes in the Gospel of Matthew: "Some will be gathered on my right hand and some on my left. I will say to those on my right, 'Come, you blessed of my Father. When I was hungry you gave me to eat . . . .' To those on my left, 'Depart from me, ye cursed, because you ignored me in your brothers and sisters, my people on this earth.' "

The *Catechism* continues:

> Christ is Lord of eternal life. The full right to judge definitively the works and hearts of men belongs to him as Redeemer of the world. He acquired this right by his cross. [By His crucifixion and death, Christ compensated for original sin and acquired the right to be judge of the living and dead.] Yet the Son did not come to judge, but to save and to give us the life he has in himself. It is by refusing grace in this life that each one judges himself, receives according to his works, and can ever condemn himself for all eter-nity by rejecting the Spirit of love [679].

It is hardly scriptural, but you may remember the book by William Blatty, *The Exorcist*, in which, in a very poignant moment, the question arises, "Can there be such a thing as diabolical possession?" The answer is given: "Sometimes I think that we really don't need the devil to bring about our condemnation. Just the lack of love in our own hearts, that's enough to condemn us."

This morning when I was reading the Divine Office, which all priests and religious and many lay people read each day, I saw a selection from a deacon, St. Ephraem, who lived and died in the fourth century. He was a great preacher. He said:

Lord, who can comprehend even one of your words? We lose more of it than we grasp, like those who drink from a living spring. For God's word offers different facets according to the capacity of the listener.

Presumably each one of us here may get different things from the *Catechism* and from the scriptural quotations in which it is rooted.

Whenever anyone discovers some part of the treasure, he should not think that he has exhausted God's word. What you have received and attained is your present share, while what is left will be your heritage. For what we could not take at one time because of our weakness, we will be able to grasp at another, if we only persevere.

Perseverance, the great answer to the struggles of this life and to salvation. If we can only persevere! If we could concentrate, for instance, as Christians, on the Word of God, on the life of Christ on this earth, on our eternal destiny. If we could concentrate, as those who hope to go to the Olympics can concentrate. They go through grueling training day after day and count it as nothing, because they hope they'll get to the Olympics, and they hope, even beyond that, to win a gold, or silver or bronze medal.

Is it too much, then, if we Christians sacrifice and do penance, especially with Lent beginning in just a handful of days; if we pray; if we try to get to Mass at some point during the week; above all, if we meditate on the Word of God? Is that too much of a sacrifice to win—not a bronze, or silver, or gold medal—but to win eternal happiness itself?

13

Who Is the Holy Spirit?
. . . And Where Is He Now?

FIRST SUNDAY OF LENT
PONTIFICAL MASS
FEBRUARY 20, 1994

Today is the First Sunday of Lent, a season that always gives us new hope and an opportunity to set aside our old lives and start all over again in preparation for Easter. We have signs of great hope all around us: today's magnificent weather, the completed rehabilitation of the cathedral organ, and, this afternoon in this cathedral, some seven hundred adults of various ages will be either beginning their entrance into the Catholic Faith or beginning their return to the Catholic Faith through the program we call the Rite of Christian Initiation of Adults. What a wonderful sign of hope this is!

I have a great letter here from a young man named Joe Polchinski. Joe is now a student up in Providence College, and he was formerly a student at Fordham Prep here in New York. He wrote me this very long letter, from which I excerpt a few passages:

> I thought you would like to know a little about some of your young people. For instance, our Fordham Prep Respect Life Club is quite active. We go to the March for Life in Washington every year, as well as the High School Leadership Conference held at the seminary. We also sponsor various pro-life meetings and activities throughout the year. Yet we meet our share of adversity even within the school itself. When I was a student there, I wrote for the school newspaper and spoke on such issues as abstinence from sex and the pro-life movement. I received a lot of criticism for it, but I did what I thought was right.
>
> I can tell you, though, it was nice to have many kids compliment and agree with what I said. Young people often get a bad rap. But you can believe me when I tell you there are so many wonderful young people in our archdiocese who are hungry for the truth. We don't drink, we don't do drugs, we don't have sex. We love Christ and His message, and, when young people don't do the right thing, I don't think it's because they refuse to, but I think a lot of times they get led down the wrong path.
>
> I've been blessed with wonderful priests who have been great leaders in

my life. [He names several priests in the archdiocese.] I tell you these good things about young people to encourage you; I know even the Archbishop of New York can get discouraged. We all need hope. Those of us who went to the World Youth Day in Denver are working hard to keep its message alive. We look forward to the New York youth day with great anticipation.

I also want you to know that I'm available, as are many others in our Respect Life Group, for whatever needs to be done for Young New York '94. It is going to be great. I'm also willing to serve you and the archdiocese in any way. Please let me know how I can be of help to you. God bless you.

Joe Polchinski.

That is a remarkable letter. Some might say it's unique, but it's not. So many I know feel the way Joe Polchinski feels. Perhaps they don't express it so eloquently as he, but they are truly signs of hope. We cannot let ourselves get discouraged, regardless of what we read in the newspapers, see on television, in the movies, and so on. There's great hope, because we have been given the gift of the Holy Spirit.

Today's session on the new *Catechism* will be dominantly about the Holy Spirit. The wonderful Scripture readings today point toward the work of the Holy Spirit that is described in the *Catechism*. Let us refresh our memories on one portion of the first reading: "God said to Noah, 'I set my bow in the clouds to serve as a sign of the covenant between me and the earth.' "

Clouds in the Old Testament are often a reference to the Holy Spirit. When the Jewish people were wandering in the desert, for instance, we are told they were led by a cloud during the day and a pillar of fire by night. This was the Holy Spirit, leading them to the Promised Land.

> When I bring clouds over the earth and the bow appears in the clouds, I will recall the covenant I have made between me and you and all living beings, so that the waters shall never again become a flood to destroy all mortal beings (Gen 9:15).

As we will see, when we talk about the Holy Spirit in this section of the *Catechism*, the flood, for which Noah built the ark to ride out with his family and with all living creatures, is a sign of the waters of baptism. We are told in the Baptismal Rite that we enter into the waters in death with Christ so that we might rise with him. The ark is representative of the Church, the Church that is filled with the Holy Spirit. The Scriptures are filled with symbolism of this sort.

In the second reading, the one from the first letter of St. Peter, there is another reference to the ark and to the flood: "At that time, a few persons . . . escaped in the ark through the water. You are now saved by a baptismal bath which corresponds to this exactly" (1 Pet 3:21).

It is in baptism that we receive the Holy Spirit. Then we become temples of the Holy Spirit, and the Holy Spirit runs through our very being. We are told in the opening to the Gospel: "The Spirit sent Jesus out toward the desert . . ." (Mk 1:12).

This is a profound mystery, because Jesus is a Person of the Blessed Trinity, equal with the Holy Spirit. Each of the three Persons of the Trinity is God, distinct from one another but not separable from one another. This is a profound mystery, but this is the human nature of Jesus, Jesus the man, driven into the desert by the Spirit. What's going to happen? He is going to be confronted with temptations and with the devil. This is a preparation for the great things He is going to do in his life, above all, of course, the crowning event, the salvation of souls.

We are asked to enter into a spiritual desert for forty days during Lent. It is a desert of solitude, a desert of thought, of reflection, of meditation, of prayer. And the devil confronted by our Lord in the desert is the devil that confronts us every day: the noonday devil, discouragement; the devils of passion; the devils of impurity; the devils of losing our tempers. But we have to recognize that the Spirit is watching over us. The Spirit *drove* Jesus into the desert, so that He, humanly speaking, would be strengthened by His temptations, as we can be strengthened by ours.

These Scripture readings prepare us for what the *Catechism* says about the Holy Spirit. The *Catechism* begins: "No one is able to call Jesus the Lord except by the Holy Spirit" (1 Cor 12:3).

We wouldn't know Christ except that we have been filled by the Holy Spirit, driven to Christ. As the *Catechism* puts it:

> . . . to be in communion with Christ, we must first have been touched by that Spirit. He comes to us and awakens faith in us. [We didn't start it ourselves. We are gifted with the Holy Spirit. Not everyone has received the Holy Spirit.] From our baptism, the initial sacrament of faith, the Holy Spirit communicates to us, intimately and personally in the Church, the life that originates in the Father and is offered to us in the Son [683].

We become living temples of the Holy Spirit. It is sad that there are so many attacks on this temple. Joe Polchinski talks about the fact that young people can be led astray, and so can all of us. There are so many attacks, so much evil that is trying to drag us down. It is so important that we try to keep these temples pure and holy, and that we encourage young people, that we give them ideals, that we remind them that they are the temples of the Holy Spirit. They are not going to laugh at that. They are not going to laugh at the idea of abstinence. Under peer pressure they may seem to ridicule it, but it is so unfortunate to read materials that say, "Well, we know young people will never be pure so we have to give them these precautions." We don't even *try* to talk to them about the purity of being temples of God the Holy Spirit.

The *Catechism* goes on:

To believe in the Holy Spirit is to profess that the Spirit is one of the persons of the Holy Trinity, of one being with the Father and the Son: "With the Father and the Son he is worshipped and glorified" (Nicene Creed) [685].

The Holy Spirit is at work with the Father and the Son from the beginning to the end of God's plan for our salvation [686].

The Church . . . is the place of our knowledge of the Holy Spirit [688].

We are filled with the Holy Spirit. Christ promised the apostles, "I will send you the Holy Spirit", and the Holy Spirit came on Pentecost. They lost their fear, they became courageous, they went out and taught and preached and worked all sorts of miracles. We learn of the Holy Spirit:

—in the Scriptures he inspired;
—in the Tradition, to which the Church Fathers are always timely witnesses;
—in the Church's Magisterium, which he assists;
—in the words and symbols of sacramental liturgy, through which the Holy Spirit brings us into communion with Christ;
—in prayer, wherein he intercedes for us;
—in the charisms and ministries by which the Church is built up;
—in the signs of apostolic and missionary life [What drives people to go off to Africa, to Asia, all over the world, to incredible hardships, except the Holy Spirit];
—in the witness of saints through whom he reveals his holiness and continues the work of our salvation [688].

The *Catechism* says:

Sent into our hearts by the Father, the Spirit of his Son is truly God. Of one being with the Father and the Son, he is inseparable from them, in both the intimate life of the Trinity and his gift of love to the world. . . . In their joint mission, the Son and the Holy Spirit are distinct but inseparable. When Christ appears, visible image of the invisible God, it is the Spirit who reveals him [689].

. . . The term "Spirit" translates the Hebrew word *ruah*, which, in its first sense, means breath, air, or wind [691].

We are told in the Book of Genesis that at the creation the Spirit of God swept across the waters, brooded over the waters, stilled and calmed the waters with peace. Then God said, "Let there be light." We are told that, at the creation of Adam and Eve, God took the dust of the earth and breathed into it the breath, the Spirit of life. Creation is by the power of the Holy Spirit.

The *Catechism* goes on:

> Jesus, when he proclaimed and promised the coming of the Holy Spirit, called him another Paraclete . . . "consoler" . . . "the Spirit of truth" [692].

> *Water* is the symbol of the Holy Spirit's action in baptism . . . just as we grow toward our first birth in water [the water in our mother's womb] so the water of baptism truly signifies that our birth into the divine life is given in the Spirit. . . . The Spirit is personally the living water springing from Christ crucified and the source of eternal life in us [694].

When Jesus met the Samaritan woman, he said to her, "I will give you living water, the Holy Spirit." The *Catechism* says:

> The symbolism of anointing with oil is also a sign of the Holy Spirit. . . . In Christian initiation, *anointing* is the sacramental sign of confirmation. . . . [We anoint at Baptism, at Confirmation, in the reception of the priesthood, in the sacrament of healing, the sacrament of the dying. All these are symbols of the Holy Spirit.] The Spirit filled Christ and the Spirit's power went out from him in his healing and saving acts. Finally, the Spirit raised Jesus from the dead [695].

> While water signifies birth and the fruitfulness of life given in the Holy Spirit, *fire* symbolizes the transforming energy of the Spirit's actions [696].

We see so many signs of fire in the Old Testament—again, the Holy Spirit as a pillar of fire leading the Israelites at night.

> John the Baptist . . . proclaimed Christ as the one who "will baptize in the Holy Spirit and fire" (Lk 1:17). Jesus would say of the Spirit: "I am come to bring fire to the earth and how I wish it were already kindled" (Lk 12:49). In the form of tongues "as of fire," the Holy Spirit rested on the disciples on the morning of Pentecost and filled them with himself [696].

> The Holy Spirit came upon the Virgin Mary and "overshadowed" her, so that she might conceive and give birth to Jesus. [He had no human father, a foster father Joseph, so the Holy Spirit conceived in, and of, and through Mary.] On the mountain of transfiguration, the Spirit in the "cloud came and overshadowed" Jesus, Moses and Elijah, Peter, James and John, and "from the cloud came a voice that said: 'This is my Son, my Chosen, listen to him'" (Lk 9:34–35) [697].

Then a dove came down. We are told in the flood story that Noah sent forth a dove, and a dove came back with a twig of olive, the branch of peace, symbolizing the coming of the Holy Spirit.

Jesus healed the sick and blessed little children by *laying hands* on them. In his name the apostles did the same. Through the laying on of the hands of the apostles, the Holy Spirit was given [699].

Christ inaugurated the proclamation of the good news by making his own this passage from the prophet Isaiah:

"The Spirit of the LORD is upon me,
because the LORD has anointed me.
He has sent me to bring good news to the poor,
to bind up the broken hearted,
to proclaim liberty to captives
and release to the prisoners,
to proclaim a year of the LORD's favor" (Is 61:1–2) [714].

The *Catechism* continues:

"There was a man sent from God, whose name was John" (Jn 1:6). John was "filled with the Holy Spirit" from his mother's womb, by Christ himself, just conceived in the Virgin's womb by the Holy Spirit. Mary's visitation to Elizabeth thus became a visit from God to his people [717].

You remember that scene. Mary went to help Elizabeth because Elizabeth was advanced in age, she was bearing John the Baptist, her first child. We are told that at Mary's greeting the infant in Elizabeth's womb leaped for joy, was cleansed of original sin in his mother's womb, as you and I are cleansed by baptism, because of the presence of Christ. This is the work of the Holy Spirit.

The *Catechism* goes on:

In the fullness of time, Mary, the all-holy Mother of God, ever-virgin, became the masterwork of the mission of the Son and the Spirit. For the first time in the plan of salvation and because his Spirit had prepared her, the Father found the dwelling where his Son and Spirit could abide among human beings [721].

God's word, engraved in the tablets of stone, was placed in that precious box called the Ark of the Covenant, lined with gold and covered with rare woods. But Mary is *the* resting place of the Word made flesh.

In Mary, the "wonders of God" that the Spirit was to fulfill in Christ and the Church began to be revealed:

The Holy Spirit *prepared* Mary by his grace. . . . She was, by pure grace, conceived without sin, the most humble of creatures, the most capable of receiving the inexpressible gift of the Almighty [722].

On the eighth of December we celebrate the beautiful Feast of the Immaculate Conception. Mary was conceived without any sin whatsoever so that she might be the resting place of Jesus.

The *Catechism* states:

> In Mary, the Holy Spirit fulfilled the plan of the Father's good pleasure. It was with and by the Holy Spirit that the Virgin conceived and gave birth to the Son of God. By the Spirit's power and Mary's faith, her virginity became uniquely fruitful [723].

Mary was a virgin, but she brought forth the Son of God, the Son of the Creator, who was going to give life to all.

The *Catechism* continues:

> Finally, through Mary, the Holy Spirit began to bring the men whom God favors into communion with Christ. The lowly were always the first to accept him: shepherds, magi, Simeon and Anna, the bridegroom of Cana, and the first disciples [725].

> At the end of this mission of the Spirit, Mary became the Woman, the new Eve ("mother of the living"), the mother of the "whole Christ." As such, she was present with the Twelve, "of one heart, devoted to prayer" (Acts 1:14), at the dawn of the "end time" inaugurated by the Spirit on the morning of Pentecost with the manifestation of the Church [726].

> The whole mission of the Son and the Holy Spirit, in the fullness of time, is contained in this: that the Son is the one anointed by the Father's Spirit since his Incarnation—Jesus is the Christ, the Messiah. . . .
> Christ's whole work is, in fact, a joint mission of the Son and the Holy Spirit [727].

> During his public life, Jesus . . . gradually disclosed the Spirit in his teaching of the multitudes, as when he revealed that his own flesh would be food for the life of the world [728].

> Only when the hour came for his glorification did Jesus *promise* the coming of the Holy Spirit, since his death and Resurrection would fulfill the promise made to the Fathers. The Spirit of truth, the other Paraclete, will be given by the Father in answer to Jesus' prayer; . . . The Holy Spirit will come and we shall know him, for he will be with us and remain with us for ever. He will teach us everything, remind us of all that Christ said to us and bear witness to him. He will lead us into all truth and glorify Christ [729].

Jesus could tell us this only because His death and Resurrection would fulfill the promise made in the Old Testament: the Messiah would come.

> When at last Jesus' hour came, the moment when he conquered death by dying, the Son commended his spirit into the Father's hands so that, "raised from the dead by the glory of the Father" (Rom 6:4), he might immediately *give* the Holy Spirit by "breathing" on his disciples. From this hour forward, the mission of Christ and the Spirit became the mission of the Church: "As the Father has sent me, so I send you" (Jn 20:21) [730].

On the day of Pentecost, seven weeks after Easter, Christ's Paschal mystery was fulfilled in the outpouring of the Holy Spirit, revealed, given and communicated as a divine person . . . [731].

On that day, the Holy Trinity was fully revealed [732].

Because we are dead or at least wounded by sin, the first effect of the gift of love is the forgiveness of our sins. The fellowship of the Spirit in the Church restores to the baptized the divine likeness lost through sin [734].

What a gift given to us!

"The Spirit is our life"; the more we renounce ourselves, the more we are guided by the Spirit [736].

Finally, the *Catechism* speaks about "The Holy Spirit and the Church": "The mission of Christ and the Holy Spirit is brought to completion in the Church, which is the Body of Christ and the Temple of the Holy Spirit" [737]. Each of us individually is a temple of the Holy Spirit, the Church is the glorious Temple of the Holy Spirit.

Thus the Church's mission is not an addition to that of Christ and the Holy Spirit . . . . In its whole being and in all its members, the Church is sent to proclaim, bear witness, make present, and spread the mystery of the communion of the Holy Trinity . . . :

"All of us who have received one and the same Spirit, that is, the Holy Spirit, are in a sense blended together with one another and with God" (St. Cyril) [738].

This is what we call the Mystical Body of Christ here on earth, of which each of us is a member.

"The Spirit helps us in our weakness . . ." [741]. What a great gift of hope! Hope, we are told, is a so-called *infused* virtue, as are faith and charity. These are gifts infused in us, poured into us by the Holy Spirit.

Gerard Manley Hopkins, the mystical poet whose poetry often is very difficult to understand, gives us a clear expression of the hope that is the Holy Spirit, the joy and the light that the Holy Spirit brings us. The poem "God's Grandeur" is reflective of the springtime that is coming upon us:

The world is charged with the grandeur of God.
   It will flame out, like shining from shook foil . . .

Generations have trod, have trod, have trod;
   And all is seared with trade; bleared, smeared with toil;
   And wears man's smudge and shares man's smell: the soil
Is bare now, nor can foot feel, being shod.

And for all this, nature is never spent;
  There lives the dearest freshness deep down things . . .

Because the Holy Ghost over the bent
  World broods with warm breast and with ah! bright wings.

14

The Church Is Here to Help Us!

SECOND SUNDAY OF LENT
FEBRUARY 27, 1994
PONTIFICAL MASS

May I ask that we offer this Holy Sacrifice for the repose of the souls of all of those who were killed in the massacre in the Middle East, for all the Palestinians, for all of the Jews, for all who were in any way hurt or killed. We pray most particularly that this horrifying event will not disrupt the peace process but that peace with justice for all will follow even more quickly.

This is the fourteenth Sunday of our treatment of the new *Catechism of the Catholic Church*. The section of the *Catechism* we will cover today tells us what the Church teaches about herself inspired by the Holy Spirit. We know there is a wide variety of viewpoints about the Church from outsiders and so-called insiders. Some see the Church as a big, wealthy, bureaucratic organization, and that's all. Some see the Church as completely irrelevant to our day, having nothing to say to any one of us, to our pains, to our sorrows, to our needs, to our salvation. Some see the Church as a place to go on Sundays for Mass. Some see the Church generally, as the apostles saw Christ in His ordinary, everyday, work-a-day life. They respected Him, but for the most part they saw Him simply as another human being, not radically different from others they had known.

We are told in today's Gospel that the three closest to Jesus—Peter, James, and John—had this remarkable experience (Mk 9:2–10). He selected them from the Twelve and took them up to the top of the mountain. There they saw what looked like a radically different Jesus. It was the same Jesus they were with every day, but now their eyes were opened, and they were filled with the Holy Spirit. They saw His face shining as the sun, His clothes dazzlingly white. This was the Transfiguration. They were to come down from the mountain and be as weak as before, sin just as frequently, even run away from Him when it was time for His crucifixion. But it had to have had an impact on their lives, an impact they remembered when it came time for the Resurrection. They had to have the coming of the Holy Spirit on Pentecost before they had the courage and the strength to preach and teach the gospel and risk their lives; nevertheless, this memory stayed with them. This was one of the reasons that Christ revealed Himself. It was the same Christ, now seen in a radically different light.

Every once in a while some of us have opportunity to see the Church that way. Sometimes we've been in pain, perhaps someone in the family has died. At the funeral, all of the meaningfulness of the Church's liturgy comes home to us. The same can happen when we bring a baby to be baptized, when there's a beautiful marriage, when we see our loved ones anointed, when the priest comes. There are so many instances when we have this kind of transfiguring experience.

This past Friday evening I was down in lower Manhattan at what we call a vicariate meeting. There were representatives of 32 parishes there; it was like the League of Nations! They have 129 Masses on the weekend—they are in French, Italian, Spanish, German, Slovenian, Polish, Cantonese, Mandarin, Tagalog for the Philippines, and so on. It was a real transfiguration experience to be reminded once again that the Church is one Body.

At the vicariate meeting a number of people got up, some quite young, and talked about prayer groups that they are in and about being members of the Legion of Mary. One young lady got up and identified herself as a member of young Catholics who work on Wall Street. The way she talked about the Church—the joy that she experiences in being able to get to go to Our Lady of Victory Parish on Wall Street for Mass each day, for a Holy Hour, what her faith means to her, the fact that she and other young Catholics, married and single, meet once a month for dinner and just share their faith—this is a transfiguration-type experience. This is really the Church.

What does the Church say about herself in the *Catechism*? First, we are told:

> Christ is the light of the peoples. . . . The Church has no other light than that of Christ [The pope and the bishops aren't the light of the Church. They simply represent Christ, who is the *only* light of the Church.]; according to a favorite image of the Church Fathers, the Church is like the moon, all its light reflected from the sun [748].

The *Catechism* goes on:

> In Christian usage, the word "church" designates the liturgical assembly, but also the local community or the whole universal community of believers. "The Church" is the people God gathers in the world. She lives on the word and the Body of Christ and so becomes Christ's Body [752].

> In the Sacred Scriptures we find a number of images of the Church [753].

The *Catechism* says:

> The Church is . . . the flock of which God himself foretold that he would
> be the shepherd, and whose sheep . . . are unfailingly nourished and led by
> Christ himself, the Good Shepherd . . . who laid down his life for his sheep
> [754].

> The Church is . . . often called God's *building* [756].

God forbid that this magnificent cathedral and all of its stone, glass, and
steel be destroyed. But you who are the building blocks of God's Church,
you *can't* be destroyed. That's the kind of mystical Church that Christ established. The *Catechism* goes on:

> "The eternal Father . . . decided to raise up men to share in the communion
> of his divine life" . . . . The Father wished to call to form his Holy Church
> all those "who believe in Christ" [759].

> The gathering of the Church is, as it were, God's reaction to the chaos pro-
> voked by sin [beginning with original sin] [761].

> The remote preparation of the calling of the people of God begins with the
> calling of Abraham, to whom God promised that he would become the fa-
> ther of a great people [762].

God called him from nowhere, called him from paganism. This was the
Abraham who was just read about in today's first reading, called by the
grace of God just as we are called to the Church (Gen 22:1–2, 9, 10–13,
15–18). The *Catechism* continues:

> The Son's task was to accomplish his Father's plan of salvation in the full-
> ness of time. Its accomplishment was the reason for his being sent. The Lord
> Jesus laid the foundation of his Church by preaching the Good News, the
> coming of God's Kingdom promised in the Scriptures throughout the ages
> [763]. [Everything that He did was preparation for establishing the Church.]

Now this is crucial. The *Catechism* says:

> The Lord Jesus endowed his community with a structure that will remain
> until the Kingdom is fully achieved. He did so above all in the choice of the
> Twelve with Peter as their leader. . . . The Twelve and the other disciples
> shared in Christ's mission and his power, but also in his lot [his suffering].
> By all his actions, Christ prepared and built his Church [765].

I just read this week a foolish article by a woman who calls herself the
president of "Catholics for a Free Choice", a tiny little group who purport
to represent Catholicism in the matter of human life. She says, "Who's the
pope? The pope's nobody. Who are the bishops? They are silly. I'm a

Catholic, but I have enough just in Christ." Well, that's not the way
Christ structured it.

The *Catechism* continues:

> ... The Church's beginning and growth were symbolized "by the blood
> and water that flowed from the open side of the crucified Jesus." As Eve
> was formed from the sleeping Adam's side, so the Church was born from
> Christ's heart pierced at his death on the cross [766].

> "When the Son had accomplished on earth the task entrusted to him by the
> Father, the Holy Spirit was sent on Pentecost that he might ever sanctify the
> Church" [767]. [Until then, the Apostles had been frightened to death.]

> The Church will reach her "consummation only in the glory of heaven,"
> when Christ will come again [769]. [Until then, we are a pilgrim people,
> weak, sinful, often suffering. That will change when Christ comes again.]

We are told in the *Catechism*:

> The seven sacraments are the signs and instruments by which the Holy
> Spirit spreads the grace of Christ, the head, throughout the Church, his
> Body [774].

> To be the sacrament of intimate *union of men with God* is the first purpose of
> the Church [775].

The Church exists for our holiness here and for our eternal salvation. It
doesn't exist simply to perform works of mercy, works of the social gospel, works of justice, of feeding the hungry, clothing the naked. These are
very important, but *the primary* purpose of the Church is to make us holy.
It is the instrument of our holiness and the instrument of our salvation.

> The Church "is the visible plan of God's love for humanity" . . . [776].

> The People of God is marked by characteristics that clearly distinguish it
> from all other religions, ethnic, political, or cultural groups found in history:
> —We become *members* of this people not by a physical birth, but . . . by
> faith in Christ and Baptism. [Jesus said to Nicodemus, "You have to be
> born again of water and the Holy Spirit."]
> —This People's *Head* is Jesus Christ (the anointed, the Messiah). Because
> the same anointing, the Holy Spirit, flows from the head into the body, the
> Church is "the messianic people." [We are a "priestly people", a "kingly
> people".]
> —Its *law* is the new commandment to love as Christ has loved us.
> —Its *mission* is to be the salt and the light of the world.
> —Its *destiny*, finally, is the Kingdom of God [eternity] . . . [782].

> In entering into the People of God by faith and Baptism, one receives a
> share in the unique vocation of this people, a *priestly* vocation [784].

We hear the demand for the ordination of women. Women and men are ordained in a certain way by Baptism to be members of the priestly people. The sacrament of Ordination is reserved for men, but all of us here constitute the priestly people of Christ.

The *Catechism* continues:

When Christ's visible presence was taken from them, he did not leave his disciples orphans, but promised to remain with them until the end of time and sent them his own Spirit [a Spirit Who is still among us] [788].

Believers who respond to God's word become members of Christ's body. . . . This is especially true of Baptism, which unites us to Christ's death and Resurrection, and the Eucharist, by which "we really partake of the Lord's body" and "are raised up to communion with him and with one another" [790]. [We are united with one another because we receive and are fed by that one unique Body and Blood of Christ.]

"In the structure of Christ's body there is also a diversity of members and functions. There is one Spirit who distributes his many gifts for the good of the Church" [791].

Christ "is the head of the body, the Church" [792].

Christ and the Church together make up the "whole Christ." The Church is one with Christ [795].

The unity of Christ and the Church . . . [is] often expressed by the image of bridegroom and bride. . . . The Lord called himself the bridegroom; St. Paul spoke of the whole Church and each of the faithful members of his Body as a bride of Christ the Lord so as to become one spirit with him [796]. [In the old days, in many religious communities, women who were becoming sisters would come in a bridal gown and then exchange the bridal gown for the religious habit.]

"What our spirit, I mean our soul, is to our members," says St. Augustine, "the Holy Spirit is to the members of Christ, or to the Body of Christ, I mean the Church" [797].

The Holy Spirit . . . works for building up the Body in love: by God's Word . . . ; by Baptism . . . ; by the sacraments . . . ; by "the grace of the apostles . . ."; by the virtues [faith, hope, and charity] . . . ; by the many special graces called charisms [which each one of us enjoys in his or her own way so each one of us is vital to the entire body] [798].

The *Catechism* tells us:

These four characteristics, inseparably linked among themselves, indicate essential features of the Church and her mission: the Church is one, holy, catholic, and apostolic [811].

The Church is one because of her source: ". . . the unity of the Persons of the Trinity in the one God, the Father, the Son and the Holy Spirit". She is one because of her founder . . . the incarnate Son, the prince of peace. . . . She is one because of her soul: "The Holy Spirit . . . [who] brings about the wonderful communion of the faithful and joins them all in intimate union with Christ." It is therefore of the essence of the Church to be one [813].

What are [the] bonds of unity? Above all, it is love which is the bond of perfection. But the unity of the pilgrim Church is also assured by visible bonds of communion:
—profession of the one only faith received from the apostles;
—common celebration of divine worship, especially of the sacraments;
—apostolic succession through the sacrament of Orders [815].

"Even at the beginning of this one and only Church of God certain schisms arose. . . . In the following centuries, more extensive dissensions appeared, and large communities came to be separated from the full communion of the Catholic Church, dissensions for which, all too often, people on both sides were to blame" [817].

All who have been justified by faith in Baptism are incorporated into Christ; they therefore have a right to be called Christians and with good reason are accepted as brothers in the Lord by the children of the Catholic Church [818].

Christ dying gives the gift of unity to his Church, but the Church must always pray and work to maintain, reinforce, and perfect the unity that Christ wills for her. Hence Jesus' prayer: "That they may all be one. As you, Father, are in me and I am in you, may they also be [one] in us, . . . so that the world may know that you have sent me" [820].

"Christ, the Son of God, who 'alone is the holy one,' with the Father and the Spirit, loved the Church as his bride and gave himself up for her in order to make her holy . . ." [823].

By *canonizing* some of the faithful, i.e., by solemnly proclaiming that they practiced heroic virtue and lived in fidelity to God's grace, the Church recognizes the power of the Spirit of holiness which is in her and sustains the hope of believers by proposing the saints as models and intercessors [828].

The word "catholic" means "universal," in the sense of "having the character of totality" or wholeness. [It is universal because it is same faith for all: rich and poor, whatever color, whatever ethnic background. All over the world the Church teaches the same thing everywhere.]
    The Church is catholic because Christ is present in her [830].

She is catholic because Christ has given her a mission to the whole human race [831].

Particular churches [like the church in New York] are catholic through their communion with the Pope, the Bishop of Rome, the successor to St. Peter [834].

Who belongs to the Catholic Church? The *Catechism* tells us:

They are fully incorporated into the society of the Church who, possessing the Spirit of Christ, accept her whole structure and all the means of salvation established in her, and are united within her visible framework with Christ, who governs her through the Supreme Pontiff and the bishops, by the bonds of profession of faith, sacraments, ecclesiastical governance, and communion [837].

For many reasons the Church acknowledges herself to be joined to those who, though baptized and so honored with the name "Christian", do not profess the faith in its entirety or do not preserve the unity of communion under the successor of Peter. Those "who believe in Christ and who have been validly baptized are in a kind of imperfect communion with the Catholic Church." With the Orthodox Churches, this communion is so profound "that it lacks little to attain the fullness that would permit a common celebration of the Lord's Eucharist" [838].

When she looks into the mystery of her own being, the Church, God's People in the New Covenant, discovers her link with the Jewish people, "the first to hear the Word of God." Unlike other non-Christian religions, the Jewish faith was already a response to the revelation of God in the Old Covenant [839].

The plan of salvation includes equally those also who acknowledge the Creator, foremost among these are the Muslims; they profess fidelity to the faith of Abraham and, with us, adore the one merciful God, judge of men on the last day [841].

The Catholic Church recognizes in other religions that search, among shadows and images, for the unknown God who is yet near since he gives life, breath, and all good things to everyone and wants all men to be saved. Thus, the Church considers all goodness and truth found in these religions "as a preparation for the Gospel, a gift from him who enlightens" all men that they "may finally have life" [843].

The Church . . . strives with her every effort to preach the Gospel to all: "Go therefore and make disciples of all nations, baptizing them in the name of the Father and of the Son and of the Holy Spirit, and teaching them to obey everything that I have commanded you. And remember, I am with you always, until the end of the age" [849].

The Church is apostolic because she was founded on the apostles. She is preserved formally, officially by the bishops, successors to the apostles, in an unbroken chain from Peter until our day.

We are reminded:

The Christian faithful are . . . called, according to the proper condition of each, "to exercise the mission" God "entrusted to the Church to fulfill in the world" [871].

There is a genuine equality of dignity and action among all of Christ's faithful, deriving from their rebirth in Christ. Because of this equality, they all contribute "to the building up of the Body of Christ," according to the condition and function proper to each [872].

The pope, bishops, priests, deacons, women and men religious, every layperson, all elements in the Body of Christ are indispensable in building up the Body of Christ.

I conclude with a very beautiful quotation from the convert, Cardinal Newman. We remarked earlier that the Church exists not simply to carry out the works of mercy and justice but dominantly for our holiness and for our salvation. Cardinal Newman was very strong on this point. He said:

> The Church aims not at making a show but at doing a work. She regards this world and all that is in it as a mere shadow, as dust and ashes compared with the value of one single soul. The Church holds that unless she can in her own way do good to souls, there is no use in doing anything. She considers the action of the world and the action of the soul simply incommensurate, viewed in their respective spheres. She would rather save the soul of one single wild bandit of Calabria. She would rather save the soul of one whining beggar at Palermo than draw a hundred miles of railroad through the length and breadth of Italy, or carry out a sanitary reform in its fullest details in every city of Sicily, except so far as these great national works tended to some spiritual good beyond them.

This is our Church—not a bloated, wealthy bureaucracy, not impersonal, not irrelevant, not a building made of stones. We are the Church, all of us here, the vital, vibrant, dynamic Body of Christ. This is the gift that Christ Himself gave us when He said to Peter, "You are the rock and on you I will build My Church and the gates of hell will not prevail against it." What a great, great gift is this, our Church.

15

We Must All Work Together

THIRD SUNDAY OF LENT

MARCH 6, 1994

PONTIFICAL MASS

Today we continue our treatment of the new universal *Catechism of the Catholic Church*. In this, our fifteenth session, we continue our study of the Creed, focusing on two articles, one that we began last Sunday, "I believe in the holy, Catholic Church", and a second, "the communion of saints".

The *Catechism* treats the Catholic Church as an institution, as it is. We say it is "hierarchically" structured, with the pope, bishops, priests, deacons, religious, laypersons. But the *Catechism* also treats the Church as the Body of Christ, the living, pulsating, dynamic, vibrant, and vital Body of Christ of which you and I are members and on which our Lord depends so very much. This is also what the Church is. Whether one speaks of the "institutional Church" or the "personal Church of Jesus", it is important to recognize that both are filled with the Holy Spirit and are indistinguishable.

We begin by looking at the Scriptures to get our lead. In the first reading we are given the Ten Commandments, the divine law (Ex 20:1–17). God gave the commandments to Moses, the officially appointed leader of the Jewish people, the Israelites. It was Moses' responsibility to articulate them carefully, to tell the people what had actually come from God—no more, no less—and to try to get them to accept the commandments and to preserve that teaching. This is the role of the Church today. God has given His word through the Church. It is the Church who is the custodian, the transmitter, the educator, in the teachings of our Divine Lord. It is the Church who is expected to try to encourage God's People to accept His word and to preserve that word, to serve as the guardian of the word so that it won't be adulterated.

In the second reading, the letter of St. Paul to the people of Corinth, St. Paul writes to this new Church, which is being marred by dissention and disagreement and the incorporation of pagan practices into Christianity (1 Cor 1:22–25). St. Paul says, in essence, "Other people can teach you other things. I teach you Christ, Christ crucified. It's an unpopular teaching. It makes demands on us. I tell you that what people think is foolish is wisdom with God, what people think is weakness is strength with God." The role of the Church, again, is to teach the *truth*. It is often difficult and often hard to live out in our lives, but the Church neither creates the truth nor can change it.

In today's fascinating Gospel, we are told about our Divine Lord cleaning out the temple (Jn 2:13–25). He is asked, "By what authority do you do this? Show us some sign." Our Divine Lord says to them, "You're looking for a sign? Destroy this temple and in three days I will rebuild it." They think, of course, that our Divine Lord is referring to the temple of bricks and mortar. But He is referring to the temple of His Body, which is going to replace every other temple. He is talking about this new faith, faith in Christ. He is talking about the establishing of His Church, rooted in and growing out of the faith of the Israelites but now, if you will, the faith Christianized, the faith of Christ. They crucified Him, they buried Him, and He rose on the third day. But our Divine Lord also said to His apostles, "I build My Church on Peter and the gates of hell will not prevail against it." In other words, "Nothing can destroy My Church."

I want to share with you what is, for me at least, a very beautiful passage from the German theologian Karl Adam's *Spirit of Catholicism*. This puts today's *Catechism* lesson in context—the love of our Church, the love of our faith—without that we don't have a great deal. Karl Adam says:

> . . . God permits so much weakness and wretchedness in the earthly Church just because He is good. . . . [T]he mystical Christ has taken so much weakness upon Himself for our sakes and for our welfare. For how might we, who are "prone to evil from our youth," who are constantly stumbling, constantly struggling, and never spotless . . . —how might we gladly adhere to a Church which displayed holiness not as a chaste hope, but as a radiant achievement? Her very beauty would be a stumbling block to us. Her glory would accuse and condemn us. How would we dare to call her . . . our mother, the mother of poor and wretched mortals? No, we need a redemptress mother, one who . . . never turns coldly away from her children, when their soiled fingers touch her, and when folly and wickedness rend her marriage robe. We need a poor mother, for we ourselves are poor.
>
> Therefore we love our Church in spite of, nay just because of, her poor outward appearance. The Catholic affirms the Church just as it is. For in its actual form the Church is to him the revelation of the divine Holiness, Justice and Goodness. The Catholic does not desire some ideal Church, a Church of the philosopher or the poet. Though his mother be travel-stained with long journeying, though her countenance be furrowed with care and trouble—yet, she is his mother. In her heart burns the ancient love. Out of her eyes shines the ancient faith. From her hands flow ever the ancient blessings. What would heaven be without God? What would the

earth be without this Church? I believe in One Holy Catholic and Apostolic Church.

That is a highly personal view of the Church, and that is what the Church is supposed to mean to us, the Church that we love, the Church that is our mother. The *Catechism* explains the structure of the Church, as it were.

> The very differences which the Lord has willed to put between the members of his body serve its unity and mission. . . . "To the apostles and their successors Christ has entrusted the office of teaching, sanctifying, and governing in his name and by his power. But the laity are made to share in the priestly, prophetic, and kingly office of Christ; they have, therefore, in the Church and in the world, their own assignment in the mission of the whole People of God" [873].

We have talked in the past about the fact that at baptism we are anointed with oil. Kings and queens are anointed with oil, so we become a "kingly people" of Christ. Prophets were anointed with oil, so we become the "prophetic people" of Christ. Priests are anointed with oil, so we become a "priestly people" of Christ.

> Christ himself is the source of ministry in the Church. He instituted the Church. He gave her authority and mission, orientation and goal . . . [874].

> No one—no individual and no community—can proclaim the Gospel to himself. [We have to get it from Christ, through the Church.] . . . No one can give himself the mandate and the mission to proclaim the Gospel. The one sent by the Lord does not speak and act on his own authority, but by virtue of Christ's authority . . . [875].

I don't have the right, for instance, to offer Mass every morning and say, "Well, *I* think this and *I* think that" and speculate all over the place. I am here because we believe that Christ sent me, but I am given His authority to teach His word and not my own.

> The Lord Jesus appointed the Twelve. . . . Chosen together, they were also sent out together. . . . And so every bishop exercises his ministry from within the episcopal college, in communion with the bishop of Rome, the successor of St. Peter [who is the Pope] and head of the college. So also the priests exercise their ministry within the *presbyterium* of the diocese, under the direction of and in conjunction with the bishop [877].

This is all bound up in the sacrament of Holy Orders. We said last week that all share in the priesthood of Baptism; the priest and the bishop are specifically in the priesthood of the sacrament of Holy Orders.

The Lord made Simon alone, whom he named Peter, the "rock" of his Church. He gave him the keys of his Church and instituted him shepherd of the whole flock [881].

The Roman Pontiff [the Pope], "by virtue of his office as Vicar of Christ, and as pastor of the entire Church," has "full, supreme and universal power, which he may always exercise freely, over the whole Church" [882].

Then the *Catechism* says that the bishops enjoy this power, this authority, only when they are in union with our Holy Father, the Pope (cf. 883).

"The individual *bishops* are the visible source and foundation of unity in their own particular Churches" [886].

Bishops, with priests as co-workers, "have as their first task proclaiming the Gospel of God to all men," in keeping with the Lord's command [888]. [That's why we are studying the *Catechism*; my first responsibility here as your bishop is to teach the Word of God.]

Christ, who is the Truth, willed to confer on the Church a share in his own infallibility in order to preserve her in the purity of the apostolic faith [889].

This is something that confuses a lot of people. Christ, of course, could not err; He was God. He gave this same power, what we call "infallibility", to our Holy Father, to Peter and to his successors, but only under very severely restricted circumstances. The Pope can err about the weather just as any weather forecaster can err. The Pope can say it's going to rain tomorrow, and it may not rain. The Pope can make mistakes in the stock market. But under certain specific conditions he cannot err: when he is speaking authoritatively as Pope, as the successor to St. Peter ("from the Chair of Peter"); when he is speaking to the entire Church all over the world (he can't say one thing binding on the people in New York and another thing binding in Kenya); and when he is explicitly defining a doctrine of faith or morals. When these circumstances are in place, and they are rarely exercised, then we say the Pope cannot err.

Last week we noted that the first purpose of the Church is to make us holy. There are many other purposes of the Church—the social gospel, working with the poor, and so on. But the primary purpose of the Church is to make us holy and to make possible our salvation. We are told in the *Catechism*:

The bishop is "the steward of the grace of the high priesthood," especially in the Eucharist, which he offers personally or whose offering he assures through the priests, his co-workers. The Eucharist is the center of the life of the particular Church [893].

Our Holy Father never tires of saying that we can become a community only in the Eucharist. If, as a bishop, I fail to try to lead a holy life, fail to try to encourage you to holiness, that's the worst failure that I could be guilty of. Nothing else would really matter if I fail in that. It doesn't mean we're not weak. As someone says, "You can't have a two-thousand-year-old institution and not expect skeletons in the closet." Sure, we have them, but they do not reflect the life of the Church filled with the Holy Spirit.

The *Catechism* continues:

> The Good Shepherd [Jesus] ought to be the model and "form" of the bishop's pastoral office. Conscious of his own weaknesses, "the bishop . . . can have compassion for those who are ignorant and erring. [We bishops are just as weak as everyone else.] He should not refuse to listen to his subjects whose welfare he promotes as of his very own children. . . . The faithful . . . should be closely attached to the bishop as the Church is to Jesus Christ, and as Jesus Christ is to the Father" . . . [896].

Next the *Catechism* talks about the laity.

> "The term 'laity' is here understood to mean all the faithful except those in Holy Orders [deacons, priests, bishops] and those who belong to a religious state approved by the Church" [897].

> "By reason of their special vocation it belongs to the laity to seek the Kingdom of God by engaging in temporal matters and directing them in accordance with God's will" [898].

> The initiative of lay Christians is necessary especially when the matter involves discovering or inventing means for permeating social, political, and economic realties with the demands of Christian doctrine and faith [899].

The laity have a grave obligation. The *Catechism* says:

> Lay people, like all the faithful, are entrusted by God with the apostolate by virtue of their Baptism and Confirmation. They have the right and duty, individually or in groups, to work so that the divine message of salvation may be known and accepted by all men throughout the world [900].

I want to read you a brief portion of a very beautiful letter from a couple who recognize this important point.

> Dear Cardinal O'Connor:
>
> With Jesus' direction my husband and I have been going into the charismatic prayer group. We are both Jewish believers and have been baptized in the Catholic Church. We've been sharing on how to witness to Jewish people.
>
> Jesus' great commission to us is to go into all the world and preach the gospel to all creation. In these difficult times we who believe in Jesus should firmly stand together in love.

Jesus is from the line of David. He was circumcised after eight days. He was barmitzvahed. The Twelve Apostles were Jewish. The Last Supper was a Jewish Seder, and He was buried in a shroud. It is apparent that the biblical Judaism is indeed the root of our Judeo-Christian heritage.

Then she quotes St. Paul to the people of Rome:

For I am not ashamed of the gospel, for it is the power of God for salvation to everyone who believes, to the Jew first and also to the Greek (Rom 1:16).

That is a very beautiful recognition of the lay apostolate, the lay obligation to reach out to others.

The *Catechism* also says that:

. . . worshipping everywhere by their holy actions, the laity consecrate the world itself to God, everywhere offering worship by the holiness of their lives [901].

Wherever you go, you take our Lord with you. As you worship God, so His graces radiate throughout the world.

We are reminded in the *Catechism*:

Lay people have the right and even at times the duty, in keeping with their knowledge, competence, and position, to manifest to the sacred pastors their opinion on matters which pertain to the good of the Church . . . [907].

That's a nice way to put it, but I have not discovered too many laity who are unwilling to give me their advice! I receive a very substantial number of letters telling me all sorts of things I should be doing, and especially where I should be going.

The *Catechism* talks about the evangelical counsels and what is called the "consecrated life". The evangelical counsels are poverty, chastity, and obedience. We are all supposed to live them to some degree, but those who consecrate themselves, who take special vows of poverty, chastity, and obedience authorized by the Church, are supposed to live these vows in a special way. To be consecrated is to "become sacred", to be set aside for what is sacred, God Himself.

The *Catechism* continues:

From the very beginning . . . there were men and women who set out to follow Christ with greater liberty, and to imitate him more closely, by practicing the evangelical counsels [918].

The *Catechism* goes on to talk about hermits who were inspired by the Holy Spirit. They went off, for instance, into the desert, and lived especially holy lives for the good of the Church at large, for the good of society at large, and did special penance and praying. A lot of these early members of the Church established beautiful religious communities that have per-dured unto this day.

The *Catechism* says:

> From apostolic times Christian virgins, called by the Lord to cling only to him with greater freedom of hearts, body, and spirit, have decided with the Church's approval to live in a state of virginity "for the sake of the King-dom of heaven" [922].

> Virgins . . . consecrated to God by the diocesan bishop . . . are betrothed mystically to Christ, the Son of God, and are dedicated to the service of the Church [923].

> Religious life was born in the East during the first centuries of Christian-ity. . . . [I]t is distinguished . . . by its liturgical character [formal prayer, praying the Divine Office in common, offering the Holy Sacrifice of the Mass together], public profession of the evangelical counsels [poverty, chas-tity, and obedience], fraternal life led in common, and witness given to the union of Christ with the Church [925].

Then we have things called "secular institutes".

> A secular institute is an institute of consecrated life in which Christian faith-ful living in the world strive for the perfection of charity and work for the sanctification of the world especially from within [928].

Right here in this congregation you might have, without your even knowing it, some members of a secular institute who live as you do in the world but are specially consecrated to the work of the Lord.

The *Catechism* says:

> Alongside the different forms of consecrated life are "societies of apostolic life" whose members without religious vows pursue the particular apostolic purpose of their society, and lead a life as brothers or sisters in common ac-cording to a particular manner of life, "strive for the perfection of charity through the observance of the constitutions" [930].

Now we come to the section of the Creed that speaks about the com-munion of saints. We are told that:

> After confessing "the holy catholic Church," the Apostles' Creed adds "the communion of saints." . . . The communion of saints *is* the Church [946].

> Baptism, the gate by which we enter into the Church, and all the sacra-ments are many sacred links uniting the faithful with one another and bind-ing them to Jesus Christ. The communion of saints must be understood as the communion of the sacraments. . . . [The majority of us here will receive our Divine Lord in Holy Communion because we are of the communion

of saints. In this sense, the word means His holy ones, here with Him in this sacrifice.] The name *communion* can be applied to all of the sacraments, for they unite us to God. . . . But . . . it is primarily the Eucharist that brings our communion with God and one another to completion [950].

Everything the true Christian has is to be regarded as a good possessed in common with everything else. [In accordance with the communion of saints] all Christians should be ready and eager to come to the help of the needy . . . and their neighbors in want [952].

As St. Paul says:

"If one member suffers, all suffer together; if one member is honored, all rejoice together. Now you are the Body of Christ, and individually members of it" [953].

At the present time some of Christ's disciples are pilgrims on earth. Others have died and are being purified [in Purgatory], while others are in glory, contemplating "in full light, God himself exactly as he is" [954].

So we have the Church here on earth, the Church of those who have gone before us, those who are in Purgatory, waiting to get to heaven, and the Church in heaven. We are all one in the communion of saints, and those who are in heaven are interceding for us. We must pray for those who are in Purgatory that they will be released from Purgatory and get to heaven; they, too, can pray for us.

The *Catechism* speaks about Mary, Mother of Christ, Mother of the Church.

The Church "recognizes and honors Mary as the true Mother of God and of the redeemer. . . . She is 'clearly Mother of the members' of Christ . . . since she has by her charity joined in bringing about the birth of believers in the Church, who are members of its head" [963].

Mary's role in the Church is inseparable from her union with Christ and flows directly from it. "Mary's union with her Son in the work of salvation is evident from the time of Christ's virginal conception" until his death; it is revealed above all at the hour of his Passion . . . [964].

After her Son's Ascension, Mary assisted the Church with her prayers at its birth. Meeting with the apostles and several women, Mary by her prayers called down "the gift of the Spirit, who had already overshadowed her at the Annunciation" [965].

"Finally the Immaculate Virgin, preserved free from every stain of original sin, when the course of her earthly life was finished, was taken up body and soul into heavenly glory, and exalted by the Lord as Queen over all things . . ." [966].

"The Church's devotion to the Blessed Virgin is intrinsic to Christian worship." [We go to Jesus through Mary.] . . . From the most ancient times the Blessed Virgin has been honored with the title of "Mother of God" . . . [971].

Finally, the *Catechism* says:

After speaking of the Church, her origin, mission, and destiny, we can find no better way to conclude than by looking to Mary. In her we contemplate what the Church already is in her mystery on her "pilgrimage of faith," and what she will be in the homeland at the end of her journey [972].

Just as we said, the Church is a pilgrim, weary, travel-stained, with a furrowed brow and wrinkled cheeks, worn out after two thousand years of carrying us, so Mary isn't simply a young lady on a holy card. She is a woman who, for all these centuries, has been carrying us worn and weary. It will be such a wonderful thing to see her face to face when we meet God. This is our Church. If only we could love her as we love a human being, and even more.

As I was preparing to reflect on this section of the *Catechism* with you, I thought of that delightful Broadway play *My Fair Lady*. Henry Higgins treats Eliza Doolittle so casually, so callously, often contemptuously, until finally she leaves him. Then he sits there sorrowing, lonely, because, he says:

> I've grown accustomed to her face.
> She almost makes the day begin. . . .
> Her smiles, her frowns, her ups, her downs
> Are second nature to me now,
> Like breathing out and breathing in. . . .
> I've grown accustomed to the trace
>   of something in the air,
> Accustomed to her face.

I think that's the way so many of us are with the Church. We just don't appreciate her when we have her. But, oh, if we ever lost her!

16

On "The Last Things"

FOURTH SUNDAY OF LENT
MARCH 13, 1994
PONTIFICAL MASS

Today we have our sixteenth session on the new *Catechism of the Catholic Church*.
I want to turn first to something very sobering, said in today's Gospel.

> God did not send the Son into the world to condemn the world, but that the world might be saved through him.
> . . . [T]he light came into the world, but men loved darkness rather than light because their deeds were wicked. Everyone who practices evil hates the light; he does not come near it for fear his deeds will be exposed (Jn 3:17, 19–20).

This reading might sound very abstract, and it might not seem to have any practical application in our lives today. But let me read you a portion of a haunting letter from Sister Mary Rose McGeady, who is the president of Covenant House. She is trying to restore Covenant House from the ruins into which it had been shattered. She describes a little colloquy between herself and a young girl.

> "I'm what they call a mule, Sister", the girl said. "They made me smuggle drugs for them. . . . They stuffed cocaine in little plastic bags and made me swallow them. . . . The drug runners made me a drug mule. Me and my friend, Michelle. Michelle is dead now. She was the same age as me.
> "Michelle and I come from London, and we did the New York run. In London they'd made us swallow bags filled with drugs. Sometimes I didn't even know what was in them.
> "A few weeks ago, Michelle and I were waiting to get picked up when she started to feel real sick. She got worse and worse, and then she collapsed on the sidewalk. When the dealers came to pick us up, they made me leave her there.
> "I found out that she died on the way to the hospital. A bag burst inside her, and the drugs killed her. And I'm next, Sister. Sooner or later. I know it. That's why I had to come here [to Covenant House]. But if they find me, they'll kill me."

"No one is going to kill you, Liz. You're safe here."

"You don't know these people, Sister. They wouldn't think twice about shooting you or anyone else."

For another hour I went around and around with Liz, trying to convince her that she was safe . . . trying to convince her that she was worth saving.

She told me about her life. How her mother needed money so she put Liz to work [as a prostitute]. She was twelve years old. Liz shook with disgust and pain when she told me how she was forced to have sex with dozens of perverted men every week.

Then, six months ago, her pimp decided he had a new use for her. He wanted her to carry drugs through customs—to be a drug "mule". Liz resisted, but her pimp said it wasn't her choice. He owned her, and she had to do what he wanted. So, out of fear, Liz became a drug mule, part of a rapidly growing herd of defenseless kids being manipulated and used by the multi-billion dollar drug and sex industry.

These greedy men in their $2,000 designer suits use kids like Liz to smuggle drugs for some unforgivable reasons. . . . One policeman I talked to recently summed it up: "These kids are the perfect puppets, Sister. They don't raise a lot of suspicion. And they're so young and so scared, they do exactly what they're told."

"The light came into the world," said St. John, "but men loved darkness rather than light because their deeds were wicked. Everyone who practices evil hates the light and does not come near it for fear his deed will be exposed." We live in a land of so much darkness, but what of the mercy of God, what of His compassion and gentleness? Surely a Liz will go to heaven when she dies, which, tragically, might be very soon. She has suffered so very much. But what of those who have tormented her, who have destroyed her life? Is there the possibility of salvation for them? They are the men of darkness, surely, and they hate the light. We are told, "The Light came into its own but its own rejected it. And yet the Light could not be overcome. The Light shines in the darkness."

We are told in the *Catechism* that at the end of the world all will be balanced, all will be rectified, with rewards and punishments: "Come, you blest of My Father, receive the kingdom prepared for you for all eternity" or "Depart from me, ye cursed, into everlasting fire." We are told in the *Catechism* that no one, absolutely no one, is beyond forgiveness, however horrible the sins have been.

In the reading of St. Paul to the people of Ephesus this morning we are told:

God is rich in mercy; because of his great love for us he brought us to life with Christ when we were dead in sin. . . . Both with and in Christ Jesus he raised us up and gave us a place in the heavens. . . . This is not your own doing, it is God's gift (Eph 2:4–6, 8).

There's not one of us here, starting with myself, who deserves this gift, who deserves to be raised up. It's strictly a gift given by God because His Son suffered and died out of love for us.

The *Catechism* says:

> It was when he gave the Holy Spirit to his apostles that the risen Christ conferred on them his own divine power to forgive sins: "Receive the Holy Spirit. If you forgive the sins of any, they are forgiven; if you retain the sins of any, they are retained" (Jn 20:22–23) [976].

> Our Lord tied the forgiveness of sins to faith and Baptism. . . . "He who believes and is baptized will be saved" (Mk 16:15–16). Baptism is the first and chief sacrament of forgiveness . . . because it unites us with Christ . . . [977].

> ". . . [But] the forgiveness we received [in Baptism] was so full and complete that there remained in us absolutely nothing left to wash away, neither original sin nor offenses committed by our own will, nor was there left any penalty to suffer in order to expiate them" [978].

Baptism is so thorough that in the early days of the Church people preferred what they called "clinical Baptism". They would wait until they were sick or dying to be baptized. The great Charlemagne was one of these. He waited until he was on his deathbed to ask for Baptism, because Baptism washes away everything, original sin and all of the sins of a lifetime. Plus the fact that, if you're baptized when you die, you're going to go to heaven, and you're not going to be around this earth to sin again. "But the grace of Baptism delivers no one", the *Catechism* says, "from the weakness of nature" [978]. Even after Baptism we can still sin.

> "If the Church has the power to forgive sins, then Baptism cannot be her only means. . . . The Church must be able to forgive all penitents their offenses, even if they should sin until the last moment of their lives" [979].

There is a beautiful little verse from an Irish poet that captures this concept of forgiveness: "Betwixt the stirrup and the ground was mercy sought and mercy found." In the flash of an eye, a horseman is forgiven the sins of a lifetime.

> It is through the sacrament of Penance that the baptized can be reconciled with God and with the Church [980].

We call it the sacrament of Reconciliation. Christ's was the ministry of picking up the pieces of broken lives.

> There is no offense, however serious, that the Church cannot forgive. Christ who died for all . . . desires that in his Church the gates of forgive-

ness should always be open to anyone who turns away from sin [982]. [This includes the hoodlums right here in New York who give these kids to pimps who use them for drugs.]

We firmly believe . . . that, just as Christ is truly risen from the dead and lives for ever, so after death the righteous will live for ever with the risen Christ and he will raise them up on the last day [989].

We believe this so strongly that St. Paul says, "If Christ has not been raised, then our preaching is in vain and your faith is in vain. . . . But in fact Christ has been raised from the dead" (1 Cor 15:14, 20) [991]. Otherwise, it would be foolish for us to be here today.

This takes us to the next part of the *Catechism*—about the Resurrection:

Jesus links faith in the resurrection to his own person: "I am the Resurrection and the life" (Jn 11:25) [994].

From the beginning, Christian faith in the resurrection has met with incomprehension and opposition. "On no point does the Christian faith encounter more opposition than on the resurrection of the body" (St. Augustine). It is very commonly accepted that the life of the human person continues in a spiritual fashion after death. But how can we believe that this body, so clearly mortal, could rise to everlasting life? [996]

The *Catechism* asks, "How do the dead rise?"

What is "rising"? In death, the separation of the soul from the body, the human body decays and the soul goes to meet God, while awaiting its reunion with its glorified body. God, in his almighty power, will definitely grant incorruptible life to our bodies by reuniting them with our souls, through the power of Jesus' Resurrection [997].

Who will rise? All the dead will rise [the Liz's *and* their tormentors], "those who have done good, to the resurrection of life, and those who have done evil, to the resurrection of judgment" (Jn 5:29) [998].

How? Christ is raised with his own body: "See my hands and my feet [He said to doubting Thomas], that it is I myself" (Lk 24–30); but he did not return to an earthly life. [He stayed here for a short time before the Ascension into heaven.] So, in him, "all of them will rise again with their own bodies which they now bear," but Christ "will change our lowly body to be like his glorious body," into a "spiritual body" [999].

This "how" exceeds our imagination and understanding; it is accessible only to faith. Yet our participation in the Eucharist already gives us a foretaste of Christ's transfiguration of our bodies [1000].

Then there is a very beautiful thought from St. Irenaeus that the *Catechism* gives us:

"Just as bread that comes from the earth, after God's blessing has been invoked upon it, is no longer ordinary bread, but Eucharist, formed of two things, the one earthly and the other heavenly: so too our bodies, which partake of the Eucharist, are no longer corruptible, but possess the hope of resurrection" [1000].

The *Catechism* continues:

When? Definitely "at the last day," "at the end of the world."

"For the Lord himself will descend from heaven, with a cry of command, with the archangel's call, and with the sound of the trumpet of God. And the dead in Christ will rise first" (1 Th 4:16) [1001].

The *Catechism* continues:

In expectation of that day, the believer's body and soul already participate in the dignity of belonging to Christ. This dignity entails the demand that we should treat with respect our own bodies, but also the body of every other person, especially the suffering [1004]. [It rules out euthanasia, assisted suicide, but rules in reverence and purity for our bodies and the bodies of others, which are the temples of Almighty God.]

In a sense bodily death is natural, but for faith it is in fact "the wages of sin" (Rom 6:23). [It came because of original sin.] For those who die in Christ's grace it is a participation in the death of the Lord [we unite ourselves with Him in our sufferings, in our death] so that we can share his Resurrection [1006].

Death is the end of earthly life. Our lives are measured by time, in the course of which we change, grow old and, as with all living beings on earth, death seems like the normal end of life. That aspect of death lends urgency to our lives: remembering our mortality helps us realize that we have only a limited time in which to bring our lives to fulfillment:

"Remember also your Creator in the days of your youth, . . . before the dust returns to the earth as it was, and the spirit returns to God who gave it" [1007].

Death is a consequence of sin. Even though man's nature is mortal, God had destined him not to die. Death was therefore contrary to the plans of God the Creator [1008]. [God didn't intend that Adam and Eve die. They brought it on themselves.]

Death is transformed by Christ. Jesus, the Son of God, despite his anguish as he faced death, accepted it in an act of complete and free submission to his Father's will. The obedience of Jesus has transformed the curse of death into a blessing [1009].

Because of Christ, Christian death has a positive meaning: "If we have died with him, we will also live with him" (2 Tim 2:11). What is essentially new about Christian death is this: through Baptism, the Christian has already "died with Christ" sacramentally . . . [1010]. [We say in the baptismal rite, "We are buried with Christ in the waters of grace so that we will rise with Christ."]

Death is the end of man's earthly pilgrimage . . . and there is no "reincarnation" after death [1013].

There's an ancient philosophy, particularly in the East, of so-called "metempsychosis", a transmigration of souls, which says we will come back as butterflies in the next life or hippopotamuses or whatever, going through constant purifications. This was really basic to the whole philosophy of Naziism. The idea of the superman was that the Aryan race would go through many, many purifications, and then it would be the ultimate race, the race of supermen.

The Church encourages us to prepare ourselves for the hour of death. "From a sudden and unforeseen death, deliver us, O Lord." We ask Mary in the *Hail Mary* to intercede for us now and "at the hour of our death." We pray to St. Joseph, who is the patron of a happy death.
    "Every action of yours, every thought, should be those of one who expects to die before the day is out" [1014]. [It could happen this very day.]

The *Catechism* continues:

The Christian who unites his own death to that of Jesus views it as a step toward him and an entrance into everlasting life. [This is why we do not fear death.] When the Church for the last time speaks Christ's words of pardon and absolution over the dying Christian, seals him for the last time with a strengthening anointing, and gives him Christ in viaticum as nourishment for the journey, she speaks with gentle assurance: "Be not afraid" [1020].

There are two judgments: the particular judgment and the general judgment. The *Catechism* says:

Death puts an end to human life as the time open to either accepting or rejecting the divine grace manifested in Christ [We can't do that after we die.] The New Testament repeatedly affirms that each will be rewarded immediately after death in accordance with his works and faith [1021].

Those who die in God's grace and friendship and are perfectly purified live for ever with Christ. They are like God for ever, for they "see him as he is," face to face (1 Jn 3:2) [1023].

This perfect life with the Most Holy Trinity is called "heaven." Heaven is the ultimate end and fulfillment of the deepest human longings, the state of supreme, definite happiness [1024].

Everything we do we do to be happy. Some people even kill themselves to be happy. Happiness is the main drive within us. That is so because we were made for heaven. St. Augustine says, "My heart was made
for Thee, O Lord, and it will not rest until it rests in Thee."

> By his death and Resurrection, Jesus Christ has "opened" heaven to us
> [1026].

> This mystery of blessed communion with God and all who are in Christ is
> beyond all understanding and description. Scripture speaks of it in images:
> life, light, peace, wedding feast . . . [and so on] [1027].

> The Church calls . . . contemplation of God in his heavenly glory "the
> beatific vision" . . . [1028].

Next the *Catechism* speaks of Purgatory. A lot of people think Purgatory
has been done away with. Not at all.

> All who die in God's grace and friendship, but still imperfectly purified, are
> indeed assured of their eternal salvation; but after death they undergo
> purification, so as to achieve the holiness necessary to enter the joy of
> heaven [1030].

> The Church gives the name *Purgatory* to this final purification of the elect,
> which is entirely different from the punishment of the damned [1031]. [We
> go through some kind of purifying fire, we are told, but it's a one-way
> ticket to heaven.]

> This teaching is based on the practice of prayer for the dead, already men-
> tioned in Sacred Scripture. . . . From the beginning the Church has hon-
> ored the memory of the dead and offered prayers . . . for them, above all
> the Eucharistic sacrifice, so that, thus purified, they may attain the beatific
> vision of God [1032]. [We can pray for the souls in Purgatory. We can earn
> indulgences for the souls in Purgatory. We can give to the poor for the
> souls in Purgatory to shorten their time in Purgatory and to speed them to
> heaven.]

Now we move on to hell. The *Catechism* says:

> We cannot be united with God unless we freely choose to love him. But
> we cannot love God if we sin gravely against him, against our neighbor or
> against ourselves. . . . To die in mortal sin without repenting and accepting
> God's merciful love means remaining separated from him for ever by our
> own free choice. [God does not put us into hell. People say, "How can a
> merciful God condemn anyone to hell?" He doesn't. We condemn our-
> selves to hell.] This state of definite self-exclusion from communion with
> God and the blessed is called "hell" [1033].

The teaching of the Church affirms the existence of hell and its eternity. Immediately after death the souls of those who die in a state of mortal sin [unforgiven, even at that last instance] descend into hell, where they suffer the punishments of hell, "eternal fire." The chief punishment of hell is eternal separation from God, in whom alone man can possess the life and happiness for which he was created and for which he longs [1035]. [We are created to know, love, and serve God in this life and to be happy with Him forever in heaven. If we miss that, that's hell.]

God predestines no one to go to hell; for this, a willful turning away from God (a mortal sin) is necessary, and persistence in it until the end. God . . . does not want "any to perish, but all to come to repentance" (2 Pet 3:9) [1037]. [When we think of Liz's tormentors, we must remember this.]

The resurrection of all the dead, "of both the just and the unjust" (Acts 24:15), will precede the Last Judgment. . . . Then Christ will come "in his glory, and all the angels with him. . . . Before him will be gathered all the nations, and he will separate them one from another as a shepherd separates the sheep from the goats, and he will place the sheep at his right hand, but the goats at the left. . . . And they will go away into eternal punishment, but the righteous into eternal life" (Mt 25:31, 32, 46) [1038].

When will the Last Judgment come? "When Christ returns in glory and only the Father knows the day and the hour; only he determines the moment of its coming" [1040].

At the end of time, the Kingdom of God will come in its fullness. . . . The universe itself will be renewed [1042].

Sacred Scripture calls this mysterious renewal, which will transform humanity and the world, "new heavens and a new earth" (2 Pet 3:13) [1043].

In this new universe, the heavenly Jerusalem, God will have his dwelling among men. "He will wipe away every tear from the eyes, and death shall be no more, neither shall there be mourning nor crying nor pain any more, for the former things have passed away" (Rev 21:4) [1044].

What a wonderful thing for a little Liz or the other kids in the street, or for all who suffer, all who have cancer, all who are lonely, all who are in difficulty—what a wonderful thing! All mourning will be gone, and all pain will pass away.

Finally, we are told in the *Catechism*:

The Creed . . . ends with the Hebrew word *amen*. This word frequently concludes prayers in the New Testament. The Church likewise ends her prayers with "Amen" [1061].

In Hebrew, *amen* comes from the same root as the word "believe." [I didn't know this, and I have been saying "Amen" all of my life. It comes from the same root as the word "believe".] Our Lord often used the word "Amen," sometimes repeated, to emphasize the trustworthiness of his teaching, his authority founded on God's truth [1062].

Thus the Creed's final "Amen" repeats and confirms its first words: "I believe." To believe is to say "Amen" to God's words, promises and commandments. . . .

"May your Creed be for you as a mirror. Look at yourself in it, to see if you believe everything you say you believe. And rejoice in your faith each day" (St. Augustine) [1064].

Jesus Christ . . . is the definite "Amen" of the Father's love for us [1065].

As we say "Amen" to this sixteenth session, we are saying "Amen" to the first and the major portion in the *Catechism*, "Amen" to the Creed, which has taken up these first sixteen Sundays.

17

There Is More to Liturgy
Than You May Think

FIFTH SUNDAY OF LENT

MASS FOR THE HOLY NAME SOCIETY, NEW YORK POLICE DEPARTMENT

MARCH 20, 1994

PONTIFICAL MASS

We begin with today's Gospel just read to us (Jn 12:20–33). Let's just re-peat a few words. Our Lord said:

> The hour has come for the Son of Man to be glorified. I solemnly assure you, unless the grain of wheat falls to the earth and dies, it remains just a grain of wheat. But if it dies it produces much fruit.
> . . . I—once I am lifted up from earth—will draw all men to myself.

"The hour has come for the Son of Man to be glorified." He means "to die on the Cross". That was His glorification—to suffer and die on the Cross. That's why He had come into the world. He says, "Only then, when I am raised up from the earth on the Cross I will draw all people to myself." I have to relate that to you police officers, who each day have no idea what's going to happen to you, only because you're a police officer. And you're giving your lives in a very special way.

Yes, I know, I read in the newspapers that more civilians are killed than police officers. Of course, there are more civilians than there are police officers. So that stands to reason. But civilians aren't killed or maligned simply because they're civilians. You are because you are police officers, because you're trying to restore and preserve a respect for human life.

Now let's go to the section of the *Catechism* for today. It's called the lit-urgy. It may sound very tedious. We'll have to go through it quickly be-cause of the time. But I wore a uniform for twenty-seven years, Navy and Marine Corps—I still wear a uniform, rather obviously. The uniform that I wore for twenty-seven years in the sea services was a uniform that reflected what we could have called, in a somewhat different way, the "lit-urgy" of being a military officer. You have a "liturgy" as police officers. What we called in the military "customs, courtesies, and traditions" are quite similar to what you carry out. We will talk about those a little bit later. But I would suggest that to you so that you can put this session into context. We are told in the *Catechism*:

> The word "liturgy" originally meant a "public work" or a "service in the name of or on behalf of the people." [That was in the ancient use of the term.] In Christian tradition it means the participation of the People of God in the "work of God." [And it's not just the Mass and the sacraments but all the work of God in which we share, that's called the liturgy in the broad sense.] Through the liturgy, Christ, our redeemer and high priest, continues the work of our redemption in, with and through his Church [1069]. [And we're all supposed to be doing that, not simply keeping the faith but spreading the faith.]

The *Catechism* goes on:

> "It was from the side of Christ as he slept the sleep of death upon the cross that there came forth 'the wondrous sacrament of the whole Church.'" For this reason, the Church celebrates in the liturgy [such as the Mass] above all the Paschal mystery by which Christ accomplished the work of our salvation [1067].

What is the Paschal mystery? His suffering and death on the Cross and His Resurrection. That's what we celebrate during the Easter period.

> In the New Testament the word "liturgy" refers not only to the celebration of divine worship but also to the proclamation of the Gospel and to active charity. In all of these situations it is a question of the service of God and neighbor [1070].

Every time you do something in the name of God, if you give help to somebody, if you give money to the poor, whatever the help may be— your work as police officers, in a sense, if you do it for God because each human being is made in the image of God—you're carrying out a "liturgy". The famous Bishop Fulton Sheen used to say that we conclude the Mass by saying, "the Mass is ended", but that in reality the Mass is continued, the Mass is extended, because, when we leave the church, as when you leave this cathedral and go back to your daily activities in your home, in your work, whatever it might be, you're supposed to be living the Mass, taking Christ with you. That's a "liturgical" action.

> The Church was made manifest to the world on the day of Pentecost by the outpouring of the Holy Spirit. [Up until then the apostles had been frightened to death, even though Christ had risen from the dead.] . . . In this age of the Church Christ now lives and acts in and with his Church . . . and [primarily] he acts through the sacraments [the seven sacraments] . . . [1076].

The *Catechism* says:

"Christ is always present in his Church, especially in her liturgical celebrations. He is present in the Sacrifice of the Mass not only in the person of his minister, 'the same now offering, through the ministry of priests, who formerly offered himself on the cross', but [he is] especially [present] in the Eucharistic species. By his power he is present in [each of] the sacraments so that when anybody baptizes [for example], it is really Christ himself who baptizes. He is present in his word [as I'm preaching now] since it is he himself who speaks when the holy Scriptures are read in the Church. [H]e is present when the Church prays and sings, for he has promised 'where two or three are gathered together in my name there am I in the midst of them' " (Mt 18:20) [1088]. [That's the case right now. Christ is here.]

The *Catechism* continues:

Christian liturgy not only recalls the events that saved us [so it's not just a memorial] but [it] actualizes them, makes them present [in the Sacrifice of the Mass]. The Paschal mystery of Christ is celebrated, not repeated [He died on the Cross in bloody fashion and for all. He dies here in a spiritual, mysterious fashion, bringing His death on the Cross to us present today.] . . . In each celebration there is an outpouring of the Holy Spirit that makes the unique mystery present [1104].

The whole liturgical life of the Church revolves around the Eucharistic sacrifice [the Mass] and the sacraments. There are seven sacraments . . . : Baptism, Confirmation . . . , Eucharist, Penance [Confession], Anointing of the Sick, Holy Orders, and Matrimony [1113].

. . . "[T]he sacraments of the new law were . . . all instituted by Jesus Christ our Lord" (Council of Trent) [1114]. [The Church couldn't say today, "We're going to start a new sacrament." Each of these seven came from Christ Himself.]

Sacraments are "powers that come forth" from the Body of Christ, which is ever-living and life-giving. They are actions of the Holy Spirit at work in his Body, the Church [1116].

The ordained ministry or [what we call] *ministerial* priesthood is at the service of the baptismal priesthood [all of you]. The ordained priesthood guarantees that it really is Christ who acts in the sacraments through the Holy Spirit for the Church [1120].

The three sacraments of Baptism, Confirmation, and Holy Orders confer, in addition to grace, a sacramental *character*. [A special seal. You get a special grace when you go to confession, in addition to the forgiveness of sins. It's called "sacramental grace". When you receive Baptism, there's a seal attached to it so you can't be baptized again if you have been validly baptized.] . . . Therefore these sacraments can never be repeated [1121].

What is the purpose of the sacraments? "To sanctify us, to make us holy, to build up the Body of Christ and . . . to give worship to [Almighty] God" [1123]. When the sacraments are appropriately celebrated, we all receive tremendous graces.

A sacrament, in a sense, works automatically. What do we mean by this? Once we say over a piece of bread "This is My Body" and over a cup of wine "This is My Blood", the Body and Blood of Christ become present, whether I'm worthy or not. I might be in the state of sin. When you come up here to receive Holy Communion, you are receiving the Body and Blood of Christ, even if you're in mortal sin. But if you are in mortal sin, you're not going to get the graces that come from the sacrament. Indeed, it can put you into further sin for receiving in the state of mortal sin. So, in a sense, the sacraments work automatically, if I may use the term, but we must try to be worthy, we must prepare ourselves to receive them.

The *Catechism* continues:

> The Church affirms that for believers the sacraments of the New Covenant are *necessary for salvation* [1129].[So this isn't just a luxury.]

> It is the whole *community*, the Body of Christ united with its Head, that celebrates. [So] liturgical services are not private functions but are celebrations of the Church which is 'the sacrament of unity' . . ." [1140]. [There's nothing private about this Mass. This is a liturgical act, a public act.]

> The celebrating assembly is the community of the baptized who, "by regeneration and the anointing of the Holy Spirit, are consecrated to be a spiritual house and a holy priesthood, that . . . they may offer spiritual sacrifices" [*Lumen Gentium*, no. 10]. This "common priesthood" is that of Christ the sole priest, in which we all participate [1141]. [We all share in the priesthood; those who are ordained, those who are simply baptized.]

> But "the members do not all have the same function" (Rom 12:4). Certain members are called by God, in and through the Church, to a special service of the community. These servants are chosen and consecrated by the sacrament of Holy Orders, by which the Holy Spirit enables them to act in the person of Christ the head, for the service of all the members of the Church. . . . [In a quite different, but somewhat analogous sense, you have a hierarchy in the Police Department. It's understood that there's one commissioner, that there are deputies, chiefs, captains, lieutenants, foot soldiers, and so on. There's a hierarchy in the Church, but very special in that hierarchy is the ordained priest or bishop.] Since it is in the Eucharist that the sacrament of the Church is made fully visible, it is in his presiding at the Eucharist that the bishop's ministry is most evident [1142].

> As a social being, man needs signs and symbols to communicate with others, through language, gestures, and actions. The same holds true for his relationship with God [1146].

So we have the external appearances of the Mass. We have the vestments. We have all sorts of special signs because we're human beings, we're not just spiritual beings. You know, a handful of years ago, after the Second Vatican Council, and blaming it on the Second Vatican Council whose fault it wasn't, some people went around tearing statues out of churches, tearing holy pictures out of churches, all the signs of devotion out of churches. They turned churches into buildings. With due respect, a lot of our churches came to look like police stations or fire houses. I have great respect for police stations and fire houses, but they are not churches. Look at this magnificent church. What a shame it would be if you would rip the statue of St. Patrick off the wall and all these others. It would not only be liturgically foolish, it would be anti-human. We are human beings when we worship God. Our bodies, our senses, need these things. That's why they're part of the liturgy. And, of course, they uplift the soul.

Signs were used by Christ Himself in His teaching, in His preaching. For instance, when Christ would heal a man who was blind, He might well wet His thumb with His tongue and then reach down and take a little bit of dirt, make mud of it, and put it on the man's eyes. The man's sight was restored, not because of the mud or because of the gesture, but because of the power of Christ.

In the sacraments, the Church uses external signs—such as water in Baptism. It's not the water that washes the soul, it's the power of Christ. But these external signs are essential elements of the sacraments.

The *Catechism* continues: "All the signs in the liturgical celebrations are related to Christ: as are sacred images of the holy Mother of God and of the saints. . . . They truly signify Christ . . ." [1161].

Further, the Church emphasizes certain days of the year and certain seasons of the year. This is all part of the liturgy. Christ rose on the first day of the week, so that's when we have a special obligation to get to Mass. Each Sunday, we celebrate the Resurrection in a very special way. We have, also, the liturgical seasons of the year. Right now, we are in the liturgical season of Lent. Then we will go into the liturgical season of Easter. Then, in due time, we will be back in the liturgical season of Advent and of Christmas, and so on. There's a rhythm to the seasons of the year. There's a rhythm to the liturgy, because, again, we're human beings, human beings made in the image and likeness of God.

The *Catechism* continues:

A church, [of course, is] "a house of prayer in which the Eucharist is celebrated and reserved, where the faithful assemble, and where is worshipped the presence of the Son of God our Savior, offered for us on the sacrificial altar for the help and consolation of the faithful . . ." [1181].

Just a couple of paragraphs to complete this portion of the *Catechism*.

On the *altar*, which is the center of the church, the sacrifice of the Cross is made present under [what we call] sacramental signs. The altar is also the table of the Lord, to which the People of God are invited [1182].

The *tabernacle* is to be situated "in churches in a most worthy place with the greatest honor" (Paul VI) [1183]. [And so we have here a beautiful gold tabernacle behind what we call the *reredos*, which is behind the altar. It's in the Chapel of Our Lady, such a fitting place because of the intimate relationship between our Lady and her Son, Jesus, who is there present in the Blessed Sacrament.]

What we call the *cathedra*, that chair up there, which is used by the bishop, is the teaching center. It's where the bishop presides over the liturgy.

Finally, . . . To enter into the house of God, we must cross a *threshold* [You came through the door. You police came marching up the center aisle through the main door.], which symbolizes passing from the world wounded by sin to the world of the new life to which all men are called. The visible church is a symbol of the Father's house toward which the People of God is journeying and where the Father "will wipe [away] every tear from their eyes" (Rev 21:4) [1186]. [In other words, we're all on a pilgrimage to heaven.]

Now, this takes us to yesterday's funeral for Police Officer Sean McDonald. I will spend just a few minutes before we finish. You were there, many of you, for the liturgy, called the Funeral Mass, an example of what we have been talking about today. Huge numbers received Holy Communion, the sacrament of the Eucharist. But in addition to this ecclesiastical liturgy, the liturgy of the Church, you of the police department had your own rituals, similar, in a sense, to liturgy. Outside the church, for instance, there was a certain order. You used a slow march. The music was appropriate. There were salutes. There was a flag-covered coffin. Taps were played. These are all rituals, a form of "liturgy" of its own.

Why does the Church have a funeral celebration within the Sacrifice of the Mass? Because our Lord laid down His life in bloody fashion on the Cross out of love for all of us to help save all of us, and mysteriously and spiritually that is extended in the Holy Sacrifice of the Mass. When we are burying someone, especially someone who has died to save others, this is the perfect way to do it, to celebrate within the Sacrifice of Christ. Sean McDonald was engaged in his own sacrifice.

A characteristic of liturgy is to worship God in an orderly, harmonious way so the Church requires that everyone pray together. We don't all come in here and do our own thing. Where such happens there is chaos. So we have an orderly way of offering the Mass. In principle, it's supposed to be done the same way by every priest. The sacraments are supposed to be carried out in principle in the same way by every priest. There are natural human variations, but essentially the rituals are the same.

What does the Police Department do? It tries to preserve harmony, order, in society, otherwise we wouldn't have civilization. We would have barbarity, we would have savagery, we would have chaos. The role of the police, if you will permit me to say so, is much like the role of a priest. Each has a vocation. I can't believe that many of you joined the police force just to get a job, even in this difficult economy. It's more than a job; it's a vocation. It's a calling to help others, to give yourselves to others. I don't know anybody who becomes a priest in order to have a "job". The priesthood is a vocation. He's called to lay down his life for others.

There's another similarity. While on occasion a priest makes headlines with scandalous behavior, the overwhelming majority of the people know that this is the exception. They get worried. They get anxious. There's a loss of credibility in the Church for a while, but it's restored because the overwhelming majority see the priest go about his business, day after day, visiting the sick, spending long hours, and so on. The same with a police officer. You have the occasional rogue cop. He makes headlines, or *she* makes headlines. How many times has that happened, given the size of the Police Department in this terribly difficult and demanding city? Of course there are corruption probes, because there is corruption. But not on the part of the overwhelming number of police officers. The people know this. The overwhelming majority of the people know that the average cop is not a rogue cop, that the average cop is a decent human being. As the average priest is weak, slips, and falls—I have to get to confession frequently. I go every week. And so police slip and fall and need the sacrament of Reconciliation.

You need the sacraments as I need the sacraments. You need the Mass as I need the Mass. The totality of your lives is in giving yourselves, so you need the Mass and sacraments in a special way. Yesterday, on a hospital visit, a man showed me a brochure that had been created to raise money for the hospital. There are a lot of ads in it from different people. There was an ad from two doctors that touched me very deeply. I copied it by hand. The doctors wrote, "The dignity of man is secure in the reality that he is created in the image and likeness of God. To reject this truth is to place the dignity and destiny of man on the shifting sands of public opinion." You don't do that. You don't leave human beings at the mercy of the arbitrary whims of other people. They're entitled to life. They're entitled to liberty. They're entitled to the pursuit of happiness. If it weren't for you, it would be utterly impossible for any of us to live in dignity. So I urge you—don't sell yourselves short, don't give up on yourselves, don't be distressed by temporary losses of credibility. Yours is a noble calling. Yours, in my judgment, is a vocation. It is appropriate that you were here today when the *Catechism* session concerned the liturgy, because you have your own "liturgies", as well as the sacred liturgy of the Church. You are more like the priesthood in your calling than you might have ever realized. Yours is a noble calling. We thank you. We thank God for you. We pray for you. We salute you.

18

What Is Baptism?

PALM SUNDAY
PONTIFICAL MASS
MARCH 27, 1994

As we enter into this Holy Week, which represents for us the holiest week in the history of the human race, let us be reminded that this is not a pageant, this is not a stage show, this is not simply a memorial of something that took place almost two thousand years ago. The purpose of this liturgy is to make present in this cathedral those same events that occurred historically once but are now living here among us. Our Divine Lord spiritually and mysteriously is present once again in the power generated by His sufferings that began in a special way on Palm Sunday and then continued through the holiest week in history. All of our Holy Week observances must be relived together with Christ, if we are to find meaning in His suffering, death, and Resurrection.

One might be led to believe that, since the reading of the Passion is featured in today's Mass, it is the heart of the Mass on Palm Sunday. It is not. The heart of the Mass is the Eucharistic Sacrifice, in which spiritually and mysteriously we have re-presented the suffering, death, and Resurrection of Jesus. Without that, this week would have no meaning. As St. Paul says to us: "If Christ didn't rise from the dead, then our faith is in vain."

At one time this was called not Holy Week but the Week of Reconciliation. The reason Christ came into this world was to pick up the pieces of our broken lives. But the emphasis should not be placed simply on the suffering and death of our Divine Lord to the exclusion of what it points toward—His Resurrection and ours. It is quite common throughout the Church all over the world that many people come to Mass on Palm Sunday who, for whatever reason, are unable to get to Mass each Sunday and holy day of the year. But all are welcome. This is indeed a week of reconciliation. If we have not been able to get to Mass, if we have not been able to practice our faith as we would like and as we know that we should, this is a wonderful week to get started all over again. In this way, when Easter is celebrated next Sunday, we will really feel that something has been accomplished. I went to confession yesterday morning, and the wonderful priest who heard my confession said: "This week you should have a sense of 'risen-ness'. You should experience the Resurrection of our Divine Lord."

Today we continue our sessions on the new *Catechism of the Catholic Church*. Appropriately, this session focuses on the sacrament of Baptism. Nothing could be more intimately keyed with the suffering, death, and Resurrection of our Divine Lord than the sacrament of Baptism. This entire week is to help make possible our salvation. That is why our Divine Lord came, to make us a "holy people" so that we will become saints and achieve everlasting happiness with Him. We first become holy when we become temples of the Holy Spirit at Baptism. St. Paul says when we are baptized we are plunged into death with Christ so that we will rise with Him.

This section of the *Catechism* begins with a preliminary word about the sacraments in general:

> Christ instituted the sacraments. . . . There are seven: Baptism, Confirmation, the Eucharist, Penance, the Anointing of the Sick, Holy Orders and Matrimony. The seven sacraments touch all the stages and all the important moments of Christian life . . . [1210].

I thought of this last night when the phone rang, and I was told that a man who might be dying was in New York Hospital. Father Mustaciuolo, my associate, and I took the holy oils and went over to the hospital and administered the Sacrament of the Sick. I thought to myself, many years ago this man was baptized, and, through all these years, at each important moment of his life, there has been a sacrament to meet his needs. His eyes lighted up when he saw what I was doing. It was clear to me that he understood, that he knew that he was in danger of death. But there was a serenity about the situation after I had anointed him. It was a wonderful experience for me, and I know it was a great joy for him. This is true of each of the sacraments properly received.

The *Catechism* says:

> Holy Baptism is the basis of the whole Christian life, the gateway to life in the Spirit, and the door which gives access to the other sacraments. Through Baptism we are freed from sin and reborn as sons of God; we become members of Christ, are incorporated into the Church and made sharers in her mission . . . [1213].

The mission of Christ is not merely the mission of the ordained priest or bishop. It is the mission of all of us. We receive certain rights and privileges with Baptism, but we also receive certain responsibilities, as we will see.

> The sacrament is called *Baptism*, after the central rite by which it is carried out: to baptize means to "plunge" or "immerse"; the "plunge" into the water symbolizes the catechumen's burial into Christ's death, from which he rises up to resurrection with him, as "a new creature" (2 Cor 5:17) [1214].

Baptism completely renovates us. The *Catechism* says:

> Since the beginning of the world, water . . . has been the source of life and fruitfulness. Sacred Scripture sees it as "overshadowed" by the Spirit of God [1218].

> The Church has seen in Noah's ark a prefiguring of salvation by baptism, for by it "a few, that is, eight persons, were saved through water" (1 Pet 3:20) [1219].

> But above all, the crossing of the Red Sea, literally the liberation of Israel from slavery of Egypt, announces the liberation wrought by Baptism [1221].

> Finally, Baptism is prefigured in the crossing of the Jordan River by which the People of God received the gift of the land promised to Abraham's descendants, an image of eternal life [1222].

> [Christ] begins his public life after having himself baptized by St. John the Baptist in the Jordan. After his resurrection Christ gives this mission to his apostles: "Go therefore and make disciples of all nations, baptizing them in the name of the Father and of the Son and of the Holy Spirit, teaching them to observe all that I have commanded you" (Mt 28:19–20) [1223].

The Church didn't dream up Baptism. This was *essential* to all of the teaching of Christ. The *Catechism* continues:

> Jesus' gesture is a manifestation of his self-emptying. The Spirit who had hovered over the waters of the first creation descended on the Christ as a prelude of the new creation, and the Father revealed Jesus as his "beloved Son" (Mt 3:16–17) [1224].

The first reading today is from a letter of St. Paul to the people of Philippi. In it he says: "Christ emptied himself and took the form of a slave, being born in the likeness of men . . . obediently accepting even death, death on a cross!" (Phil 2:7–8). That is what happens when we are baptized. We empty ourselves so that we may receive the Holy Spirit and be obedient to the Holy Spirit.

The *Catechism* says:

> In his Passover Christ opened to all the fountain of Baptism. He had already spoken of his Passion, which he was about to suffer in Jerusalem, as a "Bap-

tism" with which he had to be baptized (Mk 10:38). [He gives the name "Baptism" to his torture, his sufferings, his crucifixion, his death.] The blood and water that flowed from the pierced side of the crucified Jesus are types of Baptism and the Eucharist, the sacraments of new life. From then on, it is possible "to be born of water and the Spirit" in order to enter the Kingdom of God [1225].

That is what Jesus said when Nicodemus came to Him and asked about salvation. Jesus said, "You must first be born of water and the Spirit."

The *Catechism* says: "According to the Apostle Paul, the believer enters through Baptism into communion with Christ's death, is buried with him, and rises with him" [1227].

Next the *Catechism* brings up the question of how the sacrament of Baptism is celebrated.

The sign of the cross . . . marks with the imprint of Christ the one who is going to belong to him and signifies the grace of the redemption Christ won for us by his cross [1235].

Since Baptism signifies liberation from sin and from its instigator the devil, one or more *exorcisms* are pronounced over the candidate. [Exorcism is the ceremony used to drive out the devil.] The celebrant then anoints him with the oil . . . lays his hands on him and that individual or someone on his behalf explicitly renounces Satan [1237].

The *Catechism* tells us what is essential to Baptism.

Baptism properly speaking signifies and actually brings about death to sin and entry into the life of the Most Holy Trinity. . . . Baptism is performed in the most expressive way by triple immersion in the baptismal water [That is the way it was done in the earliest days of the Church.] From ancient times it has been possible to confer Baptism by pouring the water three times over the candidate's head [1239]. [That is what we normally do, simultaneously saying, "I baptize you in the name of the Father, and of the Son and of the Holy Spirit."]

The *anointing with sacred chrism*, perfumed oil consecrated by the bishop, signifies the gift of the Holy Spirit to the newly baptized, who has become a Christian, that is, one "anointed" by the Holy Spirit, incorporated into Christ who is anointed priest, prophet, and king [1241].

The white garment symbolizes that the person baptized has "put on Christ" (Gal 3:27), has risen with Christ. The candle, lit from the Easter candle, signifies that Christ has enlightened the neophyte. In him the baptized are "the light of the world" (Mt 5:14) [1243].

The newly baptized is now, in the only Son, a child of God entitled to say the prayer of the children of God: "Our Father" [1243].

At the Baptism of newborns the blessing of the mother occupies a special place [1245].

"Every person not yet baptized and only such a person is able to be baptized" [1246].

Since the beginning of the Church, adult Baptism is the common practice where the proclamation of the Gospel is still new. The catechumenate (preparation for Baptism) therefore occupies an important place. This initiation into Christian faith and life should dispose the catechumen to receive the gift of God in Baptism, Confirmation, and the Eucharist [1247].

Born with a fallen human nature and tainted by original sin, children also have need of the new birth in Baptism to be freed from the power of darkness and brought into the realm of the freedom of the children of God. . . . The Church and the parents would deny a child the priceless grace of becoming a child of God were they not to confer Baptism shortly after birth [1250].

Sometimes people wait many, many months for the godparents to come, for instance, from a distance. That is really not a good practice. That is not what the Church intends. The Church intends Baptism shortly after birth. A child could die without Baptism, and then an uncertainty sets in.

The *Catechism* continues:

For all the baptized, children or adults, faith must grow *after* Baptism. For this reason the Church celebrates each year at the Easter Vigil [or on Easter Sunday itself] the renewal of baptismal promises [1254].

For the grace of Baptism to unfold, the parents' help is terribly important. [Today we have instructions for the parents, usually before the child is baptized.] So too is the role of the godfather and godmother, who must be firm believers, able and ready to help the newly baptized—child or adult—on the road of Christian life [1255].

It is most unfortunate that some people get a godparent only because the person is kind of a distant friend or maybe even for political reasons or for reasons of business. That is not supposed to be the case. Being a godparent is a very solemn responsibility. Again, if the parents can't rear the child as a good devout Catholic, it is the responsibility of the godparents to do so.

The *Catechism* says:

The Lord himself affirms that Baptism is necessary for salvation. . . . The Church does not know of any means other than Baptism that assures entry into eternal beatitude . . . [1257].

The Church has always held the firm conviction that those who suffer death for the sake of the faith without having received Baptism are baptized by their death for and with Christ. This *Baptism of blood*, like the *desire for Baptism*, brings about the fruits of Baptism without being a sacrament [1258].

For *catechumens* who die before their Baptism, their explicit desire to receive it, together with repentance for their sins, and charity, assures them the salvation that they were not able to receive through the sacrament [1259].

"Since Christ died for all ... we must hold that the Holy Spirit offers to all the possibility of being made partakers, in a way known to God, of the Paschal mystery." Every man who is ignorant of the Gospel of Christ and of his Church, but seeks the truth and does the will of God in accordance with his understanding of it, can be saved. It may be supposed that such persons would have *desired Baptism explicitly* if they had known its necessity [1260].

So even those who die without being formally baptized may have the "Baptism of desire" and can still get to heaven. The *Catechism* goes on.

As regards *children who have died without Baptism*, the Church can only entrust them to the mercy of God ... [The God] who desires that all men should be saved ... allows us to hope that there is a way of salvation for children who have died without Baptism [1261].

By Baptism *all sins* are forgiven, original sin and all personal sins, as well as all punishment for sin. In those who have been reborn nothing remains that would have impeded their entry into the Kingdom of God, neither Adam's sin, nor personal sin, nor the consequences of sin, the gravest of which is separation from God [1263].

Yet certain temporal consequences of sin remain in the baptized, such as suffering, illness, death, and such frailties inherent in life as weakness of character, and so on, as well as an inclination to sin that Tradition calls *concupiscence* ... [1264].

Baptism not only purifies from all sins, but also makes the neophyte a "new creature," an adopted son of God, who has become a partaker of the divine nature" (2 Cor 5:17), a member of Christ and co-heir with him, and a temple of the Holy Spirit [1265].

The major point of this session is that the entire Christian supernatural life has its roots in Baptism. Everything that comes together this week in commemoration of and in the representation of the suffering and death of Christ, all begins for us through Baptism.

Baptism makes us members of the Body of Christ: "Therefore ... we are members one of another" (Eph 4:25). Baptism incorporates us *into the Church* [1267].

The baptized have become "living stones" to be "built into a spiritual house, to be a holy priesthood" (1 Pet 2:5). By Baptism they share in the priesthood of Christ, in his prophetic and royal mission. . . . *Baptism gives a share in the common priesthood of all believers* [1268].

Just as Baptism is the source of responsibilities and duties, the baptized person also enjoys rights within the Church: to receive the sacraments, to be nourished with the Word of God and to be sustained by the other spiritual helps of the Church [1269].

"Reborn as children of God, [the baptized] must profess before men the faith they have received from God through the Church" and participate in the apostolic and missionary activity of the People of God [1270].

It is not enough to *keep* the faith; you have to try to *share* the faith. We must share in Christ's suffering, in His death to sin. We must rise with Him and then spread the good joy to all.

Baptism seals the Christian with the indelible spiritual mark (*character*) of his belonging to Christ. No sin can erase this mark, even if sin prevents Baptism from bearing the fruits of salvation [1272].

We can be baptized but then turn away from God, but we still have that indelible mark of Baptism, and, therefore, Baptism once given cannot be repeated. When we receive someone into the Church who has been legitimately baptized in some other Christian religion, we don't repeat the Baptism. If there is any doubt, we repeat it "conditionally".

Once baptized, we are caught up by the Holy Spirit. We become truly children of God, marked indelibly with the sign of Christ, the Christ who suffered for one reason and one reason only: out of love for every one of us. Hard as it may be for us to believe, whatever sins that we may have committed, if there had been only one of us alive when Christ came to this earth, He would have come. He would have come and suffered and died. That's how much He loves us! That's why this week is so meaningful to us as we suffer and die again with Christ to be reconciled with Christ, and, above all, as we rise with Christ in the glory of Easter.

19

The Eucharist Is the Sum and Summary
of Our Faith

EASTER SUNDAY
APRIL 3, 1994
PONTIFICAL MASS

My associate Monsignor McCarthy and I had several wonderful experiences this week. Among these, of course, were the experiences of the Holy Week ceremonies, but, in addition and as part of these in a sense, we went to the wakes of the two firemen who were killed this past week, James Young and Christopher Siedenburg. In each instance we were inspired by the faith of their parents. Both mothers and both fathers spoke freely of putting the deaths of their sons into the context of Holy Week. This didn't come from me, it came from them. They all firmly believe that, having died the way they died, to save the lives of others, their sons were in heaven, they had already experienced the Resurrection of Christ. We left there truly buoyed up, recognizing the magnificent nature of our faith. What would it be like for those families if they didn't believe? What emptiness there would be in their hearts! Of course they grieve, but there's a very real sense of happiness underlying their grief, the happiness of the faith that their sons are now in heaven, experiencing the joys of the Resurrection.

We visited, too, one of our priests who is dying. He is only sixty-five years of age and is dying of cancer. I talked with him at some length. He can hardly speak, but there is no question about what he tries to express. He sees his cancer, his suffering, merely as means to an end. He has one foot in heaven. He sees himself being caught up into the Resurrection after many months of severe suffering. What a difference it makes to this man to be able to say that he firmly believes he soon will be with Almighty God in heaven.

That's what today is all about: this profound reminder that each one of us is on a pilgrimage. We are here for hardly more than a breath of life, a handful of years, and then we are destined for eternity. We are reminded in the Scriptures today that if we believe, if we live with Christ here, then surely we will live with Christ hereafter. That's the meaning of all the finery, the Easter hats, and the flowers; here it's the meaning of this Holy Sacrifice of the Mass, it's the true meaning of the words "Happy Easter".

Despite the fact that it is Easter Sunday, I continue with our nineteenth session of the new *Catechism of the Catholic Church*.

Today's session is on the Eucharist, the Blessed Sacrament, what the Church calls the "summation" of everything in our faith and, most particularly, the summation of everything that took place during Holy Week and culminates in Easter. I must confess that there's nothing I could think of that would more adequately express the essential meaning of Easter Sunday than to reflect on the Eucharist. Let us turn now to the *Catechism*. We are told:

> "At the Last Supper, on the night he was betrayed, our Savior instituted the Eucharistic sacrifice of his Body and Blood. This he did in order to perpetuate the sacrifice of the cross throughout the ages until he should come again, and so to entrust to his beloved Spouse, the Church, a memorial of his death and resurrection . . ." [1323]. [Sometimes when we think of the Last Supper we are thinking only of our Lord's death, but this was the prelude to His Resurrection.]

> The Eucharist is "the source and summit of the Christian life." . . . [I]n the Blessed Eucharist is contained the whole spiritual good of the Church, namely Christ himself, our Pasch [sacrifice] [1324].

> In brief, the Eucharist is the sum and summary of our faith [1327].

The *Catechism* goes on:

> The inexhaustible richness of this sacrament is expressed in the different names we give it.

> *Eucharist*, because it is an action of thanksgiving to God [1328].

> The *Lord's Supper*, because of its connection with the supper which the Lord took with his disciples on the eve of his Passion. . . .

> The *Breaking of the Bread*, because Jesus used this rite . . . above all at the Last Supper. It is by this action that his disciples will recognize him after his Resurrection . . . [1329].

> The *Holy Sacrifice* [*of the Mass*], because it makes present the one sacrifice of Christ the Savior and includes the Church's offering.

> The *Holy and Divine Liturgy*, because the Church's whole liturgy finds its center and most intense expression in the celebration of this sacrament. . . . [T]he *Most Blessed Sacrament* because it is the Sacrament of sacraments [1330].

Holy Communion, because by this sacrament we unite ourselves to Christ, who makes us sharers in his Body and Blood to form a single body [1331].

At the heart of the Eucharistic celebration are the bread and wine that, by the words of Christ and the invocation of the Holy Spirit, become Christ's Body and Blood [1333].

The miracles of the multiplication of the loaves, when the Lord says the blessing, breaks and distributes the loaves through his disciples to feed the multitude, prefigure the superabundance of this unique bread of his Eucharist. The sign of water turned into wine at Cana already announces the Hour of Jesus' glorification [1335].

The Lord, having loved those who were his own, loved them to the end. Knowing that the hour had come to leave this world and return to the Father, in the course of a meal he washed their feet and gave them the commandment of love. In order to leave them a pledge of this love, in order never to depart from his own and to make them sharers in his Passover, he instituted the Eucharist as the memorial of his death and Resurrection, and commanded his apostles to celebrate it until his return; "thereby he constituted them priests of the New Testament" [1337].

The *Catechism* describes the institution of the Eucharist:

And he took bread, and when he had given thanks he broke it and gave it to them saying, "This is my body which is given for you. Do this in remembrance of me." And likewise the cup after supper, saying, "This cup which is poured out for you is the New Covenant in my blood" [1339].

By celebrating the Last Supper with his apostles in the course of the Passover meal, Jesus gave the Jewish Passover its definitive meaning. Jesus' passing over to his father by his death and Resurrection, the new Passover, is anticipated in the Supper and celebrated in the Eucharist . . . [1340].

The *Catechism* continues:

It was above all on the "first day of the week," Sunday, the day of Jesus' resurrection, that the Christians met "to break bread." From that time on down to our own day the celebration of the Eucharist has been continued so that today we encounter it everywhere in the Church with the same fundamental structure. It remains the center of the Church's life [1343].

All gather together. Christians come together in one place for the Eucharistic assembly. At its head is Christ himself, the principal agent of the Eucharist. He is high priest of the New Covenant; it is he himself who presides invisibly over every Eucharistic celebration. It is in representing him that the bishop or priest acting *in the person of Christ the head* (*in persona Christi capitis*) presides over the assembly, speaks after the readings, receives the offerings, and says the Eucharistic Prayer. *All* have their own active parts to play in the celebration, each in his own way: readers, those who bring up the offerings, those who give communion, and the whole people whose "Amen" manifests their participation [1348].

Because this bread and wine have been made Eucharist, "we call this food *Eucharist*, and no one may take part in it unless he believes that what we teach is true, has received baptism for the forgiveness of sins and new birth, and lives in keeping with what Christ taught" [1355].

. . . When the Church celebrates the Eucharist, she commemorates Christ's Passover, and it is made present [Those of you who have been here during Holy Week have heard us emphasize this so frequently. This is not a memorial in terms of a tombstone. This is a memorial in which Christ is again present on the altar, very truly as present as we are present in this cathedral.]: the sacrifice Christ offered once for all on the cross remains ever present. "As often as the sacrifice of the Cross by which 'Christ our Pasch has been sacrificed' is celebrated on the altar, the work of our redemption is carried out" [1364].

The work of our salvation is still being carried out in each Mass, the power of the crucifixion, the power of the Resurrection.

The *Catechism* continues: "The sacrificial character of the Eucharist is manifested in the very words of institution: 'This is my body which is given for you' and 'This cup which is poured out for you is the New Covenant in my blood' " [1365].

We pointed out before that the priest doesn't say over the bread and wine, "These are my body and my blood." He says over the bread separately, "This is my body," and over the wine, "This is my blood." He spiritually separates them as the blood of our Divine Lord was separated from His body on the Cross. There He died in bloody fashion, in the Mass in unbloody fashion.

In the Eucharist Christ gives us the very body which he gave up for us on the cross, the very blood which he "poured out for many for the forgiveness of sins" [1365].

It is not a different body and blood in the Mass, not a different body and blood that we receive in Holy Communion. It is the same body and blood as were sacrificed on the Cross.

The *Catechism* says:

The Eucharist is thus a real sacrifice because it *re-presents* (makes present) the sacrifice of the cross because it is its *memorial* and because it *applies* its fruit [1366].

The sacrifice of Christ and the sacrifice of the Eucharist are *one single sacrifice*: "The victim is one and the same: the same now offers through the ministry of priests, who then offered himself on the cross; only the manner of offering is different." "In this divine sacrifice which is celebrated in the Mass, the same Christ who offered himself once in a bloody manner on the altar of the cross is contained and is offered in an unbloody manner" [1367].

On Easter Sunday we can say that the same Christ who rose from the dead more than nineteen hundred years ago in the Garden of the Resurrection, that same Christ rises from the dead in the Sacrifice of the Mass. The *Catechism* continues:

> *The whole Church is united with the offering and intercession of Christ.* Since he has the ministry of Peter in the Church, the *Pope* is associated with every celebration of the Eucharist, wherein he is named as the sign and servant of the unity of the universal Church. The *bishop* of the place is always responsible for the Eucharist, even when a *priest* presides; the bishop's name is mentioned . . . [1369].

> To the offering of Christ are united not only the members still here on earth, but also those already *in the glory of heaven* [1370].

> The Eucharistic sacrifice is also offered for *the faithful departed* who "have died in Christ but are not yet wholly purified," so that they may be able to enter into the light and peace of Christ [1371].

The *Catechism* continues:

> It is by the *conversion* of the bread and wine into Christ's body and blood that Christ becomes present in this sacrament [What we receive is not a piece of bread, not a drink of wine, but the Body and Blood, the soul and divinity, the entirety of the risen Christ. Each Mass is Easter Sunday.] Thus St. John Chrysostom declares:
> "It is not man that causes the things offered to become the Body and Blood of Christ, but he who was crucified for us, Christ himself. The priest, in the role of Christ, pronounces these words, but their power and grace are God's" [1375].

> ". . . by the consecration of the bread and wine there takes place a change of the whole substance of the bread into the substance of the body of Christ our Lord and of the whole substance of the wine into the substance of his blood. This change the holy Catholic Church has fittingly and properly called transubstantiation" [1376].

> The Eucharistic presence of Christ begins at the moment of the consecration and endures as long as the Eucharistic species subsist. Christ is present whole and entire in each of the species and whole and entire in each of their parts in such a way that the breaking of the bread does not divide Christ [1377].

The tabernacle was first intended for the reservation of the Eucharist in a worthy place so that it could be brought to the sick and those absent, outside of Mass. As faith in the real presence of Christ in this Eucharist deepened, the Church became conscious of the meaning of silent adoration of the Lord present under the Eucharistic species [1379].

One of my associates here is Father Gregory Mustaciuolo. He was telling me the other day about his five-year-old niece, who was discussing her catechism lessons with her mother. Her mother was reviewing different items used in the Mass, what are the names of the particular vestments, and so on. There was a drawing of a tabernacle, and she asked her daughter, "What is the name of this object here?" Her daughter hesitated for a while. She said, "I know it begins with a 't'." Her mother said, "Well, what is it for?" The five-year-old said, "Oh, that's where at the end of Mass they put the leftovers." These are "leftovers", and we can say that reverently. Each one of these "leftovers" is the totality of our Divine Lord.

The Mass is at the same time, and inseparably, the sacrificial memorial in which the sacrifice of the cross is perpetuated, and the sacred banquet of communion with the Lord's body and blood. But the celebration of the Eucharistic sacrifice is wholly directed toward the intimate union of the faithful with Christ through communion. To receive communion is to receive Christ himself who has offered himself for us [1382].

We must repeat and reemphasize this. Mary Magdalene saw Christ after the Resurrection. At first she did not recognize Him. He looked to her like the gardener, and she thought that the body had been stolen. But when she recognized Him, when He called her by name, "Mary", her heart just burst with joy for "Rabboni, Master." She was only seeing the risen Christ. Now in Holy Communion we receive the risen Christ. What should be the reaction within us if we are concentrating on what we are doing, if we are opening our hearts and our minds to our Divine Lord, if we truly believe? What does "communion" mean? It means "in union with". When we receive our Lord we are in intimate union with Him, much more than would be the case if we simply saw Him.

The *Catechism* continues:

The Lord addresses an invitation to us, urging us to receive him in the sacrament of the Eucharist: "Truly, I say to you, unless you eat the flesh of the Son of man and drink his blood, you have no life in you" [1384].

To respond to this invitation we must *prepare ourselves* for so great and so holy a moment. . . . Anyone conscious of a grave sin must receive the sacrament of Reconciliation before coming to communion [1385].

This week a tremendous number of people, becoming more and more conscious of the meaning of receiving our Divine Lord in Holy Communion, went to confession, were reconciled to our Divine Lord, and had their souls purified before approaching Him in Holy Communion. That's what we are supposed to do.

> To prepare for worthy reception of this sacrament, the faithful should observe the fast required in their Church. [We are to refrain from eating solid foods up to one hour before receiving Communion. We can drink water right up to the time we receive Communion. We have one hour, therefore, of complete fast.] Bodily demeanor (gestures, clothing) ought to convey the respect, solemnity, and joy of this moment when Christ becomes our guest [1387]. [And that should be especially true at the actual moment at which we take Christ in our hand or on our tongue.]

> The Church obliges the faithful "to take part in the Divine Liturgy on Sundays and feast days" and, prepared by the sacrament of Reconciliation, to receive the Eucharist at least once a year, if possible during the Easter season. But the Church strongly encourages the faithful to receive the Holy Eucharist on Sunday and feast days, or more often still, even daily [1389].

> Since Christ is sacramentally present under each of the species, communion under the species of bread alone makes it possible to receive all the fruit of Eucharistic grace [1390].

As with so many other things, an awful lot of people seem to think that after the Second Vatican Council all the rules went out the window. That's not true. We still have the obligation to receive Holy Communion at least once a year, and if possible that's to be during the Easter season—from now until Pentecost. Obviously, it's wonderful if we receive every Sunday, even more wonderful if we receive every day. But the absolute minimum is that we receive our Divine Lord once a year.

The *Catechism* says:

> *Holy Communion augments our union with Christ.* The principal fruit of receiving the Eucharist in Holy Communion is an intimate union with Christ Jesus. Indeed, the Lord said, "He who eats my flesh and drinks my blood abides in me, and I in him." Life in Christ has its foundation in the Eucharistic banquet: "As the living Father sent me, and I live because of the Father, so he who eats me will live because of me."

> On the feasts of the Lord, when the faithful receive the Body of the Son, they proclaim to one another the Good News that the first fruits of life have been given, as when the angel said to Mary Magdalene, "Christ is risen!" Now too are life and resurrection conferred on whoever receives Christ [1391].

So you can see that this lesson of the *Catechism* is perfectly expressive of the real meaning of Easter. How special we are! We are reminded in the first reading:

> "They killed Jesus finally, 'hanging him on a tree,' only to have God raise him up on the third day and grant that he be seen, not by all, but only by such witnesses as had been chosen beforehand by God—by us who ate and drank with him after he rose from the dead" [Acts 10:39–41].

We are special. We don't say this to be exclusive. We don't say this with any sense of contempt for those who have not been baptized into Christ, those who cannot receive our Divine Lord in Holy Communion. We say it with a sense of *awe*. We are special! We have been chosen for this. We have come to know Him, as the apostles did, in the breaking of the bread.

When the two disciples on their way to Emmaus were walking with Jesus, they didn't recognize Him. But when He went into the inn with them, they sat at the table, and He broke bread. It was then that they recognized Him. We recognize Jesus in the breaking of bread that we call the Eucharist.

Were I still a little boy this Easter afternoon, my mother and father would take me, my brother, my sisters to Holy Cross Cemetery in suburban Philadelphia. There we would lay flowers on the graves of my grandmother and grandfather, and there my father would look a little bit sad, and we would feel a little bit awed, and we would say some prayers. But never for a moment did we think that we were praying for some dust lying in those graves awaiting the resurrection of the body. We knew that our grandmother, our grandfather, wasn't in that grave. We knew that they had risen because they believed, and they were so good, and they lived such good lives. We knew that, at worst, they were in Purgatory and that our prayers could help them get to heaven. But as little kids we were more likely to believe that they were already in heaven with Almighty God. Our father spoke of them so lovingly.

We didn't always get a new pair of shoes for Easter, a new sweater, a new suit. My sisters didn't always get new dresses. But what we got on Easter Sunday was the greatest gift that parents could give to their children. We were renewed in our faith. We left that cemetery as we had left Mass earlier, reminded once again that we are here for only a short span of years and that we are destined for eternity with Almighty God. If we lose that, we are complete failures in life. We got succinctly told the entire story of the Resurrection—that Christ had died for us, that Christ lives for us, and that we have every reason to hope that if we live with Christ on this earth we will live with Him for eternity in heaven. What greater Easter gift could children be given. God bless you, and Happy Easter!

20

The Great Sacraments of Healing

SECOND SUNDAY OF EASTER
APRIL 10, 1994
PONTIFICAL MASS

Today's session on the new *Catechism of the Catholic Church* is on the sacrament of Penance and the sacrament intimately co-joined with it, if you will, the sacrament of the Anointing of the Sick. It's very possible that nothing has been so confused and so abused in the Church since the Second Vatican Council as the sacrament of Penance, the sacrament of Reconciliation, as it is now called. Many people don't get to confession anymore because they think the Second Vatican Council said that it wasn't any longer necessary. That's a *total* distortion of what the Second Vatican Council taught about this and so many other things. If we read the documents of the Council, we see that the questions of sin, of alienation from God, and of reparation, of picking up the pieces, are there. This is the teaching of the Church; the reception of the sacrament of Penance, Reconciliation, is very much a requirement of the Church today.

Only God knows how many people just so casually receive Holy Communion even if in the state of mortal sin, not having gone to confession, not having been given absolution. This was never intended by the Church. But of equal importance, as my confessor said to me yesterday morning, is that this is the great sacrament of healing, the great gift of our Divine Lord to heal us, to pick up the pieces of our broken lives.

We have just come through the season of Lent and particularly Holy Week. Throughout Holy Week, in this cathedral, we constantly preached about healing, reconciliation, forgiveness, and the mercy of God. Here's what the *Catechism* says, word for word:

> The Lord Jesus Christ, physician of our souls and bodies, who forgave the sins of the paralytic and restored him to bodily health, has willed that his Church continue, in the power of the Holy Spirit, his work of healing and salvation, even among her own members. This is the purpose of the two sacraments of healing: the sacrament of Penance and the sacrament of Anointing the Sick [1421].

There are, of course, people who know that they are sick and are terrified to go to a doctor, or afraid they are going to get bad news. You don't have to be afraid of a priest in confession.

The *Catechism* continues:

It is called the *sacrament of Penance*, since it consecrates the Christian sinner's personal and ecclesial steps of conversion, penance, and satisfaction [1423].

It is called the *sacrament of confession*, since the disclosure or confession of sins to a priest is an essential element of this sacrament [1424].

It is called the *sacrament of forgiveness*, since by the priest's sacramental absolution God grants the penitent "pardon and peace" [1424].

It is called the *sacrament of Reconciliation*, because it imparts to the sinner the life of God who reconciles: "Be reconciled to God" (2 Cor 5:20) [1424].

Jesus calls to conversion. . . . Baptism is the principal place for the first and fundamental conversion . . . that is, the forgiveness of all sins and the gift of new life [1427].

God gives us the strength to begin anew. It is in discovering the greatness of God's love that our heart is shaken by the horror and weight of sin and begins to fear offending God by sin and being separated from him [1432].

The interior penance of the Christian can be expressed in many and various ways. Scripture and the Fathers insist above all on three forms, *fasting, prayer,* and *almsgiving* . . . [1434].

Daily conversion and penance find their source and nourishment in the Eucharist, for in it is made present the sacrifice of Christ which has reconciled us with God [1436].

Reading Sacred Scripture, praying the Liturgy of the Hours and the Our Father—every sincere act of worship or devotion revives the spirit of conversion and repentance within us and contributes to the forgiveness of our sins [1437].

The seasons and days of penance . . . (Lent, and each Friday in memory of the death of the Lord) are intense moments of the Church's penitential practice [1438].

The process of conversion and repentance was described by Jesus in the parable of the prodigal son, the center of which is the merciful father: the fascination of illusory freedom, the abandonment of the father's house; the extreme misery in which the son finds himself after squandering his fortune; his deep humiliation at finding himself obliged to feed swine, and still worse, at wanting to feed on the husks of pigs ate; his reflection on all he has lost; his repentance and decision to declare himself guilty before his father; the journey back; the father's generous welcome; the father's joy—all these are characteristic of the process of conversion [1439].

We could add, of course, the beautiful story of the woman taken in adultery and thrown at the feet of our Divine Lord, whose concluding words to her were, "Has no man condemned you? Neither do I condemn you. Go now and sin no more."

The *Catechism* continues:

> Sin is before all else an offense against God, a rupture of communion with him. At the same time it damages communion with the Church. For this reason conversion entails both God's forgiveness and reconciliation with the Church [1440]. [We are *one* body in the Church. When we sin, we hurt everyone in the Church, and so we make reparation to God and to the Church by the sacrament of Penance and Reconciliation.]

> Only God forgives sins. . . . [B]y virtue of his divine authority Christ gives this power to men to exercise in his name [1441].

Some people will say, "Well, I can go right to God and be forgiven for whatever I've done." Of course they can. Who is to say that God can't forgive any sin that He wills to forgive? But that's not the way He structured His Church. That's not the way His Son left things for us. He gave His power to human beings, as we saw in today's Gospel (Jn 20:19-31). Christ appeared to the apostles. Significantly, they were behind locked doors. Why? They were afraid. But the locked doors didn't stop Christ; He just went right through. What did Christ say to them? "Peace be with you." Peace is the primary fruit of the sacrament of Penance. "Peace be with you. As the Father has sent me, so I send you." Christ is giving this authority to His apostles. Then He breathed on them and said, "Receive the Holy Spirit. If you forgive men's sins, they are forgiven them. If you hold them bound, they are held bound." This is the way our Divine Lord structured it.

The *Catechism* continues:

> In imparting to his apostles his own power to forgive sins the Lord also gives them the authority to reconcile sinners with the Church. This dimension of their task is expressed most notably in Christ's solemn words to Simon Peter: "I will give you the keys of the kingdom of heaven, and whatever you bind on earth shall be bound in heaven, and whatever you loose on earth shall be loosed in heaven" (Mt 16:19) [1444].

> The words *bind and loose* mean: whomever you exclude from your communion, will be excluded from communion with God; whomever you receive anew into your communion, God will welcome back into his. *Reconciliation with the Church is inseparable from reconciliation with God* [1445].

Of course there are people, understandably, who will say, "I don't need the Church. God is enough." Once more we can only answer, "The

Church is the body of Christ on earth. It is Christ who established the Church."

> The formula of absolution used in the Latin Church expresses the essential elements of this sacrament [1449].

Every time I administer this sacrament these words seem so beautiful to me. Yesterday when I heard them, when I was going to confession, they seemed so beautiful:

> God, the Father of mercies,
> through the death and the resurrection of his Son
> has reconciled the world to himself
> and sent the Holy Spirit among us
> for the forgiveness of sins:
> through the ministry of the Church
> may God give you pardon and peace,
> and I absolve you from your sins
> in the name of the Father, and of the Son, and of the Holy Spirit [1449].

See how the Church takes Christ's words seriously! The priest says, "I absolve you from your sins." He doesn't simply say, "I'll ask God to forgive you." Rather, he says, "I'm using the power that Christ has given me. I absolve you from your sins." In this, Christ is absolving you.

The *Catechism* continues: "Among the penitent's acts contrition occupies first place. Contrition is 'sorrow of the soul and detestation for the sin committed, together with the resolution not to sin again' " [1451].

That's the big thing. We can't just go to confession and say I did this and this and this, and as soon as I get out of the confessional I'm going to do it all over again. That's not the point. A lot of people say, "What good is confession? We know Catholics commit sins, and yet they go to confession and receive Holy Communion." There are two answers to that. We are very weak human beings, and that's why our Lord gave us this sacrament. Secondly, we have to ask, "What would we be without this? If people think that we're bad now, what would we be if we didn't get to confession?" I don't know what I could do if I didn't get to confession. I know, of course, when I go to confession that I'm going to lose my temper again tomorrow.

There are two kinds of what we call contrition, being sorry for sins— perfect and imperfect. The *Catechism* says:

> When it arises from a love by which God is loved above all else, contrition is called "perfect". Such contrition remits venial sins; it also obtains forgiveness of mortal sins if it includes the firm resolution to have recourse to sacramental confession as soon as possible [1452].

The contrition called "imperfect" . . . is born of the consideration of sin's ugliness or the fear of eternal damnation and the other penalties threatening the sinner (contrition of fear). . . . By itself . . . imperfect contrition cannot obtain the forgiveness of grave sins, but it disposes one to obtain forgiveness in the sacrament of Penance [1453].

The *Catechism* goes on to say that we are supposed to examine our conscience before we go into the confessional. It's not supposed to be helter-skelter.

Confession . . . is an essential part of the sacrament of Penance: "All mortal sins of which penitents after a diligent self-examination are conscious must be recounted . . . in confession . . ." [1456].

. . . "[A]fter having attained the age of discretion, each of the faithful is bound by an obligation faithfully to confess serious sins at least once a year." Anyone who is aware of having committed a mortal sin must not receive Holy Communion, even if he experiences deep contrition [sorrow], without having first received sacramental absolution [in the sacrament of Penance], unless he has a grave reason for receiving Communion and there is no possibility of going to confession. [I don't know what ever happened to this, why so many seem to think that this doesn't bind anymore. It *is* binding, says the new *Catechism*.] Children must go to the sacrament of Penance before Holy Communion for the first time [1457].

This has become so confused. Parishes in different parts of the country who say, "We're going to do it this way: we'll give Communion first, and then, when a child is older, we'll hear confession." That's not what the Church says. We are supposed to be one Church. The *Catechism* is very clear in its teaching. Confession precedes Communion even for little children.

Without being strictly necessary, confession of everyday faults (venial sins) is nevertheless strongly recommended by the Church. Indeed the regular confession of our venial sins helps us form our conscience, fight against evil tendencies, let ourselves be healed by Christ and progress in the life of the Spirit [1458].

We get a special grace in the sacrament of Penance. It strengthens us against future sins. It's kind of a reserve that we can lean on when we are tempted.

Many sins wrong our neighbor. One must do what is possible in order to repair the harm (e.g., return stolen goods, restore the reputation of someone slandered, pay compensation for injuries). Simple justice requires as much. . . . Absolution takes away sin, but it does not remedy all the disorders sin has caused. . . . [T]he sinner . . . must "make satisfaction for" or "expiate" his sins. This satisfaction is also called "penance" [1459].

While absolution takes away our sins, we have to do some form of penance—prayers, almsgiving, whatever it may be. The priest is supposed to try to fit the penance to the nature of the sins. I usually have to spend all of Saturday afternoon doing penance!

> . . . [B]ishops and priests, by virtue of the sacrament of the Holy Orders, have the power to forgive all sins "in the name of the Father, and of the Son, and of the Holy Spirit" [1461].

There are certain grave sins that incur what we call "excommunication", which means, in essence, that you cannot receive the Sacrament of Holy Communion or any of the sacraments of the Church until you go to confession. Some of these sins are what we call "reserved sins". Ordinarily, the priest in the confessional may not be authorized to forgive them without the authority of the bishop. The bishop frequently gives authority to all of his priests on certain occasions to forgive the sin and to wash away the excommunication.

> . . . [E]very priest who hears confessions is bound under very severe penalties to keep absolute secrecy regarding the sins that his penitents have confessed to him. He can make no use of the knowledge that confession gives him about penitents' lives. This secret, which admits of no exception, is called the "sacramental seal," because what the penitent has made known to the priest remains "sealed" by the sacrament [1467].

The priest has to die, literally has to give up his life, rather than reveal to anybody what he has heard in the sacrament of Penance.

The *Catechism* then tells us about indulgences. We still receive indulgences. We can receive indulgences for prayer, for acts of penance, for acts of sacrifice. Indulgences can take away part of what we call the temporal punishment due to sin.

We have talked before about Purgatory. If one goes to Purgatory, through an indulgence one's period in Purgatory can be shortened, and one can go directly to heaven. One can receive what we call a "plenary indulgence", when everything is forgiven. The *Catechism* says:

> "An indulgence is a remission before God of the temporal punishment due to sins whose guilt has already been forgiven, which the faithful Christian who is duly disposed gains under certain prescribed conditions through the action of the Church which, as the minister of redemption, dispenses and applies with authority the treasure of the satisfactions of Christ and the saints" [1471].

A partial indulgence removes part of the temporal punishment due to sin. A plenary indulgence removes all of the temporal punishment due to sin. Indulgences may be applied to the living or the dead [1471].

. . . [S]in has a *double consequence*. Grave sin deprives us of communion with God, and therefore makes us incapable of eternal life, the privation of which is called the "eternal punishment" of sin. . . . [E]very sin, even venial, entails an unhealthy attachment of creatures, which must be purified either here on earth, or after death in the state called Purgatory. This purification frees one from what is called the "temporal punishment" of sin [1472].

The forgiveness of sin and restoration of communion with God entail the remission of the eternal punishment of sin, but temporal punishment of sin remains [1473].

"[The] treasury [of the Church] . . . includes the prayers and good works of the Blessed Virgin Mary. . . . In the treasury, too, are the prayers and good works of all the saints, all those who have followed in the footsteps of Christ the Lord and by his grace have made their lives holy and carried out the mission the Father entrusted to them" [1477].

Regardless of what you hear in some places, we are still not supposed to have what we call general absolution except in very specific circumstances, in battle, for example, when a lot of men might be exposed to death. But even when you give general absolution to a crowd of people without their immediately confessing their sins to a priest at that time, then the individuals must get to confession as soon as they can. The *Catechism* tells us:

In case of grave necessity recourse may be had to a *communal celebration of reconciliation with general confession and general absolution*. Grave necessity of this sort can arise when there is imminent danger of death without sufficient time for the priest or priests to hear each penitent's confession. Grave necessity can also exist when, given the number of penitents, there are not enough confessors to hear individual confessions properly in a reasonable time, so that the penitents through no fault of their own would be deprived of sacramental grace or Holy Communion for a long time. In this case, for the absolution to be valid the faithful must have the intention of individually confessing their sins in the time required. The diocesan bishop is the judge of whether or not the conditions required for general absolution exist. A large gathering of the faithful on the occasion of major feasts or pilgrimages does not constitute a case of grave necessity [1483].

Now we move to the Anointing of the Sick. We are reminded that illness can lead to discouragement, to anguish, to a great fear, and so our Lord instituted this sacrament. This is not just when we are in immediate danger of death. If we get seriously sick, we should be anointed. If we are going to undergo surgery, we should be anointed. If we've been sick for an extended period of time, we can be anointed again. Even if the sickness, if I may call it such, is the sickness of old age, we can be anointed again, because the anointing of this particular sacrament not only has a spiritual effect, it has a physical effect—it can actually strengthen us and bring us back to health.

The *Catechism* says:

> Illness can lead to anguish, self-absorption, sometimes even despair and revolt against God. It can also make a person more mature, helping him discern in his life what is not essential so that he can turn toward that which is. Very often illness provokes a search for God and a return to him [1501].

> . . . [I]n the sacraments Christ continues to "touch" us in order to heal us [1504].

> The Holy Spirit gives to some a special charism of healing so as to make manifest the power of the grace of the risen Lord. But even the most intense prayers do not always obtain the healing of all illnesses [1508].

> However, the apostolic Church has its own rite for the sick, attested to by St. James: "Is any among you sick? Let him call for the elders of the Church and let them pray over him, anointing him with oil in the name of the Lord; and the prayer of faith will save the sick man, and the Lord will raise him up; and if he has committed sins, he will be forgiven" (James 5:14–15). Tradition has recognized in this rite one of the seven sacraments [1510].

> The sacrament of Anointing the Sick is given to those who are seriously ill by anointing them on the forehead and hands with duly blessed oil—pressed from olives or from other plants—saying, only once: "Through this holy anointing may the Lord in his love and mercy help you with the grace of the Holy Spirit. May the Lord who frees you from sin save you and raise you up" [1513].

> The celebration of the sacrament includes the following principal elements: the "priests of the Church"—in silence—lay hands on the sick; they pray over them in the faith of the Church—this is the epiclesis proper to the sacrament; they then anoint them with oil blessed, if possible, by the bishop [1519].

> The first grace of this sacrament is one of strengthening, peace and courage to overcome the difficulties that go with the condition of serious illness or the frailty of old age. . . . This assistance from the Lord by the power of his Spirit is meant to lead the sick person to healing of the soul, but also of the body if such is God's will. Furthermore, "if he has committed sins, he will be forgiven" (James 5:15) [1520].

Accompanying this particular sacrament, which is a very special gift of the Holy Spirit, is what we call Holy Viaticum, the receiving of Holy

Communion as we are approaching death. The word *viaticum* means "to go with you", so our Lord is going with you as you enter into eternity. This is a tremendous comfort. Generally, we speak of all of these together as the Last Rites.

The Church reminds us of this in the *Catechism* in a very beautiful passage, which concludes this section:

> In addition to the Anointing of the Sick, the Church offers those who are about to leave this life the Eucharist as viaticum. . . . [A]ccording to the words of the Lord: "He who eats my flesh and drinks my blood has eternal life, and I will raise him up on the last day" (Jn 6:54) [1524].

21

What Is the Priesthood?

THIRD SUNDAY OF EASTER

NEOPHYTES

APRIL 17, 1994

PONTIFICAL MASS

Given the special joyousness of our celebration today, I regret having to introduce a jarring note, but your prayers are critically needed, one could say desperately needed, because of a struggle taking place at this very moment here in the United Nations in New York. Some of you have read that there is a commission preparing for an International Conference on Population and Development, which will take place in Cairo in September of this year. There are forces at work—and I would like to see some evidence that the United States is not one of these forces—that, if permitted to carry out their work unrestrained, could lead to the destruction of family life throughout the world, to the introduction of concepts totally alien to what we've always considered to be our American philosophy, let alone our Judeo-Christian philosophy.

The very integrity of family life is at stake; all human life is at stake! There are efforts to advance by every means the destruction of human life through abortion, widespread contraception, and sterilization. Many African nations, Latin American nations, and Asian nations are trying valiantly to resist, but they are up against mighty forces of the West. The United States is perceived as being among those forces. It is not only the Holy See that has been combating these efforts to destroy so much that we have always believed to be inherent in our concept of the rights, dignity, and sacredness of the human person. Many nations have joined the Holy See in the struggle to resist this destructive effort to advance a new vision of sexuality, a new vision of the family at the expense and integrity of the family.

This is not in any way a light or laughing matter, so I have to ask you if you will commit yourselves to pray at least one Hail Mary a day to the Mother of all human life, to the Mother who is the paragon of family life, Mary, that this battle against the sacred will not be won. Please pray a Hail Mary for those who are engaged in the development of the preparatory documents for the Cairo Conference and pray right on through until that conference takes place. I have been following it closely, trying to write about it in my own stumbling fashion in *Catholic New York*. In my judgment it is one of the most critical attacks against everything that we have purported to be inherent in our Judeo-Christian way of life that I have experienced in what is no longer a brief lifetime. So please pray.

I cannot tell you how warmly we welcome you, those whom we call neophytes, those who are new in the full practice of everything that Christianity is supposed to mean. I look at you and wish that all of us who have been "practicing Catholicism" all our lives were as fully dedicated as you. What has happened to you is described in today's Gospel (Lk 24:35–48). You have touched the Lord. The apostles were terribly disturbed because Christ had been crucified. They thought everything was shattered. When He appeared they thought He was a ghost. He said, "Why are you disturbed? . . . Touch me, and see that a ghost does not have flesh and bones as I do." He showed them His hands and His feet. That's what happened to you.

Perhaps for years people have been telling some of you that the Church is a ghost from the ancient past. But you know that the Church is not a ghost. You know that the Church is the Body of Christ. You have been given a great grace. Only as recently as the Easter Vigil a number of you were baptized, a number of you received Holy Communion for the first time, a number of you were confirmed. What a wonderful gift that is to you, but what a wonderful gift you are to the Church! You bring this very alive, very active faith to the Body of Christ. One need only look at you and see the sense of wonder, the sense of joy.

I cannot adequately thank Sister Rose Vermette and all of those who have worked with you and influenced you: parents, husbands, wives, families, friends, godparents, teachers, sisters, pastors, everyone who has taken an interest in you. We are so grateful to them.

Our Holy Father who loves you so much hopes that the confusion in the Church will begin to end with the publishing of the new *Catechism of the Catholic Church*. The *Catechism* brings together all of the teachings of the Church from the Sacred Scriptures, the Old and the New Testament, and the traditions and the practices of the Church.

Today we are going to talk about the sacrament of Holy Orders, the sacrament of the priesthood. It couldn't be a better time to talk about it because all of you have been initiated into the priesthood. Every baptized person here shares in the priesthood of Christ.

Because I am a priest, I share in the priesthood of Christ in a very special way. Because I am a bishop, I share in the priesthood of Christ in a different special way. But it all begins at Baptism, when we come to share in the priesthood of Christ. Your priesthood is to be lived out in a different way from mine. All of us live out the priesthood for our own personal holiness and the personal holiness of each member of your families. You are given this share in the priesthood of Christ for your own holiness.

There is a special form of the priesthood called Holy Orders; it is a special sacrament that most people do not receive. It comes from Christ through the Church. It's interesting that with all of the teachers that you have had, with all the help that so many people have given you, ultimately it all focused on the Sacrifice of the Mass. You were baptized, and that made it possible then for you to receive the Body and Blood of our Divine Lord, the living Jesus. You received the living Jesus because a priest offered the Holy Sacrifice of the Mass and brought Jesus to the altar through the power of the Holy Spirit. The role of the priest in the Church is critical. While the priest is no more important than any one of you, his role is very special. This is what the *Catechism* says:

> . . . Today the word *"ordination"* is reserved for the sacrament which integrates a man as either a bishop, a priest or a deacon . . . [1538].

We'll talk about that in a moment. It has to be given by Christ through the Church. He can't just be elected by the people. He is ordained by the bishop, because it's the bishop who is given the special power to do this. That's one of the things that make a bishop different. He can ordain priests.

The *Catechism* points out:

> The chosen people [they were the Israelites, God's chosen people] was constituted . . . "a kingdom of priests and a holy nation." (Ex 19:6) [all of them, just like you]. But within the Israelites, God selected a particular tribe. There were twelve tribes of Israelites. God selected one, the tribe of Levi, and they were to be the priests. They were to serve the people in a special way. They were to offer sacrifice. They were to pray for the people [1539].

Then we are told:

> Everything that the priesthood of the Old Testament prefigured came into fulfillment in Christ Jesus, who was the "one real mediator between God and men" (1 Tim 2:5) [1544].

> The redeeming sacrifice of Christ [His crucifixion and death] is unique [it happened only once in bloody form on Calvary]; yet it is made present in the Eucharistic sacrifice of the Church. The same is true of the one priesthood of Christ. Christ is the only priest and those of us who are ordained priests derive our priesthood from him [1545]. [That's why the ordained priest is said to act in the person of Christ, and all baptized derive their priesthood from Christ, who is the only real priest.]

Each of us then exercises the priesthood in a different way. In the ordained minister we are told:

> It is Christ himself who is present to his Church as Head of his Body, in the bishop as the primary teacher and in the priest [1548, 1549].

The presence of Christ in the priest, in the bishop, however, is not to be understood as though the priest were without sins, without error, without fault. Would to God that he were. But the priest is quite capable, the bishop is quite capable, of any weakness that any of you are capable of. Those of you who are brand new in the Church can still commit sins even though you have been baptized, even though you have been to confession, and so can the priest, but the important thing is that the essential things the priest does—forgive sins, for instance, in the sacrament of Penance, change the bread into the Body of Christ and the wine into the Blood of Christ through the power of the Holy Spirit—still happen, despite any sinfulness on the part of the priest. That's a tremendously important thing to remember, because there have been religions that have said that if the priest is in the state of sin and offers Mass, then the Mass is not valid, the bread does not become the Body of Christ, the wine does not become His Blood. When the priest baptizes, if the priest is in the state of serious sin, such religions would assert, the person is not baptized. If the priest is in the sacrament of Penance forgiving sin and is himself in the state of sin, he cannot forgive the sins of others. That's not true.

Now, in other things, in his work with the people, in his general ministry, in his preaching, in his teaching, if the priest is in the state of sin, that sin adversely affects others.

Not only has the bishop the power that any priest has, and not only can he ordain other priests as well, but his is the primary responsibility for teaching. Every priest in the Church in New York, for example, where we have 413 parishes, represents the bishop. When he offers the Sacrifice of the Mass, technically he's representing the bishop. When he teaches the truths of the Catholic faith, he represents the bishop. Teachers in our Catholic schools, catechists in religious education programs outside of schools, they represent the bishop, who is the prime teacher, the prime governor. This is why, when a priest is ordained, he promises obedience to the bishop; the priest cannot function without the bishop. The bishop is not likely to do this, but he could, for grave cause, suspend a priest from his activities. So, at the very time of ordination, the priest promises obedience to the bishop. It's in the offering of the Sacrifice of the Mass, of course, that the priest reaches his fullness, the bishop reaches his fullness. What could one possibly do that would be comparable to taking the place of Christ in the Mass, saying over a piece of bread "This is My Body", over a cup of wine "This is My Blood"? That's really when we all come into our fullness.

Once ordained a priest, one is a priest forever. We hear of priests who have "given up their priesthood". We hear of priests who are "laicized". But just as, when you are baptized, you can never be baptized again, because there's an indelible, spiritual mark on your soul that's forever—it lasts for all eternity—the same is true with an ordained priest. Once he is ordained, he is ordained forever. Even though he may no longer act as a priest, or for very grave reason he may be forbidden to act as a priest, or he may be laicized, he may be relieved of the responsibilities of a priest, he may marry, he is still a priest.

A priest is ordained, as a bishop is ordained or consecrated, at the time that the bishop lays his hands on his head and prays a very special prayer of consecration. That's a characteristic of the ordained priesthood—we are consecrated. That characterizes your priesthood, as well, you who have been received into the Church. You are consecrated. What does that mean? You are made sacred. You are set apart for sacred things. You are set apart for God, who is sacredness itself. That's what we mean by consecration.

The *Catechism* continues:

> Deacons share in Christ's mission and grace in a special way. The sacrament of Holy Orders marks them with an *imprint* ("character") which cannot be removed and which configures them to Christ, who made himself the "deacon" or servant of all. Among other tasks, it is the task of deacons to assist the bishop and priests in the celebration of the divine mysteries, above all the Eucharist, in the distribution of Holy Communion, in assisting at and blessing marriages, in the proclamation of the Gospel and preaching, in presiding over funerals, and in dedicating themselves to the various ministries of charity [1570].

Now the *Catechism* asks and answers the question:

> Who can receive the Sacrament of Holy Orders? Only a baptized man receives sacred ordination [1577].

There is considerable argument about this, I know. Why does the Church ordain only men? We must cut through all of the other arguments that might seem to be very logical, or very practical, for example, that we might have more priests if we had women ordained, that they would bring a special sensitivity, or that women have a *right* to ordination. All of these might have their logic. All of these might seem reasonable. Why, then, what is the basic reason that the Church says that only men can be ordained priests? Because the Church believes that that is what Christ intended. Christ chose only men, the apostles chose only men. We can argue all we want, but this is what the Church believes. The Church believes this very, very strongly, very firmly. So it is not just a casual or arbitrary thing. It's not an anti-feminine thing. It's not a male chauvinist thing. This is what the Church *believes*. Who can reasonably argue that the Church should practice other than what the Church believes?

We might as well at this point, incidentally, make reference to something that you read in the newspaper this past week or heard on the radio or saw on television: that now girls can serve the altar as "altar girls". This has nothing to do with basic beliefs of the Church. Thus far we have had boys serving at the altar. Now it has been announced by the Holy See that, subject to the judgment of the individual bishop, girls can serve on the altar.

There are sensitivities about this. There are some who agree, some who disagree, some who will think that the Church is falling apart, others who will think that this is the beginning of women's ordination. Neither is the case. It's not the beginning of women's ordination. Rome has made that very clear. Nor is the Church going to fall apart. But as in everything, we must act with charity. This is the Church, this is the Body of Christ. We are supposed to love one another. So we try to do things with delicacy and sensitivity, not trampling on anyone's feelings. I said when I came here ten years ago that I am a man of the Church. If and when the Holy See speaks, then we will respond accordingly. Now the Holy See has spoken, and we will respond accordingly.

I want to read in conclusion a very beautiful thing that was said about the priesthood centuries and centuries ago by a man named St. Gregory of Nazianzus. It includes everybody here. It says:

> We must begin by purifying ourselves before purifying others; we must be instructed to be able to instruct, become light to illuminate, draw close to God to bring him close to others, be sanctified to sanctify, lead by the hand and counsel prudently. I know whose ministers we are, where we find ourselves and to where we strive. I know God's greatness and man's [our] weakness, but also his [our] potential. [Who then is the priest? He is] the defender of truth, who stands with angels, gives glory with archangels, causes sacrifices to rise to the altar on high, shares Christ's priesthood, refashions creation, restores it in God's image, recreates it for the world on high and, even greater, *is divinized* [made divine] *and divinizes* [helps others to become divine] [1589].

That's true of the entire priesthood, of you and of me. Not all of us who are your priests have served you well. You must pray for us. Not all who share in the priesthood of the baptized have served themselves well or the Church well. So we all must strive for holiness, and the one who preaches most to others, for him you must pray most, as St. Paul says, "Lest having preached to others I myself may become a castaway."

Saint Michael of the Saints
Trinitarian Mystic & Cancer Patron

FEAST CELEBRATED ON JUNE 8TH

mit me to welcome
ndividual I want to

rganization Sea Ca-
mmandant Captain
ts. It's a real aposto-
y get a great deal of
safe boating as well.
people who sacrifice
Rhonda, who is the
of the various of the
a who do this work,
a Cadets for getting

certain sadness and a
ight years ago on the
26th of April, the most disastrous nuclear accident in history, at Chernobyl; with joy because there has been formed by Doctor Matkiwsky and his
wife, formerly of the Ukraine, a wonderful organization "Children of
Chernobyl Relief Fund". They are here with us today. During these past
eight years they and others have been responsible for funneling millions of
dollars into all kinds of relief, most particularly medical relief and medical
projects. The fallout of the Chernobyl disaster will still affect almost certainly thousands upon thousands of young people, and the "Children of
Chernobyl Relief Fund" is one answer. They are supported in turn by the
Catholic Medical Mission Board, represented here today by an outstanding
Jesuit priest, Father Edward McMahon. The Catholic Medical Mission

185

Board, more than sixty-five years old, has raised millions of dollars for medical relief throughout the world. Early in May, Father McMahon will himself go to the Ukraine to assist further the victims of Chernobyl. Please pray for them. We welcome both of these groups warmly.

Finally, I know you will want to remember in this Holy Sacrifice the repose of the soul of former President Richard Nixon. One can transcend completely his particular political persuasions; these have nothing to do with the fact that this is a man who had tremendous respect for the Catholic Church. I personally know of the regard in which he held the Catholic Church, the many quiet, unknown things that he did in support of Church teaching. We pray for him, his wife, Pat, who preceded him in death, and for his two daughters. He so often suffered so much sadness. Let us pray during this Mass that he will now experience everlasting joy and peace.

Those of you who come here regularly or who read *Catholic New York* are aware that for several weeks I have been talking about events taking place at the United Nations by way of a commission preparing for an international meeting in Cairo in September on population and development. I have asked your prayers because of some truly shameful efforts to reject literally the whole concept of marriage as we know it, to export abortion, contraception, and sterilization, and to confuse the notions of population control and development. These efforts virtually ignore what every major economist says about development, in favor of trying to do nothing but reduce the numbers of people in the world through capricious and artificial means. I have said that I consider this one of the most important conferences that could be imagined; it could affect literally the fate of the world.

There has been a delegation from the Holy See participating in these important meetings at the United Nations. One of the members of that delegation, who has been one of the chief negotiators, is concelebrating this Mass with us, Father Martin of the Pontifical Council on International Justice and Peace. Father Martin has been carrying out what is clearly the will of our Holy Father himself and has done so valiantly, working tirelessly all through the night against great odds but not infrequently treated with contempt. I am personally grateful to Father Martin. I think that all human beings, of every race, and nation, and religious persuasion should be grateful to him. I would be grateful if Father Martin would stand so you might thank him. You will be happy to know that through your prayers and other efforts he has finally achieved some success. We shall see and continue to pray for what happens in Cairo.

* * *

Today's Gospel is almost the perfect Gospel for this *Catechism* session on the sacrament of Matrimony (Jn 10:11–18). It is one of almost everyone's favorite Gospels, when our Lord reminds us that He is the Good Shepherd who lays down His life for His sheep. Perhaps we never thought of marriage in those terms, but when a man says, "I, Joseph, take you, Mary, for my lawful wife to have and to hold from this day forward for better, for worse, for richer, for poorer, in sickness and in health, until death do us part", and she says the same to him, they are laying down their lives for each other. They truly become tender, gentle, loving shepherds to each other.

Our Lord goes on:

> "The hired hand, who is no shepherd nor owner of the sheep, catches sight of the wolf coming and runs away, leaving the sheep to be snatched and scattered by the wolf."

The hired hand has no concern for the sheep. When I reflected on this, I couldn't but think of promiscuity outside a marriage, or those who get married only for their own selfish ends. I couldn't but think of men who get women pregnant and encourage them to have abortions or abandon them with their babies. Our Lord goes on:

> "I am the good shepherd. I know my sheep and my sheep know me in the same way that the Father knows me and I know the Father."

Our Lord is using the term "know" in the Hebrew sense of the term. It doesn't mean simply intellectual knowledge, it means personal intimacy, complete unity, total communion with another party, as a husband knows his wife, a wife knows her husband. Finally, our Lord says:

> "The Father loves me for this: that I lay down my life to take it up again. No one takes it from me; I lay it down freely."

Isn't this what each party does by entering into marriage? "I lay down my life for you unconditionally", says each to the other. "No one is forcing me; this is purely voluntary. I do it for the same reason that Jesus laid down His life—I do it out of love."

We turn now to the text of the *Catechism*.

> Sacred Scripture begins with the creation of man and woman in the image and likeness of God and concludes with a vision of "the wedding-feast of the Lamb" (Rev 19:7–9) [1602].

> The vocation to marriage is written in the very nature of man and woman as they came from the hand of the Creator. Marriage is not a purely human institution despite the many variations it may have undergone through the centuries in different cultures, social structures, and spiritual attitudes. These differences should not cause us to forget its common and permanent characteristics. Although the dignity of this institution is not transparent everywhere with the same clarity, some sense of the greatness of the matrimonial union exists in all cultures [1603].

We keep learning, we keep growing spiritually. Everything changed, for example, with the coming of Christ, and marriage became a sacrament. But the very nature of the human person has always been directed toward the concept of marriage. It has always been clear to all people everywhere; it's been very basic.

> Holy Scripture affirms that man and woman were created for one another: "It is not good that the man should be alone" (Gen 1:18]. The woman, "flesh of his flesh," i.e., his counterpart, his equal, his nearest in all things, is given to him by God as a "helpmate"; she thus represents God from whom comes our help. "Therefore a man leaves his father and his mother and cleaves to his wife, and they become one flesh" (Gen 2:24). The Lord himself shows that this signifies an unbreakable union of their two lives by recalling what the plan of the Creator had been "in the beginning": "So they are no longer two, but one flesh" [1605].

This is what the Holy See has been trying desperately to uphold at the recent United Nations planning sessions for the Cairo Conference on Population and Development, scheduled for September. The very nature of man and woman, the very nature of marriage and the family is at stake.

> Every man experiences evil around him and within himself. This experience makes itself felt in the relationship between man and woman. Their union has always been threatened by discord . . . that can escalate into hatred and separation [1606].

> . . . [T]he disorder . . . does not stem from the *nature* of man and woman, nor from the nature of [marriage] relations, but from *sin*. . . . [T]he first sin had for its first consequence the rupture of the original communion between man and woman. Their relationships were distorted by mutual recriminations; their mutual attraction, the Creator's own gift, changed into a relationship of domination and lust; and the beautiful vocation of man and woman to be fruitful, multiply, and subdue the earth was burdened by the pain of childbirth and the toil of work [1607].

What happened after original sin? We are told in Genesis, the first book of the Scriptures, that God came looking for Adam and Eve but they were hiding themselves. They were now ashamed; they had discovered that they were naked, because of original sin. Until now they lived purely, freely, and naturally. God asked Adam, "Why did you do this?" What does Adam say? What a shameful thing for Adam to do. He said, "The woman made me do this." The immediate result of the first sin of the first human beings was a rupture in the marriage relationship. That's something to think about. Then Adam and Eve have children, and one kills the other—Cain kills Abel.

The *Catechism* says:

On the threshold of his public life Jesus performs his first sign—at his mother's request—during a wedding feast. The Church attaches great importance to Jesus' presence at the wedding at Cana. She sees in it the confirmation of the goodness of marriage and the proclamation that thenceforth marriage will be an efficacious sign of Christ's presence [1613].

In his preaching Jesus unequivocally taught the original meaning of the union of man and woman as the Creator willed it from the beginning [1614].

It is by following Christ, renouncing themselves, and taking up their crosses that spouses will be able to "receive" the original meaning of marriage and live it with the help of Christ. [Does that sound foolish today, that to get married, however much love there is, means that we are taking up a cross, following Christ?] This grace of Christian marriage is a fruit of Christ's cross, the source of all Christian life [1615].

The entire Christian life bears the mark of the spousal love of Christ and the Church [1617].

The *Catechism* talks about virginity for the sake of the kingdom.

From the very beginning of the Church there have been men and women who have renounced the great good of marriage to follow the Lamb wherever he goes, to be intent on the things of the Lord. . . . Christ himself has invited certain persons to follow him in this way of life, of which he remains the model [1618].

Now the celebration of marriage. The *Catechism* says:

In the Latin Rite the celebration of marriage between two Catholic faithful normally takes place during Holy Mass. . . . It is . . . fitting that the spouses should seal their consent to give themselves to each other through the offering of their own lives by uniting it to the offering of Christ for his Church made present in the Eucharistic sacrifice, and by receiving the Eucharist so that, communicating in the same Body and the same Blood of Christ, they may form but "one body" in Christ [1621].

It is therefore appropriate for the bride and groom to prepare themselves for the celebration of their marriage by receiving the sacrament of penance [1622]. [I'm not sure that's always remembered today. It used to be the case that a couple would never dream of getting married without receiving the sacrament of Penance.]

In the Latin Church, it is ordinarily understood that the spouses, as ministers of Christ's grace, mutually confer upon each other the sacrament of Matrimony by expressing their consent before the Church [1623].

This is an important point. Most of the other sacraments are administered by the priest or by the bishop, but we say that it is the man who administers the sacrament of Matrimony to the woman, the woman to the man, so they are channels, instruments of grace, to each other. The *Catechism* continues:

> The parties to a marriage covenant are a baptized man and woman, free to contract marriage, who freely express their consent. "To be free" means:
> —not being under constraint;
> —not impeded by any natural or [Church] law [1625].

> The Church holds the exchange of consent between the spouses to be the indispensable element that "makes the marriage." If consent is lacking there is no marriage [1626].

> The consent consists in a "human act by which the partners mutually give themselves to each other": "I take you to be my wife"—"I take you to be my husband." This consent that binds the spouses to each other finds its fulfillment in the two "becoming one flesh" (Gen 2:24) [1627].

We speak of the consummation of marriage; until this occurs the marriage is not yet complete.

> The consent must be an act of the will of each of the contracting parties, free of coercion or grave external fear. . . . If this freedom is lacking [in any way] the marriage is invalid [1628].

Let us turn now to a matter that many people do not understand. Some talk of "divorce" in the Church. No such thing exists. The *Catechism* reminds us that all the Church can do is declare after investigation that a particular marriage, which might seem to the whole world to be a true marriage in every way, was not so from the very beginning, and the Church then declares the marriage null and void from the beginning. If a marriage took place under fear or under coercion, it would not be a valid marriage. The *Catechism* says:

> For this reason (or for other reasons that render the marriage null and void) the Church, after an examination of the situation by the competent [Church] tribunal, can declare the nullity of a marriage, i.e., that the marriage never existed. In this case the contracting parties are free to marry, provided the natural obligations of a previous union are discharged [1629].

> The presence of the Church's minister (and also of the witnesses) visibly expresses the fact that marriage is [a Church] reality [1630].

> This is the reason why the Church normally requires that the faithful contract marriage according to the *ecclesiastical form* [1631].

> So that the "I do" of the spouses may be a free and responsible act, and so that the marriage covenant may have solid and lasting human and Christian foundations, *preparation for marriage* is of prime importance [1632].

If I am to perform a wedding, I spend many months of pre-marital discussions with the engaged couple. I find such sessions absolutely imperative. They make a tremendous difference.

The *Catechism* states:

> In many countries the situation of a *mixed marriage* (marriage between a Catholic and a baptized non-Catholic) often arises. It requires particular attention on the part of couples and their pastors. A case of marriage with *disparity of cult* (between a Catholic and a non-baptized person) requires even greater circumspection [1633].

> Difference of confession between spouses does not constitute an insurmountable obstacle for marriage . . . But the difficulties of mixed marriages must not be underestimated. They arise from the fact that the separation of Christians has not yet been overcome. . . . Disparity of cult can further aggravate these difficulties [1634].

> From a valid marriage arises *a bond* between the spouses which by its very nature is perpetual and exclusive; . . . in a Christian marriage the spouses are strengthened and . . . consecrated for the duties and the dignity of their state *by a special sacrament* [which we call Matrimony] [1638].

> The consent by which the spouses mutually give and receive one another is sealed by God himself [1639].

> Thus . . . a marriage concluded and consummated between baptized persons [in a proper way] can never be dissolved [1640. [Regardless of what you hear about easy divorces, or if you have enough money, or that kind of thing—if it is in every sense a true marriage, the Church can't undo it; it's binding by God.]

> Christ dwells with [Christian spouses], gives them the strength to take up their crosses and to follow him, to rise again after they have fallen, to forgive one another, to bear one another's burdens, to "be subject to one another out of reverence for Christ" (Eph 5:21), and to love one another with supernatural, tender, and fruitful love [1642].

> Conjugal love . . . aims at a deeply personal unity, a unity that, beyond union in one flesh, leads to forming one heart and soul; it demands *indissolubility* and *faithfulness* . . . and it has to be open to *fertility* [1643]. [It has to be open to children if God gives children. It doesn't mean that a couple *must* have all of the children physically possible, but it does mean they must be *open* to children.]

> By its very nature conjugal love requires the inviolable fidelity of the spouses. This is the consequence of the gift of themselves which they make to each other. Love seeks to be definitive; it cannot be an arrangement "until further notice." [This is why the Church will have nothing of this busi-

ness of couples living with each other to "try it out", as it were. Marriage is a definitive thing. It's a mutual self-giving.] The "intimate union of marriage . . . demands total fidelity from the spouses and requires an unbreakable union between them" [1646].

The deepest reason is found in the fidelity of God to his covenant and the union between Christ and his Church. Through the sacrament of Matrimony the spouses are enabled to represent this fidelity and witness to it. Through the sacrament, the indissolubility of marriage received a new and deeper meaning [1647].

Yet there are some situations in which living together becomes practically impossible for a variety of reasons. In such cases the Church permits the physical separation of the couple and their living apart. The spouses do not cease to be husband and wife before God and so are not free to contract a new union. In this difficult situation, the best solution would be, if possible, reconciliation. The Christian community is called to help these persons live out their situation in a Christian manner and in fidelity to their marriage bond which remains indissoluble [1649].

In fidelity to the words of Jesus Christ—"Whoever divorces his wife and marries another, commits adultery against her; and if she divorces her husband and marries another, she commits adultery" (Mk 10:11–12)—the Church maintains that a new union cannot be recognized as valid, if the first marriage was [1650]. [If the first marriage is declared null and void, then the parties are free to marry.]

Recently it was suggested by some rather prestigious theologians that there was a solution, by way of what is called the "Internal Forum", whereby a couple could live together as husband and wife, engaging in marriage relations as though their marriage were valid, and that all they would have to do was to present this to the priest in confession, and that he could permit them to follow their own consciences. The Church's teaching is very clear about this.

The *Catechism* states:

> If the divorced are remarried civilly . . . they cannot receive Eucharistic communion as long as this situation persists. For the same reason, they cannot exercise certain Church responsibilities. Reconciliation [now, I know there are some very prestigious theologians who say the contrary, but this is what the Church teaches] through the sacrament of Penance can be granted only to those who have repented for having violated the sign of the covenant and of fidelity to Christ, and who are committed to living in complete continence [1650].

In other words, a husband and wife who are only civilly married must live as brother and sister. This is not a condemnation of people. The Church knows how difficult this is, and therefore it says:

Toward Christians who live in this situation, and who often keep the faith and desire to bring up their children in a Christian manner, priests and the whole community must manifest an attentive solicitude, so that they do not consider themselves separated from the Church, in whose life they can and must participate as baptized persons:

"They should be encouraged to listen to the Word of God, to attend the Sacrifice of the Mass, to persevere in prayer, to contribute to works of charity and to community efforts for justice, to bring up their children in the Christian faith, to cultivate the spirit and practice of penance and thus implore, day by day, God's grace" [1651].

They are all welcome. There may be some here who are not validly married but living together. You are not only welcome, but you are urged to be part of this community. You are baptized into the Body of Christ. We must all pray together to support you. But you cannot simply go to confession and then be told it's perfectly all right for you to live truly as husband and wife and receive Holy Communion.

The *Catechism* goes on to talk about the family that results from marriage.

"By its very nature the institution of marriage and married love is ordered to the procreation and education of the offspring and it is in them that it finds its crowning glory."

Children are the supreme gift of marriage and contribute greatly to the good of the parents themselves. God himself said: "It is not good that man should be alone," and "from the beginning [he] made them male and female"; wishing to associate them in a special way in his own creative work, God blessed man and woman with the words: "Be fruitful and multiply." Hence, true married love and the whole structure of family life which results from it, without diminishment of the other ends of marriage, are directed to disposing the spouses to cooperate valiantly with the love of the Creator and Savior, who through them will increase and enrich his family from day to day [1652].

This is of the very nature of marriage. This is of the purpose of marriage, not only to bring children into the world but to take care of them, to educate them, to nurture them. And as the *Catechism* says:

The fruitfulness of conjugal love extends to the fruits of the moral, spiritual, and supernatural life that parents hand on to their children by education. Parents are the principal and first educators of their children. In this sense the fundamental task of marriage and family is to be at the service of life [1653].

Spouses to whom God has not granted children can nevertheless have a conjugal life full of meaning, in both human and Christian terms. Their marriage can radiate a fruitfulness of charity, of hospitality, and of sacrifice [1654].

Finally, we are told in the *Catechism*:

Christ chose to be born and grow up in the bosom of the holy family of Joseph and Mary. The Church is nothing other than "the family of God" [1655].

In our own time, in a world often alien and even hostile to faith, believing families are of primary importance as centers of living, radiant faith [1656].

Someday the whole world that will be affected by the Cairo Conference will be grateful to the Church and to those various countries that have joined the Church in insisting on this: that the world must not be alien and hostile to the family; rather it must recognize the necessity and integrity of the family and do all it can to support the family.

The *Catechism* states:

It is here that the father of the family, the mother, children, and all members of the family exercise the *priesthood of the baptized* in a privileged way "by the reception of the sacraments, prayer and thanksgiving, the witness of a holy life, and self-denial and active charity." Thus the home is the first school of Christian life and "a school for human enrichment" [1657].

23

True Love of Neighbor

FIFTH SUNDAY OF EASTER
CELEBRATION OF THE LIFE OF PIERRE TOUSSAINT
MAY 1, 1994
PONTIFICAL MASS

A very special welcome to those who are here for our annual Mass in honor of Pierre Toussaint. A number of priests are with us today who are involved in the cause of Pierre Toussaint's potential canonization.

May I say but a word about our Holy Father, because there has been so much speculation in the media. This past Tuesday evening, my associate, Monsignor McCarthy, and I had a wonderful supper with the Holy Father. He was in great spirits, the picture of health. I met with him again on Thursday, and I have never seen him looking healthier. Early Friday morning, he slipped and fell in the bathtub, a perfectly legitimate place to slip and fall, and he went to the hospital. I understand that he has a broken hip, which is being replaced, and he should be up and about within a few weeks. I personally saw no evidence for speculation that he got dizzy and fell over, he had a stroke, or anything of that sort at all. I wish that I were in the health that he's in, broken hip and all.

* * *

I'm grateful to Father Lamont Hamilton and all of the others of the Office of Black Ministry for arranging for this day. Each year I look at this congregation on this day with a mixture of great gladness and deep sadness—gladness that I see such a mix of people, of several colors and races and backgrounds, and sadness that I don't see this in this cathedral much more frequently. This cathedral is always filled on Sundays and on many other occasions, but the fact that there is a mix of this sort only on exceptional occasions suggests to me that after two thousand years of Christianity and of Catholicism, we are still separated, and we have to admit it. We are still segregated from one another, voluntarily or involuntarily, perhaps for economic or social reasons, prejudice, whatever. Our Divine Lord so longed that we would recognize that we are one body in

Him, with one Father, with no distinctions among us at all. It is so sad to note how deep prejudices still run. It is our responsibility to bring about that unity for which Christ longs.

Today I have a piece of exceptionally good news for all who are interested in the cause of canonization of Pierre Toussaint, whose remains lie beneath the high altar here in St. Patrick's Cathedral. While I was in Rome, I received a call from the Congregation for the Saints, and they told me that the history of Pierre Toussaint has been accepted and given high grades. That means that one of the major obstacles to potential canonization has now been overcome. They are quite satisfied with the account that is given of the life and the death of Pierre Toussaint.

We are going to be talking about Pierre Toussaint today, intermingling what we have to say about him with our instruction on the new *Catechism of the Catholic Church*. Some of you here, I know, have never heard of Pierre Toussaint. He was born in 1766, a slave in Haiti; he died in 1853, a free man here in New York. He came with his so-called "masters", the Berards, to New York, and here he became famous in his own day for his exceptional goodness to the poor and the sick. He himself was often treated with contempt. He died here in great sanctity, and his cause has been introduced for canonization.

Today we reach ahead in the *Catechism* to address a section very special in terms of Pierre Toussaint. The section is called "The Human Community".

First, let us look at today's Scriptures. We are told in the first reading:

> When Saul arrived back in Jerusalem he tried to join the disciples there; but it turned out that they were all afraid of him . . . (Acts 9:26).

To a degree, this was the treatment received by Pierre Toussaint here in New York. Every day for sixty years this man walked a long distance to Mass—in rain, shine, heat, and cold. Wealthy, white Catholics would pass by him in their carriages and would not pick him up, because he was black. They didn't consider him one of them, even though he was a Catholic. The Church he attended almost burned down. Largely through funds that he raised and gave, it was rebuilt. Then when he went with some friends for the great celebration of the renewal of the church, he had to sit in the back because he was black.

I return to the first reading:

> When Saul arrived back in Jerusalem . . . [t]hey even refused to believe that he was a disciple. Then Barnabas took him in charge and introduced him to the apostles. He explained to them how on his journey Saul had seen the Lord, who had conversed with him, and how Saul had been speaking out fearlessly in the name of Jesus at Damascus (Acts 9:26–31).

This was certainly true of Pierre Toussaint. No one spoke more coura-geously about Jesus than did he.

In the second reading, from the first letter of John, we are told:

His commandment is this:
we are to believe in the name of his Son, Jesus Christ,
and are to love one another as he commanded us (1 Jn 3:18–24).

This is the heart of it all. "Behold these Christians, how they love one another." That was a reason for the great conversions in the early centu-ries. "Greater love than this no one has than to lay down one's life for one's friend." This is what Pierre Toussaint did every day.

The section of the *Catechism* on "The Human Community" begins:

The vocation of humanity is to show forth the image of God and to be transformed into the image of the Father's only Son [1877].

The reason we are here is to come to know, to love, to serve God, and to be happy with Him forever in heaven. We are here to show God's im-age within us to all and to try to achieve the fullness of that image. That's what Pierre did. He saw God's image in everyone, of whatever color, whatever station in life.

In the words of the *Catechism*:

All . . . are called to the same end: God himself. There is a certain resem-blance between the union of the divine persons and the fraternity that men are to establish among themselves in truth and love. Love of neighbor is in-separable from love of God [1878].

The human person needs to live in society. Society is . . . a requirement of his nature. Through the exchange with others, mutual service and dialogue with his brethren, man develops his potential; he thus responds to his voca-tion [1879].

That's what it *should* be, that we are all helping one another to become everything that God created us to be.

The *Catechism* continues:

A *society* is a group of persons bound together organically by a principle of unity that goes beyond each of them. . . . By means of society, each man is established as an "heir" and receives certain "talents" that enrich his identity and whose fruits he must develop. He rightly owes loyalty to the communi-ties of which he is part and respect to those in authority who have charge of the common good [1880].

We are all heirs to everything that the human race has done, good and bad. Everything that we have received we have received from our forebears and from Almighty God. It is all ours, or *should* be, but many are precluded from exercising their rights to these gifts.

The *Catechism* states:

> Each community is defined by its purpose and consequently obeys specific rules; but "the *human person* . . . is and ought to be the principle, the subject and the end of all social institutions" [1881].

That's the heart of it: the human person comes first. Our Holy Father never tires of speaking of this. In his first and most basic encyclical, *The Redeemer of Man*, he says the human person is the way for the Church to follow, for the world to follow, and not vice versa. That, too, is what Pierre Toussaint recognized.

The *Catechism* continues:

> . . . "*socialization*" . . . expresses the natural tendency for human beings to associate with one another for the sake of attaining objectives that exceed individual capacities. It develops the qualities of the person, especially the sense of initiative and responsibility, and helps guarantee his rights [1882].

> Socialization also presents dangers. Excessive intervention by the state can threaten personal freedom and initiative [1883].

> God has not willed to reserve to himself all exercise of power. He entrusts to every creature the functions it is capable of performing, according to the capacities of its own nature. . . . The way God acts in governing the world, which bears witness to such great regard for human freedom, should inspire the wisdom of those who govern human communities. They should behave as ministers of divine providence [1884].

> Society is essential to the fulfillment of the human vocation. To attain this aim, respect must be accorded to the just hierarchy of values, which "subordinates physical and instinctual dimensions to interior and spiritual ones" [1886].

> The inversion of means and ends, which results in giving the value of ultimate end to what is only a means for attaining it, or in viewing persons as mere means to that end, engenders unjust structures which "make Christian conduct in keeping with the commandments of the divine Law-giver difficult and almost impossible" [1887].

> It is necessary, then, to appeal to the spiritual and moral capacities of the human person and to the permanent need for his *inner conversion*, so as to obtain social changes that will really serve him. The . . . priority of the conversion of the heart in no way eliminates but on the contrary imposes the obligation of bringing the appropriate remedies to institutions and living conditions when they are an inducement to sin, so that they conform to the norms of justice and advance the good rather than hinder it [1888].

Without the help of grace, men would not know how "to discern the often narrow path between the cowardice which gives in to evil, and the violence which under the illusion of fighting evil only makes it worse." . . . Charity is the greatest social commandment. It respects others and their rights. It requires the practice of justice, and it alone makes us capable of it. Charity inspires a life of self-giving . . . [1889].

It is so easy to wash our hands of evil. We do this, for example, by saying things like, "I am personally opposed to abortion, but I will not impose my moral principles on others." Or, "I'm personally opposed to racism, anti-Semitism, but I will not impose my beliefs on others." It is equally easy to think that the answer to overturning the existing structures is in violence. They tried to get Pierre Toussaint to do that, to join in a violent revolution. He said, in essence, "If you had seen what I have seen in Haiti, you wouldn't dream of doing that."

The *Catechism* goes on:

The authority required by the moral order derives from God: "Let every person be subject to the governing authorities. For there is no authority except from God, and those that exist have been instituted by God. Therefore he who resists the authorities resists what God has appointed, and those who resist will incur judgment" [1899].

The duty of obedience requires all to give due honor to authority, and to treat those who are charged to exercise it with respect, and, insofar as it is deserved, with gratitude and good-will [1900].

Authority does not derive its moral legitimacy from itself. It must not behave in a despotic manner, but must act for the common good as a "moral force based on freedom and a sense of responsibility":
    "A human law has the character of law to the extent that it accords with right reason, and thus derives from the eternal law. Insofar as it falls short of right reason it is said to be an unjust law, and thus has not so much the nature of law as of a kind of violence" (St. Thomas Aquinas) [1902].

Pierre Toussaint would say, "Yes, I'm a slave. Yes, I know I could have my external freedom, my 'owner' has offered it to me. But interiorly I am no slave; interiorly I am totally free."

Authority is exercised legitimately only when it seeks the common good of the group concerned and if it employs morally licit means to attain it. If rulers were to enact unjust laws or take measures contrary to the moral order, such arrangements would not be binding in conscience [1903].

I cannot, for example, accept authority that engages in creating illicit legislation, legislation that, on the face of it, is exploitative of others. How can we accept the authority that funds abortions? How could we accept the authority that supported slavery? It is illicit legislation that brings such things about.

The *Catechism* continues:

> In keeping with the social nature of man, the good of each individual is necessarily related to the common good, which in turn can be defined only in reference to the human person [1905].

> By common good is to be understood "the sum total of social conditions which allow people, either as groups or as individuals, to reach their fulfillment more fully and more easily." . . . It consists of *three essential elements*:
>
> First, the common good presupposes *respect for the person* as such. In particular, the common good resides in the conditions for the exercise of the natural freedoms indispensable for the development of human vocation, such as "the right to act according to a sound norm of conscience and to safeguard . . . privacy, and rightful freedom also in matters of religion" [1907].

When I first came to New York as Archbishop ten years ago, I was asked, "What do you think is the *real* problem in this city?" My answer was always the same, "I observed tremendous contempt for the human person." This contempt is beneath our problems of violence, drugs, hatred, racism, anti-Semitism, contempt for the human person, the failure to recognize that every human person is sacred, made in the image and likeness of Almighty God.

> Second, the common good requires the *social well-being* and *development* of the group itself. Development is the epitome of all social duties. Certainly, it is the proper function of authority to arbitrate, in the name of the common good, between various particular interests; but it should make accessible to each what is needed to lead a truly human life: food, clothing, health, work, education and culture, suitable information, the right to establish a family, and so on [1908].

It is because this concept of *development* is critical that I have been talking so frequently about the recent United Nations planning sessions for the upcoming Cairo Conference on Population and Development. During these planning sessions, most of the talk was about controlling population; very little was said about development. It is absolutely obligatory to provide everyone the help necessary for development as a person.

> Finally, the common good requires *peace*, that is, the stability and security of a just order. It presupposes that authority should ensure by morally acceptable means the *security* of society and its members. It is the basis of the right to legitimate personal and collective defence [1909].

We all have a responsibility to keep the peace, even if we have to suffer to do so.

I return to the *Catechism*.

> . . . [I]t is in the *political community* that [the common good's] most complete realization is found. It is the role of the state to defend and promote the common good of civil society, its citizens, and intermediate bodies [1910].

> The common good is always oriented towards the progress of persons. "The order of things must be subordinate to the order of persons, and not the other way around." This order is founded on truth, built up in justice, and animated by love [1912].

Pierre Toussaint recognized this. No matter what was happening around him, he gave himself to the human person. When there was a terrible plague that was virtually decimating New York, many people were running away. Pierre went to the people afflicted with the plague to treat them with his own hands. He taught those who were ignorant reading, writing, and music. He was a very intelligent man but also a very *giving* man.

The *Catechism* continues by talking about "Responsibility and Participation".

> "Participation" is the voluntary and generous engagement of a person in social interchange. . . . This obligation is inherent in the dignity of the human person [1913].

> Participation is achieved first of all by taking charge of the areas for which one assumes *personal responsibility*: by the care taken for the education of his family, by conscientious work, and so forth, man participates in the good of others and society [1914].

All colors, all races must participate together. We cannot abdicate. We cannot simply blame others for our problems. We have to take personal responsibility. The *Catechism* reminds us:

> As with any ethical obligation, the participation of all in realizing the common good calls for a continually renewed conversion of the social partners. . . . Much care should be taken to promote institutions that improve the conditions of human life [1916].

> It is incumbent on those who exercise authority to strengthen the values that inspire the confidence of the members of the group and encourage them to put themselves at the service of others [1917].

Sometimes we elect people, or people are appointed, who seem intent on destroying family values, for example. What good does that do for society? It is the obligation of elected and appointed authority to *enhance* the values of society.

> Society ensures social justice when it provides the conditions that allow associations or individuals to obtain what is their due, according to their nature and their vocation [1928].

Lots of things that are thought of as "welfare" now are *owed* to people: opportunity for a decent living, opportunity for decent housing, opportunity for decent food, for decent health care. These shouldn't be considered welfare. These are owed by the very fact that we enjoy the dignity of being human persons.

> Social justice can be obtained only in respecting the transcendent dignity of man. The person represents the ultimate end of society, which is ordered to him:
> "What is at stake is the dignity of the human person, whose defense and promotion have been entrusted to us by the Creator, and to whom the men and women at every moment of history are strictly and responsibly in debt" (John Paul II) [1929].

> Respect for the human person entails respect for the rights that flow from his dignity as a creature. These rights are prior to society and must be recognized by it. They are the basis of the moral legitimacy of every authority: by flouting them, or refusing to recognize them in its positive legislation, a society undermines its own moral legitimacy. If it does not respect them, authority can rely only on force or violence to obtain obedience from its subjects. It is the Church's role to remind men of good will of these rights, and to distinguish them from unwarranted or false claims [1930].

> Respect for the human person proceeds by way of respect for the principle that "everyone should look upon his neighbor (without any exception) as 'another self,' above all bearing in mind his life and the means necessary for living it with dignity" [1931].

Do we look at one another that way? Let's be honest. Why do we have racism, anti-Semitism? Does a white person look at a black person and say, "There is an inferior"? Does a black person look at a white person and say, "There is someone who is no good just because he or she is white"? The *Catechism*, the formal, official teaching of the Catholic Church, tells us that's wrong.

> No legislation could by itself do away with the fears, prejudices, and attitudes of pride and selfishness which obstruct the establishment of truly fraternal societies. Such behavior will cease only through the charity that finds in every man a "neighbor," a brother [1931].

At the same time, we do need appropriate legislation. The *Catechism* reminds us:

The duty of making oneself a neighbor to others and actively serving them becomes even more urgent when it involves the disadvantaged, in whatever area this may be. "As you did it to one of the least of these my brethren, you did it to me" (Mt 25:40) [1932].

Created in the image of the one God and equally endowed with rational souls, all men have the same nature and the same origin. Redeemed by the sacrifice of Christ, all are called to participate in the same divine beatitude: all therefore enjoy an equal dignity [1934].

Every form of social or cultural discrimination in fundamental personal rights on the grounds of sex, race, color, social conditions, language, or religion must be curbed and eradicated as incompatible with God's design [1935].

On coming into the world, man is not equipped with everything he needs for developing his bodily and spiritual life. He needs others. Differences appear tied to age, physical abilities, intellectual or moral aptitudes, the benefits derived from social commerce, and the distribution of wealth. The "talents" are not distributed equally [1936].

This is why we have our inner-city schools. They are terribly difficult to maintain. We've tried to resist closing the doors of those schools. Eighty-five percent of the youngsters in our Catholic, inner-city schools are black or Hispanic.

There exist also *sinful inequalities* that affect millions of men and women. These are in open contradiction of the Gospel:
"Their equal dignity as persons demands that we strive for fairer and more humane conditions. Excessive economic and social disparity between individuals and peoples of the one human race is a source of scandal and militates against social justice, equity, human dignity, as well as social and international peace" [1938].

The principle of solidarity, also articulated in terms of "friendship" or "social charity," is a direct demand of human and Christian brotherhood [1939].

Solidarity is manifested in the first place by the distribution of goods and remuneration for work. It also presupposes the effort for a more just social order where tensions are better able to be reduced and conflicts more readily settled by negotiation [1940].

Socio-economic problems can be resolved only with the help of all the forms of solidarity: solidarity of the poor among themselves, between rich and poor, of workers among themselves, between employers and employees in a business, solidarity among nations and peoples. International solidarity is a requirement of the moral order; world peace depends in part upon this [1941].

The *Catechism* teaches that black against black, white against white, white against black, black against brown, whatever it may be, it is all wrong. Regardless of what the past has been. Finally, we are reminded:

> The virtue of solidarity goes beyond material goods. In spreading the spiritual goods of the faith, the Church has promoted, and often opened new paths for, the development of temporal goods as well. And so throughout the centuries has the Lord's saying been verified: "Seek first his kingdom and his righteousness, and all these things shall be yours as well" (Mt 6:33) [1942].

I suggest to everyone here—white, black, Asian, whoever may be here today—that this was the life of Pierre Toussaint, a black man formerly a slave. "Seek first the kingdom of God and his righteousness, and all these things shall be yours as well." That is why we have his remains under the high altar with the former bishops of this diocese. And that is why, please God, the day will come soon that our Holy Father will declare before all the world, "this black slave was truly and is now a saint of God".

24

What Will Make Us Truly Happy?

SIXTH SUNDAY OF EASTER
MOTHER'S DAY
MAY 8, 1994
PONTIFICAL MASS

This morning I spoke with Vina Drennan, the extraordinarily courageous wife of Captain John Drennan, one of three firemen who died as the result of that devastating fire in which they were suddenly and without warning burned so horribly. All three firemen were Catholic. Captain Drennan will be buried on Wednesday from this cathedral.

Mrs. Drennan is not Catholic. She expressed great respect toward our faith, especially about the Holy Sacrifice of the Mass. She expressed her great love of the Mass, the comfort that she receives from it. She is very gratified for that reason that the Mass will be here in St. Patrick's Cathedral, where so many people will be able to attend. Mrs. Drennan asked me to thank all of you. She said that the people of New York have been utterly fantastic in the support they have expressed all through this lonely period when her husband was suffering so horribly. She said that the prayers of the entire city of New York have been extraordinary, and she is very grateful.

Because it is Mother's Day, I want to transmit the contents of a letter that I received yesterday.

Your Eminence,
I ask you this favor with all my heart.
Please announce baby Nicole Ficarra in all your Masses.
On Friday, April 22, a car ran a red light and struck the door of the car Nicole was in, right where she was sleeping.
Nicole is a sweet three-year-old baby. She is paralyzed from the neck down. The doctors . . . tell her parents, Roseann and Paul, that Nicole has only a one percent chance of recovering from her injuries.
Nicole is conscious but unable to talk.
Her mother says Nicole looks at her with tears rolling down her cheeks. We are praying for Nicole but we need your help for a miracle.
I ask you in the name of the Lord Jesus to pray and announce her name in your Masses.

... Knowing your prayers and Masses will be for Nicole, she will get well. I know Jesus will hear. To help the pain and suffering her parents are going through right now, if you could let them know baby Nicole is in your prayers, this would help them get through this.

This very lovely lady who wrote this letter signs her name, and I will write to Nicole's parents and try to talk with them. I am sure you would want me to assure them that you are praying for them and for their baby, Nicole Ficarra.

This is not a very happy Mother's Day letter, and yet it's essential to the nature of motherhood—this kind of worrying, this kind of sacrifice. This is the essence of what our Divine Lord was talking about when He said something that sounded perhaps very cruel. You remember the scene. Our Lord was in a house working a miracle and someone came in and said, "Your mother is outside waiting to see You." Our Lord said, "My mother! Who is my mother? Those who do the will of My Father in heaven, they are My mother." Mary would not have been hurt by this; she would have understood. That's what she was all about. That's what motherhood is all about: to do the will of Almighty God and to transmit this to children.

This concept is repeated in another form in today's Gospel.

"As the Father has loved me, so I have loved you. Live on in my love. You will live in my love if you keep my commandments, even as I have kept my Father's commandments, and live in his love" (Jn 15:9–10].

This leads us into today's *Catechism* session. The title of this particular section of the *Catechism* is "Life in Christ". It concerns itself with carrying out the will of Almighty God when it is relatively easy and when it is difficult and explains how our lives can be models of the life of Christ. The *Catechism* begins:

... Christians are called to lead . . . a life "worthy of the gospel of Christ" (Phil 1:27). They are made capable of doing so by the grace of Christ and the gifts of his Spirit, which they receive through the sacraments and through prayer [1692].

Following Christ and united with him, Christians can strive to be "imitators of God as beloved children, and walk in love" (Eph 5:1–2) by conforming their thoughts, words, and actions to the "mind . . . which is yours in Christ Jesus" (Phil 2:5), and by following his example [1694].

... Christians have become the temple of the Holy Spirit. . . . Healing the wounds of sin, the Holy Spirit renews us interiorly through a spiritual transformation . . . [1695].

It is a wonderful thing to think about, that women who have conceived children have conceived lives within that same temple, the temple of the Holy Spirit.

The *Catechism* states:

The way of Christ "leads to life"; a contrary way "leads to destruction" (Mt 7:13) [1696].

I don't know if you saw the front page of the *New York Times* this morning. There is a poignant, bitter story about the incredible rapidity with which the use of heroin is growing once again. It describes a wealthy, young individual in a kind of a hole-in-the-wall in San Francisco, waiting for someone to come to whom he gives a hundred dollars in return for some heroin. The article says that the place is always packed with affluent-looking people. Trying to relieve what? Their loneliness? Their sorrow? The *Catechism* reminds us that the way of *Christ* leads to life.

The *Catechism* continues:

The dignity of the human person is rooted in his creation in the image and likeness of God . . . [1700].

How distorted that creation can become through sin, drugs, drunkenness, and promiscuity! The *Catechism* continues:

It is in Christ, "the image of the invisible God" (Col 1:15), that man has been created "in the image and likeness" of the Creator. It is in Christ, Redeemer and Savior, that the divine image, disfigured in man by the first sin, has been restored to its original beauty and ennobled by the grace of God [1701].

We were fashioned after Christ, and Christ is perfect. We were disfigured through original sin and our own sins, and then Christ came and permitted Himself to be disfigured, in order that we might be restored to His image.

The *Catechism* tells us:

Endowed with "a spiritual and immortal" soul, the human person is "the only creature on earth that God has willed for its own sake." From his conception, he is destined for eternal beatitude [1703].

In recent years there has been a wonderful emphasis on the environment, on the preservation of whales and all sorts of things. That is all very good. But the only being brought into existence that "God has willed for its own sake", says the *Catechism*, is the human person. Everything else is made for the use of human beings, not for the abuse of human beings. Sometimes we are given the impression that the very *use* of the environment is wrong. That's foolish. God created the environment for us: the animals, the trees, the plants, the flowers, the seas, the sun, the moon, the stars. They are all created for us, not vice versa. We cannot subordinate the human person for any of these.

The *Catechism* continues:

> The human person participates in the light and power of the divine Spirit. By his reason, he is capable of understanding the order of things established by the Creator. By free will, he is capable of directing himself toward his true good. He finds his perfection "in seeking and loving what is true and good" [1704].

We have reason and will. We find our perfection in seeking and loving what is true and good, not what is fraudulent, not what is evil.

In the words of the *Catechism*:

> By his reason, man recognizes the voice of God which urges him "to do what is good and avoid what is evil." Everyone is obliged to follow this law [called the natural moral law], which makes itself heard in conscience and is fulfilled in the love of God and of neighbor. Living a moral life bears witness to the dignity of the person [1706].

> "Man, enticed by the Evil One, abused his freedom at the very beginning of history." He succumbed to temptation and did what was evil. He still desires the good, but his nature bears the wound of original sin. He is now inclined to evil and subject to error [1707].

> By his Passion, Christ delivered us from Satan and from sin. He merited for us the new life in the Holy Spirit. His grace restores what sin has damaged in us [1708].

The *Catechism* goes on to talk about the Beatitudes.

> The Beatitudes are at the heart of Jesus' preaching. . . .
> Blessed are the poor in spirit, for theirs is the kingdom of heaven.
> Blessed are those who mourn, for they shall be comforted.
> Blessed are the meek, for they shall inherit the earth.
> Blessed are those who hunger and thirst for righteousness, for they shall be satisfied.
> Blessed are the merciful, for they shall obtain mercy.
> Blessed are the pure in heart, for they shall see God.
> Blessed are the peacemakers, for they shall be called sons of God.
> Blessed are those who are persecuted for righteousness' sake, for theirs is the kingdom of heaven.
> Blessed are you when men revile you and persecute you and utter all kinds of evil against you falsely on my account. Rejoice and be glad, for your reward is great in heaven (Mt 5:3–10) [1716].

Then we are told in the *Catechism*:

The Beatitudes respond to the natural desire for happiness. This desire is of divine origin: God has placed it in the human heart in order to draw us to the One who alone can fulfill it [1718].

Isn't everything we do something that we *think* is going to make us happy? Even people who commit suicide, I'm convinced, do so because they think they are going to get out from under their misery and are going to be happier than they are. We believe that even evil things that we do are going to make us happy. But God has put in us this desire for happiness that can be satisfied *only* by the good, only by God Himself.

The *Catechism* states:

The Beatitudes reveal the goal of human existence, the ultimate end of human acts . . . [1719].

God put us in the world to know, to love, to serve him, and so to come to paradise. . . . With beatitude, man enters into the glory of Christ and into the joy of the Trinitarian life [1721].

The beatitude we are promised confronts us with decisive moral choices. . . . It teaches us that true happiness is not found in riches or well-being, in human fame or power, or in any human achievement—however beneficial it may be—such as science, technology and art, or indeed in any creature, but in God alone, the source of every good and of all love:
"All bow down before wealth. Wealth is that to which the multitude of men pay an instinctive homage. They measure happiness by wealth; and by wealth they measure respectability. . . . It is a homage resulting from a profound faith . . . that with wealth one may do all things. Wealth is one idol of the day and notoriety is the second . . . Notoriety, or the making of a noise in the world—it may be called "newspaper fame"—has come to be considered a great good in itself, and a ground of veneration" (John Henry Cardinal Newman) [1723].

Most of you here weren't born during the great crash of 1929. I was a kid then, but old enough to read the newspapers and to know of the great number of millionaires who jumped out of twentieth-story windows because they lost their money in the crash. All their happiness was in wealth, they thought. How very sad.

The *Catechism* continues:

God created man a rational being, conferring on him the dignity of a person who can initiate and control his own actions [1730].

Sometimes perhaps we wish we didn't have free will. We have to make choices, and then we are rewarded or perhaps punished accordingly.

The *Catechism* explains:

Freedom is the power, rooted in reason and will, to act or not to act, to do this or that, and so to perform deliberate actions on one's own responsibility. By free will one shapes one's own life [1731].

The more [we] do what is good, the freer [we] become. There is no true freedom except in the service of what is good and just. The choice to disobey and do evil is an abuse of freedom and leads to "the slavery of sin" [1733].

Freedom makes man *responsible* for his acts to the extent that they are voluntary [1734].

St. Thomas talks about habits of good and habits of evil. When your will is right, when it's disciplined, when you've been trained and educated, when you have a good mother, a good father, you grow up in the *habit* of doing good. Sometimes it's difficult, but it's a lot easier than if we didn't have that pattern. Similarly, people can grow up in the habit of doing evil.

The *Catechism* continues:

Imputability and responsibility for an action can be diminished or even nullified by ignorance, inadvertence, duress, fear, habit, inordinate attachments, and other psychological or social factors [1735].

Freedom is exercised in relationships between human beings. Every human person, created in the image of God, has the natural right to be recognized as a free and responsible being. All owe to each other this duty of respect. The *right to the exercise of freedom*, especially in moral and religious matters, is an inalienable requirement of the dignity of the human person. This right must be recognized and protected by civil authority within the limits of the common good and public order [1738].

Freedom and sin. Man's freedom is limited and fallible. . . . From its outset, human history attests the wretchedness and oppression born of the human heart in consequence of the abuse of freedom [1739].

Threats of freedom. The exercise of freedom does not imply a right to say or do *everything*. . . . [T]he economic, social, political and cultural conditions that are needed for a just exercise of freedom are too often disregarded or violated. . . . By deviating from the moral law man violates his own freedom, becomes imprisoned within himself, disrupts neighborly fellowship, and rebels against divine truth [1740].

We must remember that "freedom does not imply a right to say or do everything". We say this is a "free" country and that the government can't tell us what to do. But freedom doesn't mean you can do anything you want. Try jumping off the Empire State Building. You can say, "I'm free. I can jump off the Empire State Building." But what will the result be!

The *Catechism* moves to something tremendously important and very complex. It is almost a complete contradiction of the whole idea that all we have to do is to "feel good". It rejects the notion that if a certain thing that attracts us feels good, then it's all right. What the *Catechism* says here is not hair-splitting. This is not the old business that was ridiculed or argued about how many angels can stand on the head of a pin. This says:

> Human acts, that is acts that are freely chosen in consequence of a judgment of conscience, can be morally evaluated. They are either good or evil [1749].

> The morality of human acts depends on:
> —the object chosen;
> —the end in view or the intention;
> —the circumstances of the action [1750].

> The *object* chosen is a good toward which the will deliberately directs itself. . . . Objective norms of morality express the rational order of good and evil, attested to by conscience [1751].

> In contrast to the object, the *intention* resides in the acting subject. Because it lies at the voluntary source of an action and determines it by its end, intention is an element essential to the moral evaluation of an action [1752].

> A good intention (for example, that of helping one's neighbor) does not make behavior that is intrinsically disordered, such as lying and calumny, good or just. *The end does not justify the means.* . . . On the other hand, an added bad intention (such as vainglory) makes an act evil that, in and of itself, can be good (such as almsgiving) [1753].

> The *circumstances*, including the consequences, are secondary elements of a moral act. They contribute to increasing or diminishing the moral goodness or evil of human acts (for example, the amount of a theft). They can also diminish or increase the agent's responsibility (such as acting out of a fear of death). Circumstances of themselves cannot change the moral quality of acts themselves: they can make neither good nor right an action that is in itself evil [1754].

> It is therefore an error to judge the morality of human acts by considering only the intention that inspires them or the circumstances (environment, social pressure, duress or emergency, etc.) which supply their context. There are acts which, in and of themselves, independently of circumstances and intentions, are always gravely illicit by reason of their object; such as blasphemy and perjury, murder and adultery. One may not do evil so that good may result from it [1756].

Abortion is always an evil. The person committing the abortion may not think of it as such, may not even subjectively be committing a mortal sin, because of confusion, ignorance, and other forces that may diminish culpability, but in itself it's a grave evil. Adultery is an evil. We can say, "I love this person so much", and that's understandable. You can get swept off your feet, but that doesn't make it a good.

The *Catechism* goes on to discuss the passions, the strong feelings that drive us. These can be good. Love is a good feeling, but love itself can be distorted, can be perverted.

> In themselves passions are neither good nor evil. They are morally qualified only to the extent that they effectively engage reason and will. . . . It belongs to the perfection of the moral or human good that the passions be governed by reason [1767].

> Strong feelings are not decisive for the morality or the holiness of persons; they are simply the inexhaustible reservoir of images and affections in which the moral life is expressed. Passions are morally good when they contribute to a good action, evil in the opposite case. The upright will orders the movements of the senses it appropriates to the good and to beatitude; an evil will succumbs to disordered passions and exacerbates them. Emotions and feelings can be taken up into the virtues, or perverted by the *vices* [1768].

The *Catechism* goes on to talk about moral conscience.

> Deep within our conscience we discover a law which we have not laid upon ourselves but which we must obey. Its voice, ever calling us to love and to do what is good and to avoid evil, sounds in our hearts at the right moment. . . . For we have in our hearts a law inscribed by God. . . . [C]onscience is our most secret core and our sanctuary. There we are alone with God whose voice echoes in our depths [1776].

> Man has the right to act in conscience and in freedom so as personally to make moral decisions. "He must not be forced to act contrary to his conscience. Nor must he be prevented from acting according to his conscience, especially in religious matters" [1782].

> The education of the conscience is a lifelong task. . . . Prudent education teaches virtue; it prevents or cures fear, selfishness and pride, resentment arising from guilt, and feelings of complacency, born of human weakness and faults. The education of the conscience guarantees freedom and engenders peace of heart [1784].

> In the formation of conscience the Word of God is the light for our path; we must assimilate it in faith and prayer and put it into practice. We must also examine our conscience before the Lord's Cross. We are assisted by the gifts of the Holy Spirit, aided by the witness or advice of others and guided by the authoritative teaching of the Church [1785].

The *Catechism* tells us we must always follow our conscience but we have to make sure that our conscience is properly informed. Many people are brought up today without any moral training at all, without any real knowledge of the difference between good and evil. Our consciences must be informed by the Word of God in the Scriptures, by God's law, by the teaching of the Church. It's only after our conscience is thoroughly informed that we can then say, "I must follow what my conscience tells me." Moreover, our consciences can be dulled by constant sin, by the habit of evil.

In the first chapter of his letter to the people of Rome, St. Paul reminds us of those who have so long lived in sin that their minds, their consciences, have become completely darkened. He says very bluntly, "Now men live with men and women live with women and carry out all sorts of perversions, and they think it is all right. Their culture tells them it is all right. Their conscience tells them it is all right. But because their consciences have been darkened, have become callous, they no longer know the difference between good and evil."

I return very briefly to today's Gospel, in which our Lord says:

> It was not you who chose me,
> it was I who chose you
> to go forth and bear fruit.
> Your fruit must endure,
> so that all you ask the Father in my name
> he will give you (Jn 15:16–17).

To you who are mothers, may I say that *your* fruit must endure, in the sense that children you have borne must be prepared to live their lives in Christ here on earth, so that they will share His joy in eternity. What nobler task could there be for a mother, to prepare her children accordingly. It is surely for this that our Lord can say to you, "It was not you who chose me; it was I who chose you."

25

Virtue and the Art of Living

SEVENTH SUNDAY OF EASTER
MAY 15, 1994
WHITE PONTIFICAL MASS

Welcome to our annual "White Mass", honoring those in the medical and health care professions. Yesterday morning, in this cathedral, eleven new priests were ordained for the Church of New York. They were consecrated, as St. Paul says, "taken from among men for the things that pertain to God".

As I was conducting the ordination ceremony, reflecting on the fact that those of you in health care would be here today, I couldn't but think of the similarity because, in a very real way, you are consecrated. There is a beautiful portion of today's Gospel that speaks of consecration, and I think it is as pertinent to you in health care as it is to priests and bishops.

Our Lord is talking to His Father at the Last Supper, and He says of His apostles,

> "I gave them your word, and the world has hated them for it; they do not belong to the world, any more than I belong to the world. I do not ask you to take them out of the world, but to guard them from the evil one. They are not of the world, any more than I am of the world. Consecrate them by means of truth" (Jn 17:14–17).

One could extend this profound statement to all of the professions, to those in the media, in communications, to those in law and engineering, to all husbands, wives, mothers, and fathers. As Christians we are consecrated, set apart. We are not fully of this world. That constitutes a very difficult burden, because it is very difficult to achieve this balance of which Christ speaks. We live in the world and have obligations to the world, yet He has taken us out of the world and consecrated us to Himself.

In a sense, we are all involved in the health care professions as recipients of health care, or as well as providers of health care, and that which is critical to all of us if we are going to live "consecrated" lives is the subject of this particular catechetical session on the *virtues*. It is one of the most important sections, I think, in the entire *Catechism*. We are told:

> Whatever is true, whatever is honorable, whatever is just, whatever is pure, whatever is lovely, whatever is gracious, if there is any excellence, if there is anything worthy of praise, think about these things (Phil 4:8) [1803].

In this letter to the people of Philippi, St. Paul describes the ordinary, decent, generous, faithful, loyal, responsible human being each of us is expected to be.

In the words of the *Catechism*:

> A virtue is an habitual and firm disposition to do the good. It allows the person not only to perform good acts, but to give the best of himself. The virtuous person tends toward the good with all his sensory and spiritual powers; he pursues the good and chooses it in concrete actions.
> The goal of a virtuous life is to become like God [1803].

There has just been published a remarkable book, by a Doctor H. P. Dunn of New Zealand, called *Ethics for Doctors, Nurses and Patients*. I have selected some brief portions particularly pertinent to this section of the *Catechism* and to the health care professions. We read in Dr. Dunn's book:

> Is the private and personal life of the doctor of any concern to the patients or to anyone else? Must he live a virtuous and ethical life? . . . The answer is naturally that no one is free to indulge in . . . personal vices least of all doctors and nurses and those in positions of trust in society. Patients have the right to be protected from such practitioners [(New York: Alba House, 1994), p. 150].

The question of "private virtue" is a question asked of *all* people in public life. We are told frequently that it is no business of people what a campaigner for public office does in his personal life, what an office holder, a lawyer, a doctor, even a priest does in his personal life. But Dr. Dunn says:

> If a person has a serious moral flaw in his character in one facet of life, it will eventually affect his whole life. [This is certainly my experience as a priest and bishop.] Medicine depends not only on love, but also on justice and truth. Science depends on truth. The researcher must be absolutely honest and reliable, even if clinical results disprove his precious thesis. To quote Hippocrates . . . the ideal is: "In purity and holiness I shall pass my life . . ." (p. 150).

The *Catechism* says:

> The virtuous man is he who freely practices the good [the good not done out of empty show, not done out of force, but out of a sense of virtue].

The moral virtues are acquired by human effort. They are the fruit and seed of morally good acts; they dispose all the powers of the human being for communion with divine love [1804].

Then the *Catechism* takes up what are called the "cardinal" virtues:

Four virtues play a pivotal role and accordingly are called "cardinal": prudence, justice, fortitude and temperance . . . [1805].

These virtues are talked about by Aristotle and Plato. They are the moral virtues inherent in the natural moral law that we are all supposed to be practicing. Then the *Catechism* gives the definitions:

Prudence is "right reason in action," writes St. Thomas Aquinas, following Aristotle. It is not to be confused with timidity or fear, nor with duplicity or dissimulation. . . . It is prudence that immediately guides the judgment of conscience. The prudent man determines and directs his conduct in accordance with this judgment. With the help of this virtue we apply moral principles to particular cases without error and overcome doubts about the good to achieve and the evil to avoid [1806].

I don't know any profession today that is confronted with more potential for confusion in choosing between what is right and what is wrong than the health care professions. With all of the new sophisticated technology, with the potential for keeping people alive, letting them die, "putting them out of their misery", trying to care for mother and child in cases of very difficult pregnancies, the virtue of prudence is a tremendously important virtue. We have to be very careful about criticizing and certainly indicting those in health care who honestly believe that they are doing the patient good, even though what they are doing may be morally and objectively evil. We have to be sensitive and sympathetic. We have to teach rather than to condemn.

The *Catechism* says:

Justice is the moral virtue that consists in the constant and firm will to give their due to God and neighbor. . . . Justice toward men disposes one to respect the rights of each and to establish in human relationships the harmony that promotes equity with regard to persons and to the common good . . . [1807].

The only sound basis for any health care program, presidential or any other, is whether it is based on *justice*. Does it give everyone his or her due? Life is the first thing owed to us. That is the first that is due. Dr. Dunn talks about this very beautifully. He quotes Pope John Paul II, speaking to working groups of the Pontifical Academy of Sciences:

"Scientists and physicians are called to place their skill and energy at the service of life. They can never, for any reason or in any case, extinguish it. . . .

[E]uthanasia is a crime in which one must in no way cooperate or even consent to. Scientists and physicians must not regard themselves as the lords of life but as its skilled and generous servants" (p. 53).

Dr. Dunn writes of something I found startling, and I have been in the pro-life movement for a long time. This is a report of the annual meeting of the American Medical Association in Louisville, Kentucky.

. . . [T]his body [the AMA] representing as it does the physicians of the land, publicly expresses its abhorrence of the unnatural and now rapidly increasing crime of abortion; it avows its true nature as no simple offense against public morality and decency, no misdemeanor, no attempt upon the life of the mother, but the wanton and murderous destruction of her child (p. 87).

The American Medical Association said that in 1859! What has changed the mind of the American Medical Association? New scientific findings? No. All the scientific findings point to the fact that the unborn is truly a human being. So why the change? Is it a political change, a "politically correct" change, a change for the sake of popularity?

The *Catechism* goes on:

Fortitude is the moral virtue that ensures firmness in difficulties and constancy in the pursuit of the good. . . . The virtue of fortitude enables one to conquer fear, even fear of death, and to face trials and persecutions. It disposes one even to renounce and sacrifice his [or her own] life in defense of a just cause [1808].

It is a difficult life for physicians, nurses, and all in health care. They have to be courageous. You who fight for justice for health care workers—for those who empty bed pans, for those who sweep the floors—have to be courageous. I am absolutely insistent that we do everything we possibly can to provide a just wage for those who work in health care, particularly in our Catholic hospitals. They are owed justice, and it may take fortitude or courage to assure that they get justice.

The *Catechism* says:

Temperance is the moral virtue that moderates the attraction of pleasures and provides balance in the use of created goods. It ensures the will's mastery over instincts and keeps desires within the limits of what is honorable [1809].

We all have desires that can run away from us, instincts that can overcome us. The *Catechism* quotes a beautiful passage from St. Augustine, summarizing the cardinal virtues:

To live well is nothing other than to love God with all one's heart, with all one's soul, with all one's efforts; from this it comes about that love is kept whole and uncorrupted (through temperance). No misfortune can disturb it (and this is fortitude). It obeys only [God] (and this is justice), and is careful in discerning things, so as not to be surprised by deceit or trickery (and this is prudence) [1809].

Then the *Catechism* takes up the theological virtues:

The theological virtues are the foundation of Christian moral activity; they animate it and give it its special character. They inform us and give life to all the moral virtues. They are infused by God into the souls of the faithful to make them capable of acting as his children and of meriting eternal life. . . . There are three theological virtues: faith, hope and charity [1813].

Faith is the theological virtue by which we believe in God and believe all that he has said and revealed to us, and that the Holy Church proposes for our belief, because he is truth itself [1814].

That's where a physician or nurse can be so helpful to show his or her own faith. When I visited many hundreds of persons with AIDS, I discovered something that has been infinitely more important to them than any physical or medical help we can give them: the opportunity to talk about their own spiritual state, the opportunity to talk about their fears and anxieties, their hope for the future. Overwhelmingly, with exceptions, they believe they are going to die, and many, many do not believe that death is the end; they are worried about the future. A doctor or a nurse can do so much to help relieve such anxieties by spiritual example, not trying to force Catholicism on anyone, but treating people with spiritual gentleness.

After the Ordination Mass yesterday, I said Mass in a parish significantly distant from here. I blessed the school and then participated in the crowning of Mary and blessed a new statue of St. Joseph. There were many people present. As I was walking among them, I would bless all the little children, the little babies especially. Always the parents would smile and say, "Thank you." Then I saw a little baby in a carriage, and because I've spent much of my life working with retarded children, I recognized this child as such. I bent down and gave the child a special blessing, and then said to the mother, "How wonderful it is of you to take care of this child! What a great gift God has given the world in this child. [And I deeply believe that.] What an equal gift God has given this child and the world in having a mother who will take care of this child with such love." That's what it seems to me health care professionals can do in taking care of their patients, in taking care of everyone who comes to them.

The *Catechism* continues:

Hope is the theological virtue by which we desire the kingdom of heaven and eternal life as our happiness, placing our trust in Christ's promises and relying not on our own strength, but on the help of the grace of the Holy Spirit [1817].

The virtue of hope . . . keeps us from discouragement; it sustains [us] during times of abandonment; it opens up [our] hearts in expectation of eternal beatitude [1818].

Christian hope unfolds from the beginning of Jesus' preaching in the proclamation of the beatitudes. The *beatitudes* raise our hope toward heaven as the new Promised Land; they trace the path that leads through the trials that await the disciples of Jesus. . . . Hope is expressed and nourished in prayer, especially in the Our Father, the summary of everything that hope leads us to desire [1820].

Many of us say the Our Father every day. What a prayer it is for the health care professions! "Our Father who art in heaven, hallowed be thy name." It is God's will that is sacred. We want to bring His Kingdom on earth working with our patients, with our children at home. It is a wonderful prayer of hope.

The *Catechism* concludes its section on hope in this way:

We can therefore hope in the glory of heaven promised by God to those who love him and do his will. In every circumstance, each one of us should hope, with the grace of God, to persevere "to the end" (Mt 10:22) and to obtain the joy of heaven, as God's eternal reward for the good works accomplished with the grace of Christ. In hope, the Church prays for "all men to be saved" (1 Tim 2:4). She longs to be united with Christ, her Bridegroom, in the glory of heaven:

"Hope, O my soul, hope. You know neither the day nor the hour. Watch carefully, for everything passes quickly, even though your impatience makes doubtful what is certain, and turns a very short time into a long one. Dream that the more you struggle, the more you prove the love that you bear your God, and the more you will rejoice one day with your Beloved, in a happiness and rapture that can never end" (St. Teresa of Avila) [1821].

The *Catechism* then speaks of the virtue of charity.

Charity is the theological virtue by which we love God above all things for his own sake, and our neighbor as ourselves for the love of God [1822].

Jesus makes charity the *new commandment.* . . . "This is my commandment, that you love one another as I have loved you" (Jn 15:12) [1823].

Christ died out of love for us, while we were still "enemies" (Rom 5:10). The Lord asks us to love as he does, even our *enemies*, to make ourselves the neighbor of those farthest away, and to love children and the poor as Christ himself [1825].

The Apostle Paul has given an incomparable depiction of charity: "Charity is patient and kind, charity is not jealous or boastful; it is not arrogant or rude. Charity does not insist on its own way; it is not irritable or resentful; it does not rejoice at wrong, but rejoices in the right. Charity bears all things, believes all things, hopes all things, endures all things" (1 Cor 13:4–7) [1825].

"If I . . . have not charity," says the Apostle, "I am nothing." Whatever my privilege, service, or even virtue, "If I . . . have not charity, I gain nothing" (1 Cor 13:1–4). Charity is superior to all the virtues. It is the first of the theological virtues: "So faith, hope, charity abide, these three. But the *greatest of these is charity*" (1 Cor 13:13) [1826].

The *fruits* of charity are joy, peace, and mercy; charity demands beneficence and fraternal correction; it is benevolence; it fosters reciprocity and remains disinterested and generous; it is friendship and communion [1829].

I conclude with a suggestion offered by Dr. Dunn in his very beautiful book. Sometimes we demand things of physicians, of nurses, of others that are unjust, uncharitable. Sometimes we accuse the health care professionals of all sorts of things of which they are not guilty. We lump them all together, and we stereotype them. How often do we say, "All that doctor wants is his money. This doctor rides around in a Cadillac. This doctor has a big house", and so on. The laborer is worthy of his or her hire. We have to be careful that patients don't demand immoral and unethical practices: the cutting of tubes, for instance, to bring about infertility, the prescription of condoms for purposes of artificial contraception, abortion, and now the growing tendency of euthanasia and assisted suicide. This is as much an obligation of patients as of the health care professionals.

Dr. Dunn suggests to all medical or health care people that we have the Hippocratic oath. There is a Jewish medical oath, there is a Muslim medical oath, there is an Asian medical oath. But whereas we have had many pronouncements on medical care, on moral, ethical practices, and our Holy Father has said so many important things, we don't really offer to those graduating from medical colleges or nursing schools or others who work in our hospitals and in health care an opportunity to take a Christian oath. Dr. Dunn offers one that I think is very beautiful:

O God, in the name of the Father, the Son, and the Holy Spirit. I pledge that in the practice of Medicine I shall with Your help adhere to the principles of love and justice. I shall make the service and welfare of my patient my first duty, which will take precedence over the interests of society or the state.

Anything which the patient tells me in confidence will be respected and will not be revealed during life or after death.

I shall not participate in or facilitate artificial contraception, sterilization or induced abortion. I shall not directly bring about the death of any patient, normal or abnormal, healthy or in a terminal illness.

I shall accept with gratitude any financial rewards which You grant me but shall not allow the pursuit of wealth to dominate my practice or to influence my clinical decisions.

I shall regard my teachers with gratitude and respect, and I shall foster among my colleagues an atmosphere of friendship and cooperation. In presenting scientific papers I shall repudiate any dishonesty, knowing that we have a duty to truth in our elucidation of the mysteries of Your creation in the human body.

In purity and holiness I shall pass my life and practice my profession. My soul will be strengthened by daily prayer, weekly Mass and frequent reception of Your sacraments.

I ask the Blessed Virgin Mary and St. Joseph to bless my family life, and I pray that You will give me a share in the wisdom and courage of Our Lord Jesus Christ in undertaking this medical apostolate. Amen (p. 29).

Thank you, our doctors, our nurses, all our health care workers, including those who keep our hospitals and clinics clean. Thank you for all that you do to enhance the lives of the rest of us.

God bless you.

26

On the Sacrament of Confirmation

PENTECOST SUNDAY
CONFIRMATION OF THE HANDICAPPED
MAY 22, 1994
PONTIFICAL MASS

Welcome all of you from wherever you have come on this beautiful feast of Pentecost. It is a great, great feast of the Church.

We are very happy and privileged to have with us today Ambassador and Mrs. Raymond Flynn. Ambassador Flynn is the Ambassador from the United States to our Holy Father. I am sure you will want to welcome them in a special way.

We have a rival from Melbourne, Australia. Father William McCarthy is the Dean of St. Patrick's Cathedral in Melbourne. He has come to show us how we should do things in St. Patrick's Cathedral in New York! He is welcome nonetheless.

But more important than anyone else here, without exception, we have sixteen very, very special visitors. They are here to receive the sacrament of Confirmation on the glorious feast of Pentecost. They are very special in many ways as we will talk about later when we talk about the sacrament of Confirmation.

We are grateful to those parents who are here, teachers, volunteers, those who are in various residential facilities who have made it possible for these very special young people to be here. We are particularly grateful to have with us Sr. Joan Curtin, coordinator for Religious Education, and Anne Coghlan, Director of Special Religious Education.

Those of you who come regularly to this solemn pontifical Mass will have noted that we are not using incense today, because a number of our special individuals being confirmed have difficulty breathing, so we never use the incense.

It is particularly fitting that we pray during this Mass for the repose of the soul of Mrs. Jacqueline Kennedy Onassis. I know that you will do so with great reverence and great affection.

There is a special reason, purely coincidental, to pray for Mrs. Onassis during this Mass. Prior to President Kennedy's taking office, very little attention was paid to retardation here in the United States. I was working in the field at the time, and I know very well how few were the facilities, how indifferent a tremendous number of people were, except those, of course, with a retarded child in the family. With the advent of President Kennedy, and I am sure strongly encouraged by his wife, much of this changed. We are especially grateful for that. It is a special reason today for remembering her as we celebrate the glorious feast of Pentecost, the coming of the Holy Spirit, by confirming sixteen youngsters with varying degrees of handicaps.

* * *

Today we continue our sessions on the new *Catechism of the Catholic Church*. Whereas we have already treated the other six sacraments, we saved the sacrament of Confirmation specifically for today.

The Sacred Scriptures today give us the essence of the sacrament. We are told in the first reading from the Acts of the Apostles that the apostles were gathered together, still fearful, even though they had seen our Divine Lord after He had risen from the dead (Acts 2:1–11). Our Lord had done what He said He would do, be crucified and rise from the dead. Then He appeared to them. You would think they would have been filled with courage, but they weren't, because they hadn't yet been filled with the Holy Spirit. Our Lord told them it was necessary that He leave the earth before the Holy Spirit would come upon them. And that's what happened on the first Pentecost Sunday. They were gathered together in fright behind locked doors, and then suddenly a wind roared through the house, filling every room. People from every known country of the day were gathered outside for what was the Jewish feast of Pentecost. They heard this roaring wind. Then tongues of fire came down on the apostles. It filled them with the Holy Spirit and made it possible for them to be understood in every language.

Immediately the apostles went out and began to preach the crucified and risen Jesus. They were filled with courage because of the Holy Spirit. Pentecost was the first Confirmation. The same thing will happen here today, without the roaring wind, without seeing any tongues of fire. The Holy Spirit will come upon these sixteen individuals and fill them with all of the same graces that filled the apostles.

We might not have taken much notice of the second reading. It is the very special letter of St. Paul to the people of Corinth. St. Paul reminds us:

> There are different gifts but the same Spirit; there are different ministries but the same Lord; there are different works but the same God who accomplishes all of them in every one. . . .

The body is one and has many members, but all the members, many though they are, are one body; and so it is with Christ (1 Cor 12:4–7, 12].

The same is true of these sixteen about to be confirmed. Each one is different, as each one of us is different, but all are one in the Body of Christ.

Let us look briefly at what the *Catechism* has to say. We are reminded:

Baptism, the Eucharist and the sacrament of Confirmation together constitute the "sacraments of Christian initiation," whose unity must be safeguarded. . . . [T]he reception of the sacrament of Confirmation is necessary for the completion of baptismal grace. For "by the sacrament of Confirmation, [the baptized] are more perfectly bound to the Church and are enriched with a special strength of the Holy Spirit. Hence they are, as true witnesses of Christ, more strictly obliged to spread and defend the faith by word and deed" [1285].

We separate them today for a variety of reasons spelled out in the *Catechism*.

The *Catechism* says:

In the Old Testament the prophets announced that the Spirit of the Lord would rest on the hoped-for Messiah for his saving mission. The descent of the Holy Spirit on Jesus at his baptism by John was the sign that this was he who was to come, the Messiah, the Son of God. He was conceived of the Holy Spirit; his whole life and his whole mission are carried out in total communion with the Holy Spirit whom the Father gives him "without measure" (Jn 3:34) [1286].

As the Holy Spirit came down upon Mary and filled her with Christ, the Holy Spirit came in a very special way, the *Catechism* says, on Pentecost Sunday:

"From that time on the apostles, in fulfillment of Christ's will, imparted to the newly baptized by the laying on of hands the gift of the Spirit that completes the grace of Baptism. . . . The imposition of hands is rightly recognized by the Catholic tradition as the origin of the sacrament of Confirmation, which in a certain way perpetuates the grace of Pentecost in the Church" (Paul VI) [1288].

Very early, the better to signify the gift of the Holy Spirit, an anointing with perfumed oil (*chrism*) was added to the laying on of hands. This anointing highlights the name "Christian," which means "anointed" and derives from that of Christ himself whom God "anointed with the Holy Spirit" (Acts 10:38). This rite of anointing has continued ever since, in both East and West. For this reason the Eastern Churches call this sacrament *Chrismation*, anointing with chrism, or *myron* which means "chrism." In the West, *Confirmation* suggests both the ratification of Baptism, thus completing

Christian initiation, and the strengthening of baptismal grace—both fruits of the Holy Spirit [1289].

During the prayer before Confirmation, I will extend my hands, calling upon the Holy Spirit. Then I will place my hand on the head of each individual being confirmed and anoint the forehead of each individual with oil. Oil is a sign of healing and strength. We are told in the *Catechism*:

> Anointing, in Biblical and other ancient symbolism, is rich in meaning: oil is a sign of abundance and joy; it cleanses (anointing before and after a bath) and limbers (the anointing of athletes and wrestlers); oil is a sign of healing, since it is soothing to bruises and wounds; and it makes radiant with beauty, health, and strength [1293].

> Anointing with oil has all these meanings in the sacramental life. The pre-baptismal anointing with the oil of catechumens signifies cleansing and strengthening; the anointing of the sick expresses healing and comfort. The . . . anointing with the sacred chrism in Confirmation and Ordination is the sign of consecration . . . [1294].

When I have my hands raised, this is the prayer that I will be saying: "All-powerful God, Father of our Lord Jesus Christ, by water and the Holy Spirit you freed your sons and daughters from sin and gave them new life. Send your Holy Spirit upon them to be their helper and guide" [see 1299].

The prayer continues to list the seven special gifts of the Holy Spirit that each of these individuals will receive: the spirit of wisdom and understanding, the spirit of right judgment and courage, the spirit of knowledge and reverence, the spirit of wonder and awe in God's presence. How we need the spirit of reverence today to remind us of the sacredness of every human life in a world filled with violence and drugs, in a world of wars, a world of hunger and homelessness, in a world where more than one and a half million babies are put to death every year. How we need this gift of reverence!

Then I anoint the forehead of the person to be confirmed with oil and say, "Be sealed with the Gift of the Holy Spirit." I put my hand on the head of the individual, and that is the Confirmation. That is an indelible mark, just like Baptism. And just as we can be validly baptized only once, so we can be confirmed only once. As the *Catechism* tells us:

> Like Baptism which it completes, Confirmation is given only once, for it too imprints on the soul an *indelible spiritual mark*, the "character," which is the sign that Jesus Christ has marked a Christian with the seal of his Spirit by clothing him with power from on high so that he may be his witness [1304].

It is appropriate that immediately before the Confirmation those about to be confirmed repeat their baptismal promises, because Confirmation completes Baptism.

The *Catechism* says:

> *In the Latin Rite*, the ordinary minister of Confirmation is the bishop. Although the bishop may for grave reasons concede to priests the faculty of administering Confirmation, it is appropriate from the very meaning of the sacrament that he should confer it himself, mindful that the celebration of Confirmation has been temporally separated from Baptism for this reason. Bishops are the successors of the apostles. They have received the fullness of the sacrament of Holy Orders. The administration of this sacrament by them demonstrates clearly that its effect is to unite those who receive it more closely to the Church, to her apostolic origins and to her mission of bearing witness to Christ [1313].

The *Catechism* reminds us that there are twelve fruits of the Holy Spirit: charity, joy, peace, patience, kindness, goodness, generosity, gentleness, faithfulness, modesty, self-control, and chastity [see 1832]. These gifts make it possible for us to fulfill our mission of bearing witness to Christ.

I would like to say a special word to the individuals about to be confirmed and their families, helpers, teachers, and others. You who are to be confirmed are very important to me because you are very important to Almighty God, Who made every one of you. He made each one of you in a very special way. Every one of you was baptized, and when you were baptized our Lord came inside you.

Some of you cannot walk; some of you cannot talk. There is one of you here who cannot hear, and one who cannot see. But our Lord is still in you, and you can do so many things. The most important thing that you do is to let our Lord be inside you. Even if you cannot talk to other people you can talk to our Lord, because you don't need a voice to talk to our Lord. Even if you cannot see other people, you can see our Lord inside you, because He *is* inside. It is just like your heart. You know you have a heart even though you cannot *see* your heart. Today in Confirmation the Holy Spirit is going to come upon you.

I would like to say just a few words to you who are parents, you who are teachers, all of you who have helped these very special people. This is a wonderful, wonderful work.

More than fifty years ago, a child was born to cousins of mine. It was their eleventh child. Anyone with any experience would have known immediately that this was a Down's syndrome child, but they had no way of knowing this. All they knew was their child was "slow", and most of you know what that means. So they went to the doctor. You are not going to believe this, but this doctor looked at the child and said, "Your child has Down's syndrome, and it's your fault for having too many children." Imagine! That's what people used to have to put up with. Some people still do. I know some of you parents have suffered very, very much. Whether it is another disability, whether it's brain damage, whether it's Down's syndrome, whether it's cerebral palsy, whatever it is, you have suffered a great deal. But you have been so generous. There is no group of people in the world that I admire more than I admire you. That goes for parents, grandparents, brothers, sisters, teachers, volunteers, and everybody who helps.

Do you know there was a day when a youngster like these youngsters here could not even receive Holy Communion, and no one paid any attention to them? But look at the attention you give them. You pour out your lives for them. I know that just because I say I admire you doesn't make it easy. It is a day-after-day, night-after-night responsibility. It is always in your mind, it is always in your heart.

The coming of the Holy Spirit is very important for you, too, to give *you* wisdom. What a great gift wisdom is, especially when so many people, maybe even yourselves, ask "Where did you go wrong? Why did God punish you? Why wasn't your child completely healthy like every other child? What sin did you commit?" That should all be erased from your mind because of the wisdom, the courage, and above all the reverence of the Holy Spirit. You can look at your child, you can look at yourself, and say, "Here is a sacred person."

Does it really matter in the long run if anybody else loves us, so long as God loves us? This life is only a pilgrimage. Some of us live for sixty, seventy, eighty years. Some of us die very young. The little child that I talked about with Down's syndrome, about whom that doctor said, "It's your fault for having too many children", was buried a couple of years ago at about the age of fifty. What a joy she was to her family, and how she brought that family together in love! There's a tremendous potential in those who don't seem to have the same potential as the rest of us physically, mentally, or emotionally. Some of these youngsters have won medals in the Special Olympics. But that's not the important thing. The important thing is that they are made in the image and likeness of God. The important thing is that all of you, whether blood relatives or not, who give yourselves to them are going to receive tremendous graces from God in return.

27

God's Law Is the Law of Love

TRINITY SUNDAY
MAY 29, 1994
PONTIFICAL MASS

I understand that there was supposed to appear over this weekend a CBS poll on the beliefs of Catholics. Maybe it has appeared, but I haven't seen it. What I did see in this morning's *New York Times* was the beginning of a series giving very lengthy treatment on problems being experienced by the Catholic Church in the United States. The installment that I read this morning was very well done. It wasn't an attack on the Church. It pointed out some very serious problems. All studies and surveys, of course, have to be questioned in terms of the numbers of people questioned, the questions asked, and how were they asked. Presuming the accuracy of the findings and the reporter's treatment, it is very important that we know what the problems are. We have to face these problems.

The findings tell us that there are a number of Catholics who don't recognize the importance of the Mass, a number of Catholics who don't recognize the importance of much of Church teaching. There are also findings which suggest that a number of Catholics accept almost casually contraception, abortion, and divorce.

These problems highlight the need for the new *Catechism of the Catholic Church*, which will be published in English on the twenty-second of June. They emphasize the continuing need for education in our faith. Only about 25 percent of our Catholic youngsters go to Catholic schools, and there they get only a fraction of formal religious education. They get a good bit by their surroundings, of course. Seventy-five percent of Catholic children are in public schools, and, whereas I have tremendous respect for our public school teachers, who work so valiantly, they are by law prevented from teaching anything religious. Public schools are purely secular, and, in some instances, sadly, children are taught the *opposite* of what we believe, at least by inadvertence. Many of our laws teach us the opposite of what the Church teaches, and the law is the great teacher in the United States. Since abortion was legalized, over twenty years ago, youngsters being brought up in this country are taught that the *law* says abortion is all right, so it must be all right. The law has misled in tremendous numbers.

The media does an awful lot of good things, but some in the media treat marriage with contempt and treat sexual promiscuity very casually.

These are of the air that we breathe. It is not enough that the Church try to improve teaching, try to reach more people, try to use modern means of communications. Day after day we try to teach the truths of our Catholic faith. But we have to look to the media, we have to look to popular entertainment, which can be so misleading. We have to look to law. We have to look to our whole political system, which can, at times, be very misleading. We have to look to political leaders who represent themselves as Catholics but whose lives may not be very Catholic, who may take positions for political expediency that aren't very Catholic. All of these things affect us, and they affect us very profoundly. It really goes without saying, of course: good things aren't "news".

Today we are going to be talking about some aspects of the *Catechism* that won't make news: the fact that this is Trinity Sunday, that we believe in God the Father, God the Son, God the Holy Spirit. The fact that the Holy Spirit has descended upon the world is not going to make news. But I remember a few years ago, in the *New York Post*, the front page was devoted to the fact that I suggested that the devil may be roaming around the world today. There's nothing new about that, but it made news. I am not faulting anyone for this. I am just puzzling through what it is that brings it about that so many Catholics either don't understand the faith, don't know the faith, or don't practice the faith. There are many forces at work.

Trinity Sunday is a glorious feast. Today's Gospel reminds us that our Lord sent the apostles forth saying, "Go, therefore, and make disciples of all nations. Baptize them in the name of the Father and of the Son and of the Holy Spirit" (Mt 28:16–20). That is key doctrine. It is one of the teachings we need for salvation. We have already treated the Trinity, and today we will continue with the *Catechism* and the section on law and sin.

Today's first reading is from the book of Deuteronomy, the fifth book of the Old Testament. Deuteronomy technically means, in Greek, "second law". In Exodus, the second book of the Old Testament, Moses was called up to Mount Sinai by God and given the law, the Ten Commandments. In the book of Deuteronomy these commandments are spelled out more fully, so it is called the "second law". It is a further exposition of the law of Almighty God. We are told:

> You must know now and fix in your heart that the LORD is God in the heavens above and on earth below, and that there is no other. You must keep his statutes and commandments which I enjoin on you today, that you

and your children after you may prosper and that you may have long life on
the land which the LORD, your God, is giving you forever (Dt 4:39–40).

All law that comes from God is the law of love. Deuteronomy begins
with the Israelites being told by God, in essence: I have chosen you out of
all others because I love you so much. I give you My law because I love
you so much, because, if you keep My law, then you are going to be truly
happy.

In the *Catechism* we are told first about God's mercy and sin.

> The Gospel is the revelation in Jesus Christ of God's mercy to sinners. The
> angel announced to Joseph: "You shall call his name Jesus, for he will save
> his people from their sins" (Mt 1:21). The same is true of the Eucharist, the
> sacrament of redemption [1846].

> Sin is an offense against reason, truth, and right conscience; it is failure in
> genuine love for God and neighbor caused by a perverse attachment to cer-
> tain goods [1849].

Here is the Trinity at work. We are all made in the image of the Trinity; we are social beings. We owe *love* to God, to ourselves, to our fellow
human beings. Anytime we violate that law of love we are sinning.

Sin is an offense against God. . . . Sin sets itself against God's love for us
and turns our hearts away from it. Like the first sin, it is disobedience, a
revolt against God through the will to become "like gods" (Gen 3:5),
knowing and determining good and evil. Sin is thus "love of oneself even
to contempt of God" [1850].

The *Catechism* says:

> There are a great many kinds of sins. Scripture provides several lists of them
> [1852].

> Sins can be distinguished according to their objects, as can every human act;
> or according to the virtues they oppose, by excess or defect; or according to
> the commandments they violate. They can also be classed according to
> whether they concern God, neighbor, or oneself; they can be divided into
> spiritual and carnal sins, or again as sins in thought, word, deed, or omission
> [1853].

This is an important distinction that still exists. The main distinction between mortal and venial sin is that *mortal* sin is death-dealing. Mortal sin
kills the soul and completely alienates us from Almighty God.

In the words of the *Catechism*:

> *Mortal sin* destroys charity in the heart of man by a grave violation of God's
> law; it turns man away from God, who is his ultimate end and his happiness,
> by preferring an inferior good to him.

Venial sin allows charity to remain, even though it offends and wounds it [1855].

Money, drink, drugs, ambition, pride, power, sex, all of these are inferior to God. If we have to turn away from God for these things, then they are sinful. And if they are so serious that they kill the soul and put us in danger of death, then they are mortal sins.

The *Catechism* states:

> Mortal sin, by attacking the vital principle within us—that is, love— necessitates a new initiative of God's mercy and a conversion of heart which is normally accomplished within the setting of the sacrament of reconciliation [1856].

Normally, if we have committed mortal sins, the only route to forgiveness is through the sacrament of Penance. Some people living in mortal sin think that they can receive Holy Communion without going to confession. That is not the teaching of the Church. God can directly forgive our sins no matter what the sins are, but our Lord said to the apostles, "Whose sins you shall forgive, they are forgiven. Whose sins you shall not forgive, they are not forgiven." That is the reason for the sacrament of Penance. You can die the death of the martyr without confession, and your sins would be forgiven. But the ordinary course is confession, absolution, and penance.

The *Catechism* says:

> For a *sin* to be *mortal*, three conditions must be met all at the same time: "Mortal sin is sin whose object is grave matter and which is also committed with full knowledge and deliberate consent" [1857].

We have to understand fully what we are doing. Many people are confused today by so many forces around us. We are confused by the example of others, confused, as I said, by entertainment, and so on. Sometimes we really aren't fully aware that something is seriously sinful. Then there is the third requirement: we must really be determined to do this. We must have full consent of the will. A gun in your back doesn't leave you free. You may be all stirred up with passion. Someone can even kill in passion and it may not be a mortal sin. Someone could engage in sexual relations outside of marriage, and it wouldn't necessarily be a mortal sin because the reason might be so clouded by passion. Every situation has to be assessed in itself.

The *Catechism* explains:

> *Unintentional ignorance* can diminish or even remove the imputability of a grave offense. But no one is deemed to be ignorant of the principles of the moral law, which are written in the conscience of every man. The promptings of feelings and passions can also diminish the voluntary and free charac-

ter of the offense, as can external pressures or pathological disorders. Sin committed through malice, by deliberate choice of evil, is the gravest [1860].

Although we can judge that an act is in itself a grave offense, we must entrust the judgment of persons to the justice and mercy of God [1861].

I can say to someone, "You are living in mortal sin", but I cannot say what God is going to do. God may say, "This pitiful person does understand, but this person is trying to be good and continues to slip and fall", or "This person is confused by all sorts of circumstances." We have to leave judgment to God.

The *Catechism* says:

Venial sin . . . impedes the soul's progress in the exercise of the virtues and the practice of the moral good; it merits temporal punishment. Deliberate and unrepented venial sin disposes us little by little to commit mortal sin [1863].

There are no limits to the mercy of God, but anyone who deliberately refuses to accept his mercy by repenting, rejects the forgiveness of his sins and the salvation offered by the Holy Spirit. Such hardness of heart can lead to final impenitence and eternal loss [1864].

Sin creates a proclivity to sin; it engenders vice by repetition of the same acts. This results in perverse inclinations which cloud conscience and corrupt the concrete judgment of good and evil. Thus sin tends to reproduce itself and reinforce itself, but it cannot destroy the moral sense at its root [1865].

Vices can be classified according to the virtues they oppose, or also be linked to the *capital sins* which Christian experience has distinguished. . . . They are called "capital" because they engender other sins, other vices. They are pride, avarice, envy, wrath, lust, gluttony, and sloth or acedia [1866].

We have a grave responsibility not only for our own personal sins but for those sins that we encourage in others.

The *Catechism* moves from the violation of law to law itself. The heading in the *Catechism* is "God's Salvation: Law and Grace". We can get the wrong idea of law and view it simply as something restrictive, prohibitive. But law is supposed to help lead to happiness. We have all been wounded by original sin. Despite all of our evil inclinations, how can we get to heaven?

The *Catechism* says:

Called to beatitude but wounded by sin, man stands in need of salvation from God. Divine help comes to him in Christ through the law that guides him and the grace that sustains him [1949].

The moral law is the work of divine Wisdom [1950].

Law is a rule of conduct enacted by competent authority for the sake of the common good. The moral law presupposes the rational order, established among creatures for their good and to serve their final end, by the power, wisdom, and goodness of the Creator. All law finds its first and ultimate truth in the eternal law [1951].

There are different expressions of the moral law, all of them interrelated: eternal law—the source, in God, of all law; natural law; revealed law, comprising the Old Law and the New Law, or Law of the Gospel; finally, civil and ecclesiastical laws [1952].

The moral law finds its fullness and its unity in Christ. Jesus Christ is in person the way of perfection [1953].

The natural law expresses the original moral sense which enables man to discern by reason the good and the evil, the truth and the lie:
"The natural law is written and engraved in the soul of each and every man, because it is human reason ordaining him to do good and forbidding him to sin . . ." (Leo XIII) [1954].

The "divine and natural" law shows man the way to follow so as to practice the good and attain his end. The natural law states the first and essential precepts which govern the moral life. . . . Its principal precepts are expressed in the Decalogue. This law is called "natural," not in reference to the nature of irrational beings, but because reason which decrees it properly belongs to human nature.
"The natural law is nothing other than the light of understanding placed in us by God; through it we know what we must do and what we must avoid. God has given this light or law at the creation" (St. Thomas Aquinas) [1955].

The natural law, present in the heart of each man and established by reason, is universal in its precepts and its authority extends to all men. It expresses the dignity of the person and determines the basis for his fundamental rights and duties:
"For there is a true law: right reason. It is in conformity with nature, is diffused among all men, and is immutable and eternal; its orders summon to duty; its prohibitions turn away from offense. . . . To replace it with a contrary law is a sacrilege; failure to apply even one of its provisions is forbidden; no one can abrogate it entirely" (Cicero) [1956].

The natural law is *immutable* and permanent throughout the variations of history. . . . The rules that express it remain substantially valid. Even when it is rejected in its very principles, it cannot be destroyed or removed from the heart of man. It always rises again in the life of individuals and societies [1958].

The natural law exists all over the world for all peoples: Jews, Protes-
tants, Catholics, Muslims, pagans. There is a natural law that runs through
all things. It runs through our hearts, our minds. If you take a knife and
stab yourself, you are going to wound yourself, maybe you are going to
kill yourself. It is against nature to do that. This is simply a reflection of
the Divine Law. When we do things that are unnatural, somehow they
hurt us, somehow they hurt others, they violate the world. Intelligence
and common sense are basic in natural law.

The *Catechism* says:

> The natural law, the Creator's very good work, provides the solid founda-
> tion on which man can build the structure of moral rules to guide his
> choices. It also provides the indispensable moral foundation for building the
> human community. Finally, it provides the necessary basis for the civil law
> with which it is connected, whether by a reflection that draws conclusions
> from its principles, or by additions of a positive and juridical nature [1959].

> The precepts of natural law are not perceived by everyone clearly and im-
> mediately. In the present situation sinful man needs grace and revelation so
> moral and religious truths may be known "by everyone with facility, with
> firm certainty and with no admixture of error" (Pius XII) [1960].

It should be easy for most people to see what is natural. But, again, we
get clouded by our environment. Our culture is cancerous in terms of the
unnatural, the sinful, that which is hostile to us. We breathe it not only in
the air, but culturally, spiritually, morally. And, as St. Paul says in his letter to the people of Rome, our hearts become callous, our minds become
darkened, so we can no longer tell the difference between that which
used to be very clear to us. There are some things in our culture today
that we accept almost without question that previously we thought were
horrible. Again, I use abortion as an example. There was a day we ab-
horred abortion, but now we have become accustomed to it. We have
heated arguments about whether it is right or wrong. Euthanasia and
assisted suicide are all becoming very popular. Our minds get clouded,
our hearts get callous.

The *Catechism* reminds us of the Old Law.

> God, our Creator and Redeemer, chose Israel for himself to be his people
> and revealed his Law to them, thus preparing for the coming of Christ. The
> Law of Moses expresses many truths naturally accessible to reason [1961].

> The Old Law is the first stage of revealed Law. Its moral prescriptions are
> summed up in the Ten Commandments. The precepts of the Decalogue lay
> the foundations for the vocation of man fashioned in the image of God;
> they prohibit what is contrary to the love of God and neighbor and pre-
> scribe what is essential to it [1962].

The Old Law is a *preparation for the Gospel.* "The Law is a pedagogy and a prophecy of things to come" (St. Irenaeus). It prophesies and presages the work of liberation from sin which will be fulfilled in Christ [1964].

Christ came to fulfill the old law. The law that He gives us is summarized in this: "Love the Lord your God with your whole heart, your whole soul, your whole mind, your whole strength, and love your neighbor as yourself."

The *Catechism* speaks of the New Law:

> The New Law or the Law of the Gospel is the perfection here on earth of the divine law, natural and revealed. It is the work of Christ and is expressed particularly in the Sermon on the Mount. It is also the work of the Holy Spirit and through him it becomes the interior law of charity: "I will establish a New Covenant with the house of Israel. . . . I will put my laws into their minds, and write them on their hearts, and I will be their God, and they shall be my people" (Heb 8:8) [1965].

> The Law of the Gospels "fulfills," refines, surpasses, and leads the Old Law to its perfection. In the Beatitudes, the New law *fulfills the divine promises* by elevating and orienting them toward the "kingdom of heaven." It is addressed to those open to accepting this new hope with faith—the poor, the humble, the afflicted, the pure of heart, those persecuted on account of Christ—and so marks out the surprising ways of the Kingdom [1967].

> The Law of the Gospel requires us to make the decisive choice between "the two ways" and to put into practice the words of the Lord. It is summed up in the *Golden Rule,* "Whatever you wish that men would do to you, do so to them; this is the law and the prophets" (Mt 7:12).
> The entire Law of the Gospel is contained in the *"new commandment"* of Jesus, to love one another as he has loved us [1970].

Every law that has ever come from God is a law of love. They protect us from ourselves, from one another, and lead us to eternal happiness. This is why we say that every civil law, every law of any government at whatever level, must be in accordance with the law of God, the law of love expressed in the natural moral law. Any law of any government, no matter how reasonable it may look, must be in accord with the divine law, the natural moral law, or it is in violation of the very nature of human beings, in violation of our relationship with God.

This section of the *Catechism* concludes with a summary of the New Law as a law of love, grace, and freedom.

> The New Law is called a *law of love* because it makes us act out of the love infused by the Holy Spirit, rather than from fear; a *law of grace,* because it confers the strength of grace to act, by means of faith and the sacraments; a *law of freedom,* because it sets us free from the ritual and juridical observances

of the Old Law, inclines us to act spontaneously by the prompting of charity and, finally, lets us pass from the condition of a servant who "does not know what his master is doing" to that of a friend of Christ . . . [1972].

If the law of love given us by Almighty God prevailed throughout all of history, we wouldn't have a Memorial Day, because there would be no wars. During this Memorial Day, let us try to love one another and everyone we meet as made in the image and likeness of God, as a concrete contribution to the reduction of hatred, violence, and war in the world.

28

We Need God's Grace

THE FEAST OF CORPUS CHRISTI

JUNE 5, 1994

PONTIFICAL MASS

While I could never pretend to be a war hero, I have lived in a hole in the ground filled with mud, with shells flying over. I have prowled through a jungle with men who did not know which moment might be their last. And I have seen men die beside me. Therefore, I hate war with a passion, and believe that very few wars in history have been morally justified. But I do not agree with those who have been protesting against our honoring those brave men and women of so many nations who sacrificed so much, even gave their lives, in the invasion of Normandy and in other theaters of World War II. In my judgment, no matter what mistakes we may have made, such as carpet bombing, if ever our waging any war in history has been justified, certainly our entering World War II was justified as an effort to stop the incredible evil of Nazism, an effort to bring to an end a holocaust that took the lives of six million Jews and many millions of Christians and others, an effort to prevent the advance of a force that could have enslaved the entire world.

I have seen a flyer that is being passed out protesting the fact that we honor those who have died, implying that our entrance into Normandy was an act of aggression. The flyer mentions Haiti. I would think it disastrous were American forces to invade Haiti. I have repeatedly, from this pulpit, pleaded for mercy, compassion, and justice for Haitians, and against the maltreatment they have suffered. But I cannot accept the criticism of the United States celebrating our efforts to free Europe, or the criticism of those churches that ring their bells today in honor of that effort in Europe, including the liberation of Rome. Thank God that so many were willing to sacrifice so very much. Rather than being ashamed of what was done, I am proud to stand before you as an American.

Many men and women lost their lives in that war. If so many were prepared to give their lives to save the world materially, how much our Divine Lord must have loved us to have given His Body and Blood for our eternal life. This is what the celebration of the Feast of the Body and Blood of Christ really means.

We are told at the conclusion of the Gospel, "After singing songs of praise Jesus and the apostles walked to the Mount of Olives" (Mk 14:26). His crucifixion loomed before Him. There His blood was going to drench the ground in the horror of His suffering. There He was going to cry out to God, His Father, "Let this cup of suffering pass from Me. Nevertheless, not My will but Thine be done." It is only because of the crucifixion, the death of our Divine Lord, that we have His Body and Blood in Holy Communion. It was only because of that Last Supper that we have the Sacrifice of the Mass today. And it is only because of His crucifixion and death that eternal life is possible for us. Christ always raises the natural up to the super-natural. When we receive His Body and Blood we are swept up into His divinity.

Today's *Catechism* session addresses not the Body and Blood of Christ, but the question of grace and justification, a tremendously important issue, most particularly since the Reformation in Germany. There have been very bitter arguments about how we are "justified", that is, how our sins are forgiven, how we are saved.

About justification the *Catechism* says:

> Through the power of the Holy Spirit we take part in Christ's Passion by dying to sin, and in his Resurrection by being born to a new life; we are members of his Body which is the Church, branches grafted onto the vine which is himself [1988].

At the Last Supper, Christ talked so beautifully of His being the vine and our being the branches.

The *Catechism* goes on:

> The first work of the grace of the Holy Spirit is *conversion*, effecting justification. . . . "Justification is not only the remission of sins, but also the sanctification and renewal of the interior man" [1989].

Conversion is a complete interior turnaround—when we come to see things in a completely different light. We live under the light of eternity, and that illuminates things in a different way. Conversion brings about justification.

We are told further:

> Justification has been *merited for us by the Passion of Christ* who offered himself on the cross as a living victim, holy and pleasing to God, and whose blood has become the instrument of atonement for all of our sins [1992].

These include whatever sins we have committed in war when blood was shed as an instrument of ultimate peace.

The *Catechism* goes on to speak of grace. We are told:

Our justification comes from the grace of God. Grace is *favor*, the *free and undeserved help* that God gives us to respond to his call to become his children, his adopted children, partakers of the divine nature and of eternal life [1996].

The whole concept of grace, this great mystery, has perhaps been expressed as beautifully as anywhere in that haunting song with its haunting melody, "Amazing Grace," now sung in Catholic as well as in Protestant churches. That song was written by a slave runner. He transported slaves and sold them in England and then in America. He treated the slaves horribly. Ultimately he was converted from this, and that is when he wrote "Amazing Grace". "Amazing grace, how sweet . . . that saved a wretch like me. I once was lost and now I am found." There can hardly be a much better explanation of grace than that.

The Church, as the *Catechism* tells us, divides graces into various categories.

Sanctifying grace is an habitual grace, a stable and supernatural disposition that perfects the soul itself to enable it to live with God, to act by his love [2000].

It is a habit of being, as the author Flannery O'Connor would call it. It is a habit of being good, a habit of being oriented to Almighty God. It is a habit of asking what God wants. When we live this way, habitually, we sin only by exception. This is because of sanctifying, habitual grace.

Then there is what we call *actual grace*. Actual grace is what comes to us so that we will perform good acts or avoid evil acts. For example, we may find ourselves in terrible temptation. If we turn toward God, God will give us the grace to overcome the temptation. This is an important point: that we must respond to God by *seeking* His grace.

In the words of the *Catechism*:

God's free initiative demands *man's free response*, for God has created man in his image by conferring on him, along with freedom, the power to know him and love him. The soul only enters freely into the communion of love. God immediately touches and directly moves the heart of man. He has placed in man a longing for truth and goodness that only he can satisfy. The promises of "eternal life" respond, beyond all hope, to this desire [2002].

Then the *Catechism* reminds us:

There are *sacramental graces*, peculiar to each of the sacraments [2003].

When we go regularly to receive the sacrament of Reconciliation, the sacrament of Penance, then we receive special graces as bulwarks against temptation, especially if we have habits of special sins. The more frequently we get to confession, the more sacramental grace we get to help us in that particular matter.

Those who are married validly receive sacramental graces, the graces of the sacrament of Marriage to meet the needs unique to the state of marriage. A priest receives the sacramental grace of the sacrament of Holy Orders, to meet the needs unique to the priesthood.

The *Catechism* tells us:

> Since it belongs to the supernatural order, grace *escapes our experience* and cannot be known except by faith. We cannot therefore rely on our feelings or our works to conclude that we are justified and saved [2005].

The *Catechism* then goes on to talk about merit. It is a word we use commonly enough. If a youngster in school works hard and gets special marks, he or she is said to merit these marks. If a police officer does what he or she is supposed to do, then he or she merits pay. If the police officer doesn't do what is supposed to be done, then that pay isn't merited. What we get from God is really never merited; it is always a free gift of God. Did any one of us here, including myself, merit to become Catholic? Did we merit to be called to salvation? Did we merit having Christ love us so much that He died for us? Frequently I feel disappointed in myself. I don't merit God's graces or the grace of salvation. I certainly don't merit to be a priest. But our Lord suffered and died for me because of my weakness.

I read a very foolish thing in the newspaper the other day. A woman said, "I have a 'divine right' to be a priest." *No one* has a divine right to be a priest. I don't have a divine right to be standing here before you. I was called by the Church. We believe that the Holy Spirit was given to me in a special way in the sacrament of Holy Orders. I had no right to that. Who was I? Mr. and Mrs. O'Connor's boy who got into a lot of mischief, who was never very smart. Then one day our Holy Father appointed me the Cardinal Archbishop of New York. The same Pope or another could remove me. Wouldn't you think it stupid if I stood here and said that I have a "divine right" to be here, just because of who I am? No one has a right to be called to the priesthood.

The *Catechism* states:

> With regard to God, there is no strict right to any merit on the part of man. Between God and us there is an immeasurable inequality, for we have received everything from him, our Creator [2007].

The *Catechism* goes on to talk about Christian holiness: "We know that in everything God works for good with those who love him . . ." [2012].

This may seem difficult to understand. Being in a wheelchair, for example, hardly seems to be a good. Yet somehow God is at work. God is sustaining those of you in wheelchairs. Somehow God let these things happen to you, and somehow God brings good out of it. The wheelchair itself is not a good. To have neurological damage is not in itself a good. But God brings good out of it. God brings good out of all suffering. We are told in the *Catechism*:

> The way of perfection comes by way of the Cross. There is no holiness without renunciation and spiritual battle. Spiritual progress entails mortification that gradually leads to living in the peace and joy of the happiness of heaven, of the so-called Beatitudes [2015].

There was not much joy and happiness on the beaches in Normandy, in the sea, in the air. But in God's mysterious way, through that suffering a horrifying evil was overcome. I believe that all war is evil, but there are times that it is the lesser of evils, as I believe that Allied involvement in World War II was the lesser of the evils that were taking place and that would have continued had that war not been fought.

The *Catechism* continues with the subject of "The Church, Mother and Teacher":

> It is in the Church, in communion with all the baptized, that the Christian fulfills his or her vocation. From the Church we receive the Word of God containing the teachings of "the law of Christ" (Gal 6:2). From the Church we receive the grace of the sacraments that sustains us on the "way." From the Church we learn the *example of holiness* and recognize its model and source in the all-holy Virgin Mary; we discern it in the authentic witness of those who live it; we discover it in the spiritual tradition and long history of the saints who have gone before us . . . [2030].

As Chesterton puts it, "The Church doesn't exist because we are not sinners but because we *are* sinners." The Church is made up of people like you and me. We are sinners. Humanly the Church is weak, yet, filled with the Holy Spirit, the Church helps us toward our salvation. How tragic if we can't depend on the teaching of the Church, if we have to question everything that comes from the pope, if we say, for example, "Who is he to say that women cannot be ordained", or whatever it might be. That is the Church. That is our structure. That is what it means to be a Catholic. Clearly there is room for honest disagreement over non-substantive issues. We cannot simply pick and choose. If that's to be the case, then spiritually we are members of some other congregation or community and not spiritually members of the Catholic Church, even though we may call ourselves such. Nor do I understand how some can call themselves Catholic and reject the teaching of the Holy Father in the most vitriolic and abusive language, as though he has no right to teach at all.

The next section of the *Catechism* concerns "Moral Life and the Magisterium of the Church".

The Church, the "pillar and bulwark of the truth," "has received this solemn command of Christ from the apostles to announce the saving truth" (1 Tim 3:15). "To the Church belongs the right always and everywhere to announce moral principles, including those pertaining to the social order, and to make judgments on any human affairs to the extent that they are required by the fundamental rights of the human person or the salvation of souls" [2032].

The *Magisterium of the Pastors of the Church* in moral matters is ordinarily exercised in catechesis and preaching, with the help of the works of theologians and spiritual authors. Thus from generation to generation, under the aegis and vigilance of the pastors, the "deposit" of Christian moral teaching has been handed on, a deposit composed of a characteristic body of rules, commandments, and virtues proceeding from faith in Christ and animated by charity. Alongside the Creed and the Our Father, the basis for this catechesis has traditionally been the Decalogue which sets out the principles of moral life valid for all men [2033].

The authority of the Magisterium extends also to the specific precepts of the *natural law*, because their observance, demanded by the Creator, is necessary for salvation. In recalling the prescriptions of the natural law, the Magisterium of the Church exercises an essential part of its prophetic office of proclaiming to men what they truly are and reminding them of what they should be before God [2036].

The *Catechism* tells us about precepts of the Church. As with so many other things, many people seem to believe that what we call the precepts of the Church went out the window with the Second Vatican Council. Not at all. The *Catechism* spells them out for us.

The first precept ("You shall attend Mass on Sundays and holy days of obligation.") requires the faithful to participate in the Eucharistic celebration when the Christian community gathers together on the day commemorating the Resurrection of the Lord [2042].

I am told that there was a day that even in some Catholic high schools Catholic teachers were telling students, "You don't have to go to Mass on Sunday. Go if you like. It's a nice thing to do but there is no requirement." That is nonsense! We are bound under pain of mortal sin when it is humanly possible for us to get to Mass on Sundays. This is not the case when we are sick, when there is some emergency situation. This has always been the case.

The *Catechism* continues:

The second precept ("You shall confess your sins at least once a year.") ensures preparation for the Eucharist by the reception of the sacrament of reconciliation, which continues Baptism's work of conversion and forgiveness [2042].

Many people today think we can just receive Communion and never go to confession. We are bound to go *at least* once a year. We are certainly bound to go anytime we commit mortal sins. I try to get to confession every Saturday. As I have said before, undoubtedly I sin more than anybody in New York, because I don't see too many people at confession on Saturday. But that's all right. I know I need it.

The third precept ("You shall humbly receive your Creator in Holy Communion at least during the Easter season.") guarantees as a minimum the reception of the Lord's Body and Blood in connection with the Paschal feasts, the origin and center of the Christian liturgy [2042].

The fourth precept ("You shall keep holy the holy days of obligation.") completes the Sunday observance by participation in the principal liturgical feasts which honor the mysteries of the Lord, the Virgin Mary, and the saints [2043].

The fifth precept ("You shall observe the prescribed days of fasting and abstinence.") ensures the times of ascesis and penance which prepare us for the liturgical feasts; they help us acquire mastery over our instincts and freedom of heart [2043].

This is another thing that a lot of people think has gone out the window. We are supposed to fast and abstain during Lent and at other particular times. On Good Friday, for example, we are supposed to abstain from meat, and we are supposed to fast during the day. This still binds. The Second Vatican Council didn't change any of this.

Finally, we have the obligation, within our means, to support the Church. This doesn't mean we have to starve ourselves. But someone has to pay for our schools, someone has to pay for our hospitals, someone has to pay for our churches. Anyone who wants to subtract from any contribution to the cathedral what he or she thinks is my salary, feel free—I don't get one!

29

"What Must I Do to Have Eternal Life?"

A Look at the Ten Commandments, Starting with the First

TEXT PREPARED FOR SUNDAY
JUNE 12, 1994

It was hot and sticky last night, and noisy. I tried to sleep with the window open. Some kind of high-powered machinery whined in the street, and even at three A.M., cars roared by. I thought of today's Gospel and of Jesus' words to the crowd:

> "This is how it is with the reign of God. A man scattered seed on the ground. He goes to bed and gets up day after day. Through it all the seed sprouts and grows without his knowing how it happened" (Mk 4:26–27).

Despite all the noise in the world, the clatter, the chaos; despite our ignoring it, ridiculing it, violating it, rejecting it, God's law works quietly and inevitably in all things. All our thoughts, our words, our works are scattered on the world throughout the course of each day. And as we sow, we reap, for good or for bad, for happiness or for unhappiness, for love or for hatred, for salvation or damnation, in accordance with the law of God that governs all.

"What must I do to have eternal life?" a young man asked Jesus. "Keep the commandments", Jesus answered. That's the way the section of the new *Catechism* begins in its treatment of the Ten Commandments. The Ten Commandments, in general, and the first commandment, in particular, constitute the contents of this twenty-ninth session of our 41 sessions on the *Catechism*. With few exceptions, this time I will simply let the text speak for itself.

Cardinal O'Connor was in Rome on June 12. This homily was prepared for the *Catechism* series published by *Catholic New York*. It was not given at St. Patrick's Cathedral.

THE TEN COMMANDMENTS

I. "TEACHER, WHAT MUST I DO . . . ?"

"Teacher, what good deed must I do, to have eternal life?" To the young man who asked this question, Jesus answers first by invoking the necessity to recognize God as the "One there is who is good," as the supreme Good and the source of all good. Then Jesus tells him: "If you would enter life, keep the commandments." And he cites for his questioner the precepts that concern love of neighbor: "You shall not kill, You shall not commit adultery, You shall not steal, You shall not bear false witness, Honor your father and mother." Finally Jesus sums up these commandments positively: "You shall love your neighbor as yourself" (Mt 19:16–19) [2052].

When someone asks him, "Which commandment in the Law is the greatest?" (Mt 22:36), Jesus replies: "You shall love the Lord your God with all your heart, and with all your soul, and with all your mind. This is the greatest and first commandment. And a second is like it: You shall love your neighbor as yourself. On these two commandments hang all the Law and the prophets" (Mt 22:37–40). The Decalogue must be interpreted in light of this twofold yet single commandment of love, the fullness of the Law [2055].

II. THE DECALOGUE IN SACRED SCRIPTURE

The word "Decalogue" means literally "ten words" (Ex 34:28). God revealed these "ten words" to his people on the holy mountain. . . . They are pre-eminently the words of God. They are handed on to us in the books of *Exodus* and *Deuteronomy.* . . . it is in the New Covenant in Jesus Christ that their full meaning will be revealed [2056].

. . . [T]he "ten words" point out the conditions of a life freed from slavery of sin. The Decalogue is a path of life [2057].

III. THE DECALOGUE IN THE CHURCH'S TRADITION

In fidelity to Scripture and in conformity with the example of Jesus, the tradition of the Church has acknowledged the primordial importance and significance of the Decalogue [2064].

The division and numbering of the Commandments have varied in the course of history. The present catechism follows the division of the Commandments established by Saint Augustine, which has become traditional in the Catholic Church [2066].

The Ten Commandments state what is required in the love of God and love of neighbor. The first three concern love of God, and the other seven love of neighbor [2067].

IV. THE UNITY OF THE DECALOGUE

The Decalogue forms a coherent whole. Each "word" refers to each of the others and to all of them; they reciprocally condition one another. The two tables shed light on one another; they form an organic unity. To transgress one commandment is to infringe all the others. One cannot honor another person without blessing God his Creator. One cannot adore God without loving all men, his creatures. The Decalogue brings man's religious and social life into unity [2069].

V. THE DECALOGUE AND THE NATURAL LAW

The Ten Commandments belong to God's revelation. At the same time they teach us the true humanity of man. They bring to light the essential duties, and therefore, indirectly, the fundamental rights inherent in the nature of the human person [2070].

The commandments of the Decalogue, although accessible to reason alone, have been revealed. To attain a complete and certain understanding of the requirements of the natural law, sinful humanity needed this revelation:

"A full explanation of the commandments of the Decalogue became necessary in the state of sin because the light of reason was obscured and the will had gone astray."

We know God's commandments through the divine revelation proposed to us in the Church, and through the voice of moral conscience [2071].

VI. THE OBLIGATION OF THE DECALOGUE

Since they express man's fundamental duties towards God and towards his neighbor, the Ten Commandments reveal, in their primordial content, *grave* obligations. They are fundamentally immutable, and they oblige always and everywhere. No one can dispense from them. The Ten Commandments are engraved by God in the human heart [2072].

Jesus summed up man's duties toward God in this saying: "You shall love the Lord your God with all your heart, and with all your soul, and with all your mind" (Mt 22:37). This immediately echoes the solemn call: "Hear, O Israel: the LORD our God is the one LORD" (Dt 6:4).

God has loved us first. The love of the One God is recalled in the first of the "ten words." The commandments then make explicit the response of love that man is called to give to his God [2083].

The First Commandment

I am the LORD your God, who brought you out of the land of Egypt, out of the house of bondage. You shall have no other gods before me. You shall not make for yourself a graven image, or any likeness of anything that is in heaven above, or that is in the earth beneath, or that is in the water under the earth; you shall not bow down to them or serve them (Ex 20:2–5).

"The first commandment embraces faith, hope and charity" [2086].

Faith

Our moral life has its source in faith in God who reveals His love to us [2087].

The first commandment requires us to nourish and protect our faith with prudence and vigilance, and to reject everything that is opposed to it. There are various ways of sinning against faith:

Voluntary doubt about the faith disregards or refuses to hold as true what God has revealed and the Church proposed for belief. *Involuntary doubt* refers to hesitation in believing, difficulty in overcoming objections connected with the faith, or also anxiety aroused by its obscurity. If deliberately cultivated doubt can lead to spiritual blindness [2088].

Incredulity is the neglect of revealed truth or the willful refusal to assent to it. "*Heresy* is the obstinate post-baptismal denial of some truth which must be believed with divine and catholic faith, or it is likewise an obstinate doubt concerning the same; *apostasy* is the total repudiation of the Christian faith; *schism* is the refusal of submission to the Roman Pontiff or of communion with the members of the Church subject to him" [2089].

Hope

When God reveals Himself and calls him, man cannot fully respond to the divine love by his own powers. He must hope that God will give him the capacity to love Him in return and to act in conformity with the commandments of charity. Hope is the confident expectation of divine blessing and the beatific vision of God; it is also the fear of offending God's love and of incurring punishment [2090].

The first commandment is also concerned with sins against hope, namely, despair and presumption:

By *despair*, man ceases to hope for his personal salvation from God, for help in attaining it or for the forgiveness of his sins. Despair is contrary to God's goodness, to his justice—for the Lord is faithful to his promises—and to his mercy [2091].

There are two kinds of *presumption*. Either man presumes upon his own capacities (hoping to be able to save himself without help from on high), or he presumes upon God's almighty power or his mercy (hoping to obtain forgiveness without conversion and glory without merit) [2092].

Charity

Faith in God's love encompasses the call and the obligation to respond with sincere love to divine charity. The first commandment enjoins us to love God above everything and all creatures for him and because of him [2093].

"HIM ONLY SHALL YOU SERVE"

Adoration

Adoration is the first act of the virtue of religion. To adore God is to acknowledge him as God, as the Creator and Savior, the Lord and Master of everything that exists, as infinite and merciful Love [2096].

Prayer

The acts of faith, hope and charity enjoined by the first commandment are accomplished in prayer [2098].

Sacrifice

It is right to offer sacrifice to God as a sign of adoration and gratitude, supplication and communion [2099].

Outward sacrifice, to be genuine, must be the expression of spiritual sacrifice [2100].

Promises amd Vows

In many circumstances, the Christian is called to make *promises* to God. Baptism and Confirmation, Matrimony and Holy Orders always entail promises [2101].

"A *vow* is a deliberate and free promise made to God concerning a possible and better good which must be fulfilled by reason of the virtue of religion." A vow is an act of *devotion* in which the Christian dedicates himself to God or promises him some good work [2102].

The Church recognizes an exemplary value in the vows to practice the *evangelical counsels* [2103].

I might add here to the *Catechism*'s mention of the evangelical counsels the fascinating words of St. Anthony of Padua:

The man who is filled with the Holy Spirit speaks in different languages. These different tongues are different ways of witnessing to Christ, such as humility, poverty, patience and obedience; we speak in those languages when we reveal in ourselves these virtues to others. Actions speak louder than words; let your words teach and your action speak.

I wonder how many of us who first heard as children "Actions speak louder than words", know that these words came from St. Anthony of Padua?

In any event, it is consoling to recognize how many religious men and women the world over take vows to live lives of poverty, chastity, and obedience, evangelical counsels that witness to Christ in extraordinary ways.

THE SOCIAL DUTY OF RELIGION
AND THE RIGHT TO RELIGIOUS FREEDOM

"All men are bound to seek the truth, especially in what concerns God and his Church, and to embrace it and hold on to it as they come to know it." This duty derives from "the very dignity of the human person." It does not contradict a "sincere respect" for different religions which frequently "reflect a ray of that truth which enlightens all men," nor the requirement of charity, which urges Christians "to treat with love, prudence and patience those who are in error or ignorance with regard to the faith" [2104].

"Nobody may be forced to act against his convictions, nor is anyone to be restrained from acting in accordance with his conscience in religious matters in private or in public, alone or in association with others, within due limits." This right is based on the very nature of the human person, whose dignity enables him freely to assent to the divine truth which transcends the temporal order. For this reason it "continues to exist even in those who do not live up to their obligation of seeking the truth and adhering to it" [2106].

"If because of the circumstances of a particular people special civil recognition is given one religious community in the constitutional organization of a state, the right of all citizens and religious communities to religious freedom must be recognized and respected as well" [2107].

The right to religious liberty is neither a moral license to adhere to error, nor a supposed right to error, but rather a natural right of the human person to civil liberty, i.e., immunity, within just limits, from external constraint in religious matters by political authorities. This natural right ought to be acknowledged in the juridical order of society in such a way that it constitutes a civil right [2108].

"YOU SHALL HAVE NO OTHER GODS BEFORE ME"

The first commandment forbids honoring gods other than the Lord who has revealed Himself to His people. It proscribes superstition and irreligion [2110].

Superstition

Superstition is the deviation of religious feeling and of the practices this feeling imposes. It can even affect the worship we offer the true God, e.g., when one attributes an importance in some way magical to certain practices otherwise lawful or necessary [2111].

Idolatry

The first commandment condemns *polytheism*. It requires man neither to believe in, nor to venerate, other divinities than the one true God [2112].

Idolatry not only refers to false pagan worship. It remains a constant temptation to faith. Idolatry consists in divinizing what is not God [2113].

Permit me to suggest that this might be one of the most important warnings in the entire *Catechism*.

Call someone an idolater, and he or she would be outraged. "You're insulting my intelligence. You think I would worship a totem pole? You think I'm a savage?" Yet how easy is it for money to become our god, or sex, or drugs, or alcohol, or gambling, or ambitions? How easy is it to put a big job, a big house, a big car, a big bank account before everything else? Aren't these highly common forms of idolatry?

It might be worth reminding ourselves here, for a moment, of what idolatry is *not*, because, at times, we Catholics have been accused of it. A statue of Mary is not an *idol*, nor is a picture of the Sacred Heart of Jesus, nor an image of a saint. We don't *adore* these. They are merely reminders to us. We don't pray *to* them. They have no power in themselves. I have a painting of my mother and father in my room and a picture of my sister on my desk. They are reminders of loved ones.

Divination and Magic

All forms of *divination* are to be rejected: recourse to Satan or demons, conjuring up the dead or other practices falsely supposed to "unveil" the future.

Consulting horoscopes, astrology, palm reading, interpretation of omens and lots, the phenomena of clairvoyance, and recourse to mediums all conceal a desire for power over time, history and, in the last analysis, other human beings, as well as a wish to conciliate hidden powers. They contradict the honor, respect and loving fear that we owe to God alone [2116].

All practices of *magic and sorcery,* by which one attempts to tame occult powers, so as to place them at one's service and have a supernatural power over others—even if this were for the sake of restoring their health—are gravely contrary to the virtue of religion. These practices are even more to be condemned when accompanied by the intention of harming someone, or when they have recourse to the intervention of demons. Wearing charms is also reprehensible. *Spiritism* often implies divination or magical practices; the Church for her part warns the faithful against it. Recourse to so-called traditional cures does not justify either the invocation of evil powers or the exploitation of another's credulity [2117].

Irreligion

God's first commandment condemns the main sins of irreligion: tempting God, in words or deeds, sacrilege, and simony [2118].

Tempting God consists in putting his goodness and almighty power to test by word or deed. Thus Satan tried to induce Jesus to throw himself down from the Temple and, by this gesture, force God to act. Jesus opposed Satan with the word of God: "You shall not put the LORD your God to the test" [2119].

Sacrilege consists in profaning or treating unworthily the sacraments and other liturgical actions, as well as persons, things or places consecrated to God. Sacrilege is a grave sin especially when committed against the Eucharist, for in this sacrament the true Body of Christ is made substantially present for us [2120].

Simony is defined as the buying or selling of spiritual things [2121].

Atheism

"Many . . . of our contemporaries either do not at all perceive, or explicitly reject, this intimate and vital bond of man to God. Atheism must therefore be regarded as one of the most serious problems of our time" [2123].

The name "atheism" covers many very different phenomena. One common form is the practical materialism which restricts its needs and aspirations to space and time. Atheistic humanism falsely considers man to be "an end to himself, and the sole maker, with supreme control, of his own history." Another form of contemporary atheism looks for the liberation of man through economic and social liberation. "It holds that religion, of its very nature, thwarts such emancipation by raising man's hopes in a future life, thus both deceiving him and discouraging him from working for a better form of life on earth" [2124].

Since it rejects or denies the existence of God, atheism is a sin against the virtue of religion [2125].

Atheism is often based on a false conception of human autonomy, exaggerated to the point of refusing any dependence on God [2126].

Agnosticism

Agnosticism assumes a number of forms. In certain cases the agnostic refrains from denying God; instead he postulates the existence of a transcendent being which is incapable of revealing itself, and about which nothing can be said. In other cases, the agnostic makes no judgment about God's existence, declaring it impossible to prove, or even to affirm or deny [2127].

It is time to conclude this twenty-ninth session on the *Catechism*. I do so with a brief comment on this matter of agnosticism, which is often enough only another word for laziness, or even for cowardice. "I can't be bothered thinking about God. If there is a God, what's the difference? He certainly has nothing to do with me." But then, there's the story of the agnostic who was drowning and cried out: "O God, if there be a God, save my soul, if I have a soul."

Agnosticism is a sad state of affairs. The agnostic can seem so sophisticated. He can seem to know all the answers. He appears to be so clever in brushing off the questions that really matter. Yet even while the *agnostic* sleeps, the seed in the ground sprouts and grows, despite his not knowing how it happens. And the law of God works on.

30

God's Name Is Holy

On the Second Commandment

FATHER'S DAY
JUNE 19, 1994
PONTIFICAL MASS

Last week we began looking at the *Catechism*'s treatment of the Ten Commandments. We focused on the first commandment, "I am the LORD your God; you shall not have strange gods before Me." Today we continue with the second commandment, "You shall not take the name of the LORD your God in vain" (Ex 20:7).

We are told in the *Catechism*:

> The second commandment *prescribes respect for the Lord's name.* Like the first commandment, it belongs to the virtue of religion and more particularly it governs our use of speech in sacred matters [2142].

> Among all of the words of Revelation, there is one which is unique: the revealed name of God. God confides his name to those who believe in him; he reveals himself to them in his personal mystery. The gift of a name belongs to the order of trust and intimacy. "The Lord's name is holy." For this reason man must not abuse it. He must keep it in mind in silent, loving adoration. He will not introduce it into his own speech except to bless, praise, and glorify it [2143].

That is not strange from a human perspective. We introduce ourselves by name. We introduce one friend to another by name. Those who are in love often have a special name for the person whom they love. The first question that Moses asked Almighty God when God told him He wanted him to go to lead His people out of slavery to the Egyptians was, "Who shall I say sent me? What is your name?"

We know, of course, how easy it is to slip into the habit of using the name of the Lord, the name of Jesus, the name of Christ in vain, or even how easily we say, "Oh, my God", or something of that sort. The Scriptures tell us that the name is to be used only with adoration, only as a blessing.

The *Catechism* continues:

Respect for the name of God is an expression of the respect owed to the mystery of God himself and to the whole sacred reality it evokes [2144].

To understand this commandment adequately, we have to understand the Jewish respect for names, especially in the Old Testament. For example, in the first book of the Old Testament we are told that God gave Adam the power to name everything. This meant that Adam had dominion over everything. In addition, in the Old Testament it was always the father who named the new baby, indicating that the father was taking the place of God the Father.

The Jews had such respect for the name of God that they never used that most intimate name that He used for Himself, that is, the one that He gave to Moses. When Moses asked, "Who shall I say sent me?" God answered, "Yahweh, He who is. I am who am." He was saying to Moses, tell them God the Creator, God who is everything, sent you. In this way God revealed Himself and in that sense gave Himself to Moses, making Himself vulnerable. Recognizing this, with great reverence and respect, the Jews never used the name "Yahweh". The Jewish rabbis devised a hundred fifty names for God, such as "Adoni", so they wouldn't use the name Yahweh. That is how sacred they considered the name to be.

Today's Gospel, for example, concludes with the apostles having just gone through this terrifying experience where they think they are drowning, while our Lord is asleep. They wake Him in fear and perhaps in some resentment. Our Lord calms the winds and the waves, and the apostles say, "Who can this be that the wind and the sea obey him? What is his name?" His name reveals everything—Jesus, He who saves.

We are told in the *Catechism*:

The faithful should bear witness to the Lord's name by confessing the faith without giving way to fear. [We should all be able to say, I am proud of being a Christian, a follower of Christ. I am never ashamed of that, under any circumstances, and I try to behave accordingly.] Preaching and catechizing should be permeated with adoration and respect for the name of our Lord Jesus Christ [2145].

The second commandment *forbids the abuse of God's name*, i.e., every improper use of the names of God, Jesus Christ, but also of the Virgin Mary and all the saints [2146].

Promises made to others in God's name engage the divine honor, fidelity, truthfulness, and authority. They must be respected in justice. To be unfaithful [to a promise we made] is to misuse God's name and in some way to make God out to be a liar [2147].

So often we will say, "As God is my judge, I tell you that this is true." If it is not true, then we are making God out to be a liar.

> *Blasphemy* is directly opposed to the second commandment. It consists in uttering against God—inwardly or outwardly—words of hatred, reproach, or defiance, in speaking ill of God, in failing to respect Him in one's speech, in misusing His name. . . . The prohibition of blasphemy extends to language against Christ's Church, the saints, and sacred things. It is also blasphemous to make use of God's name to cover up criminal practices. . . . The misuse of God's name to commit a crime can provoke others to repudiate religion.
> Blasphemy is contrary to the respect due God and his holy name. It is in itself a grave sin [2148].

> *Oaths* which misuse God's name, though without the intention of blasphemy, show lack of respect for the Lord. The second commandment also forbids *magical use* of the divine name [2149].

Just saying the name "Jesus" over and over again may be a very holy thing to do, but if we think that just saying that name has some magical power attached to it, we are mistaken. If we think we are going to make it rain, for instance, or we are going to make the sun shine by invoking God's name, that is superstitious, and that is one of the original reasons for this commandment.

The *Catechism* continues:

> The second commandment *forbids false oaths.* Taking an oath or swearing is to take God as witness to what one affirms. It is to invoke the divine truthfulness as a pledge of one's own truthfulness [2150].

> A false oath calls on God to be a witness to a lie [2151].

Perjury is even a civil offense, one of the worst civil offenses that can be committed in a courtroom. A witness is asked, "Do you swear to tell the truth, the whole truth, and nothing but the truth, so help you God?" If he or she answers, "I do", and then does not tell the truth, that is perjury, and it is a serious civil offense.

The *Catechism* says:

> A person commits *perjury* when he makes a promise under oath with no intention of keeping it, or when after promising on oath he does not keep it. Perjury is a grave lack of respect for the Lord of all speech. Pledging oneself by oath to commit an evil deed is contrary to the holiness of the divine name [2152].

Secret societies, crime syndicates, for instance, who swear in blood in God's name to commit various crimes, are obviously atrocities.

> Jesus teaches that every oath involves a reference to God and that God's presence and his truth must be honored in all speech. Discretion in calling

upon God is allied with a respectful awareness of his presence, which all our assertions either witness to or mock [2153].

For years and years the great guardians of the Holy Name of Jesus have been Holy Name Societies. Unfortunately they don't seem to be as popular or strong as they once were. They are still to be encouraged. The Holy Name Society is a wonderful reminder that we are made in the image of God and that we must keep His name holy.

The *Catechism* says:

> The holiness of the divine name demands that we neither use it for trivial matters, nor take an oath which on the basis of the circumstances could be interpreted as approval of an authority unjustly requiring it. When an oath is required by illegitimate civil authorities, it may be refused. It must be refused when it is required for purposes contrary to the dignity of persons or to ecclesial communion [2155].

We are told in the *Catechism* about Christian names:

> The sacrament of Baptism is conferred "in the name of the Father and of the Son and of the Holy Spirit" (Mt 28:19). In Baptism, the Lord's name sanctifies man, and the Christian receives his name in the Church. This can be the name of a saint, that is, of a disciple who has lived a life of exemplary fidelity to the Lord. The patron saint provides a model of charity; we are assured of his intercession. The "baptismal name" can also express a Christian mystery or Christian virtue. "Parents, sponsors and the pastor are to see that a name is not given which is foreign to Christian sentiment" (Canon 855) [2156].

It is not uncommon today for people to want to give their youngster, let us say, the last name of the mother or the name of George Washington, or Lincoln, or someone like that. I must confess that when I baptize, if a name like that is given, I always add Mary, if it's a girl, or Joseph, if it's a boy, and that goes on the baptismal certificate with the other name, whatever it may be.

The *Catechism* continues:

> The Christian begins his day, his prayers and his activities with the Sign of the Cross: "in the name of the Father and of the Son and of the Holy Spirit. Amen." The baptized person dedicates the day to the glory of God and calls on the Savior's grace which lets him act in the Spirit as a child of the Father. The sign of the cross strengthens us in temptations and difficulties [2157].

It is a travesty, and so sad, that some people today refuse to say, "In the name of the Father and of the Son and of the Holy Spirit." They will say something like "In the name of the creator, the redeemer, and the sanctifier" because they don't want to call God Father. That is very, very foolish. In God are all traits, masculine and feminine, fatherly and motherly traits. But Christ called God His Father. Christ it is who gave us the formula, "Going therefore, teach all nations, baptizing them in the name of the Father and of the Son and of the Holy Spirit." We cannot change that formula. A Baptism would be invalid if we did not use that formula. The *Catechism* continues:

> God calls each one by name. Everyone's name is sacred. The name is the [image, as it were] of the person. It demands respect as a sign of the dignity of the one who bears it [2158].

When our Lord called the apostles, He didn't just say, "You fellows come and follow Me." He called Simon—"From now on your name will be Peter." "Nathaniel, you will be Bartholomew." He called *each one of them by name.*
The *Catechism* tells us:

> The name one receives is a name for eternity. In the kingdom, the mysterious and unique character of each person marked with God's name will shine forth in splendor. "To him who conquers . . . I will give a white stone, with a new name written on the stone which no one knows except him who receives it" (Rev 2:17). "Then I looked, and Lo, on Mount Zion stood the Lamb, and with him a hundred and forty-four thousand who had his name and his Father's name written on their foreheads" (Rev 14:1) [2159].

I would like to add just a word about this being Father's Day, in conjunction with this particular commandment and our Lord's calling God His Father. The name "father" conjures up so much. Last night I telephoned the father of a 22-year-old man who was killed in an accident while trying to save someone else's life. I reminded the father that our Lord was trying to save our lives when He was killed. The father said to me what one would expect, or at least hope, a father would say. He said, "I would gladly change places with him. I would gladly give my life for my son." That's the essence of being a father.

A couple of weeks ago we had in this cathedral several hundred couples who had been married fifty years. As I looked at the mothers and fathers who came up the aisle—some of them very old, some of them handicapped—I thought of the tremendous sacrifices that most of them have made for their children, in some cases some of the abuse that they have taken. They have never stopped loving their children. To look at them it was a far cry from the Greek drama *Oedipus Rex*, in which Oedipus unknowingly kills his father and then unknowingly marries his own mother. Nothing so tangled these couples' lives as that. Fidelity to each other, fidelity to and sacrifice for their children, characterizes their lives.

Most of us have had an opportunity to live normal lives, and if our fathers have gone before us, we remember them with fondness. Sadly, it's not true of all, we can't be naïve about it. I know if I were a kid on a red-hot day like this and my father were alive now, he would take me fishing. That kind of thing is one of my wonderful memories, and I think they contributed significantly to my being a priest.

I wish everyone had had such experiences. Everyone hasn't had. But today is a day to try to forget bitterness, if we have any, to forget animosity between fathers and sons and daughters. Today is a day to remember those who have gone before or those who are still living, with a great sense of gratitude for their having given us the gift of life. Perhaps when we come to the Our Father in the Mass, all of us can pray the Our Father for our own fathers and for all of the fathers who are here today.

This week we will have many, many visitors in town. All of us are reminded as Catholics, as Christians, particularly during this heat, which tends to make us lose our reason and at times our temper, we are reminded of the words of our Divine Lord, "By this shall everyone know that you are My followers, that you love one another." We are never acting on behalf of the Church, we are never bringing honor to the Church, when we treat with contempt those with whom we disagree, whether that contempt be expressed physically, mentally, or orally.

31

Keeping the Sabbath Holy

On the Third Commandment

THIRTEENTH SUNDAY OF THE YEAR
JUNE 26, 1994
PONTIFICAL MASS

Every time I go to confession, as I did yesterday, my homily is a little bit better the next day. Perhaps some of you are thinking, "Why doesn't he go to confession every day?" or, "If he thinks his homilies are better after he goes to confession, how bad they must be before he goes to confession!"

I mention this because I go to confession to a wonderful, elderly priest who always reflects on the Gospel of the Sunday. Yesterday, for example, he talked about the wonder and beauty of today's Gospel (Mk 5:21–43). For at least ten years this poor woman has suffered with terrible hemorrhaging. No doctors can do anything about it. Then she reaches out to touch Jesus' robe, saying, "If I could touch the hem of his robe I will be cured." A sense of awe went through her entire body, and she was completely healed.

The priest-confessor talked to me in terms of hope, about having hope and trusting in Jesus. Reflecting on this all day yesterday, I thought of an application of this concept to our entire society and to the Church in society. There are many who see society hemorrhaging morally. All of our old values seem to be disappearing before our eyes. Many people reject and even ridicule marriage and the family. We are told that we should welcome new ways of living and forget the old, that we should encourage new forms of freedom, of liberty.

William Butler Yeats would put it as he did put it in his day, "Mere anarchy is loosed upon the world. . . . The center cannot hold." We know that the center *can* hold and the center *will* hold, because the center is Christ. Pope John Paul II never tires of reminding us that this is a Christocentric world, everything revolves around the Lord Jesus.

The other night I was interviewed by Charlie Rose of the "Charlie Rose Show". He asked me if I thought that the people in this country were less religious today. In essence, he was asking if religion is a dead issue. We talked about the moral fiber of the country, the general chaos that we seem to see, the hemorrhaging. But I answered, "No, people aren't less religious today. Come to St. Patrick's Cathedral on any Sunday, at least until the hot weather comes, and you will see standing-room-only crowds. There are so many millions of deeply devout, spiritually, religiously committed people in our land."

The Church is not dead. It is like that young girl in today's Gospel. We are told that they came to Christ and they said this young girl was dead. The Gospel says: "Jesus disregarded the report that had been brought and said: 'Fear is useless. What is needed is trust' " (Mk 5:36).

We are told in the Gospel that in Jesus' time, in His own time, He went to the home of the little girl, and the people were understandably wailing and mourning. He said to them, "This little girl is not dead, she is asleep." And they ridiculed Him. Then He reached out and touched her, and she was whole again.

I think that is the way it is with religion, with morality, with the Church. Perhaps they look dead, but all we have to do is to reach out and touch the hem of Jesus' robe or let Him touch us. He's not far from the Church. His living Body is the Church. We need not fear whatever happens anywhere.

In the Old Testament, in the beautiful Twenty-third Psalm, we are told, "The Lord is my shepherd, I shall not want. He leads me through green pastures. He restores my soul." Then the Psalm says something very beautiful, which is particularly applicable to our *Catechism* session today: "He has prepared a banquet for me in the sight of my foes. My cup runneth over." We are at that banquet now.

This is a reference to the Holy Sacrifice of the Mass, the banquet of the Lord, where the cup of His Blood runs over, giving us new life, washing this world, purifying it even when the world doesn't want to be purified. The Blood of Christ washes over even those who want to live in their sins.

The third commandment, which is the subject of our *Catechism* session today, is the third of those three that refer directly to Almighty God: the first, "I am the LORD your God; you shall not have strange Gods before me"; the second, "You shall not take the name of the LORD in vain"; the third, "Remember to keep holy the Sabbath."

I read from the *Catechism*:

> Remember the sabbath day, to keep it holy. Six days you shall labor, and do all your work; but the seventh day is a sabbath to the Lord your God; in it you shall not do any work (Ex 20:8–10).

That is taken from the Book of Exodus, the story of the exit of the Israelites from slavery to the Egyptians, during which period Almighty God gave to Moses the Ten Commandments.

The *Catechism* gives us several reasons why the sabbath day is holy. The first it gives is:

> The third commandment of the Decalogue [the Ten Commandments] recalls the holiness of the sabbath: "The seventh day is a sabbath of solemn rest, holy to the LORD" (Ex 31:15) [2168].

Why is this? We are told that God created the world in six days. We don't know that they were days of twenty-four hours. They could be millions of light years. Apparently, however, the world was created in phases. On the seventh day, we are told, God rested, that is, He did not create. We keep the day after God had completed creation holy because He had given us this wonderful gift. He stopped creating for a time, and so we join Him in that period of rest.

The *Catechism* gives us a second reason why we keep the sabbath holy:

> Scripture also reveals in the Lord's day *a memorial of Israel's liberation* from bondage in Egypt: "You shall remember that you were a servant in the land of Egypt, and the LORD your God brought you out thence with mighty hand and outstretched arm; therefore the LORD your God commanded you to keep the sabbath day" (Dt 5:15) [2170].

That was true liberation. We use the word "liberation" today so easily, but true liberation is liberation from sin. Even the liberation from slavery to the Egyptians was a symbol of liberation from sin.

The third reason the *Catechism* gives for keeping the Sabbath day holy is:

> God's action is the model for human action. If God "rested and was refreshed" on the seventh day, [we] too ought to "rest" and should let others, especially the poor, "be refreshed" (Ex 31:17). The sabbath brings everyday work to a halt and provides a respite. It is a day to protest against the servitude of work and the worship of money [2172].

This goes back a long way. After he became a convert to Christianity, the emperor Constantine, in the year 321, promulgated a civil law saying there will be no work done on Sundays. He exempted farmers, because they were dependent on the weather and so on to get their crops in. So it was actually an emperor who first established in civil society what we are told in the commandments.

The *Catechism* says:

> Jesus rose from the dead "on the first day of the week." Because it is the "first day," the day of Christ's Resurrection recalls the first creation. Because it is the "eighth day" following the sabbath, it symbolizes the new creation ushered in by Christ's Resurrection. For Christians it has become the first of all days, the first of all feasts, the Lord's Day—Sunday [2174].

Why did early Christians emphasize that Sunday was the Lord's day? Because Nero and other pagan emperors demanded to be called "lord", because lord meant God. They really believed they were divine. The Christians refused to call Nero and the others "lord". They said, "Christ is our Lord. Christ is our God." They converted the name Sunday, which was a pagan term for worship of the sun. They said, "Christ is our sun. Christ is the Light of the World. Sunday is the day that we will celebrate."

The *Catechism* continues:

> Sunday is expressly distinguished from the sabbath which it follows chronologically every week [which is still observed by our Jewish brothers and sisters]; for Christians its ceremonial observance replaces that of the sabbath [2175].

> The celebration of Sunday observes the moral commandment inscribed by nature in the human heart to render to God an outward, visible, public and regular worship "as a sign of his universal [generosity] to all" (St. Thomas Aquinas) [2176].

In other words, it just makes sense. It is a natural part of things. God has given us His wonderful gifts, so it is very part of our nature to thank God. "The Sunday celebration of the Lord's Day and his Eucharist is at the heart of the Church's life" [2177].

This is the primary way we celebrate Sunday. Whatever else happens today, this is the most important. This is the heart and soul of our faith. This is the heart and soul of our Sunday. This is the spiritual, mysterious renewal of our Lord's suffering and death on the Cross. This, for us, is another Easter, another day of Resurrection.

We are told in the *Catechism*:

> This practice of the Christian assembly dates from the beginnings of the apostolic age. The Letter to the Hebrews reminds the faithful "not to neglect to meet together, as is the habit of some . . ." (Heb 10:25) [2178].

The polls always want to know how many people come to Mass. You might tell them to go back to the first century and find out how many people came then! Maybe it is not very different, because in this letter to the Hebrews, which was written very early, 70 A.D. or something of that sort, we are told not to neglect meeting together as some do.

We are told in the *Catechism*, and this again shows us there is nothing new under the sun:

> Tradition preserves the memory of an ever-timely exhortation: Come to Church early, approach the Lord, and confess your sins, repent in

prayer. . . . Be present at the sacred and divine liturgy, conclude its prayer
and do not leave before the dismissal. . . . We have often said: "This day is
given to you for prayer and rest. This is the day the Lord has made, let us
rejoice and be glad in it" [2178].

How many pastors have you heard in various parish churches throughout the country and the world saying, "Don't be standing in the back and
leaving after Communion is over." I remember when I was a kid growing
up in St. Clement's Parish in Philadelphia, the good-natured butt of jokes
in the parish was one family who lived immediately across the street. They
lived maybe fifty feet from the church, and they were always the last ones
for Mass on Sunday!

The *Catechism* talks briefly about the parish:

A parish . . . is the place where all the faithful can be gathered together for
the Sunday celebration of the Eucharist. The parish initiates the Christian
people into the ordinary expression of the liturgical life: it gathers them together in this celebration; it teaches Christ's saving doctrine; it practices the
charity of the Lord in good works and brotherly love [2179].

There are always recommendations coming in that we should do
away with parishes. Today parish lines and boundaries are not respected
in every case. You can go to Mass wherever you want, and of course
you should be able to do so. Some say it should be more free-wheeling
and that we shouldn't have parishes. We have too many churches,
they'll say. That is so, however, because of the Eucharist. Again, Pope
John Paul II is constantly telling us that it is the Eucharist that makes us
a community.

It is difficult to capture, to maintain, a sense of community. We really
have to work at it. It is not impossible, however, because we have the Eucharist. This is what makes community in a parish. A parish community
should engage in good works by feeding the hungry, clothing the naked,
housing the homeless, and meeting the other needs of the community.
The Eucharist must be at the heart of it all.

We are told in the *Catechism*:

The precept of the Church specifies the law of the Lord more precisely:
"On Sundays and other holy days of obligation the faithful are bound to
participate in the Mass" [2180].

God said, "Remember to keep holy the sabbath." The Church specifies
how this will be done, saying, "We will make that Sunday, and the Mass
will be the central act of worship." Somehow the idea spread after the
Vatican Council that it was no longer obligatory to go to Mass on Sunday.

As I mentioned before, I have been told that, even in some of our Catholic high schools, students were told, "You don't have to go to Mass. You should go out of love. You should go because it is a good thing to do." Of course you should go out of love because it's a good thing to do! But the Church still says it's a mortal sin if we deliberately miss Mass on Sundays or holy days of obligation. God has the right to oblige us; the Church has the right to oblige us. Even more, we should recognize that it's a wonderful privilege and a wonderful gift.

We come here and find the hemorrhage of blood is stemmed. Our sorrows, our cares, our problems are recognized. Christ does reach out to us. Christ does raise us from the dead. Going to Mass on Sunday is an obligation. Summertime is no exception.

We are told in the *Catechism*:

> If because of a lack of a sacred minister or for other grave cause participation in the celebration of the [Mass] is impossible, it is specifically recommended that [we do something. We take part in sacred readings. We pray the rosary. We spend some time in prayer. But the idea is we try to keep the day holy] [2183].

> On Sundays and other holy days of obligation, the faithful are to refrain from engaging in work or activities that hinder the worship owed to God, the joy proper to the Lord's Day, the performance of the works of mercy, and the appropriate relaxation of mind and body. Family needs or important social service can legitimately excuse from the obligation of Sunday rest. The faithful should see to it that legitimate excuses do not lead to habits prejudicial to religion, family life, and health [2185].

There is a lot of conflict on this in our day. Common sense has to prevail. There are a lot of police officers working today. Last night the mayor told me there would be six thousand officers on duty today. They are there for our good and for the good of all society. They are needed to work today.

When I was a kid, we were told we had to refrain from servile work, which meant manual labor. I remember my mother would never sew on Sunday. If you had a hole in your sock, that is the way you went to school on Monday! My mother would sew it on Monday night, because she could not work on Sunday. Clearly we are in a very, very complex society. The important thing, once again, is that we truly try within our hearts, within our beings to rest in the Lord, to rest with the Lord, to feel serene in the Lord on Sunday.

Early Church legislation about keeping holy the sabbath and getting to Mass on Sunday emphasized above all that we should make a very special effort to refrain from any evil on Sundays. You are supposed to do that always, but on Sunday we are supposed to be particularly scrupulous about that. You have to figure your own way. You know the needs of your families. You know whether you have to work manually or not. We have to do our best to rest in the Lord, to delight in the Lord.

32

"Honor Your Father and Your Mother"

On the Fourth Commandment

May I ask you please to remember in this Holy Sacrifice of the Mass a wonderful lady who died this past year at the age of ninety-six, Josephine Azzara. During those ninety-six years she was totally devoted to the Church, said two Rosaries a day, and lived in a spirit that exemplifies everything good in our holy faith.

Today we return to our reflections on the *Catechism*, which we began on the First Sunday of Advent in 1993. I understand that since its publication the *Catechism* has sold more than two million copies, that another two million are on order, and that it is being very widely used throughout the United States by Catholics and by a significant number of non-Catholics. This is a wonderful thing. We hope that much of the confusion that has existed will be dissipated.

Before we ended these sessions on the final Sunday in June, we had completed three of the Ten Commandments. Today we move to the fourth commandment: "Honor your father and your mother, that your days may be long in the land which the Lord your God gives you" (Ex 20:12). The *Catechism* says:

> . . . God has willed that, after him, we should honor our parents to whom we owe life and who have handed on to us the knowledge of God. We are obliged to honor and respect all those whom God, for our good, has vested with his authority [2197].

How wonderful if this commandment would be lived bilaterally in every home and in all society, with honor and respect between parents and children, brothers and sisters, and toward all lawful authority and on the part of all lawful authority toward those whom it governs.

The *Catechism* says:

This commandment is expressed in positive terms of duties to be fulfilled. It introduces the subsequent commandments which are concerned with particular respect for life, marriage, earthly goods, and speech. It constitutes one of the foundations of the social doctrine of the Church [2198].

The fourth commandment is addressed expressly to children in their relationship to their father and mother, because this relationship is the most universal. It likewise concerns the ties of kinship between members of the extended family. It requires honor, affection and gratitude toward elders and ancestors [2199].

This takes me to this lady, Josephine Azzara, who died earlier this year. Apparently there were some unfortunate circumstances surrounding the Mass and the funeral of this noble lady, and her niece wrote to me about it in a long, poignant letter. In just one paragraph of this letter she gives an epitaph, a tribute that I think all of us would be proud to have on our own tombstones. She says:

My aunt's name was Josephine Azzara, and she was born in Sicily in 1898. She spent the first seventeen years of her life in a Catholic orphanage [because her dad had come here to the United States to establish himself]. Because of these formative years, her relationship with nuns and priests was exceptional. To her they were the symbol of the parents she lacked. The sisters taught her to sew, and she became their seamstress. They taught her to love God and her church, and she, until the day she died, said her Rosary two times every day.

That's all. Her name was never in the newspapers. She wasn't famous. She wasn't wealthy. She was just a good woman, a good Catholic, the kind we should honor. We are honoring her in this Mass, and this is why I ask you to remember her in a special way. Her niece's family's concerns about her are a great reminder of the teaching of the fourth commandment.

The *Catechism* goes on:

[The fourth commandment] extends to the duties of pupils to teachers, employees to employers, subordinates to leaders, citizens to their country and to those who administer or govern it.

This commandment includes and presupposes the duties of parents, instructors, teachers, leaders, magistrates, those who govern, all who exercise authority over others or over a community of persons [2199].

Then it talks about the family in God's plan and the nature of the family. Here's what it says:

The conjugal community is established upon the consent of the spouses. Marriage and the family are ordered to the good of the spouses and to the procreation and education of children [2201].

A man and a woman united in marriage, together with their children, form a family [2202].

Today there are all sorts of definitions of "family". This is the definition the Church gives us in accordance with the fourth commandment.

This institution is prior to any recognition by public authority, which has an obligation to recognize it [2202].

In creating man and woman, God instituted the human family and endowed it with its fundamental constitution. Its members are persons equal in dignity [2203].

We could not be speaking of this commandment on a more timely occasion than today because tomorrow begins in Cairo, Egypt, the extremely important International Conference on Population and Development, under the auspices of the United Nations. You have read a good deal about it in the newspapers, and you have very possibly read a number of attacks on our Holy Father. Indeed, in a major newspaper there was an advertisement signed by a number of dissident groups, accusing him of oppression of women, of trying to impose his will on others, and so on.

In preparation for this conference and in the preparatory document for the conference, it was clear that some of those who will participate in the conference were committed to trying to make abortion on demand a universal right, and, therefore, every nation would have to make abortion available—indeed, perhaps subsidize it. More than this, there were attacks on the traditional family in the draft document. The idea was proposed that there are many forms of family, and we have to get rid of the idea that only a husband and wife and children constitute a family. There were various other perversions in this preparatory draft document, as well.

Thank the good Lord, some nations, such as our own, have now adopted the position that abortion should not be forced on the nations of the world, that abortion should not be looked at as a means of so-called "family planning". Some new understandings about the sacredness of traditional definitions of the family have appeared in the words of those speaking for the United States. But in the meanwhile, our Holy Father has made very, very clear that the future of the world is literally at stake; that, particularly throughout the so-called Third World, if this draft document prevailed, misery would be unparalleled, unborn infants would be massacred in almost incredible numbers, and the whole notion of the family, and therefore the stability of society, could be turned upside down. Our Holy Father has been speaking for all peoples, and now many, many nations have joined him. Those who initially tried to isolate the Pope, calling him an anachronism, saying that he wasn't speaking for the women of the world when exactly the opposite is true, they have had to change their tune.

The *Catechism* goes on, speaking of family and society. It says:

> The family is the *original cell of social life.* . . . Authority, stability and a life of relationships within the family constitute the foundations for freedom, security and fraternity within society. The family is the community in which, from childhood, one can learn moral values, begin to honor God, and make good use of freedom [2207].

> The family should live in such a way that its members learn to care and take responsibility for the young, the old, the sick, the handicapped, and the poor [2208].

So, for example, in today's second lesson, St. James tells us:

> Your faith in our Lord Jesus Christ glorified must not allow of favoritism. Suppose there should come into your assembly a man fashionably dressed, with gold rings on his fingers, and at the same time a poor man dressed in shabby clothes. Suppose further you were to take notice of the well-dressed man and say, "Sit right here, please"; whereas you were to say to the poor man, "You can stand!" or "Sit over there by my footrest." Have you not in a case like this discriminated in your hearts?
>
> Listen. Did not God choose those who are poor in the eyes of the world to be rich in faith and heirs of the kingdom he promised to those who love him? (James 2:1–5).

How wonderful if this kind of love and charity were taught in every family!

The *Catechism* goes on to state:

> The family must be helped and defended by appropriate social measures. . . . Following the principle of subsidiarity, larger communities should take care not to usurp the family's prerogatives or interfere in its life [2209].

Prior to the opening of the Cairo Conference, the Pope urged the large nations of the world not to try to impose their particular values, especially perverse values, on smaller nations.

With regard to "usurping the family's prerogatives" or "interfering in its life", we are reminded that our schools exist to educate, not to alienate children from the values of their families. Schools do not exist to argue, on grounds that families don't teach their children certain things, that these things to which families object must be taught in schools, especially in a perverse way contradicting the values of families under the title of, for example, "multi-culturalism".

The *Catechism* continues:

. . . Civil authority should consider it a grave duty "to acknowledge the true nature of marriage and the family, to protect and foster them, to safeguard public morality and promote domestic prosperity" [2210].

How difficult it must be for parents today to see their young children get into a subway where now, we are told, it is legal for women to travel naked to the waist. The government has a responsibility to maintain public morality. It is absolutely preposterous that something like this is condoned, merely that a few may exercise what they consider to be their rights, without any consideration of others.

The *Catechism* continues:

The political community has a duty to honor the family, to assist it, and to ensure especially:
—the freedom to establish a family, have children, and bring them up in keeping with the family's own moral and religious convictions;
—the protection of the stability of the marriage bond and the institution of the family.

The family has special rights, and marriage has special rights. Simply because people decide to live together without the benefit of marriage does not mean that the laws should then extend to them the same rights and benefits extended to married people.

The *Catechism* continues its list of these rights:

—the freedom to profess one's faith, to hand it on, and raise one's children in it, with the necessary means and institutions;
—the right to private property, to free enterprise, to obtain work and housing, and the right to emigrate;
—in keeping with the country's institutions, the right to medical care, assistance for the aged, and family benefits . . . .

The bishops of the United States have strongly taught not only the desirability but the necessity of some kind of extensive health care that would take care of even the poorest of the poor. We have refused to accept abortion under the title of health care. We do not, we will not accept any health care proposal that demands, for instance, that our Catholic institutions support or provide abortion. That, too, would be an outrage.

The *Catechism* calls also for these rights for families:

—the protection of security and health, especially with respect to dangers like drugs, pornography, alcoholism, etc.;
—the freedom to form associations with other families and so to have representation before civil authority [2211].

Isn't it amazing that we are forbidden in public schools to teach moral values, but we can teach many, many things that lead to various kinds of crimes and to perversion? Without moral values, how can you teach youngsters that taking drugs is wrong? Merely because it hurts their bodies? We know it leads to crime. We know it leads to all sorts of perversion.

The *Catechism* goes on:

> The divine fatherhood is the source of human fatherhood; this is the foundation of the honor owed to parents. The respect of children, whether minors or adults, for their father and mother is nourished by the natural affection born of the bond uniting them. It is required by God's commandment [2214].

> As long as a child lives at home with his parents, the child should obey his parents in all that they ask of him when it is for his good or that of the family. "Children, obey your parents in everything, for this pleases the Lord" (Col 3:20). Children should also obey the reasonable directions of their teachers and all to whom their parents have entrusted them. But if a child is convinced in conscience that it would be morally wrong to obey a particular order, he must not do so.

> As they grow up, children should continue to respect their parents. They should anticipate their wishes, willingly seek their advice, and accept their just admonitions. Obedience toward parents ceases with the emancipation of the children; not so respect, which is always owed to them. This respect has its roots in the fear of God, one of the gifts of the Holy Spirit [2217].

> The fourth commandment reminds grown children of their *responsibilities toward their parents*. As much as they can, they must give them material and moral support in old age and in times of illness, loneliness, or distress [2218].

How beautiful it is when you see young people taking care of their parents, their grandparents, their aunts, their uncles! The *Catechism* states:

> Filial respect promotes harmony in all of family life; it also concerns *relationships between brothers and sisters* [2219].

> For Christians a special gratitude is due to those from whom they have received the gift of faith, the grace of Baptism and life in the Church. These may include parents, grandparents, other members of the family, pastors, catechists, and other teachers or friends [2220].

> The fecundity of conjugal love cannot be reduced solely to the procreation of children, but must extend to their moral education and their spiritual formation. . . . The right and the duty of parents to educate their children are primordial and inalienable [2221].

> Parents must regard their children as *children of God* and respect them as *human persons* [2222]. [That's the answer to child abuse.]

A MOMENT OF GRACE

Parents have the first responsibility for the education of their children [2223]. [They must educate them in the virtues.]

Parents should teach their children to avoid the compromising and degrading influences which threaten human societies [2224].

Through the grace of the sacrament of marriage, parents receive the responsibility and privilege of *evangelizing their children*. Parents should initiate their children at an early age into the mysteries of the faith of which they are the "first heralds" for their children. They should associate them from their tenderest years with the life of the Church (*Lumen Gentium*, no. 11). A wholesome family life can foster interior dispositions that are a genuine preparation for a living faith and remain a support for it throughout one's life [2225].

Parents have a grave responsibility to give good example to their children. But parents cannot do it alone. If the law doesn't help them, if the schools don't help them, if the media don't help them, parents feel as though they are drowning in trying to give good example to their youngsters and educate them in the virtues.

The *Catechism* continues:

Education in the faith by the parents should begin in the child's earliest years [2226].

No child is too young for the parents to start teaching the child to make the Sign of the Cross, for example. Unfortunately, today we will find youngsters come into the confessional, and they don't know the Our Father, the Hail Mary, the Sign of the Cross, or the Act of Contrition.

The *Catechism* continues:

As those first responsible for the education of their children, parents have the right to *choose a school for them* which corresponds to their own convictions. This right is fundamental [2229].

We talk so much in this country about "free choice" and "pro-choice". The fact is that parents do not really have a choice. Approximately 75 percent of youngsters in Catholic families go to public schools out of necessity, not out of choice. I am not damning or condemning the public schools. But if parents want to send them to Catholic schools, they should be able to. They cannot because they cannot afford it, yet they are taxed to support public schools. What kind of equity is that? Parents do not have a choice. The public school may be wonderful, but real choice means that when they want to send them to Catholic schools or to any other religious school—Lutheran, Jewish, or whichever—they should be given that freedom.

The *Catechism* continues:

Some forgo marriage in order to care for their parents or brothers and sisters, to give themselves more completely to a profession, or to serve other honorable ends. They can contribute greatly to the good of the human family [2231].

Family ties are important but not absolute. Just as the child grows to maturity and human and spiritual autonomy, so his unique vocation which comes from God asserts itself more clearly and forcefully. Parents should respect this call and encourage their children to follow it. They must be convinced that the first vocation of the Christian is to *follow Jesus*: "He who loves father or mother more than me is not worthy of me; and he who loves son or daughter more than me is not worthy of me" (Mt 10:37) [2232].

Parents should welcome and respect with joy and thanksgiving the Lord's call to one of their children to follow him in virginity for the sake of the Kingdom in the consecrated life or in priestly ministry [2233].

God's fourth commandment also enjoins us to honor all who for our good have received authority in society from God. It clarifies the duties of those who exercise authority as well as those who benefit from it [2234].

Those who exercise authority should do so as a service. . . . No one [in public office] can command or establish what is contrary to the dignity of persons and the natural law [2235].

Political authorities are obliged to respect the fundamental rights of the human person. They will dispense justice humanely by respecting the rights of everyone, especially of families and the disadvantaged. . . . Political rights are meant to be exercised for the common good of the nation and the human community [2237].

The loyal collaboration of [those subject to authority] includes the right, and at times the duty, to voice their just criticisms of that which seems harmful to the dignity of persons and to the good of the community [2238].

I don't often quote politicians, Democrat or Republican. I will suggest here that Senator Moynihan was really on to something when he said that we have been "defining deviancy downward", so that anything goes in society. That is an abdication of public responsibility.

The *Catechism* continues:

It is the *duty of citizens* to contribute along with the civil authorities to the good of society in a spirit of truth, justice, solidarity and freedom. The love and service of *one's country* follow from the duty of gratitude and belong to the order of charity. Submission to legitimate authorities and service of the common good require citizens to fulfill their roles in the life of the political community [2239].

Submission to authority and co-responsibility for the common good make it morally obligatory to pay taxes, to exercise the right to vote, and to defend one's country [2240].

The more prosperous nations are obliged, to the extent they are able, to welcome the *foreigner* in search of the security and the means of livelihood which he cannot find in his country of origin [2241].

Political authorities, for the sake of the common good for which they are responsible, may make the exercise of the right to immigrate subject to various juridical conditions [2241].

It is not for me to say how many immigrants there should be from any country but we must recognize the moral dimension in our immigration policy. Whether we are talking about Haitians or Cubans or anyone else, we cannot let people die, we cannot let people suffer, simply because it may be inconvenient or difficult for us to accept them. They must be thought of as sacred human persons made in the image of God, before being thought of as Haitians, Cubans, Somalians, Rwandans, or anything else. The *Catechism* continues:

The citizen is obliged in conscience not to follow the directives of civil authorities when they are contrary to the demands of the moral order, to the fundamental rights of persons or the teachings of the Gospel. *Refusing obedience* to civil authorities, when their demands are contrary to those of an upright conscience, finds its justification in the distinction between serving God and serving the political community. "Render to Caesar the things that are Caesar's, and to God the things that are God's" (Mt 22:21) [2242].

In no way does this justify killing. During the summer, some in the press attacked the Church for the killing of an abortion doctor in Florida. This is preposterous. Because the Church teaches that it is wrong to kill unborn children, we are accused of stirring up people to kill abortion doctors? Categorically, unconditionally, the killing of doctors who commit abortions is murder, it is forbidden by the fifth commandment. There is no question about the Church's teaching in this regard.

We are reminded in the *Catechism*:

Every institution is inspired, at least implicitly, by a vision of man and his destiny, from which it derives the point of reference for its judgment, its hierarchy of values, its line of conduct. Most societies have formed their institutions in the recognition of a certain preeminence of man over things. Only the divinely revealed religion has clearly recognized man's origin and destiny in God, the Creator and Redeemer [2244].

It is part of the Church's mission "to pass moral judgments even in matters related to politics, whenever the fundamental rights of man or the salvation of souls requires it [2246].

Someone must continue to be a conscience of society, and we will not be intimidated by those who accuse us of being political when we point out grave aberrations in the public order committed—in some instances—by public officials. This is not encouraging anyone to vote for or to vote against any individual. This we avoid. But we cannot avoid our responsibility to comment on what we see as the moral dimensions in public policy.

33

Real Justice

On the Seventh Commandment

TWENTY-FOURTH SUNDAY OF THE YEAR
LABOR DAY MASS
SEPTEMBER 11, 1994
PONTIFICAL MASS

Today we continue our study of the new *Catechism of the Catholic Church*. Our session today will focus on the seventh commandment, which most completely expresses the social teaching of the Church, particularly in areas of special concern to labor. And because today we honor labor, it is most appropriate.

First, however, I want to go back to today's second reading. It is taken from the letter of St. James, written around 45 A.D. To me it synthesizes everything that could be said, everything that should be said, about what our relations with one another should be, and in a very special way what relations between employers and employees, labor and management should be.

St. James asks the question, "What good is it to profess faith without practicing it?" Our Lord Himself said, "Many people cry out to me 'Lord, Lord', but their hearts are far from me." St. James asks:

> What good is it to profess faith without practicing it? Such faith has no power to save one, has it? If a brother or sister has nothing to wear and no food for the day, and you say to them, "Good-bye and good luck! Keep warm and well fed," but do not meet their bodily needs, what good is that? So it is with the faith that does nothing in practice. It is thoroughly lifeless (James 2:14–16).

This spells out what we call the social gospel, the gospel of justice and of charity, the gospel of carrying what we purport to believe into action.

I watch a lot of parades. During those parades I get many hats and many T-shirts. Frequently, the hats and the T-shirts will have some poignant message on them, something very clear and meaningful. This is especially true during the Labor Day Parade. If I were going to create a T-shirt for this purpose, I would select these words from St. James and put them right up and down the T-shirt: "If a brother or sister has nothing to wear and no food for the day, and you say to them, 'Good-bye and good luck! Keep warm and well fed', but do not meet their bodily needs, what good is that?" What good is that? This is not simply a Christian teaching, a teaching only from the Gospels. This is deeply rooted in the Old Testament, what we call the Jewish Scriptures, and it is spelled out quite explicitly in the Ten Commandments from beginning to end.

The seventh commandment is a negative-sounding commandment—"You shall not steal"—but it is actually talking about how we treat one another, how we respect one another, how we respect one another's time, property, efforts, and labor. The *Catechism* says:

> The seventh commandment forbids unjustly taking or keeping the goods of one's neighbor and wronging him in any way with respect to his goods. It commands justice and charity in the care of earthly goods and the fruits of men's labor. For the sake of the common good, it requires respect for the universal destination of goods and respect for the right to private property. Christian life strives to order this world's good to God and to fraternal charity [2401].

The Church has been teaching this kind of thing all through its history, but it has come into full blossom since 1891 and the encyclical of Pope Leo XIII called *Rerum Novarum* or *Of New Things*. We will see in a few moments why it has that title. The *Catechism* goes on:

> The goods of creation are destined for the whole human race. However, the earth is divided up among men to assure the security of their lives, endangered by poverty and threatened by violence. The appropriation of property is legitimate for guaranteeing the freedom and dignity of persons and for helping each of them to meet his basic needs and the needs of those in his charge. It should allow for a natural solidarity to develop between men [2402].

It can hardly be argued that one of the triggering factors in the breakdown of the Soviet Union was what the Polish unions called "solidarity".

The *Catechism* continues: "In his use of things man should regard the external goods he legitimately owns not merely as exclusive to himself but common to others also, in the sense that they can benefit others as well as himself" [2404]. As St. James said, it is no good to say good-bye and good luck, keep warm and well fed, but not meet peoples' bodily needs. That is a lifeless faith.

The *Catechism* says:

> Even if it does not contradict the provisions of civil law, any form of unjustly taking and keeping the property of others is against the seventh com-

mandment: thus, business fraud; paying unjust wages; forcing up prices by taking advantage of the ignorance or hardship of another [2409].

Civil law may allow a number of these things, but the moral law does not. We are still suffering, all of us, because of the manipulations of savings and loans, a major scandal for which the country, that means all working people, are still paying.

The *Catechism* continues:

> . . . The following are also morally illicit: speculation in which one contrives to manipulate the price of goods artificially, in order to gain an advantage to the detriment of others; corruption in which one influences the judgment of those who must make decisions according to law; appropriation and use for private purposes of the common goods of an enterprise; work poorly done [Work poorly done means taking money for what has not been done. Stealing is not simply the pickpocket in the subway or a robbery at Tiffany's. Stealing is an exercise of injustice toward anyone else's rights, depriving anyone of that which is his or her due.]; tax evasion; forgery of checks and invoices; excessive expenses and waste. Willfully damaging private or public property is contrary to the moral law and requires reparation [2409]. [Sometimes, unfortunately, this is done during strikes. It is always self-defeating, as well as immoral.]

> *Promises* must be kept and *contracts* strictly observed to the extent that the commitments made in them are morally just [2410]. [It used to be good enough just to shake hands. Now contracts are very, very complex, but, to the degree that they are morally just, they must be kept.]

In the plays of Shakespeare you find that beyond the law is honor, a plain, old-fashioned virtue. Or, as we read in *Spartacus*, "The law often allows what honor forbids."

The *Catechism* continues: "In virtue of commutative justice, *reparation for injustice* committed requires the restitution of stolen goods to their owner" [2412]. It is not enough to be sorry for having stolen, to be sorry for depriving someone of his or her rights. There must be restitution.

The *Catechism* continues:

> The seventh commandment forbids acts or enterprises that for any reason—selfish or ideological, commercial or totalitarian—lead to the *enslavement of human beings*, to their being bought, sold and exchanged like merchandise, in disregard for their personal dignity [2414].

These are not dead, abstract words in the *Catechism*. We have to keep looking at various of our practices. Corporate takeovers, for example, may be carried out with civil justice but not moral justice. Very often today people don't know for whom they work, *who* actually owns the company, and so this personal touch is lost and makes lawful negotiations very difficult. We have seen that happen right here in this city, when out-of-town companies own what seems to be a local corporation. Then, when it comes time for workers to bargain, they are bargaining with faceless out-of-towners in the person of their representatives here.

Is it possible that in some corporate takeovers pension funds are plundered, and people who have worked for a lifetime find themselves without jobs and without pensions? This is stealing. This is a gross violation of the seventh commandment.

The *Catechism* talks explicitly about the social doctrine of the Church. It says: "The Church receives from the Gospel the full revelation of the truth about man. . . . She teaches him the demands of justice and peace in conformity with divine wisdom" [2419].

Pope John Paul II is *constantly* preaching about the dignity of the human person, of *all* human persons, with emphasis on the working person. He gets discredited by so many, he gets blamed for so much, but so many ignore what he fearlessly says about our obligations toward one another.

The *Catechism* continues:

> The Church makes a moral judgment about economic and social matters, "when the fundamental rights of the person or the salvation of souls requires it" [2420].

> The social doctrine of the Church developed in the nineteenth century when the Gospel encountered modern industrial society with its new structures for the production of consumer goods, its new concept of society, the state and authority, and its new forms of labor and ownership. The development of the doctrine of the Church on economic and social matters attests the permanent value of the Church's teaching at the same time as it attests the true meaning of her Tradition, always living and active [2421].

At the risk of being tedious and sounding abstract, let me spend a moment on this. This passage is talking about the period in the Church immediately following Karl Marx, who lived from 1818 to 1883. Pope Leo XIII came out with his encyclical *Of New Things* in 1891 precisely because there had been a revolution in society. Everything had been turned topsy-turvy. The industrial revolution had taken place, and all sorts of new attitudes had developed.

Karl Marx taught the principle of so-called economic determinism, which argued that the economy determined everything. By "the economy" Karl Marx meant money. Money was the determinant of everything. Free will meant nothing. The place of God meant nothing. The dignity of the human person meant nothing. It sounded as though it was for the purpose of helping the human person, but it was exactly the opposite. Marx borrowed from the philosopher-historian Hegel, who believed that class struggle, class conflict, is absolutely inevitable. It is in the very nature of things that the "have-nots" will always turn against the "haves". Then there will be a period of equilibrium. Then it starts all over again, as though there were no free will, as though we couldn't bargain intelligently, in dignified civil human fashion, with one another, respecting one another as made in the image and likeness of God. This is what Karl Marx was saying. It was part of his teaching—that only by bloody revolution could equity and justice be brought about.

It was against this that Pope Leo XIII was speaking in *Of New Things*. This is why he fostered and encouraged the development of unions, of working peoples' associations, of voluntarily coming together, of recognizing that we are social human beings, that we naturally should unite out of justice, out of charity, out of self-protection. We should do this voluntarily, not by force and not letting any superior force—state, management, whoever it might be—prevent us from negotiating in good faith as human beings.

The *Catechism* continues: "Any system in which social relationships are determined entirely by economic factors is contrary to the nature of the human person and his acts" [2423].

What we have to ask today in our own country is: Even though communism has generally been dissipated, do we have a mirror image of it or of economic determinism? Is it still money that matters most?

The *Catechism* says: "A theory that makes profit the exclusive norm and ultimate end of economic activity is morally unacceptable. . . . It is one of the causes of the many conflicts which disturb the social order [2424].

The profit motive is a legitimate motive. But do we exist *only* for profit, *only* for money? Does that determine everything? Are people good or bad in accordance with whether they have money or don't have money? Are industrialists good or bad in accordance with how much profit they make or don't make? Is a union leader good or bad in proportion to how much more money he or she can get for workers, regardless of how, regardless of whether it is just? That's the mirror image of economic determinism. It is just as bad if it is practiced in capitalism as if it is practiced in communism.

The *Catechism* continues:

A system that "subordinates the basic rights of individuals and of groups to the collective organization of production" is contrary to human dignity [2424].

The Church has rejected the totalitarian and atheistic ideologies associated in modern times with "communism" or "socialism." She has likewise refused to accept, in the practice of "capitalism," individualism and the absolute primacy of the law of the marketplace over human labor [2425].

We cannot permit abstract laws, so-called historical laws, to rob us of free will.

Economic life is not meant solely to multiply goods produced and increase profit or power; it is ordered first of all to the service of persons, of the whole man, and of the entire human community [2426].

The *Catechism* talks about human work in very exalted terms:

Human work proceeds directly from persons created in the image of God and called to prolong the work of creation by subduing the earth, both with and for one another. Hence work is a duty. . . . Work honors the Creator's gifts and the talents received from him. It can also be redemptive. By enduring the hardship of work in union with Jesus, the carpenter of Nazareth and the one crucified on Calvary, [we] collaborate in a certain fashion with the Son of God in his redemptive work. . . . Work can be a means of sanctification and a way of animating earthly realities with the Spirit of Christ [2427].

In work, the person exercises and fulfills in part the potential inscribed in his nature. . . . Work is for man, not man for work.
    Everyone should be able to draw from work the means of providing for his life and that of his family, and of serving the human community [2428].

Economic life brings into play different interests, often opposed to one another. This explains why the conflicts that characterize it arise. Efforts should be made to reduce these conflicts by negotiation that respects the rights and duties of each social partner: those responsible for business enterprises, representatives of wage earners (for example, trade unions), and public authorities when appropriate [2430].

We have to have the right to negotiate but somehow, somewhere, in my judgment, we have gone wrong. Sometimes it appears that we think ourselves back in the early decades of this century. We want to use the same tools, the same instruments, in negotiation. For example, in 1938 the Supreme Court of the United States delivered a decision that, in my judgment, was terribly destructive of the whole concept of negotiation, if not actually immoral—the decision that authorized permanent replacements for striking laborers.

We are still using that today. It was used in the newspaper strike here in New York quite recently. The threat of permanent replacements makes it a charade to say that working people have the right to negotiate and the right to strike. The right to strike should be exercised *only* after all negotiations in good faith have been exhausted.

Is the move to strike the first step taken? Is it used as an instrument of threat? Do we believe that management negotiates with labor, instead of human persons negotiating with human persons? Have we lost something, or are we losing something, something that must be restored, something vital to true, honest, effective, productive, and fruitful negotiations between persons in management and persons who constitute the labor force? Management is not negotiating with unions; *persons* in management are negotiating with *persons* in unions.

Pope John Paul II said, "The primacy of man over the instrument of capital, the primacy of the person over things, the priority of human labor over capital—upon this we must insist." *Then* we will get rid of the potential of violence. *Then* we will get rid of the strike as the first approach rather than the last. *Then* we will get rid of the arrogant use of power.

Something has gone wrong. I can say that as an employer myself and on behalf of everyone in a position in the Church who must exercise equity, justice, and charity for those who work for the Church, with the Church, to those who build for the Church, to those who work in Church offices. Each is a person, as I am supposed to be a person. We have to right whatever it is that is wrong. We cannot start out from the principle of "How can I get more? How can I give less?" This to me is enormously important.

The *Catechism* takes up justice and solidarity among nations and reminds us of the almost singular voice of our Holy Father in Cairo, trying to bring about justice and charity for all the peoples of the world, rather than an obsession with population control. It seems to me that labor should be on this side, rather than on the side of those obsessed with reducing the number of people in the world. Labor should be on the side of those who opt for development, rather than the side of those intent on reducing the numbers of black peoples, and Hispanic peoples, and other peoples who are non-white labor. Pragmatically, that is where the jobs are: to build dams in the Third World, to provide engineers and agriculturalists for the Third World, to help develop the enormous resources in the Third World and throughout the world.

The *Catechism* says:

> God blesses those who come to the aid of the poor and rebukes those who turn away from them [2443].

> "The Church's love for the poor . . . is a part of her constant tradition." . . . Love for the poor is even one of the motives for the duty of working so as to "be able to give to those in need" (Eph 4:28). It extends not only to material poverty but also to the many forms of cultural and religious poverty [2444].

> The works of mercy are charitable actions by which we come to the aid of our neighbor in his spiritual and bodily necessities. Instructing, advising, consoling, comforting are spiritual works of mercy, as are forgiving and

bearing wrongs patiently. The corporal works of mercy consist especially in feeding the hungry, sheltering the homeless, clothing the naked, visiting the sick and imprisoned, and burying the dead [2447].

In its various forms—material deprivation, unjust oppression, physical and psychological illness and death—*human misery* is the obvious sign of the inherited condition of frailty and need for salvation in which man finds himself as a consequence of original sin [2448].

It has been clearly demonstrated for any who are willing to listen with an open mind that there can be more than enough food for anyone who could be born. But we have to work. Work is a great gift and a great privilege.

I can never preach in this cathedral about work without being again reminded of the beauty of the cathedral itself. I didn't build it. It was built by management. Archbishop John Hughes had to take the risks of management. It was built physically by the hands of working people, by the hands of artists, as is everything done by human beings: a beautiful piece of music, a beautiful work of art, the molding of bricks, the digging of sewers, the emptying of bed pans, the administration of medicines, the practice of surgery, the typing of letters—all of these are the work of human hands. Even if the work is done by machines, they are machines created by the human mind. How we must respect this! And how I, who profit so much, as do we all, by the work of others, must respect everyone who contributes to society. Everything that we wear, everything that we eat, is the result of the work of human hands.

In this Mass, when we offer the bread to Almighty God that we believe becomes the Body of His Son, we call it "the work of human hands". We offer the wine, the "fruit of the vine, and the work of human hands" to become the Blood of the Son of God. What reverence and what respect we must have!

Not too long ago I was criticized for saying at a union rally that I am proud to be the son of a union man. Let me tell you I am proud to have my responsibilities in management. I am proud of all of the wonderful people in the Archdiocese of New York in management who help the archdiocese, who help the poor, who help keep kids in our schools, who help keep our hospitals open, people in corporate management in the corporate structure. I am proud of all of them. I am proud and humbled to be the Cardinal Archbishop of New York. But the title of which I am as proud as any that I could ever have is the title of being the son of a union man! God bless you.

34

"What Is Truth?"

On the Eighth Commandment

In today's session on the new *Catechism of the Catholic Church* we will look at the eighth commandment: "You shall not bear false witness against your neighbor." It is found in the second book of the Old Testament, the book that describes the escape of the Israelites from the Egyptians (Ex 20:16). We are told in the *Catechism*:

> The eighth commandment forbids misrepresenting the truth in our relations with others. This moral prescription flows from the vocation of the holy people to bear witness to their God who is the truth and wills the truth [2464].

This is a very important definition that not everyone understands. No one can claim to understand it fully, but *God is truth*, and therefore this whole world, everything in the world, and particularly all relationships between and among human beings, are supposed to reflect Almighty God, since we are made in the image and likeness of Him. If God is truth, then truth is required in all of our dealings with one another and with ourselves, of course.

The *Catechism* continues:

> The Old Testament attests that *God is the source of all truth*. His Word is truth. His Law is truth. His "faithfulness endures to all generations" (Ps 119:90). Since God is "true," the members of his people are called to live in the truth (Rom 3:4) [2465].

> In Jesus Christ, the whole of God's truth has been made manifest. "Full of grace and truth," he came as the "light of the world," he *is the Truth* (Jn 1:14; 8:12). "Whoever believes in me may not remain in darkness" (Jn 12:46). The disciple of Jesus continues in his word so as to know "the truth [that] will make you free" and that sanctifies (Jn 8:32). [Truth is not intended to enslave; quite the contrary. We cannot be afraid of the truth.

Truth is the greatest liberating force possible, because God is truth.] To follow Jesus is to live in "the Spirit of truth," whom the Father sends in his
name and who leads "into all the truth" (Jn 16:13). To his disciples Jesus
teaches the unconditional love of truth [2466].

The *Catechism* goes on to say that by our nature we tend toward the
truth, so we are obliged to honor and bear witness to it [see 2467].

If the world were in a perfect state, we would all be totally truthful in
everything that we do and everything that we are, because that is the way
we are made. We reach out for the truth, not for falsehood. However, as
St. Paul reminds us in the first chapter of the Letter to the Romans, we
get corroded and calloused. Our minds get darkened by repeated sin and
by living in a culture that just drenches us with falsehood, a culture the
falsehood of which eats into our very beings, eats into our souls. Our
minds are darkened, and we get it all mixed up, and we introduce perversions into our society and then consider the perversions to be the equiva-
lent of the purely natural. This would not be the case except that our
minds are darkened first by original sin and then by the steadiness of repeated sin and by breathing the air of this culture.

The other night some of us in the house watched William Buckley's
"Firing Line". This special two-hour program was a debate between those
who believe that government should support the work of religion in the
world at large—that moral principle cannot be confined to churches and
to homes—and those who oppose this concept on the grounds of the so-
called "separation of Church and State". It was a fascinating program. It
was easy to see how the truth can be manipulated, can be distorted.

For example, one of those totally committed to the position that
there must be absolute separation between Church and State and that
religion is only for the home and for churches made a very radical statement. He said that in Cairo recently, at the International Conference on
Population and Development, one single force (the Church), by objecting to one sentence in a huge document prepared for this conference,
was able to bring the conference to a halt. That statement was sheer
nonsense! The position of the Holy See was that the overwhelming focus of the document was on population control, and practically no time
was given to development, to feeding the hungry and clothing the
naked and housing the homeless, to engineering and agricultural reform,
to getting the wealthy world to assist the undeveloped world in developing. That was supposed to be the thrust of the conference. I read the
document very, very carefully, and in my assessment at least 95 percent
of it was devoted to population control and maybe 5 percent to development. When this individual said that by objecting to one sentence in
the document the Holy See was bringing the entire conference to a

halt, I doubt very much that he intended a deliberate lie. I have to believe that he is ignorant of the document. But if one is ignorant of the document, he should not be on television telling the whole world what it said. These are the kinds of "lies" that simply permeate our society. Sometimes they are not thought of as lies, but, at a minimum, they are falsehoods.

The *Catechism* quotes St. Thomas Aquinas and speaks of the practicality of the eighth commandment: "Men could not live with one another if there were not mutual confidence that they were being truthful to one another" [2469].

This was also brought up in the debate on Friday evening. You can talk all you want about keeping moral principles and religion out of the marketplace, out of the public square, out of political life. But the reality is that chaos results. On what do we base, for example, our acceptance in public life of the fact that we have to believe one another? If anything that a public official says can be a lie, what trust can there be? Truth is not something we create or manufacture. There must be an objective source, a moral law. How can we keep religion out of the marketplace? If we do that, then we abdicate completely to the forces of secularism, and our government is supporting pure secularism.

A young student in a state university called me last night. She is taking a new course, and in the opening session the professor began by talking about our cultural milieu. He said, in essence, "I want to tell you how people can advance beyond their culture. I was once a Catholic, but then I saw the foolishness of it all, so I gave all that up. I have advanced beyond Catholicism." This is a professor in a state-run, taxed-supported university bashing the Catholic Church needlessly. We are supposed to accept this? We are not supposed to respond?

In the recent past, the National Endowment for the Arts has given *tax money* for projects that have ridiculed the teaching of the Church, have ridiculed our moral values. We have accepted that, at times, on the grounds that not everything can be controlled or should be controlled in society, or it would be a despicable totalitarian society. But, oh, what meticulous care is used to assure that the Church has no "governmental" forum in which to respond. The eighth commandment is a far more important commandment than we might sometimes realize, because falsehood so readily permeates our society.

We are told in the *Catechism*:

Before Pilate, Christ proclaims that he "has come into the world, to bear witness to the truth" (Jn 18:37). The Christian is not to "be ashamed then of the testifying to our Lord" (2 Tim 1:8). In situations that require witness to the faith, the Christian must profess it without equivocation, after the example of St. Paul before his judges. We must keep "a clear conscience toward God and toward men" (Acts 24:16) [2471].

When Christ was brought before Pilate, and the people were howling for his blood, Pilate said, in essence, "I cannot find any fault in this innocent man, so I wash my hands of it. I am a public official, and I look at the accusation against him as lies, but I wash my hands. I turn this matter over to the people." How can we have public order, how can we have dignified, intelligent public policy, if that is the behavior of public officials?

Pilate asked Jesus, "What is truth?" Then, before Jesus had opportunity to answer, he walked away. We do that also. Do we really want to know the truth, the truth that sets us free?

We have just listened to the Gospel from St. Mark (Mk 9:30–37). Jesus was teaching His disciples, we are told: "The Son of Man is going to be delivered into the hands of men who will put him to death; three days after his death he will rise." That was the truth, but the disciples did not want to believe that. As a matter of fact, Peter said to Jesus, "Stop talking such nonsense. We will protect you!" This was Christ, the Son of God, telling them He was going to suffer and die. Still, they did not want to believe.

The teachings of the Catholic Church can be hard teachings, teachings that include suffering, teachings that include self-discipline, teachings that include, according with all of the commandments, that we live according to truth. What do some people say? Foolish things, such as, "This will all change, won't it, after this Pope dies?" I don't know how often I am asked this. Television interviewers will say to me, "Don't you think what a lot of people say is true, that when this Pope dies, then the Church will forget all this stuff about abortion?" The Pope did not create this teaching, but we don't like to accept the hard truth, some of us.

The disciples went on talking about who would be the greatest among them when Christ established His Kingdom. Forget all this about sacrifice, self-discipline, the commandments, the law, and the crucifixion of Christ. What are *we* going to get out of all this? That is what they were asking. That is why He brought a little child before them, an example of what we are all supposed to be: innocence, goodness, truth.

It is very difficult to get people to accept truth as an absolute. Truth is treated so cynically. Oscar Wilde, for instance, said, "Truth in matters of religion is simply the opinion that has survived." In other words, any opinion is as good as any other.

A number of years ago, an English poet-essayist named Coventry Patmore wrote an essay called "The Rod, the Root and the Flower". He said:

Tolerance as it is now widely practiced can be completely misleading. It will not do for truth to say to falsehood, "I will tolerate you if you will tolerate me." The most powerful solvent is the strongest opposite. We can best move this world by making it clear that we stand upon another.

That is the truth of the Gospel. For the truth of the Gospel Christ was crucified. Christ was not crucified because of His miracles. Christ was not crucified for being kind and gentle and compassionate with people. He was all of that. But the people could not stand His teaching, and that is why He was crucified. People could not accept the truth.

The *Catechism* continues:

> Martyrdom is the supreme witness given to the truth of the faith: it means bearing witness even unto death. The martyr bears witness to Christ who died and rose, to whom he is united by charity. He bears witness to the truth of faith and of Christian doctrine. He endures death through an act of fortitude. "Let me become the food of the beasts, through whom it will be given me to reach God" [2473].

St. Ignatius of Antioch spoke these words and compared this to that bread that is ground to become the Body of the Son of God, the grapes that are crushed to become the wine that will be the Son of God, Whom we receive in Holy Communion.

The *Catechism* says:

> The Church has painstakingly collected the records of those who persevered to the end in witnessing to their faith. These are the acts of the Martyrs. They form the archives of truth written in letters of blood:
>
> "I bless you for having judged me worthy from this day and this hour to be counted among your martyrs. . . . You have kept your promise, God of faithfulness and truth. For this reason and for everything, I praise you, I bless you, I glorify you through the eternal and heavenly High Priest, Jesus Christ, your beloved Son. Through him, who is with you and the Holy Spirit, may glory be given to you, now and in the ages to come. Amen" (*Martyrium Polycarpi* 14, 2–3) [2474].

> *False witness and perjury.* When it is made publicly, a statement contrary to the truth takes on a particular gravity. In court it becomes false witness. When it is under oath, it is perjury. Acts such as these contribute to condemnation of the innocent, exoneration of the guilty, or the increased punishment of the accused. They gravely compromise the exercise of justice and the fairness of judicial decisions [2476].

Obviously, if a witness is lying, perjuring himself or herself, then someone could be sentenced to life in prison.

The *Catechism* says:

> Respect for the reputation of persons forbids every attitude and word likely to cause them unjust injury. [Whoever does this] becomes guilty:

—of *rash judgment* who, even tacitly, assumes as true, without sufficient foundation, the moral fault of a neighbor;

—of *detraction* who, without objectively valid reason, discloses another's faults and failings to persons who did not know them;

—of *calumny* who, by remarks contrary to the truth, harms the reputation of others and gives occasion for false judgments concerning them [2477].

One of the most distasteful things to happen to me from time to time is to receive an anonymous letter, particularly one telling me something nefarious about a priest. Even should it be true or the essence of it be true, it is so sad that people can be protected by anonymity, and then I am forced to try to do something about it, purely on the basis of an anonymous charge.

We have had some tragic events in the Church in the past few years. There are few things that could equal the tragedy of pedophilia. There have been some priests accused, found guilty, even now serving prison sentences. Huge fines have been paid. *No one* can possibly defend this kind of action. One can call it a sickness, and it may well be, but victims are terribly, terribly hurt. The scandal that rips the Church is frightening, so one does not want to defend against true charges of this sort. But how easy it is today to make false charges of this nature and then to remain anonymous. We now have a diocesan policy that requires that, if an allegation of this sort is made, then the priest must go through all sorts of psychological testing, investigations, and so on, and even when he is found totally innocent, purer than the driven snow, what has it done to him? What has it done to his reputation? I think anonymous letters of this sort are despicable things, and they are violations of the eighth commandment.

We are told in the *Catechism*:

To avoid rash judgment, everyone should be careful to interpret insofar as possible his neighbor's thoughts, words and deeds in a favorable way [2478].

Detraction and calumny destroy the *reputation and honor of one's neighbor.* Honor is the social witness given to human dignity, and everyone enjoys a natural right to the honor of his name and reputation and to respect. Thus, detraction and calumny offend against the virtues of justice and charity [2479].

Every word or attitude is forbidden which by *flattery, adulation, or complaisance* encourages and confirms another in malicious acts and perverse conduct. Adulation is a grave fault if it makes one an accomplice in another's vices or grave sins. Neither the desire to be of service nor friendship justifies duplicitous speech. Adulation is a venial sin when it only seeks to be agreeable, to avoid evil, to meet a need, or to obtain legitimate advantages [2480].

Every offense committed against justice and truth entails the *duty of reparation* . . . [2487].

We cannot lie about someone and cause damage and then not make restitutions. When I went to confession last week, I told the very smart priest that I had been unjust and uncharitable in thought and word. I thought he would just let it go at that and tell me to say a Hail Mary. But the priest said, "Make a little meditation on the person you were unjust to, and then do something nice for that person." Then I had to go into the chapel and think about this person. At first it started to backfire, because the more I thought of him the madder I got at him. I thought I was right in what I did. But I had to simmer down and recognize that this person is made in the image and likeness of God, and it was my pride that was hurt. He did not do any damage to me. Then I had to figure out something nice I could do for him, and that was not easy. But that is the way it is supposed to be, to balance the books, to make reparation.

Some in the media who try very hard to speak the truth tell me of the terrible prejudices in the minds and hearts of *some* others in the media who are grossly ignorant of what the Catholic Church really teaches. Instead of informing themselves, they remain prejudiced against everything the Church does and report accordingly in prejudice. The public deserves the truth, whether about the Church or anything else.

We deserve the truth right now about Haiti. As I wrote in *Catholic New York* this week, it is not for me to determine military matters, that is for the Commander-in-Chief of the Armed Forces. It is not for me to determine whether we should invade another country, that is for the President or the Congress, as appropriate. But it *is* for me as a citizen, it is for all of us, to plead that questions be asked about the moral dimensions of what we do as a nation. It is very difficult to determine the moral dimensions unless we know the truth. So we have to ask: "Do we really know the truth about Haiti?" "Do we really know what will happen if an invasion occurs?" "Do we really know what the aftermath will be?" "Do we really have a sense of the numbers who might be killed?" We are told that this invasion is in the national interest of the United States. It is not for me to determine this, but it is for me to ask, for everyone to ask: "Why is it in the national interest of the United States?" We have stumbled into too many wars without asking ourselves in advance about the morality of entering into war, and then, once we enter into war, about the morality of the way in which we wage the war.

I found in many years of military life that often the military themselves were far more scrupulous than they were given credit for in trying to determine how they could best contain damage, how they could save innocent, human lives, the lives of non-combatants. But policy-makers must recognize these issues before we enter into a war. What does an invasion mean but some kind of war, small or large, short or long. We cannot live with lies. I am not suggesting for a single moment that anyone in the administration in the United States is lying. I am saying only that an obligation of Christians, of all peoples, is to ask: "What is the truth?" It is the truth and the truth alone that sets us free.

May I ask, please, that, especially during the next few days, whatever your personal beliefs or your political positions, you will pray that a just and peaceful resolution be found to the situation in Haiti and between Haiti and the United States that will not require intervention of armed forces. Pray particularly for those members of the armed forces who will be the ones called upon if there is an intervention. Each human life is sacred, whether one is lost or a thousand are lost. Pray for their families who have to make the sacrifices. Pray for the Haitians themselves, that they will come to peace and to justice in their own land and that none of those will experience death because of a conflict between Haiti and the United States.

35

Against This Culture of Death

On the Fifth Commandment

RED MASS
TWENTY-SIXTH SUNDAY IN ORDINARY TIME
SEPTEMBER 25, 1994
PONTIFICAL MASS

A very special welcome today to the members of the bar, the members of the legal profession, and all of those who are involved with the law as a profession. Today is the annual Red Mass, and the priests wear red vestments, symbolic of our calling upon the Holy Spirit to infuse the minds and hearts of those ultimately responsible for the administration of justice with the dedication to the truth.

Honorable members of the bench, respected counsellors, you are among friends. We are very happy to have you. We thank you for attempting to assure justice from the smallest to the largest set of circumstances. Today we continue our sessions on the *Catechism of the Catholic Church*, and today's session is most pertinent to the legal profession.

Yesterday morning we had a beautiful Mass in this cathedral for persons with disabilities. The church was filled with persons in wheelchairs, persons with cerebral palsy, many blind, a large group of deaf, and many mentally retarded. It was a very moving, deeply touching sight. I have celebrated Mass hundreds of times now, in this cathedral, and have never felt more deeply moved. But there were not only the physically handicapped and the mentally retarded here. There was love. This cathedral was just flowing with love; it was palpable. There was love, dedication, commitment, self-sacrifice, sacrifice on the part of parents, guardians, and others responsible for taking care of those who could not take care of themselves. This is not the sacrifice of an hour or two each day, but a twenty-four-hour-a-day sacrifice. Any of you who have a helpless child, a retarded child, or someone in a wheelchair, you know that this is a twenty-four-hour-a-day job. You are constantly confined yourselves. Your whole life is preoccupied. That is why the love was so evident.

Following the Mass, I thought of something that I had read from an article by Nat Hentoff, reprinted in the Winter 1993 edition of the *Human Life Review*. Mr. Hentoff talks about the year 1971, when abortion was legalized in New York State, and he quotes an editorial on WCBS Radio in New York that "attempted to define abortion as an act of compassion: 'It is one sensible method of dealing with such problems as overpopulation, illegitimacy, and possible birth defects. . . .' "

I looked out yesterday at hundreds of parents and others who might well have aborted these children. Many of them, surely, had advance notice of the probability of some kind of a defect. Mr. Hentoff quotes the rest of what the announcer said: "It is one way of fighting the rising welfare rolls and the increasing number of child-abuse cases."

Then Mr. Hentoff quotes a 1992 article that appeared in the *New York Observer*:

> Free, cheap abortion is a policy of social defense. To save ourselves from being murdered in our beds and raped on the streets, we should do everything possible to encourage pregnant women who don't want the baby and will not take care of it to get rid of the thing before it turns into a monster. . . .

What do you think the reaction would have been if I had read that yesterday to those parents and others who were here?

I had a second Mass yesterday in the afternoon in this cathedral, with another crowd of people—older adults, many of them in wheelchairs. Many had very difficult problems, problems with mobility, sight problems, the onset of various diseases, and so on. There are a quarter of a million people in the State of New York over the age of 65 and seventy-two thousand over the age of 85. Again, my heart was moved because one could just *see* all of the love present. There were many husbands and wives here who had been taking care of each other for many years and have had no intention of abandoning each other. And I was reminded of something that Patrick Buchanan wrote, also quoted in the *Human Life Review* (Spring 1993):

> Seventy-year-old Mr. Gale, suffering from emphysema and heart disease, volunteered to be gassed on February 15. According to the Final Action, however, 45 seconds after Mr. Gale pulled the death mask over his face and started the flow of lethal carbon monoxide, he "became flushed, agitated, breathing deeply, saying, 'Take it off.' "
>
> [The doctor] complied. Twenty minutes later, Mr. Gale asked that the mask be put back on. "He again flushed, became agitated . . . and said, 'Take it off,' once again." This time, the mask was left on.

There is nothing romantic about euthanasia or assisted suicide. I would ask those who would argue that a 95-year-old lying in a hospital bed, feeling useless, should be entitled to have herself, himself, put to death: How about the 16-year-old girl disappointed in a romantic affair? A 16-year-old girl in this state has the right to abortion, as you know. Should she have the same right to take her own life? There are efforts to legalize euthanasia and assisted suicide throughout the land. One referendum after another is being confronted.

What is happening to us as a people? Why is it happening? Why is there so much violence against human life? Why are there so many teens with guns? One out of eight youngsters is carrying a gun or a lethal weapon. Why this culture of death? There are many reasons; sociologists could adduce them, judges and lawyers could adduce them, as well.

Certainly one reason for the culture of death that is of concern to us within the context of the *Catechism* and of this Mass is that we have so often come to substitute law (civil law) for sin (moral law). *Sin* is a word that has almost disappeared from our social vocabulary. If mentioned, it is often laughed at or considered a matter of mere personal opinion. People say things such as, "Who are you to tell me that something is sinful?" If something is civilly lawful, we assume that it is morally lawful. We have an entire generation that has been reared to believe, for example, that abortion is morally okay because abortion is civilly "okay", it is legal. The government funds abortion. We respect government, hence abortion must be okay.

The natural moral law says abortion is not okay, and the Divine Law says it is not okay. Because we have this constant, now habitual and chronic, substitution of the law for a sense of morality, we have a situation that, it seems to me, John Adams warned us that we would have. You will recall that he was the first Vice-President and the second President of the United States. Here is what he had to say:

> We have no government armed with power capable of contending with human passions unbridled by morality and religion. Our constitution was made only for a moral and religious people. It is wholly inadequate to the government of any other.

I don't accept much of modern writings about the Fathers of the Constitution. If one reads their own writings, one finds that they believed in original sin. They believed in our inclination to sin. This was the context in which they formulated the Constitution. They did not have to say this in the Constitution. They believed this with every breath: that we are weak, sinful human beings. They tried, therefore, to design a constitution that would fit for a virtuous people, but, as Adams said, it would never fit for those who reject virtue.

Today, if we interpret the Constitution out of context, without the intention of its framers, we come up with something quite different and something that has demonstrably been unable to govern us in peace and in harmony. Unfortunately, we have increasing evidence of this. That is part of the reason, it seems to me, that we are in danger of not working and not succeeding as a society.

This takes us to the fifth commandment, which is elucidated in this session of the *Catechism*: "You shall not kill" (Ex 20:13). Found in the Tablets of the Law given to Moses during the Exodus from slavery to the Egyptians, it could really have been written for the legal profession, for the judicial profession. Our Divine Lord, hundreds and hundreds of years later, said: "You have heard that it was said to the men of old, 'You shall not kill: and whoever kills shall be liable to judgment.' But I say to you that every one who is angry with his brother shall be liable to judgment" (Mt 5:21–22).

The *Catechism* quotes the Congregation for the Doctrine of the Faith, the preserver of the traditions of our teachings: "God alone is the Lord of life from its beginning until its end: no one can under any circumstance claim for himself the right directly to destroy an innocent human being" [2258].

Then the *Catechism* talks about what happened after original sin. The first effect of original sin, we believe, was that Adam and Eve turned against each other, with Adam blaming Eve and Eve, then, blaming the Devil. The second major social effect was the first murder. We are told in the *Catechism*:

> In the account of Abel's murder by his brother Cain, Scripture reveals the presence of anger and envy in man, consequences of original sin, from the beginning of human history. . . . God declares the wickedness of this fratricide: "What have you done? The voice of your brother's blood is crying to me from the ground. And now you are cursed from the ground, which has opened its mouth to receive your brother's blood from your hand" (Gen 4:10–11) [2259].

The *Catechism* goes on:

> The deliberate murder of an innocent person is gravely contrary to the dignity of the human being, to the golden rule, and to the holiness of the Creator. The law forbidding it is universally valid: it obliges each and everyone, always and everywhere [2261].

It is valid in Rwanda. It is valid in Croatia, in Bosnia-Herzegovina. It is valid in Somalia. It is valid in Haiti. It is the same, unchanging moral law. The *Catechism* says:

> In the Sermon on the Mount, the Lord recalls the commandment, "You shall not kill" (Mt 5:21), and adds to it the proscription of anger, hatred, and vengeance. Going further, Christ asks his disciples to turn the other cheek,

to love their enemies. He did not defend himself and told Peter to leave his sword in its sheath [2262].

Then the *Catechism* talks about "legitimate defense":

The legitimate defense of persons and societies is not an exception to the prohibition against the murder of the innocent that constitutes intentional killing. "The act of self-defense can have a double effect: the preservation of one's own life; and the killing of the aggressor. . . . The one is intended, the other is not" [2263].

Love toward oneself remains a fundamental principle of morality. Therefore it is legitimate to insist on respect for one's own right to life. Someone who defends his life is not guilty of murder even if he is forced to deal his aggressor a lethal blow [2264].

This introduction of *love* as a fundamental principle of morality is so important. We are told that the first commandment is: "Love the Lord thy God with thy whole heart, thy whole soul, thy whole mind, and thy whole strength." The second, we are told, is like this: "Love thy neighbor as thyself." You who sit on the bench see so much violence, so much contempt for human life. Why is there much of this? If we do not love ourselves, if we do not have any sense of self-worth, if we do not recognize that *we* are made in the image and likeness of God, then it is most unlikely that we will think this about others.

The *Catechism* says: "Legitimate defense can be not only a right but a grave duty for someone responsible for another's life, the common good of the family or of the state" [2265].

Then the *Catechism* addresses an issue that gets kicked around as a political football, so easily, so glibly.

Preserving the common good of society requires rendering the aggressor unable to inflict harm. For this reason the traditional teaching of the Church has acknowledged as well-founded the right and duty of legitimate public authority to punish malefactors by means of penalties commensurate with the gravity of the crime, not excluding, in cases of extreme gravity, the death penalty. For analogous reasons those holding authority have the right to repel by armed force aggressors against the community in their charge [2266].

Although it is being muddled in the newspapers, and being muddled by various people today, the Church teaches very clearly that the state, having as its primary obligation to protect the lives of its citizens, has the right to exercise capital punishment. The bishops have recommended against this for reasons in part given here in the *Catechism*:

If bloodless means are sufficient to defend human lives against an aggressor and to protect public order and the safety of persons, public authority should limit itself to such means, because they better correspond to the concrete conditions of the common good and are more in conformity to the dignity of the human person [2267].

The bishops argue against the use of capital punishment. Many argue that it does not deter capital offenses. Many argue that it contributes to the spiral of violence. These may be sound arguments, but the Church nevertheless teaches that the state has the *right* to administer capital punishment for capital offenses. We must make these distinctions. They may be unpopular with those who want the Church to say something else, but this is the teaching of the Church: we recommend against the use of capital punishment, but we recognize the right of the state to use capital punishment. It is interesting that some of those who tell the Church to stay out of things like abortion, calling it a matter of "choice" and claiming it as a matter for the civil law to determine, emphasize separation of church and state. However, when it comes to capital punishment, these same people say, "The Church teaches that we should not use capital punishment." Suddenly Church teaching becomes very important to them!

The *Catechism* goes on: "The fifth commandment forbids *direct and intentional killing* as gravely sinful. The murderer and those who cooperate voluntarily in murder commit a sin that cries out to heaven for vengeance" [2268].

Here we are again. It is not simply a civil offense, a criminal offense against the law, it is a *sin*. That is the essence of it.

Infanticide, fratricide, parricide, and the murder of a spouse are especially grave crimes by reason of the *natural* bonds which they break. [These are natural bonds on which all of society depends.] Concern for eugenics or public health cannot justify any murder, even if commanded by public authority [2268].

The fifth commandment forbids doing anything with the intention of *indirectly* bringing about a person's death. The moral law prohibits exposing someone to mortal danger without grave reason, as well as refusing assistance to a person in danger [2269].

Those of you who deal with insurance law and who may be involved with the crafting of health-care packages must remember this. You cannot exclude those who have the right to protection by the state. If unborn babies are human beings, how can one propose to the public a health-care package that funds the killing of unborn babies? They have the right to the same defense of their health as anyone else.

The *Catechism* says:

The acceptance by human society of murderous famines, without efforts to remedy them, is a scandalous injustice and a grave offense. Those whose usurious and avaricious dealings lead to the hunger and death of their brethren in the human family indirectly commit homicide, which is imputable to them [2269].

The letter of St. James read to us today said:

You rich, weep and wail over your impending miseries. Your wealth has rotted, your fine wardrobe has grown moth-eaten, your gold and silver have corroded, and other corrosion shall be a testimony against you; it will devour your flesh like a fire. See what you have stored up for yourselves against the last days. Here, crying aloud, are the wages you withheld from the farmhands who harvested your fields. The shouts of the harvesters have reached the ears of the Lord of hosts. You lived in wanton luxury on the earth; you fattened yourselves for the day of slaughter (James 5:1–6).

He is talking to all of us, but he is certainly talking to those of you in corporation law. Sometimes there is certain, if indirect, responsibility for some international activities directly opposed to the fifth commandment. The *Catechism* is clear about the defense of human life.

Human life must be respected and protected absolutely from the moment of conception. From the first moment of his existence, a human being must be recognized as having the rights of a person—among which is the inviolable right of every innocent being to life [2270].

Since the first century the Church has affirmed the moral evil of every procured abortion. This teaching has not changed and remains unchangeable. Direct abortion, that is to say, abortion willed either as an end or a means, is gravely contrary to the moral law:
[The document called the *Didache* of the twelve apostles in the first century says very clearly:] "You shall not kill the embryo by abortion and shall not cause the newborn to perish" [2271].

What of those who try to argue so speciously that the Church has changed its positions? They will say that St. Thomas was not certain when the soul entered the body of the unborn. That is right; the biology of his day was not certain. But St. Thomas said that from the instant of conception abortion is gravely sinful. Many leave that part out. In today's Gospel, our gentle and compassionate Lord warns that, rather than lead astray one of the simple believers, it would be better for a man to be plunged into the sea with a great millstone fastened around his neck.

If your hand is your difficulty, cut it off! Better for you to enter life maimed than to keep both hands and enter Gehenna. . . . If your foot is your undoing, cut it off! Better for you to enter life crippled than to be thrown into

Gehenna with both feet. If your eye is your downfall, tear it out! Better for you to enter the kingdom of God with one eye than to be thrown with both eyes into Gehenna (Mk 9:42–47).

For "hand", for "foot", for "eye" substitute "money", or "political ambition", or "political power", and our Lord is saying, in essence, "If you twist and distort the truth, and you give scandal, and you pretend that the Church teaches something for your own ends, better to cut off your money, your status, your political prestige or ambition, because you are endangering your soul.

The *Catechism* tells us: "Formal cooperation in an abortion constitutes a grave offense. The Church attaches the canonical penalty of excommunication to this crime against human life" [2272].

At the same time the Church is most compassionate and most merciful. The Church does not condemn a poor, wandering woman, weak, misled, confused, not knowing where to turn, who has an abortion. It is very understandable. The Church pleads that she pick up the pieces of her life and start all over again. The Church is always ready to forgive. But the Church also teaches, as the *Catechism* tells us:

> The inalienable right to life of every innocent human individual is a *constitutive element of a civil society and its legislation*.
>
> "The inalienable rights of the person must be recognized and respected by civil society and the political authority. These human rights depend neither on single individuals nor on parents; nor do they represent a concession made by society and the state; they belong to human nature and are inherent in the person by virtue of the creative act from which the person took his origin. Among such fundamental rights one should mention in this regard every human being's right to life and physical integrity from the moment of conception until death" [2273].

We recognize the restrictions placed on those who sit on the bench. They cannot willy-nilly deny the interpretations of the Constitution by the Supreme Court. We *hope* that many of you recognize the immorality of some of these interpretations. We said at the outset that we respect you, and we respect your limitations. All that the Church asks of you, all that God asks of you, is that you do your very best within the light of human reason, praying for divine guidance. Simultaneously, respectfully, we remind you that, in a sense, you, perhaps together with the medical profession, are the first line of defense for human life. If it be true, as Thomas Jefferson said, that the *only* reason for the existence of government is to protect the life of its people, then clearly you have the gravest of obligations as representatives of government to do everything within your power to extend the protection of human life to the weakest of the weak, the poorest of the poor, the most vulnerable of the vulnerable.

We thank you sincerely for what you attempt to do, and we pray that you will be inspired by divine guidance. You are remembered in this Mass in a very special way.

36

To Protect and Cherish
That Which Is So Sacred

On the Sixth and Ninth Commandments

THIRTY-SECOND SUNDAY IN ORDINARY TIME
NOVEMBER 6, 1994
PONTIFICAL MASS

It is wonderful to be back with you here in St. Patrick's Cathedral for this Mass, after the longest month in my life, which was spent in Rome. Despite the fact that I was with our Holy Father every day, my heart was always with you in this cathedral. Before I left Rome, Pope John Paul II asked me to extend to you his very special love.

Today we welcome a special group of about fifty-five people who are involved in the Cardinal's Leadership Project. Like so many other wonderful things in this archdiocese, it was begun by Cardinal Cooke in 1982. It has been headed by Father John O'Keefe, who is celebrating this Mass with us. The Cardinal's Leadership Project is for the development of Latino leadership in the Latino community. About one hundred graduates have gone through the program during their junior and senior year of high school. The project has many, many meetings and a lot of disciplined training. The students spend five weekends in a retreat-like atmosphere here in the archdiocese. Members of the Cardinal's Leadership Project are here under the leadership of Mr. George Cabrero. We welcome them as a very vital element in the life of the Church in New York.

* * *

Many of you are aware that on the First Sunday of Advent of 1993 we began reflecting, chapter by chapter, on the new *Catechism of the Catholic Church*. At that time it had not even yet been published in English. It was

Pope John Paul II appointed Cardinal O'Connor to serve as one of three co-presidents of the Synod on the Consecrated Life. His Eminence was in Rome from October 1 through October 31, 1994. His series of homilies on the *Catechism* resumed on November 6, 1994.

our expectation that we would finish prior to the First Sunday of Advent of this year, 1994, which is only a few Sundays away. We won't quite make it, but you will be happy to learn that we have only another five sessions after this one. Today we will study the sixth and the ninth commandments in outline form, quoting selectively from the *Catechism*.

The older I get, the more I become my father, by which I mean that my father had certain strong ideas about a number of things and constantly drilled them into me. Through the years I have absorbed them. Today's Gospel was one of my father's favorites (Mk 12:38–44). It is about the scribes, other public officials, and those who are famous who always seek the highest honors. In so many cases, the lives of such people leave a great deal to be desired. What distressed my father was that the street cleaner or the woman who scrubs the office buildings at night in order to raise a family, people who are trying to live a decent, valiant life, may be treated as dirt themselves. That is truly sad. Certainly this is applicable to the sixth and ninth commandments: "Thou shalt not commit adultery" (Ex 20:17), and "Thou shalt not covet thy neighbor's wife" (Ex 20:14).

It is so sad that today we have virtually institutionalized promiscuity. We have honored it so that we can turn on television, look at movies, look in the media and see people who apparently have nothing but contempt for the divine commandments, for the natural moral law—yet they are treated with such prestige. I suspect that if some of them walked in here now, we would be tempted even to applaud them. It is not for me to judge or to condemn individual persons—that is up to Almighty God. But we are speaking about practices, about gross, crude, chronic violations of the divine commandments. While we do not want to condemn individuals, we have to ask ourselves how this has influenced us and our children.

The sixth and the ninth commandments are negatively worded, but for positive purposes. In the Book of Exodus we are told: "Thou shalt not commit adultery." In the Gospel of Matthew our Divine Lord says: "You have heard that it was said, 'You shall not commit adultery.' But I say to you that every one who looks at a woman lustfully has already committed adultery with her in his heart" (Mt 5:27–28). Our Lord broadened the definition of adultery, taking it outside the context of a married woman or man to all acts of impurity, indecency, uncleanness.

The whole notion of these commandments is positive to remind us of the beauty of marriage, of the beauty of the legitimate use of the sexual capacity, of the beauty of being a man or woman, of the beauty of love. These must be safeguarded, and this is the purpose of the sixth and ninth commandments—to protect, to cherish, that which is so sacred.

We are told in the *Catechism*:

"God created man in his own image . . . male and female he created them" (Gen 1:27); He blessed them and said, "Be fruitful and multiply" (Gen 1:18); "When God created man, he made him in the likeness of God. Male and female he created them, and he blessed them . . ." (Gen 5:1–2) [2331].

Sexuality is part of our whole being, not just our body. It is part of our mind, part of our heart, part of our spirit, part of our way of thinking and feeling. But, as the *Catechism* reminds us:

"In creating men 'male and female,' God gives man and woman an equal personal dignity" . . . [2334].

Each of the two sexes is an image of the power and tenderness of God, with equal dignity though in a different way. The union of man and woman in marriage is a way of imitating in the flesh the Creator's generosity and [fruitfulness]: "Therefore a man leaves his father and his mother and cleaves to his wife, and they become one flesh" (Gen 2:24). All human generations proceed from this union [2335].

When Jesus came to this earth, it was to restore creation to the purity of its origins [see 2336]. Before original sin, Adam and Eve took no note of the fact that they were naked. They had nothing to be ashamed about until original sin; then the perfect order created by God was destroyed, and Adam and Eve came to have illicit desires, which they did not have before.

St. John Chrysostom lived in the fourth century and died very early in the fifth century. He was called the "golden-tongued preacher". Everything that he has to say he says beautifully, but perhaps nothing more beautifully than this, which he suggests young husbands should say to their wives:

I have taken you in my arms and I love you, and I prefer you to my life itself. For the present life is nothing, and my most ardent dream is to spend it with you in such a way that we may be assured of not being separated in the life reserved for us [2365].

In other words, we are not created simply for this life but for eternal happiness with God. That is the real meaning of love. St. John says, "I place your love above all things, and nothing would be more bitter or painful to me than to be of a different mind than you."

The *Catechism* goes on to talk about chastity and purity:

Chastity means the successful integration of sexuality within the person and thus the inner unity of man in his bodily and spiritual being. Sexuality, in which man's belonging to the bodily and biological world is expressed, becomes personal and truly human when it is integrated into the relationship of one person to another, in the complete and lifelong mutual gift of a man and a woman [in marriage] [2337].

I do not believe many of the surveys that tell us that there is no such thing as young men and women today who are chaste, who are virgins. It is just not true in my experience. I give a lot of retreats to young people. I hear a lot of confessions. Sure we slip and fall, all of us. You are never beyond this particular temptation until you are at least thirty days dead. But to write young people off as though they have no control over themselves at all, that is very unjust and unfair.

We are told in the Catechism: "Chastity includes an *apprenticeship in self-mastery* which is a training in human freedom" [2339]. That is a wonderful thing to say, particularly on this day, when there are more than twenty thousand people running the marathon. How many weeks, months, and years so many of them have trained, have disciplined themselves, have fasted, have gotten up at ungodly hours to run six, ten, twenty miles and more in a day! That is self-discipline, and that is what chastity requires. The alternative is clear, says the Catechism. Either we govern our passions and find peace, or we let ourselves be dominated by them and become unhappy.

Wouldn't you think that with all the lurid advertising, with all of the lust portrayed in the movies and on television, that there would be tremendous happiness in those who give themselves over to these lusts? But how many are really happy? Do the happy go from one marriage to the next, to the next, or from living with this person to that person? Are they truly happy?

If you ride through Times Square, you will see the displays of the disgraceful movies and shows. Ask yourselves: Are those young or older women and men who perform, who strip themselves in these two-bit, hole-in-the-wall places for the curious, for the lustful, are they happy? You have to feel sorry for them.

We are reminded in the Catechism:

"[Our] dignity require[s us] to act out of conscious and free choice, as moved and drawn in a personal way from within, and not by blind impulses in [ourselves] or by mere external constraint. [We] gain such dignity when, ridding [ourselves] of all slavery to the passions, [we] press forward to our goal by freely choosing what is good . . ." [2339].

Chastity represents an eminently personal task; it also involves a *cultural effort*, for there is "an interdependence between personal betterment and the improvement of society." Chastity presupposes respect for the rights of the person [myself and everyone else] . . . [2344].

There are various forms of chastity. Sometimes we think only of religious sisters, brothers, or priests as chaste. Back in the fourth century St. Ambrose said: "There are three forms of the virtue of chastity: the first is that of [married people], the second that of widows and the third that of virgins. We do not praise any one of them to the exclusion of the others" [2349].

We are all called to chastity by our Baptism. We are called to discipline. Married people are called to be faithful to each other, to exercise their procreative rights, their expression of love, but even then with appropriate discipline and modesty and exclusively with each other. That requires chastity, to discipline ourselves against temptations that are opposed to marriage. Those who are engaged to marry must practice chastity, waiting until the day of their marriage to engage in the possibilities that marriage provides.

I often think about what one might call "secondary virginity". There are many people—older and younger—who have slipped and fallen. They are always worried about the past. They hear the word "virgin" or "virginity", and there is deep guilt within them. I think there is such a thing as "secondary virginity". We can let Christ pick us up, and we can start all over again. We try to consecrate ourselves, in marriage or out of marriage, to purity and to decency. This, I think, is very, very real. It is why Christ came to earth—to pick up the pieces of broken lives. Once we have slipped and fallen, that does not mean that the possibility of purity, of chastity, of decency, or even of a new type of virginity is over.

The *Catechism* goes on to talk about the terrible pornography to which we are subjected today and the kinds of things that pornography so often leads to, such as rape, one of the most horrible of crimes, incest, and sexual abuse of the young within their own families or by others. This last crime is most tragic, of course, when carried out by someone respected by society, someone whom society trusts with children: teachers or priests. What scandal have we had in the Church, in all the history of the Church, comparable to the scandal of child abuse by priests? Why is it such a scandal, why does it tear us apart? Of course we are angry because someone we trusted abused that trust. But it is more than that. We recognize that it is perverse. We recognize that it is unnatural. But we should also recognize that the pornography of the day can lead to activities of this sort.

There are heterosexually oriented persons, there are homosexually oriented persons. The *Catechism* reminds us we must respect both, but both are obliged by chastity whatever their orientation. The *Catechism* says:

> [Those] who have . . . homosexual tendencies . . . must be accepted with respect, compassion, and sensitivity. Every sign of unjust discrimination in their regard should be avoided. These persons are called to fulfill God's will in their lives and, if they are Christians, to unite to the sacrifice of the Lord's Cross the difficulties they may encounter . . . [2358].

The *Catechism* talks about "The Love of Husband and Wife". Yesterday I witnessed the marriage of a very lovely young couple here in Our Lady's Chapel. I have known the bride from the time she was about a minute old. I was amazed and delighted when they picked this unusual reading for the Mass. It is in the *Catechism*:

> Tobias got out of bed and said to Sarah, "Sister, get up, and let us pray and implore our Lord that he grant us mercy and safety." So she got up, and they began to pray and implore that they might be kept safe. Tobias began by saying, "Blessed are you, O God of our fathers. . . . You made Adam, and for him you made his wife Eve as a helper and support. From the two of them the race of mankind has sprung. You said, 'It is not good that the man should be alone; let us make a helper for him like himself.' I now am taking this kinswoman of mine, not because of lust, but with sincerity. Grant that she and I may find mercy and that we may grow old together." And they both said, "Amen, Amen." Then they went to sleep for the night (Tob 8:4–9) [2361].

This, again, is the kind of thing that gives me so much hope—that a young couple should select a reading like that. That shows deep faith, and a deep desire to be holy.

The *Catechism* goes on to talk a great deal about the purpose of marriage, the purpose of the sexual capacity—to express love, companionship, to fulfill the desire for two people to be one with each other—never separated from the possibility of having children. This does not mean that every marital relation must result in children, but that possibility can never be artificially prevented.

There is an opportunity here to talk about things such as natural family planning. Couples, of course, have the right and the responsibility to think about the number of children that they believe God wants them to have. That is within their competence. But it is the *means* by which such is done that the Church talks about, the means that always emphasizes the sacredness of human life.

The *Catechism* says:

> When it is a question of harmonizing married love with the responsible transmission of life, the morality of the behavior does not depend on sincere intention and evaluation of motives alone; but it must be determined by objective criteria, criteria drawn from the nature of the person and his acts, criteria that respect the total meaning of mutual self-giving and human procreation in the context of true love; this is possible only if the virtue of married chastity is practiced with sincerity of heart [2368].

> By safeguarding both these essential aspects, the unitive and procreative, the conjugal act preserves in its fullness the sense of true mutual love and its orientation toward man's exalted vocation to parenthood [2369].

Thus the innate language that expresses the total reciprocal self-giving of husband and wife is overlaid, through contraception, by an objectively contradictory language, namely, that of not giving oneself totally to the other. This leads not only to a positive refusal to be open to life but also to a falsification of the inner truth of conjugal love, which is called upon to give itself in personal totality . . . [2370].

The state has a responsibility for its citizens' well-being. In this capacity it is legitimate for it to intervene to orient the demography of the population. This can be done by means of objective and respectful information, but certainly not by authoritarian, coercive measures. The state may not legitimately usurp the initiative of spouses, who have the primary responsibility for the procreation and education of their children. It is not authorized to promote demographic regulation by means contrary to the moral law [2372].

Techniques that entail the dissociation of husband and wife, by the intrusion of a person other than the couple (donation of sperm or ovum, surrogate uterus), are gravely immoral. These techniques (heterologous artificial insemination and fertilization) infringe the child's right to be born of a father and mother known to him and bound to each other by marriage. They betray the spouses' "right to become a father and a mother only through each other" [2376].

Techniques involving only the married couple (homologous artificial insemination and fertilization) are perhaps less reprehensible, yet remain morally unacceptable. They dissociate the sexual act from the procreative act. The act which brings the child into existence is no longer an act by which two persons give themselves to one another, but one that "entrusts the life and identity of the embryo into the power of doctors and biologists and establishes the domination of technology over the origin and destiny of the human person" [2377].

The *Catechism* talks about the pain suffered by men and women who want to have children but are not able to do so. There is the possibility of adoption. That is always limited, despite the fact that we have one million five hundred thousand abortions every year in this country. How wonderful it would be if those children were made available for adoption! A couple without children can come to recognize the power of spiritual parenting. They can pray for the children of the world. They can pray for women who are tempted to have abortions.

I must make mention of a new phenomenon called a "trial marriage", where people live together and "see if it works out". That is not a marriage [2391], nor is a "free union" a marriage [2390].

The *Catechism* clearly explains Church teaching on adultery and divorce, which it calls "Offenses against the Dignity of Marriage."

Adultery is an injustice. He who commits adultery fails in his commitment. He does injury to the sign of the covenant which the marriage bond is, transgresses the rights of the other spouse, and undermines the institution of marriage by breaking the contract on which it is based. He compromises the good of human generation and the welfare of children who need their parents' stable union [2381].

Between the baptized, "a ratified and consummated marriage cannot be dissolved by any human power or for any reason other than death" [2382].

The *separation* of spouses while maintaining the marriage bond can be legitimate in certain cases provided for by canon law.

If civil divorce remains the only possible way of ensuring certain legal rights, the care of the children, or the protection of inheritance, it can be tolerated and does not constitute a moral offense [2383].

Divorce is a grave offense against the natural law. It claims to break the contract, to which the spouses freely consented, to live with each other till death. Divorce does injury to the covenant of salvation, of which sacramental marriage is the sign. Contracting a new union, even if it is recognized by civil law, adds to the gravity of the rupture: the remarried spouse is then in a situation of public and permanent adultery [2384].

It can happen that one of the spouses is the innocent victim of a divorce decreed by civil law; this spouse therefore has not contravened the moral law. There is a considerable difference between a spouse who has sincerely tried to be faithful to the sacrament of marriage and is unjustly abandoned, and one who through his own grave fault destroys a canonically valid marriage [2386].

The *Catechism* explores the teaching of the ninth commandment, "You shall not covet your neighbor's wife", and this thing that we call "concupiscence", the way the flesh works against the spirit. I think it is helpful to remind ourselves that we were given the grace through Baptism to fight against concupiscence, but we have to struggle constantly, receive the sacrament of Penance, receive the Holy Eucharist if we are in the state of grace, and guard our modesty.

Modesty is a very important virtue to safeguard decency. But no matter how we try, we are always going to have our temptations. I think it is helpful for everyone to know that there is hardly a man or a woman in the world who escapes these temptations, these desires. They are part of our very being. It is not sinful to have the desires. It is sinful if we let them take over. The monk in the monastery, the nun, the hermit in the desert can never be certain that they will not have temptations. We are all in this same ship of life together. We are all very much human beings. If you meet people who say they have never had a temptation against chastity in their lives, you better see if they are made of iron, because temptations against chastity are part and parcel of the fallen human race. They are part and parcel of our inheritance of original sin.

I encourage you to study in greater detail the sixth and ninth commandments as presented in the new *Catechism*. They are beautiful expressions of Almighty God's great love for the human person.

37

What Is Important in Life?

On the Tenth Commandment

THIRTY-THIRD SUNDAY OF THE YEAR
NOVEMBER 13, 1994
PONTIFICAL MASS

Welcome to all from wherever you come. We are always pleased to have with us our seminarians from St. Joseph's Seminary that they may see you who, one day, please God, they will serve as priests and that you may see them.

We are delighted to have with us a number of Missionary Sisters of Charity, Mother Teresa's sisters, including several postulants. It is always a great joy to have them pray with us in this cathedral.

Those of you who have come here regularly know that starting on the First Sunday of Advent last year we embarked on weekly reflections on the new *Catechism of the Catholic Church*, which is more like an encyclopedia than a catechism. Today we will explore the tenth commandment.

The tenth commandment is: "You shall not covet . . . anything that is your neighbor's. . . . You shall not desire your neighbor's house, his field, or his manservant, or his maidservant . . ." (Ex 20:17); in other words, you shall not covet anything that belongs to anyone else. Covetousness is the sense of deep, burning envy or a willingness to do anything to get whatever another person has. Our Lord puts it, "For where your treasure is, there will your heart be also" (Mt 6:21).

During the thirty days that I was in Rome participating in the Synod on Consecrated Life, a very unassuming woman humbly sat in an assigned seat, the same seat at every session for thirty days—from nine in the morning until twelve-thirty in the afternoon and from five in the evening until seven in the evening. She sat there during that entire time and was invited to speak only once, since there were some three hundred participants. She never moved out of that chair. She was Mother Teresa of Calcutta. It was as though she were a nobody, totally unimportant, just one of everyone else. There was no envy in this woman, no complaints that she was not given star billing, no coveting what others might be saying. She said what she had to say. All the while Mother Teresa sat there, praying her rosary beads, and one could see personified in her the words of our Lord, "Where your treasure is, there is your heart."

Mother Teresa's heart is truly with the poor. She does not have huge programs. She does not have big bureaucracies. She just does whatever she can for the poor. I have known Mother Teresa for a long time. I have never seen her do anything for herself. This is the model that our Lord speaks of.

The *Catechism* says:

> The tenth commandment unfolds and completes the ninth, which is concerned with concupiscence of the flesh. [Concupiscence, this uncontrolled burning, yearning, came with original sin, in which we lost control of ourselves.] It forbids coveting the goods of another, as the root of theft, robbery, and fraud, which the seventh commandment forbids. "Lust of the eyes" leads to the violence and injustice forbidden by the fifth commandment. Avarice [or greediness], like fornication, originates in the idolatry prohibited by the first three prescriptions of the Law. The tenth commandment concerns the intention of the heart; with the ninth, it summarizes all the precepts of the Law [2534].

"Thou shalt not covet" summarizes all of the ten commandments, because the ten commandments were designed by Almighty God to give us balance, to give us peace, to show us how to live. If our hearts are filled with greed, if we are constantly envying others, if we never have enough, then we cannot be living as God intended us to live.

> The sensitive appetite leads us to desire pleasant things we do not have, e.g., the desire to eat when we are hungry, or to warm ourselves when we are cold. These desires are good in themselves; but often they exceed the limits of reason and drive us to covet unjustly what is not ours and belongs to another or is owed to [another] [2535].

So often we want to have what others have, or we want to be what others are, because we are not satisfied with being ourselves. Why aren't we satisfied with being ourselves? God made us as we are. The dissatisfaction comes from not being what God made us to be, from destroying that image. We are not satisfied with ourselves, and we think if we would be somebody else, if we had what others have, then we would be happy.

The *Catechism* continues:

> The tenth commandment forbids *greed* and the desire to amass earthly goods without limit. It forbids *avarice* arising from the passion for riches and their attendant power. It also forbids the desire to commit injustice by harming our neighbor in his temporal goods.

"When the Law says, 'You shall not covet,' these words mean that we should banish our desires for whatever does not belong to us. Our thirst for another's goods is immense, infinite, never quenched. Thus is written: 'He who loves money never has money enough'" [2536].

St. Francis of Assisi was so wise he recognized that everything we own owns us. It might be useful to us, it might even be necessary to our work or whatever, but in a way it owns us. If you own an automobile, you have to put fuel in it, you have to get a license plate for it, you have to keep it in working condition. So it owns you in a certain way. St. Francis did not want to be owned by anything. This is something that has to be taught to children, a real sense of values. What is important in life?

In the ordinary home does a child *have to have* his or her own television in his or her own room? Do kids *have* to go to what the world considers the best of schools? Is it always "Keep up with the Joneses" or "Get ahead of others"? Are children taught the real meaning of spiritual and interior poverty and putting things in perspective?

The *Catechism* continues:

It is not a violation of this commandment to desire to obtain things that belong to one's neighbor, provided this is done by just means [but not by theft, not by wishing evil to others] [2537].

The tenth commandment requires that *envy* be banished from the human heart [2538].

The *Catechism* goes on to talk of the story of King David. In those days a man like David was allowed many, many wives. David saw Bathsheba, the wife of one of his soldiers, and he wanted her, despite the fact that he had many wives of his own. David wanted Bathsheba so much that he had Uriah, Bathsheba's husband, killed. That is real covetousness. That is the evil that can lead to the worst of crimes. As the *Catechism* says, "Through the devil's envy death entered the world" (Wis 2:24). The devil so envied God that the devil tempted Adam and Eve to defy God, to demand that God give them what God knew was not fit for them. They had everything they needed, everything imaginable. But it wasn't enough.

The *Catechism* continues:

Envy is a capital sin. It refers to the sadness at the sight of another's goods and the immoderate desire to acquire them for oneself, even unjustly. When it wishes grave harm to a neighbor it is a mortal sin [2539].

Samuel Johnson, the writer, made a very astute observation. He said, "Envy desires not so much its own happiness as another's misery." It is so often the case that, if we cannot have something, we do not want anyone else to have it.

St. Augustine saw envy as "*the* diabolical sin." "From envy are born hatred, detraction, calumny, joy caused by the misfortune of a neighbor, and displeasure caused by his prosperity" [2539].

St. John Chrysostom, the "golden-tongued preacher", said:

Would you like to see God glorified by you? Then rejoice in your brother's progress and you will immediately give glory to God. Because his servant could conquer envy by rejoicing in the merits of others, God will be praised [2540].

While I was in Rome recently, I called one of our priests in St. Vincent's Hospital. He had already lost one leg through diabetes, and when I called him he had just had the other leg removed. Instead of feeling sorry for himself, despite the pain, despite the emptiness, he said, "Please tell the Holy Father that I am offering the loss of my legs in order that his leg will heal more rapidly." That's exactly the opposite of covetousness, of envy.

The *Catechism* continues: "Jesus enjoins his disciples to prefer him to everything and everyone, and bids them 'renounce all that [they have]' for his sake and that of the Gospel" (Lk 14:33) [2544].

We are told by St. Paul about Jesus, "He emptied himself, taking upon himself the form of a slave." This is exactly the opposite of greed, of avarice, of envy, of covetousness. Shortly before His Passion, our Lord told His disciples about the poor widow of Jerusalem who, out of her poverty, gave all that she had to live on. The precept of detachment from riches is obligatory for entrance into the Kingdom of heaven, quite the opposite of the two disciples James and John, who asked if they could sit at His right and left hand when they came into His Kingdom. Our Lord said, "That is not for Me to give. Will you drink of My suffering with Me?"

The *Catechism* continues:

Blessed are the poor in spirit (Mt 5:3). The Beatitudes reveal an order of happiness and grace, of beauty and peace. Jesus celebrates the joy of the poor, to whom the Kingdom already belongs [2546].

Yesterday I baptized a baby in a hospital; the baby was not a patient. The parents of the baby were there because their father is a patient, completely helpless with a disease that just radiates through an entire family and has struck this man down from the prime of health. The whole family was there at the baptism. His wife said to me, "His children and grandchildren—they don't have money, but how rich we are!" That is the opposite of covetousness, of greed, of envy.

The *Catechism* continues:

The Lord grieves over the rich, because they find their consolation in the abundance of goods (Lk 6:24). "Let the proud seek and love earthly king-

doms, but blessed are the poor in spirit for theirs is the Kingdom of
heaven." Abandonment to the providence of the Father in heaven frees us
from anxiety about tomorrow. Trust in God is a preparation for the blessed-
ness of the poor. They shall see God [2547].

That is the meaning of the Our Father. "Give us this day our daily
bread", nevertheless, let *Your* will be done, as our Lord did in the Garden
of His suffering just as He was about to die. He said, "I do not want to suffer and die. Nevertheless, not My will but Yours be done."

The *Catechism* continues: "Desire for true happiness frees [us] from [our]
immoderate attachment to the goods of this world so that [we] can find
[our] fulfillment in the vision and beatitude of God" [2548].

Many politicians come to see me, those campaigning for office, those in
office. They come not because I am anybody or can do anything for them;
I just happen to be the Archbishop of New York. Despite what one sometimes reads in the newspapers, I tell all of them the same thing—Democrat,
Republican, or whatever they are. I remind them that our Lord said,
"What can it profit a man that he gain the whole world and suffer the loss
of his own soul?" That is what a campaigner for office has to remember,
that is what one *in* office has to remember, whatever their religious persuasion. A person may be very prestigious and may have all sorts of earthly
power. If that is what that person wants, fine. But what does it profit a man
if he gain the whole world and suffer the loss of his own soul? I do not imply that everyone in public office or campaigning for office will suffer the
loss of his or her soul, but that has to be the fundamental principle.

The *Catechism* continues: "Whoever sees God has obtained all the goods
of which he can conceive" [2548]. This is why St. Thérèse, the Little
Flower, could say, "It is easy to have everything; just want God."

> In order to possess and contemplate God, Christ's faithful mortify their
> cravings and, with the grace of God, prevail over the seductions of pleasure
> and power [2549].

We have to discipline ourselves. There is no question that we have many
very, very poor people. There are many people with modest incomes who
are struggling. Nevertheless, a tremendous number of us live pretty well. I
live too well. We have to keep mortifying ourselves, continuing to discipline ourselves, continuing to give to others, continuing to give to the poor.

That, I think, is in large measure what today's Gospel was reminding us
of. This earthly life is going to end.

> Jesus said to his disciples: "During that period, after trials of every sort, the
> sun will be darkened, the moon will not shed its light, stars will fall out of
> the skies, and the heavenly host will be shaken. Then men will see the Son
> of Man coming in the clouds with great power and glory. He will dispatch

his messengers and assemble his chosen from the four winds, from the farthest bounds of earth and sky. Learn a lesson from the fig tree. Once the sap of its branches runs high and it begins to sprout leaves, you know that summer is near" (Mk 13:24–28).

Each of us knows that the end of our life is coming. We don't know when. In one of my morning Masses at seven-thirty in the cathedral this past week, I met a beautiful lady, beautiful in her holiness, and her three grown children. Just the day before, her husband had died; it was a totally unexpected death. He had a minor accident that resulted in an aneurysm and was dead in no time. We just don't know when judgment is coming, so we have to ask ourselves: What does anything mean? This life is all so transient. Our Lord says, "No one knows the exact hour or day, neither the angels in heaven or even the Son, but only the Father."

It is heartening to look at the *New York Times* review of books and see that our Holy Father's book *Crossing the Threshold of Hope* is number one on the best-seller list. That is so heartening because it is a book filled with *hope*, it is a book that gives us perspective, a book that gives us balance, a book that asks the question, "What does it profit us if we gain the whole world but suffer the loss of our own souls?" This book is not a threatening book, it is not a condemning book. It is a gentle, reassuring book, a book filled with hope. The fact that it is selling such a tremendous number of copies all over this land and has been published in thirty-one different languages suggests how deep is the desire for peace, for consolation, for hope. We cannot get that from this world but only from above.

"Prayer Is a Surge of the Heart"

THIRTY-FOURTH SUNDAY OF THE YEAR
NOVEMBER 20, 1994
CHRIST THE KING
PONTIFICAL MASS

Welcome to all of you from wherever you come! As always, it is a joy to be with you, a special joy on this beautiful Feast of Christ our King.

Each morning in our house attached to the cathedral, before we do almost anything else, the six of us who live there—two bishops, three priests, and myself—pray together in common the Divine Office. The Divine Office, as you know, is prayed by priests, by men and women religious throughout the world, and by many laypersons. It is a very beautiful custom. The Opening Psalm for Sunday, the Feast of Christ the King, is this:

> O God, you are my God, for you I long;
> for you my soul is thirsting.
> My body pines for you
> like a dry, weary land without water.
> So I gaze on you in the sanctuary
> to see your strength and your glory.

> For your love is better than life,
> my lips will speak your praise.
> So I will bless you all my life,
> in your name I will lift up my hands.
> My soul shall be filled as with a banquet,
> my mouth shall praise you with joy.

> On my bed I remember you.
> On you I muse through the night
> for you have been my help;
> in the shadow of your wings I rejoice.
> My soul clings to you;
> your right hand holds me fast.

I open with that Psalm from the Divine Office because those of you who come regularly to the cathedral know that we have been studying the new *Catechism of the Catholic Church*. We have now reached the final portion of the *Catechism*, the fourth section, which is a particularly beautiful section on prayer, that which is so important to our spiritual lives, to our spiritual survival.

As you know so well, if you have a candle burning brightly within some kind of glass enclosure, and then you cover the glass to shut off the air, the candle sputters and dies. That is the way our souls become without prayer—they just slip into darkness. This is a particularly auspicious Sunday to open the *Catechism* section on prayer because it is the Feast of Christ the King. What do we mean by calling Christ "the King"? Is He kind of a super-president, someone like the king in *The King and I* or *King Lear*? Christ is nothing of that sort at all. Christ says in this Gospel, "My kingdom does not belong to this world" (Jn 18:33–37).

In the first reading from Daniel (Dan 7:13–14), we are told, "His dominion is an everlasting dominion." This is not an everlasting world here, nor is our Kingdom of this world. It would be a pretty sad joke on humanity if this were it. Some of us are happy for a time, but how often we are gloomy. Some of us are healthy, but how often are we ill. Some of us feel secure, but how often are we lonely, how often are we besieged by death, by disease, by terrible things that happen in our families. Surely, if this life were everything, it would be a huge joke. We believe that this is only the beginning. We are all on pilgrimage.

Our Kingdom does not belong to this world because we are members of the Body of Christ, and we belong with Christ for all eternity. So often we repeat those beautiful words of St. Augustine, "My heart was made for you, O Lord, and it will not rest until it rests in you."

Many people find prayer very difficult, something very mysterious and perplexing. Prayer is not the language of this world. We might say that prayer does not come naturally because we are dealing with the supernatural. We are trying to relate to Christ our King in a supernatural way.

In the Archdiocese of New York we have Mass every Sunday in thirty different languages, and even that does not satisfy the wide variety of ethnic groups that we have. This afternoon I will celebrate Mass in this cathedral for Hispanics, and it will be packed. We have Masses in French, German, Italian, Vietnamese, Chinese, and so on throughout the Archdiocese. People want to pray in their own language. The language of prayer is a special language, and we have to work at learning that language. To some it may not come so easily.

The *Catechism* section on prayer begins with a beautiful saying from St. Thérèse of Lisieux: "For me, prayer is a surge of the heart; it is a simple look turned toward heaven, it is a cry of recognition and of love, embracing both trial and joy." How she was tried! So often we think of St.

Thérèse as a rose, but her life was filled with thorns and suffering. Some of her most poignant prayers were prayers telling God of her loneliness, of her sense of emptiness, of the darkness that she experienced, of the discouragement. That is what makes St. Thérèse a beautiful model in this our day, when we experience so many of these same things. St. Thérèse felt such horrible physical punishment. She had a terrible case of tuberculosis. She hemorrhaged a great deal, and her body was racked with pain.

St. John Damascene says, "Prayer is the raising of one's mind and heart to God or the requesting of good things from God." "But [the *Catechism* reminds us] when we pray, do we speak from the height of our pride and will, or 'out of the depths' of a humble and contrite heart?" [2559].

There are a number of Navy people here today whom I happen to know. There is a very beautiful custom in the Navy that has a profound meaning. In the name of good order and discipline, on the quarterdeck of every ship there is someone who stands watch, called the "officer of the deck". On a smaller ship the officer of the deck may be a very junior enlisted person, on a larger ship a quite senior officer. No matter who wants to go on to that ship, including the Secretary of the Navy or the Chief of Naval Operations, he or she says to that perhaps lowly officer of the deck, "I request permission to come aboard." Only when the words come, "Permission granted", does even the most senior officer or dignitary go aboard, even if it is the President of the United States. In a sense, this is the way that God is with us. He wants to be with us wherever we go, but He will not force His way into our hearts in prayer. God *asks* our permission, no matter how lowly we are, no matter how sinful we are. God wants so very much to be intimately intertwined with us, but He will not enter without our saying "Yes, God, you are permitted." It is a strange and wonderful mystery.

The *Catechism* tells us:

> Where does prayer come from? Whether prayer is expressed in words or gestures, it is the whole man who prays. But in naming the source of prayer, Scripture speaks sometimes of the soul or the spirit, but most often of the heart (more than a thousand times). According to Scripture, it is the *heart* that prays. If our heart is far from God, the words of prayer are in vain [2562].

> The heart is our hidden center, beyond the grasp of our reason and of others; only the Spirit of God can fathom the human heart and know it fully. The heart is the place of decision, deeper than our psychic drives. It is the place of truth, where we choose life or death [2563].

The philosopher Pascal says, "The heart has its reasons that reason never knows." In an unusual passage in Shakespeare's *Henry VIII*, we are told, "In prayer the lips ne'er act the winning part, Without the sweet concurrence of the heart." Although Henry VIII probably prayed devoutly before he chopped off the head of each wife, his heart was not in his prayers!

The *Catechism* reminds us that we are always in search of God. "In the act of creation, God calls every being from nothingness into existence. . . . All religions bear witness to man's essential search for God" [2566].

There is a beautiful book by Dr. Viktor Frankl, who was a Jewish psychiatrist in a concentration camp under the Nazis. When he was finally released, he wrote the book *Man's Search for Meaning*, probing the deepest searches of the human heart for a relationship with God, particularly through prayer.

The *Catechism* continues:

> [We] may forget [our] Creator or hide from his face; [we] may run after idols or accuse [God] of having abandoned [us]; yet the living and true God tirelessly calls each person to that mysterious encounter known as prayer [2567].

You remember that beautiful poem "The Hound of Heaven", by Francis Thompson, who wandered into drugs, sexual permissiveness, alcohol, and literally became a bum until his conversion, when he wrote:

> I fled Him, down the nights and down the days;
>   I fled Him, down the arches of the years;
> I fled Him down the labyrinthine ways
>   Of my own mind; and in the midst of tears
> I hid from Him . . .

Always running. Then Francis Thompson tells us that "the Hound of Heaven" ran ever-faster, always pursuing him until He caught him. It is told beautifully in Psalm 139:

> Where could I go to escape from you?
>   Where could I get away from your presence?
> If I went up to heaven, you would be there;
>   if I lay down in the world of the dead, you would be there.
> If I flew away beyond the east
>   or lived in the farthest place in the west,
> you would be there to lead me,
>   you would be there to help me.
> I could ask the darkness to hide me
>   or the light around me to turn into night,

but even darkness is not dark for you,
and the night is as bright as the day.
Darkness and light are the same to you.

The *Catechism* then goes on to give us descriptions of prayer in the Old Testament. There are many examples given [see 2569–75]: the prayer of Abraham, for example, when God said that he was to go off into a strange land and that his people would be more numerous than the stars in the sky, the sands on the shore; the prayer of Noah; the prayer of Abel, who offered the first fruits of the field to God; the story of the burning bush, when Moses is tending the sheep of his father-in-law in the desert. He looks over and sees a bush aflame at the foot of the mountain. He rushes toward it and suddenly comes the voice of God saying, "Moses, take the shoes from off your feet, for the ground on which you stand is holy ground"; in other words, this is a place of prayer, a place of reverence like the temple, like this cathedral, like the tabernacle, like this sacred altar.

We are told in the *Catechism*: "Moses converses with God often and at length, climbing the mountain to hear and entreat him and coming down to the people to repeat the words of his God for their guidance" [2576].

Often the symbol of prayer on the mountaintop is used. The most popular sermons of Dr. Martin Luther King, Jr., were those sermons when he talked about his being on the mountaintop.

The *Catechism* talks about the prophets in the Old Testament and the many forms of prayer.

The *Catechism* goes on to talk about the Book of Psalms, called the "Psalter", which is the word for praise. Earlier I read from a Psalm prayed at Morning Prayer. The Psalms were collected for worship by the Jewish assembly. One hundred fifty of them were put into five books. St. Ambrose describes them beautifully:

> What is more pleasing than a psalm? David expresses it well: "Praise the Lord, for a psalm is good: let there be praise of our God with gladness and grace!" Yes, a psalm is a blessing on the lips of the people, praise of God, the assembly's homage, a general acclamation, a word that speaks for all, the voice of the Church, a confession of faith in song [2589].

If you have trouble praying or even if you do not pray, I would very strongly recommend that you turn to the Psalms. You can just select them at random. One is more beautiful than the next. There are Psalms for periods of sadness, depression, and loneliness, Psalms of pain, Psalms when you lose someone in death. There are Psalms of joy, Psalms of thanksgiving. They are so beautiful, so uplifting. They can help answer this search in our hearts. So you might try to pray the Psalms, even if you read one each day. You may find it worthwhile.

The *Catechism* then speaks about prayer in the New Testament, reminding us that:

The drama of prayer is fully revealed to us in the Word who became flesh and dwells among us [2598].

The Gospel according to St. Luke emphasizes the action of the Holy Spirit and the meaning of prayer in Christ's ministry. Jesus prays *before* the decisive moments of his mission . . . [2600].

You recall that even before Christ began His public life He went into the desert and prayed and fasted for forty days. That was characteristic of everything He did. Often Christ would go out into the desert or pray on a mountaintop. The *Catechism* says:

Jesus often draws apart to pray *in solitude*, on a mountain, preferably at night. He *includes all men* in his prayer, for he has taken on humanity in his incarnation, and he offers [us] to the Father when he offers himself [2602].

I remember a time years ago when life was a little bit chaotic. I went to visit the Carthusian hermitage up in the woods of Vermont. I sat in a little hut with an aluminum roof with a man named Father Boylan, who was the prior there. It was pouring cats and dogs, and there was this cacophony of sound beating on the roof. I could hardly hear what Father was saying. Suddenly the rain stopped, and he said, "Listen to the silence." He was not just talking about the silence after the storm. He was talking about the silence of God found in our own hearts. Our Lord said to His apostles, "Come apart with Me and rest awhile." That is prayer.

I remember many, many nights during my many years at sea. It is a most extraordinary experience to be out on the deck of a ship on what we call the "fantail", sometimes with a group of very ordinary sailors, praying the Rosary, with a hundred million stars and pure air and the water rushing by. You just feel the presence of God in that kind of solitude. All of us need this solitude, even if it is a minute a day. Father James Keller used to write books called *Three Minutes a Day*, little stories to bring us back to ourselves, to bring us back to God.

The *Catechism* continues: "When the hour had come for him to fulfill the Father's plan of love, Jesus allows [us] a glimpse of the boundless depth of his prayer" [2605]. Remember His prayer of anguish. In the Garden of Gethsemane Jesus actually sweat blood. That is how intensely Jesus was praying. "Father, take suffering away from Me." Yet, what made it a valid prayer? "Nevertheless," Jesus said, "not My will but Thine be done." That is always the secret of prayer.

Jesus tells us many, many times, "Ask, and you shall receive. Knock, and it shall be opened to you. Seek, and you shall find." Many people say,

"Well, I pray, but I never get what I pray for." What we seek has to be in accordance with the will of God. We must add always, "Nevertheless, not my will but Thine be done", because God knows infinitely better than we do. Oscar Wilde, the real sceptic or cynic, says, "When the gods wish to punish us, they answer our prayers." There is some truth in that.

The *Catechism* completes this first section on prayer by references to the prayer of Mary. Two of these prayers, I think, are particularly beautiful. When Mary was a young girl, committed to virginity, the angel appeared to her out of nowhere. The angel says, "God wants you to be the mother of His Son." What a shock! This was to change Mary's entire life so radically. But what was Mary's prayer? "Behold the handmaid of the Lord; let it be done to me according to your word." This is a perfect prayer.

A second prayer of Mary's is equally perfect. Remember the marriage feast of Cana, when the newly married couple are so embarrassed because they have run out of wine for their excessive number of guests? It was Mary who noted it. This is so important for us to remember. Mary always knows what is going on and wants to help. Mary went to Jesus. She did not argue. She did not even ask Him anything. She said, "Son, they do not have any more wine." Then Mary just took for granted what Jesus would do. She went to the wine steward, and she said, "Do whatever He tells you."

39

At the Heart of All Prayer

FIRST SUNDAY OF ADVENT
NOVEMBER 27, 1994
PONTIFICAL MASS

Welcome to all on this glorious First Sunday of Advent! Congratulations for being able to break through the traffic. Every year at this time I ponder on whether we should move St. Patrick's Cathedral or ask them to move the tree at Rockefeller Center, because the proximity of these two places makes it almost impossible to move about during this season.

We are here with great joy to begin this very beautiful season of the Church's year. I should wish you a Happy New Year, since this is the first day of what we call the Liturgical Year. Last Sunday, the feast of Christ the King, ended what we call the Ordinary Year in the Church's season. Today we begin all over again with a new sense of life.

It is good to have our auxiliary bishop and my right-hand-man, Bishop Mansell, concelebrating today. He does not have much opportunity to be with us at this Mass because on weekends he is all over the Archdiocese, offering Masses, administering the sacrament of Confirmation, and laying cornerstones, all of which I am very grateful for, because, if Bishop Mansell did not work so hard, I would have to start!

* * *

Yesterday, I read in one of the New York newspapers, I forget which, that fifteen years ago our Holy Father, Pope John Paul II, had been recorded on tape praying the Rosary. Now, fifteen years later, that has been released as a compact disc and is a best-seller. It is near the top of all compact disc sales. Recently, there was a disc of Gregorian chant that is up toward the top of the list. Our Holy Father's book *Crossing the Threshold of Hope* is being printed in thirty-one different languages and is on the top of the best-seller list in the *New York Times* and elsewhere. The *Catechism*, commissioned by Pope John Paul II, has sold several million copies and is constantly being reprinted. What does all of this suggest, in what we so often think of as a terribly jaded age, but that there is this deep hunger for something beyond: a hunger to be reminded that this life is only the beginning, that all of the pain and suffering will one day be washed away; a hunger for support in this life so that we can go through this pilgrimage achieving some kind of serenity and peace; a hunger for a spiritual life that is best reflected in prayer, prayer of every type, the prayer of the Rosary, the prayer of the singing of the Psalms, and so on. That is what Advent is about: the spirit of prayer.

Our sessions on the new *Catechism of the Catholic Church* are almost complete. During Advent we are doing the final section of the *Catechism*, which is on prayer. This is so appropriate, because this is the period of expectancy, of prayer, of getting ready. It is the period during which we are reminded of the longing of the entire human race for the potential of salvation after original sin. It is the period during which we are reminded of the longing of the Israelites when they were on pilgrimage in the desert, after having escaped from slavery to the Egyptians—wandering, weary, lost, confused, just as are we so often, praying that they would get to the Promised Land, which is the symbol of heaven. Advent is a reminder of those nine months of prayer in which surely Mary engaged, praying to the Father, praying to the Son within her, awaiting His advent, awaiting His birth on Christmas Day. It is so appropriate, therefore, that we try during this period of Advent—with all the hustle and bustle, with all of the pseudo-Christmas carols being blasted out on the streets, all of the activities attendant to preparation for Christmas—to enter into a season of recollection, a season of reminder, a season in which we reflect on what today's Gospel reflects on: the second coming of Christ. Glorious as was His coming on Christmas Day, His first advent, the second advent will be of immeasurable glory. It is at that coming when all of us will be judged, each of us personally and individually. That will be the advent we hope will assure us of eternal happiness.

In the Gospel today (Lk 21:25–28, 34–36), as in the second reading today, we are reminded that that advent can come for any one of us at any moment. It could come today, and we would be facing Almighty God for all eternity. Hence, our Lord concludes this portion of the Gospel by saying, "Be on guard lest your spirits become bloated with indulgence and drunkenness and worldly cares. The great day will suddenly close in on you like a trap." Christ can come like a thief in the night. Christ concludes by saying, "Pray constantly for the strength to escape whatever is in prospect, and to stand secure before the Son of Man."

In the second reading, of St. Paul to the people of Thessalonia (1 Th 3:12–4:2), St. Paul gives the people an important reminder. St. Paul wrote to the people of Thessalonia because they were being persecuted for their faith. This was perhaps in the year 50 or 60. Some of them were getting terribly confused, particularly about when Christ would be coming. They thought that Christ was going to come immediately in their day, what was called the "parousia", the second coming of Christ. St. Paul writes to tell the people of Thessalonia, "No, this is not the case. We do not know specifically when our Lord will come in the second coming." Just as our Lord had told the apostles "It is not for you to know the day or the hour, just be on your guard, just watch and just pray", St. Paul says the same thing to those early Christians, "Be on your guard, watch and pray. He can come for any of you at any time."

St. Paul concludes this beautiful letter to the people of Thessalonia: "Be joyful always, pray at all times, be thankful in all circumstances. This is what God wants from you in your life in union with Christ Jesus. Do not restrain the Holy Spirit; do not despise inspired messages" (1 Th 5:16–20). We must open ourselves to the coming of the Holy Spirit.

Last week we spoke of prayer in very general terms, particularly about prayer in the Old Testament. We emphasized the prayer that we call the Psalms and strongly recommended that each of us each day pray one of the Psalms, because they are so helpful and so pertinent.

The *Catechism* then begins the section called "In the Age of the Church". This refers to the age following the coming of the Holy Spirit at Pentecost. Our Divine Lord's apostles had seen Him after He had risen from the dead, after their hopes had been shattered by the crucifixion; and they were happy to see Him, to touch Him, and to eat with Him. Yet, when our Divine Lord ascended into heaven, He seemed to have left them for good, despite His promise that He would send the Holy Spirit. The apostles were fearful. They lacked courage. They did not go out to spread the gospel as our Lord had told them to. They would frequently lock themselves in an upper room out of fear. But during that time, we are told, they would pray, and so this section of the *Catechism* begins: "On the day of Pentecost, the Spirit of the Promise [Christ's promise] was poured out on the disciples, gathered 'together in one place' (Acts 2:1). While awaiting the Spirit, 'all these with one accord devoted themselves to prayer' (Acts 1:14)" [2623].

Mary was there, not out of fear but to support and comfort the apostles. Then, suddenly, the Holy Spirit came upon them with a big burst of wind that shook the house, tongues of fires that leaped out upon them. And their prayer was then filled with the Holy Spirit. They went out and preached courageously. They were willing to die for the faith. That was the difference made by the Holy Spirit, Who comes to us in prayer.

The *Catechism* talks about the types of prayer. It begins with blessing and adoration. We do not usually think of blessing as a prayer. In the Mass today, for example, we will say "Blessed are You, Lord God of all creation. Through Your goodness we have this bread to offer, which earth has given and human hands have made. It will become for us the bread of life." The prayer of blessing is called a dialogue with God [see 2626].

In the Divine Office that we read this morning, we read the canticle from Daniel:

> Bless the Lord, all you works of the Lord.
> Praise and exalt him above all forever.
> Angels of the Lord, bless the Lord.
> You heavens, bless the Lord.
> All you waters above the heavens, bless the Lord.
>
> All you hosts of the Lord, bless the Lord.
> Sun and moon, bless the Lord.
> Stars of heaven, bless the Lord.
>
> Every shower and dew, bless the Lord.
> All you winds, bless the Lord.
> Fire and heat, bless the Lord.
> Cold and chill, bless the Lord.

This is a beautiful prayer of blessing.

Yesterday I was in an airplane, and one of the flight attendants came and sat beside me for a moment and asked me, "Will you give me a blessing?" I said a little prayer over her. This is a very beautiful, common, Hispanic custom. Many times when I meet Hispanics in New York, even on the street, they will ask me for a blessing.

We have many examples of prayers of blessing in various "sacramentals", such as the lighting of the Advent wreath, which is a form of prayer. We use a blessing prayer of sorts when we go to confession and say "Bless me, Father, for I have sinned."

The *Catechism* continues with the prayer of adoration.

> *Adoration* is the first attitude of human beings acknowledging that we are creatures before our creator. It exalts the greatness of the Lord who made us and the almighty power of the Savior who sets us free from evil [2628].

The prayer of adoration must include a sense of reverence. We must have a sense of reverence for the Christ we will receive in Holy Communion today. If we are really going to pray, we must try to concentrate when we come up here, despite all of the distractions, despite the number of people in this packed cathedral. We must try to achieve this one-to-one union with Christ. I always ask the ushers to be very gentle in directing people toward a particular priest when the lines get heavy, so that there is no pushing or sharpness. This should be a moment of great reverence, as when Almighty God called to Moses from the burning bush. When Moses was arriving, He said, "Take the shoes from off your feet, because the ground on which you stand is holy ground."

There is an Irish television personality named Eamonn Andrews. Because he is very famous, and he articulates so beautifully and is a trained speaker, the parish asked him if he would be a reader at Mass. He agreed, but he said, "You have to give me time to prepare." One Saturday a youngster came to his door and said, "Father wants you to read tomorrow." He refused. He explained why in these words:

> The word of God, as far as I am concerned, is something which is absolutely precious. It means an awful lot to me. I have made a lot of sacrifices during my life because of the convictions I have about the Gospel, and therefore I will not take the Gospel for granted.
>
> You have asked me to come along tomorrow to go out and read something I never saw before. If I were doing a television program I would spend a whole week planning and preparing it. I will not go out there just to read in front of the people without putting a lot of preparation into it; without having it explained to me. I want to know what it is about. I want to know what the people are to get out of it. I want to pray about it [*Quotes and Anecdotes for Preachers and Teachers*, Anthony P. Castle (Great Britain: Kevin Mayhew Ltd, 1979), p. A48].

That is reverence for the word of God. That is why, believe it or not, I spend so much time in preparing for these homilies. However horrible they may seem to you, think of what they would be if I did not prepare!

The next kind of prayer, we are told, is the prayer of petition.

> . . . [B]y prayer of petition we express awareness of our relationship with God. We are creatures who are not our own beginning, not the masters of adversity, not our own last end. We are sinners who as Christians know that we have turned away from our Father. Our petition is already a turning back to him [2629].

Whenever we ask God for something we are turning back to Him, because all of us have turned away from Him at one time or other, perhaps many times a day. Therefore, says the *Catechism*, very insightfully:

> The first movement of the prayer of petition is *asking forgiveness*, like the tax collector in the parable: "God, be merciful to me a sinner!" (Lk 18:13). It is a prerequisite for righteous and pure prayer. . . . Asking forgiveness is the prerequisite for both the Eucharistic liturgy and personal prayer [2631].

Whatever formula we use before the Mass, we pray for God's mercy as we are entering into this Holy Sacrifice, which is the great act of petition, the great act of adoration, the great act of praise, and the great act of thanksgiving. The Mass must begin with an expression of sorrow for our sins.

This moves us then to the prayer of intercession. Yesterday, as I walked along the street, someone said to me, "Say one for me." I hear that so often. People will stop me, not because I am anybody, but because I am a priest. They see the collar, and they will stop me and say, "Father, my wife is sick. She just learned she has cancer. Will you say a prayer for her?" Or "I have just lost my job. Will you say a prayer for me?" This is what is called prayer of intercession. It goes all the way back, as far as we know, at least to the days of Abraham. It is a very unselfish form of prayer.

We can pray for the souls in Purgatory. So often we forget that. Since the Second Vatican Council—not *because* of the Second Vatican Council—we hardly ever talk about the souls in Purgatory. The fact is that if, when we die, we still have to "balance the books" for things done wrongly in this life, we go to Purgatory, a place of purification, because, as our Lord said, "It is those of clean heart who will see God, who will get to heaven." It is a one-way street to heaven, but there is still some kind of suffering attached to it, and we can speed souls out of Purgatory with our prayers of intercession.

Next, the prayer of thanksgiving is spoken of in the *Catechism*:

> Thanksgiving characterizes the prayer of the Church which, in celebrating the Eucharist, reveals and becomes more fully what she is. . . . The thanksgiving of the members of the Body participates in that of their Head [2637].

The very word *Eucharist* means a "thanksgiving". The Eucharistic prayer is a prayer of thanksgiving. We have just celebrated the civil feast of Thanksgiving. So often we forget that that feast was established in the early days of our republic as a thanksgiving to Almighty God for delivery from religious persecution in Europe, a delivery from the elements here. It was a feast in thanksgiving for survival in this new world. Did we celebrate it in that fashion, this civil feast that we call Thanksgiving?

The *Catechism* goes on and speaks of the prayer of praise. The 150th psalm is a beautiful example of a prayer of praise. It reads:

> Praise God in his holy place,
>   praise him in his mighty heavens.
> Praise him for his powerful deeds,
>   praise his surpassing greatness.
> O, praise him with sound of trumpet,
>   praise him with lyre and harp.
> Praise him with timbrel and dance,
>   praise him with strings and pipe.
> Let everything that lives and that breathes
>   give praise to the Lord!

See why I recommend that, if it is possible for you, it is so wonderful to pray a Psalm each day? Psalms fit every mood, a mood of sorrow, a mood of joy.

St. Augustine says that he who sings prays twice. This is why we have music during the sacred liturgy. The *Catechism* says: "Praise is the form of prayer which recognizes most immediately that God is God. It [praises] God for his own sake and gives him glory, quite beyond what he does, but simply because HE IS" [2639].

The *Catechism* then goes into the tradition of prayer. It is a long tradition, as old, presumably, as the human race. This section focuses dominantly on the tradition of Christian prayer.

Yesterday my associate Monsignor McCarthy made an insightful observation. There was something on television about exercise. We were talking about how books on exercise often prove to be best-sellers. People can do exercises on television and make a fortune, with presumably many people following in their own homes. Physical exercise has become the thing of the day. That is so in large measure because we are generally a sedentary population. Monsignor McCarthy remarked, "Doesn't that suggest the need for what St. Augustine or St. Ignatius called spiritual exercises?" The muscles of our souls can get so flabby or never even be developed. To exercise is to work. The *Catechism* says: "Prayer cannot be reduced to the spontaneous outpouring of interior impulse: in order to pray one must have the will to pray" [2650].

We must say, "I am going to pray now." It takes an act of will to come to Mass. Some people can find all sorts of reasons for not going to Mass: they do not like the Mass; the Mass is too crowded, or there are not enough people there; the singing is bad; the preaching is bad. There can be all sorts of reasons for staying in bed. It takes an act of will to come to Mass. We try to make the Mass as beautiful as we can. We try to make it as prayerful as we can. But we have to remember that the first Mass was not a very pleasant experience. The first Mass was offered by Christ on the Cross. Christ was hot, sticky, covered with His own blood. People were screaming at Him. It was noisy, and soldiers were clattering dice at the foot of the Cross, gambling over who would get Christ's garment. We have to work at prayer.

The *Catechism* goes on to what are called the theological virtues: faith, hope, and charity. I recommend that you read this section in the *Catechism*. They are beautifully expressed.

> One enters into prayer as one enters into liturgy: by the narrow gate of faith [2656].

We are surely not here now because our parents force us to go to Mass.

We are here because we believe. We believe that a piece of bread will become the Body of the Son of God, a cup of wine will become His Blood. This is a tremendous act of faith.

> The Holy Spirit, who instructs us to celebrate the liturgy in expectation of Christ's return, teaches us to pray in *hope* [2657].

Following the Our Father in the Holy Sacrifice of the Mass is the very beautiful prayer: "Deliver us, Lord, from every evil and grant us peace in our day. In Your mercy keep us free from sin and protect us from all anxiety, as we wait in joyful hope for the coming of our Savior, Jesus Christ." Prayer must reflect hope.

Finally, love is the source of all prayer. The *Catechism* quotes very beautifully from the Curé of Ars, St. John Vianney:

> "I love you, O my God, and my only desire is to love you until the last breath of my life. I love you, O my infinitely lovable God, and I would rather die loving you, than live without loving you. I love you, Lord, and the only grace I ask is to love you eternally. . . . My God, if my tongue cannot say in every moment that I love you, I want my heart to repeat it to you as often as I draw breath" [2658].

The *Catechism* goes on to remind us that the heart of all prayer is Jesus Christ. *He* is what prayer is essentially all about for us who are Christians. St. Patrick wore on his breastplate: "Christ before me, Christ behind me, Christ above me, Christ beneath me, Christ all around me, Christ in the mouth of friend and stranger." That is really the meaning of prayer.

The *Catechism* goes on to speak of the Hail Mary with a great sense of love and affection. It takes the Hail Mary apart, phrase by phrase. We will turn to this section next week.

Just a few words on expressions of prayer, forms of prayer. There is, obviously, vocal prayer. We will engage in that in responses to the Mass, for instance. We have the prayer of meditation, in which we reflect on various events in the life of our Divine Lord, for instance. We may read a passage of the Gospels and then think about them. We think about Christ Himself.

Then we have this mysterious thing, the prayer of contemplation. The *Catechism* says:

> Contemplation is a *gaze* of faith, fixed on Jesus. "I look at him and he looks at me": This is what [the Curé] of Ars used to say about his prayer before the tabernacle. This focus on Jesus is a renunciation of self. His gaze purifies our heart; the light of the countenance of Jesus illumines the eyes of our heart and teaches us to see everything in the light of his truth and his compassion for all men [2715].

One writer put it, "The poet enters into life himself in order to create. The contemplative enters into God to be created." The Sisters of Life who are here today have what is called a "contemplative-active" vocation. They spend lengthy periods before the Blessed Sacrament simply contemplating the grandeur and the glory of God, of Jesus. Their activity on behalf of human life is an extension of this union with Christ, their sense of the sacredness of every human person, derived from their sense of the sacredness of Christ Himself.

A lot of people do not appreciate the meaning of contemplation. Often they see it as a wasted life. Many, many years ago I was the spiritual advisor of a young woman who was a magnificent artist and had a great professional career already under way, with a bright future ahead. She decided to enter the Carmelites and become a contemplative. Many people thought this would be a terrible waste of her talent. They blamed her. They almost cursed her. "What right do you have to waste your talent in this fashion?" Imagine! She wanted to spend her life in adoring God in contemplation.

There was a pragmatic result to this. Her superiors asked her to continue her painting and sculpturing. Some of her works are known now all over the world, even though she as the artist is unknown, which is as she wants it to be, because she is lost in contemplation of the great unknown whom we call Almighty God.

40

More on Prayer

SECOND SUNDAY OF ADVENT
DECEMBER 4, 1994
PONTIFICAL MASS

Welcome to St. Patrick's Cathedral on this joyful Second Sunday of Advent. As usual, there are so many special, distinguished individuals here that we cannot begin to acknowledge them all. Everyone here, however, is extremely distinguished in the sight of Almighty God.

Starting on the First Sunday of Advent in 1993 we launched into a weekly reflection on successive phases of the *Catechism*, chapter by chapter. The week before last we began the final section of the *Catechism*, which is on prayer. Despite the brevity of time allotted to this section, it is crucial to all of the others and gives meaning to all of the others. Today we continue in talking about prayer.

Today's Gospel says that "John went about the entire region of the Jordan proclaiming a baptism of repentance" (Lk 3:1–6). I went to my regular confessor yesterday, and he noted that while the term *repent* can be traced to other words meaning "penance", he said there is also a theory that it comes from the French *repenser*, to rethink. This reminded me that Advent is a time for rethinking our lives, asking ourselves about past or present sins. My confessor made the further point that, unless rethinking leads to conversion, then it is useless. John went about proclaiming a baptism of repentance that led to the forgiveness of sins.

The Gospel goes on to say:

> A herald's voice in the desert, crying,
> "Make ready the way of the Lord,
>   clear him a straight path.
> Every valley shall be filled
>   and every mountain and hill shall be leveled.
> The windings shall be made straight
> and the rough ways smooth" . . . (Lk 3:5–6).

Advent is a period of prayer. But our prayers are going to be heard only if we try to do what John the Baptist urged us: clean up whatever must be cleaned up; get rid of any debris in our hearts and in our souls; fill up the valleys, the emptiness; fill them up with grace; knock down any obstacles to union with God. Prayer can be a struggle because it requires repentance for sins.

You will recall there is a wonderful example in Shakespeare's *Hamlet*, reflecting both the power of prayer and the way in which prayer can be perverted. It reflects further, I think, in a very dramatic way. In Shakespeare's *Hamlet*, Claudius, Hamlet's uncle, has killed Hamlet's father and taken Hamlet's mother to be his wife and has made himself king. Hamlet is constantly looking for a way to kill the new king, Claudius. Hamlet comes upon Claudius, who is on his knees in prayer. Hamlet thinks for a moment that Claudius is helpless—"Now I can kill him with ease." But Hamlet stops just as he is drawing his sword to slay his uncle. He says,

> Now might I do it pat, now he is praying;
> And now I'll do 't: and so he goes to heaven:
> And so am I revenged . . .
> A villain kills my father; and for that,
> I, his sole son, do this same villain send
> To heaven.

That was the belief in the power of prayer that Hamlet was expressing, that no matter what sins we have committed, if we pray to Almighty God for forgiveness, should we die in that moment being sincerely sorry for our sins, wanting to get to confession without the opportunity available, we can be forgiven. That is the power of prayer of repentance, prayer asking God's forgiveness out of love.

Hamlet was reflecting a profound belief of the Church, but what he did not know was that what Claudius was saying is a reminder of what John the Baptist said in the Gospel. Claudius, on his knees, said:

> O, my offense is rank, it smells to heaven;
> It hath the primal eldest curse upon 't,
> A brother's murder. Pray can I not,
> Though inclination be as sharp as will:
> My stronger guilt defeats my strong intent.
>   . . . what form of prayer
> Can serve my turn? 'Forgive me my foul murder?'
> That cannot be, since I am still possess'd
> Of those effects for which I did the murder,
> My crown, mine own ambition, and my queen.
> May one be pardon'd and retain the offense?

He finishes this false prayer with those famous words:

My words fly up, my thoughts remain below:
Words without thoughts never to heaven go.

That is what John the Baptist is saying, in essence. Prayer is to establish, to intensify an intimate relationship with our Divine Lord. Unless we put aside those things that separate us, unless we repent of our sins, then our prayer consists of mere words.

The *Catechism* takes up this section on prayer by reminding us that:

There is no other way of Christian prayer than Christ. Whether our prayer is communal or personal, vocal or interior, it has access to the Father only if we pray "in the name" of Jesus. The sacred humanity of Jesus is therefore the way by which the Holy Spirit teaches us to pray to God our Father [2664].

That is what made the prayer of the blind man so wonderful. He just kept crying out, "Jesus, Son of David, have mercy on me." Nothing could quiet him. The crowds tried to push him aside. He wanted to get to Jesus. He raised his voice above the crowds with that simple prayer, "Jesus, Son of David, have mercy on me." Jesus hears the blind man and asks, "What would you have me do?" "Lord, that I may see." Obviously, there is much more than physical sight symbolized in the Gospel. When we pray "Lord, that I may see", we are asking: let me see myself as I am. Let me see what my relationship to You should be. Let me see You as You are. "Jesus, Son of David, have mercy on me."

The *Catechism* continues: "[T]he one name that contains everything is the one that the Son of God received in his incarnation: Jesus. . . . The name 'Jesus' contains all: God and man and the whole economy of creation and salvation" [2666].

Jesus said, "Pray always."

The invocation of the holy name of Jesus is the simplest way of praying always [2668].

The prayer of the Church venerates and honors the *heart of Jesus* just as it invokes his most holy name. It adores the incarnate Word and his Heart which, out of love for men, he allowed to be pierced by our sins. Christian prayer loves to follow the *way of the cross* in the Savior's steps. The stations from the Praetorium to Golgotha and the tomb trace the way of Jesus, who by his holy Cross has redeemed the world [2669].

The Holy Spirit, whose anointing permeates our whole being, is the interior Master of Christian prayer. He is the artisan of the living tradition of prayer. To be sure, there are as many paths of prayer as there are persons who pray, but it is the same Spirit acting in all and with all. It is in the communion of the Holy Spirit that Christian prayer is prayer in the Church [2672].

We are told in the Scriptures, "There is no other name under heaven by which we can be saved, except through the name of Jesus."

The *Catechism* makes the point: "In prayer the Holy Spirit unites us to the person of the only Son, in his glorified humanity, through which and in which our . . . prayer unites us in the Church with the Mother of Jesus" [2673].

So many people do not understand praying through Mary. We are not idolizing Mary, as though she were a goddess. We do not create statues and kneel before them, as would pagans kneeling before, let us say, a totem pole or a pagan god. We pray to Jesus through Mary. Why is this? The *Catechism* says:

> Mary gave her consent in faith at the Annunciation and maintained it without hesitation at the foot of the Cross. Ever since, her motherhood has extended to the brothers and sisters of her Son "who still journey on earth surrounded by dangers and difficulties." Jesus, the only mediator, is the way of our prayer; Mary, his mother and ours, is wholly transparent to him: she "shows the way" . . . [2674].

Remember that famous, little, sentimental poem that Archbishop Fulton Sheen used to recite so beautifully? In it he says to Mary, "God was just your little boy, and you know the way." Mary points us to Jesus.

Then the *Catechism* takes up the Hail Mary, perhaps the most beautiful and simplest of all prayers.

> *Hail Mary*: the greeting of the angel Gabriel opens this prayer. It is God himself who, through his angel as intermediary, greets Mary. Our prayer dares to take up this greeting to Mary with the regard God had for the lowliness of his humble servant and to exult in the joy he finds in her.

> *Full of grace, the Lord is with thee*. These two phrases of the angel's greeting shed light on one another. Mary is full of grace because the Lord is with her. The grace with which she is filled is the presence of him who is the source of all grace [2676].

It is kind of circular. Mary is filled with Jesus, so she is full of grace, because Jesus is the source of all grace. Mary is grace because she possesses Jesus.

The *Catechism* continues: "*Blessed art thou among women and blessed is the fruit of thy womb, Jesus*" [2676].

Mary went to visit Elizabeth, having learned that Elizabeth, advanced in age, perhaps in her sixties, is going to have a child. Mary knows, therefore, that Elizabeth would need help. We are told in the *Catechism*: " 'Filled with the Holy Spirit', Elizabeth is the first in the long succession of generations who have called Mary 'blessed' " (Lk 1:41, 48) [2676].

The *Catechism* talks about Abraham, the Father of the Jews, who came literally from nowhere, was selected by Almighty God out of a bunch of pagans. Abraham knew very, very little about the true God. But God chose Abraham. He did not know why, and we do not know why. God said to Abraham, "Have faith, and your children, and your children's children, generation after generation, will be as multitudinous as the stars in the heaven, the sands on the seashore."

The *Catechism* says:

Mary, because of her faith, became the mother of believers, through whom all nations of the earth receive him who is God's own blessing: Jesus, the "fruit of thy womb" [2676].

Holy Mary, Mother of God: With Elizabeth we marvel, "And why is this granted me, that the mother of my Lord should come to me?" (Lk 1:43) [2677].

We say "Holy Mary, Mother of God" with that same sense of wonder. Mary, you are so real! You are so near to me. You are so kind. You do anything that I ask that is for my good. "Holy Mary, Mother of God, pray for us sinners now and at the hour of our death."

The *Catechism* continues: "We give ourselves over to [Mary] now, in the Today of our lives. And our trust broadens further, already at the present moment, to surrender 'the hour of our death' wholly to her care" [2677].

Recently, it was voted by a very narrow margin in the State of Oregon that henceforth physician-assisted suicide would be legal. No one who believes that Mary is prepared to tend us at the hour of our death could vote in that fashion. It is Mary who is prepared to take any suffering we may experience and unite it with the sufferings of Christ on the Cross to give it immense power. It is Mary who is prepared to put her hand on our brow, to soothe us, to comfort us, to console us, to assure us that soon we shall see her Son face to face. That is the ultimate answer to this cheapening of human life.

The *Catechism* continues: "Medieval piety in the West developed the prayer of the rosary as a popular substitute for the Liturgy of the Hours" [2678].

There were periods in the Church, of course, when people could not read or write. That is when the Rosary was introduced. Usually, we say only one third of that: the Joyful Mysteries, the Sorrowful Mysteries, or the Glorious Mysteries. The totality of the Rosary is one hundred and fifty Hail Marys, paralleling the one hundred and fifty Psalms, reflecting the way in which the Church adapts to all ages, to all needs, to all educational backgrounds, to all languages, to the rich and to the poor.

The *Catechism* reminds us of the tremendous power of the saints, once again a teaching of the Church so little understood today. When I am going to baptize a baby, I plead with parents to give their baby the name of a saint. There are thousands of names of saints and various derivatives of these saints. For instance, the Irish "Sheila" is the derivative of the Italian "Cecilia". If people only knew the saints, only knew the way in which the saints can intercede for us, they would recognize how wonderful it is to have a saint as a patron.

My patron saint is St. John Fisher, who is the only bishop in England who refused to knuckle down to King Henry VIII and take the "supremacy oath" declaring that Henry was both pope and king in England. For this St. John Fisher was imprisoned and had his head cut off. I pray to St. John Fisher that I never be imprisoned or have my head cut off! He gives me strength and courage. It is worth reflecting on.

We are reminded in the *Catechism*:

> The *Christian family* is the first place of education in prayer. . . . For young children in particular, daily family prayer is the first witness of the Church's living memory as awakened patiently by the Holy Spirit [2685].

Kids do not always like to pray. I remember when I was a little kid and my father had the family Rosary. We had to say the Rosary on our knees. We could not even say the Rosary at the dinner table. I remember squirming and getting up off one knee and down on the other, but I learned the Rosary and the meaning of prayer. I learned the habit of prayer. It is worth thinking about.

The *Catechism* continues: "Ordained ministers [priests] are also responsible for the formation in prayer of their brothers and sisters in Christ" [2686]. No priest can give what he does not have. We cannot encourage others to pray if we do not pray ourselves.

There is a famous little scene in Albert Camus' *The Plague*, in which he talks about a lawyer in France who knew every train schedule. He knew exactly when every train would leave the station, when it would arrive at its destination, where all the crossings were. He knew everything about trains, but he never rode a train. A priest might be able to preach up a storm about prayer, but he cannot teach anybody unless he prays himself.

Many religious have consecrated their whole lives to prayer—hermits, monks, and nuns—since the times of the desert fathers, those who went into the desert to be alone with God. The interesting thing is that hundreds and hundreds of people came out from the cities to get advice and counsel from these individuals, men and women who had gone to live in caves to do nothing but pray. It reminds us of the importance of all catechetical teaching. So much of it has to do with interior prayer.

But the *Catechism* says: "The memorization of basic prayers offers an essential support to the life of prayer, but it is important to help learners savor their meaning" [2688].

It is so sad for me, when hearing confessions, to see the numbers of well-meaning people, even grown adults, who do not know the Sign of the Cross or an Act of Contrition. They do not know a Hail Mary. That is a great loss, and we have to try to correct it.

The *Catechism* talks about prayer groups. There are a lot of prayer groups today, which is a wonderful thing. Many, many people meet to pray together and support one another.

Finally, the *Catechism* talks about a "prayer corner" in homes. I go into homes in the South Bronx among the poorest of the poor, largely Hispanic. No matter how tiny their apartment or house is, many of them will have a corner with a statue of Mary or a statue of the Sacred Heart with a votive light. These are kinds of reminders that are tremendously important for youngsters growing up.

The *Catechism* reminds us:

> ... [P]rayer is a battle. Against whom? Against ourselves and against the wiles of the tempter who does all he can to turn [us] away from prayer, away from union with God. We pray as we live, because we live as we pray [2725].

The *Catechism* talks about experiencing failure in prayer, dryness, as though the prayer means nothing.

> Finally, our battle has to confront what we experience as *failure in prayer*: discouragement during periods of dryness; sadness that, because we have "great possessions," we have not given all to the Lord; disappointment over not being heard according to our own will; wounded pride, stiffened by the indignity that is ours as sinners; our resistance to the idea that prayer is a free and unmerited gift; and so forth. The conclusion is always the same: what good does it do to pray? To overcome these obstacles, we must battle to gain humility, trust, and perseverance [2728].

> The habitual difficulty in prayer is *distraction* [2729].

> Another difficulty, especially for those who sincerely want to pray, is *dryness* [2731].

Permit me to conclude by reading briefly from the autobiography of that woman who was so often thought of as the model of prayer; she is thought of in such sweet sentimental terms, St. Thérèse, the Little Flower. She is always pictured with roses, as though life were very easy, but she suffered terribly from tuberculosis. She hemorrhaged a great deal, but she also suffered a very great deal from discouragement, from spiritual dryness. St. Thérèse says:

When my heart, weary of the enveloping darkness, tries to find some rest and strength in the thought of an everlasting life to come, my anguish only increases. It seems to me that the darkness itself, borrowing the voice of the unbeliever, cries mockingly, "You dream of a land of light and fragrance, you believe that the Creator of these wonders will be yours forever, you think to escape one day from the mists in which you now languish. Hope on! Hope on! Look forward to death! It will give you, not what you hope for, but a night darker still, the night of utter nothingness!"

This description of what I suffer . . . is as far removed from reality as the painter's rough outline from the model he copies, but to write more might be to blaspheme . . . even now I may have said too much. May God forgive me! He knows how I try to live by faith, even though it affords me no consolation. I have made more acts of faith during the past year than in all the rest of my life [Dorothy Day, *Thérèse* (Springfield, Ill.: Templegate, 1960), p. 160].

If St. Thérèse, the Little Flower, had trouble praying, be of good heart. Do not give up!

The *Catechism* addresses an issue regarding prayer that is important for many people: does God hear our prayers? The *Catechism* says:

Some . . . stop praying because they think their petition is not heard. Here two questions should be asked: Why do we think our petition has not been heard? How is our prayer heard, how is it "efficacious"? [2734].

In the first place, we ought to be astonished by this fact: when we praise God or give him thanks for his benefits in general, we are not particularly concerned whether or not our prayer is acceptable to him. On the other hand, we demand to see the results of our petitions. What is the image of God that motivates our prayer: an instrument to be used? or the Father of our Lord Jesus Christ? [2735].

"You ask and do not receive, because you ask wrongly. . . ." God cannot answer us, for he desires our well-being, our life [2737].

"Do not be troubled if you do not immediately receive from God what you ask him; for he desires to do something even greater for you, while you cling to him in prayer" (Evagrius Ponticus, *De oratione* 34).

Jesus also prays for us—in our place and on our behalf. All our petitions were gathered up, once for all, in his cry on the Cross and, in his Resurrection, heard by the Father. . . . If our prayer is resolutely united with that of

Jesus, in trust and boldness as children, we obtain all that we ask in his name, even more than any particular thing: the Holy Spirit himself, who contains all gifts [2741].

The *Catechism* reminds us that the most important thing to remember is "*It is always possible to pray*" [2743].

The *Catechism* quotes St. John Chrysostom: "It is possible to offer fervent prayer even while walking in public or strolling alone, or seated in your shop, . . . while buying or selling, . . . or even while cooking" [2743].

"The Prayer of the Hour of Jesus" is the final portion of this section of the *Catechism*:

When "his hour" came, Jesus prayed to the Father. His prayer, the longest transmitted by the Gospel, embraces the whole economy of creation and salvation, as well as his death and Resurrection. The prayer of the Hour of Jesus always remains his own, just as his Passover "once for all" remains ever present in the liturgy of his Church [2746].

Christian Tradition rightly calls this prayer the "priestly" prayer of Jesus. It is the prayer of our high priest, inseparable from his sacrifice, from his passing over (Passover) to the Father to whom he is wholly "consecrated" [2747].

Jesus fulfilled the work of the Father completely; his prayer, like his sacrifice, extends until the end of time. . . . Jesus, the Son to whom the Father has given all things, has given himself wholly back to the Father . . . [2749].

By entering into the holy name of the Lord Jesus we can accept, from within, the prayer he teaches us: "Our Father!" [2750].

Our sessions on the *Catechism* will end next week with the final section on the Our Father.

41

"Lord, Teach Us to Pray"

On the Our Father

THIRD SUNDAY OF ADVENT
DECEMBER 11, 1994
PONTIFICAL MASS

Today is Gaudete Sunday. As you know, *gaudete* means "rejoice". On this Third Sunday of Advent we rejoice in a special way because Christmas is very near. Those of you who have been coming here regularly, however, rejoice, I know, for another reason. Today is the final session of our homilies on the new *Catechism of the Catholic Church*, with which I have successfully bored you for an entire year!

With us today are some of our seminarians from St. Joseph's Seminary. I mention them particularly today, with their rector, Monsignor Edwin O'Brien, because we are making very special efforts to intensify the spiritual formation of our seminarians. Some fifteen of our seminarians are spending this year in a separate house in Northampton, Pennsylvania, where they are engaged exclusively in spiritual formation. They are away from their normal studies, away from the routine of seminary life, doing nothing but trying to probe the depths of the spiritual life to find out what this Spirit St. John talks about, this Holy Spirit Who baptizes in fire, wills of them.

Beginning early in 1995, all of the priests of the Archdiocese will be participating in a year-long program of intensive spiritual renewal. Retreat after retreat will take place, directed toward this same effort—to intensify the spirituality and, therefore, to intensify the holiness of the priests of this Archdiocese. We have come to realize that no matter how academically well-formed our priests may be, no matter how intelligent, no matter how many languages they can speak, if they are not holy men, then they cannot serve you, God's people, as you deserve.

Why does the Church exist? Primarily to help us save our souls. No one can give what he does not have. We will be saved through holiness, the holiness of Christ that we share, that we live. Those who teach us, those who lead us, therefore, must be models of holiness. They must be steeped in prayer. I mention them, therefore, particularly today, because this final catechetical session on the *Catechism* is exclusively on prayer.

As a number of you know, some three years ago it was my great privilege to establish a religious institute called the Sisters of Life, whose charism is the sacredness of human life, enhancing a sense of the sacred, raising our consciousness about the sacredness of the life of the unborn, the sacredness of the life of the person dying of terminal cancer, and so on. Why do I mention the Sisters of Life? Because they are a contemplative/active community. They spend hours in prayer, and the work in which they engage is simply an extension of that prayer that gives a new dimension, a new life, to their work. This final session of the *Catechism* focuses on the prayer that we call the Lord's Prayer, obviously because it was taught by our Lord: the Our Father.

The *Catechism* tells us:

> Jesus "was praying at a certain place, and when he ceased, one of his disciples said to him, 'Lord, teach us to pray, as John taught his disciples'" (Lk 11:1). In response to this request the Lord entrusts to his disciples and to his Church the fundamental Christian prayer. St. Luke presents a brief text of five petitions, while St. Matthew gives a more developed version of seven petitions. The liturgical tradition of the Church has retained St. Matthew's text [2759].

> Very early on, liturgical usage concluded the Lord's Prayer with a doxology. In the *Didache*, we find, "For yours are the power and the glory forever." The *Apostolic Constitutions* add to the beginning: "the kingdom," and this is the formula retained to our day in ecumenical prayer. . . . The *Roman Missal* develops the last petition in the explicit perspective of "awaiting our blessed hope" and of the Second Coming of our Lord Jesus Christ (Titus 2:13). Then comes the assembly's acclamation, or the repetition of the doxology from the Apostolic Constitutions [2760].

The Our Father is in the very center of this liturgical prayer that we call the Mass.

Our Lord tells us to pray always. Tertullian, who lived in the fourth century, and St. Augustine say basically the same thing about the Our Father. Tertullian says the Lord's Prayer "is truly the summary of the whole gospel" [2761]. The *Catechism* says:

> After showing how the psalms are the principal food of Christian prayer and flow together in the petitions of the Our Father, St. Augustine concludes:
> "Run through all the words of the holy prayers [in Scripture], and I do not think that you will find anything in them that is not contained and included in the Lord's Prayer" [2762].

That is a mighty statement to make!

In his letter to the people of Philippi, which was read to us as the second reading today, St. Paul says:

Rejoice in the Lord always! I say it again. Rejoice! Everyone should see how unselfish you are. The Lord himself is near. Dismiss all anxiety from your minds. Present your needs to God in every form of prayer and in petitions full of gratitude. Then God's own peace, which is beyond all understanding, will stand guard over your hearts and minds, in Christ Jesus (Phil 4:4–7).

This is Christ Jesus' own prayer, so it is not surprising that it includes all other prayer, every form of prayer, all of the teachings of the Gospels, in a way, all of the teachings of the Church.

The *Catechism* continues:

The traditional expression "the Lord's Prayer"—*oratio Dominica*—means that the prayer to our Father is taught and given to us by the Lord Jesus. The prayer that comes to us from Jesus is truly unique: it is "of the Lord" [2765].

The first communities prayed the Lord's Prayer three times a day, in place of the "Eighteen Benedictions" customary in Jewish piety [2767].

According to the apostolic tradition, the Lord's Prayer is essentially rooted in liturgical prayer:
"[The Lord] teaches us to make prayer in common for all our [brothers and sisters]. For [Christ] did not say '*my* Father' who art in heaven, but '*our*' Father, offering petitions for the Common Body" [2768].

This last passage is a quotation from St. John Chrysostom, the great preacher of the early centuries of the Church. What a wonderful reminder! Every time we pray the Our Father, even though we are alone, even though we may be praying the Rosary, for example, and certainly here in the Holy Sacrifice of the Mass, we do not simply say "my Father", we say "our Father". We ask the petitions for "*us*", not just for "*me*". It is the common prayer of the Church.

In all the liturgical traditions, the Lord's Prayer is an integral part of the major hours of the Divine Office [prayed each day by priests, deacons, religious, and many laypersons]. In the three sacraments of Christian initiation [Baptism, Communion, and Confirmation] the ecclesial character of the Our Father is especially evident [2768].

In the *Eucharistic liturgy* [in the Mass] the Lord's Prayer appears as the prayer of the whole Church and there reveals its full meaning and efficacy [2770].

The *Catechism* presents the Our Father petition by petition, beginning with "Our Father who art in heaven". It makes a wonderful point that we dare to call God "our Father". We are so accustomed to that that we perhaps think nothing of it. But speaking of God as "our Father" was not true for all of those centuries before Christ; it came only with Christ.

When Moses was called by Almighty God, he was told, "Take the shoes from off your feet, for the ground on which you stand is holy ground." Then God gave Moses the mandate to deliver His people from slavery to the Egyptians. Moses asked Him, very understandably, "Who shall I say sent me? I am nobody. I am a shepherd. Who is going to believe me?" God simply said, "I AM WHO AM. Tell them HE WHO IS sent you." It was only through Jesus that we began to think of God as "our Father".

There are so many arguments about whether God is father or mother. They are unfortunate and divisive but certainly understandable arguments. In God, of course, there are feminine and masculine characteristics, as we label these categories. But God is a profound mystery. When Christ referred to God, He referred to Him as "our Father". If He had referred to Him as "our mother", they are the words we would be using. It is sufficient to know that God is undefinable in human terms, but that Christ called Him "our Father", and Christ is His Son.

The *Catechism* says:

> Before we make our own this first exclamation of the Lord's Prayer, we must humbly cleanse our hearts of certain false images drawn "from this world." *Humility* makes us recognize that "no one knows the Son except the Father, and no one knows the Father except the Son and anyone to whom the Son chooses to reveal him," that is, "to little children" (Mt 11:25–27). The *purification* of our hearts has to do with paternal or maternal images, stemming from our personal and cultural history, and influencing our relationship with God. God our Father transcends the categories of the created world [2779].

> We can invoke God as "Father" because *he is revealed to us* by his Son become man and because his Spirit makes him known to us [2780].

> When we pray to the Father, we are *in communion with him* and with his Son, Jesus Christ [2781].

> Praying to our Father should develop in us two fundamental dispositions:
> First, *the desire to become like him*; though created in his image, we are restored to his likeness by grace; and we must respond to this grace [2784].
> Second, *a humble and trusting heart* that enables us "to turn and become like children" (Mt 18:3): for it is to "little children" that the Father is revealed [2785].

> "Our" Father refers to God. The adjective, as used by us, does not express possession, but an entirely new relationship with God [2786].

[I]f we pray the Our Father sincerely, we leave individualism behind, because the love that we receive frees us from it. The "our" at the beginning of the Lord's Prayer, like the "us" of the last four petitions, excludes no one. If we are to say it truthfully, our divisions and oppositions have to be overcome [2792].

That is not only divisions and oppositions within families, among friends, between friends and enemies, but divisions throughout the world. St. Paul says, "In Christ there is no East or West, there is no Greek, there is no Jew." Everyone has God as his Father, so we can truly say "our Father" and include the entire world.

The *Catechism* explores the meaning of the words "Who art in heaven":

This biblical expression does not mean a place ("space"), but a way of being; it does not mean that God is distant, but majestic [2794].

When the Church prays "our Father who art in heaven," she is professing that we are the People of God, already seated "with him in the heavenly places in Christ Jesus" and "hidden with Christ in God" (Eph 2:6); yet at the same time, "here indeed we groan, and long to put on our heavenly dwelling" [2796].

The *Catechism* then takes up each of the petitions:

After we have placed ourselves in the presence of God our Father . . . the Spirit . . . stirs up in our hearts seven petitions, seven blessings [2803].

The first series of petitions carries us toward him, for his own sake: *thy* name, *thy* kingdom, *thy* will [be done]! It is characteristic of love to think first of the one whom we love. In none of the three petitions do we mention ourselves [2804].

This is the kind of love that a couple may have toward each other. In those marriages that are very good and very solid, they are good and solid in large measure because each thinks of the other first. Those of you who are widows and widowers, I am sure that you still think of the husbands and wives who have died. If you are lonely, it is because you have lost the one that you love, the one who came first in your lives.

The *Catechism* continues:

The second series of petitions unfolds . . . as an offering up of our expectations, that draws down upon itself the eyes of the Father of mercies. They go up from us and concern us from this very moment, in our present world: "give *us* . . . [this day our daily bread]; forgive *us* . . . [our trespasses]; lead *us* not [into temptation]; deliver *us* . . . [from all evil] . . ." [2805].

These petitions are centered on us, but we are asking God's mercy.

The *Catechism* moves to "hallowed be thy name". It says:

The term "to hallow" is to be understood here not primarily in its causative sense (only God hallows, makes holy), but above all in an evaluative sense: to recognize as holy, to treat in a holy way. . . . Beginning with this first petition to our Father, we are immersed in the innermost mystery of his Godhead and the drama of the salvation of our humanity. Asking the Father that his name be made holy draws us into his plan of loving kindness for the fullness of time, "according to his purpose which he set forth in Christ," that we might "be holy and blameless before him in love" (Eph 1:9, 4) [2807].

The holiness of God [the hallowness, if you will] is the inaccessible center of his eternal mystery. What is revealed of it in creation and history, Scripture calls "glory," the radiance of his majesty. In making us in his image and likeness, God "crowned [us] with glory and honor," but by sinning [we] fell "short of the glory of God" (Ps 8:5). From that time on, God was to manifest his holiness by revealing and giving his name, in order to restore [us] to the image of [the] Creator (Col 3:10) [2809].

In the promise to Abraham, and the oath that accompanied it, God commits himself but without disclosing his name. He begins to reveal it to Moses and makes it known clearly before the eyes of the whole people when he saves them from the Egyptians: "he has triumphed gloriously" (Ex 15:1). From the covenant of Sinai onwards, this people is "his own" and it is to be a "holy (or "consecrated" . . .) nation," because the name of God dwells in it [2810].

In spite of the holy Law that again and again their Holy God gives them—"You shall be holy, for I the LORD your God am holy"—and although the Lord shows patience for the sake of his name, the people turn away from the Holy One of Israel and profane his name among the nations (Ezek 20:9) . . . [2811].

I do not know about you, but I must confess that when I pray the Our Father I so often pray it so glibly; it just kind of rolls off my lips. What a difference it makes when you think in these terms that the *Catechism* raises. When we say "hallowed be thy name", we are going right at the center of the mystery of who is God.

With Moses, as I mentioned earlier, God simply defined Himself as "HE WHO IS". But when Christ came, we are told:

Finally, in Jesus the name of the Holy God is revealed and given to us, in the flesh, as Savior, revealed by what he is, by his word, and by his sacrifice. . . . At the end of Christ's Passover, the Father gives him the name that is above all names: "Jesus Christ is Lord, to the glory of God the Father" (Phil 2:9–11) [2812].

I do not know how many of you may have heard Kathleen Battle last night on public television, singing beautiful Christmas melodies. She sang about the name of Jesus. Some call Him this, some call Him that, but

His name is Jesus, His name is Emmanuel. She sang it with such reverence. It was, again, a great reminder. We are told there is no other name under heaven by which we may be saved, except by the name Jesus. Jesus is God, and Jesus calls God His Father. He is the second Person of the Blessed Trinity.

The *Catechism* says:

> This petition [hallowed be thy name] embodies all the others. Like the six petitions that follow, it is fulfilled by *the prayer of Christ*. Prayer to our Father is our prayer, if it is prayed *in the name* of Jesus. In his priestly prayer, Jesus asks: "Holy Father, protect in your name those whom you have given me" (Jn 17:11) [2815].

Why are we all sons and daughters of God our Father? Because Christ made us His brothers and sisters, so we are adopted as children of God. Then we say, "thy kingdom come".

> The Kingdom of God lies ahead of us. It is brought near in the Word incarnate, it is proclaimed throughout the whole Gospel, and it has come in Christ's death and Resurrection [2816].

> In the Lord's Prayer, "thy kingdom come" refers primarily to the final coming of the reign of God through Christ's return. But, far from distracting the Church from her mission in this present world, this desire commits her to it all the more strongly [2818].

> "The kingdom of God [is] righteousness and peace and joy in the Holy Spirit" (Rom 14:17) [2819].

> By a discernment according to the Spirit, Christians have to distinguish between the growth of the Reign of God and the progress of the culture and society in which they are involved. This distinction is not a separation. Man's vocation to eternal life does not suppress, but actually reinforces, his duty to put into action in this world the energies and means received from the Creator to serve justice and peace [2820].

The *Catechism* continues: "thy will be done on earth as it is in heaven". What is God's will?

> Our Father "desires all men to be saved and to come to the knowledge of the truth" (1 Tim 2:3–4). . . . His commandment is "that you love one another; even as I have loved you . . ." (Jn 13:34). This commandment summarizes all the others, and expresses his entire will [2822].

> In Christ, and through his human will, the will of the Father has been perfectly fulfilled once for all. Jesus said on entering into this world: "Lo, I have come to do your will, O God" (Heb 10:7) [2824].

We ask our Father to unite our will to his Son's, in order to fulfill his will, his plan of salvation for the life of the world. We are radically incapable of this, but united with Jesus and with the power of his Holy Spirit, we can surrender our will to him and decide to choose what his Son has always chosen: to do what is pleasing to the Father [2825].

When we pray the Our Father, we say "Thy will be done." That is running a big risk. Do we really want God's will to be done in our lives? Are we sincere, are we honest about that, or are we focused always on our own will? I know how difficult it is for me. It is usually what *I* want, what *I* will. I should be asking, what does God will for me, for those I try to serve?

The *Catechism* says:

> By prayer we can discern "what is the will of God" and obtain the endurance to do it (Rom 12:2). Jesus teaches us that one enters the kingdom of heaven not by speaking words, but by doing "the will of my Father in heaven" (Mt 7:21) [2826].

That is what our seminarians are trying to do. Monsignor O'Brien is giving them a series of talks on what we call "pastoral theology" that are really about the spirituality of being a whole person, of becoming a priest, of carrying out the will of God.

Our Lord says, "Not everyone who cries out to Me 'Lord, Lord', will enter the kingdom of heaven, but those who do the will of My Father in heaven, they will enter the kingdom of heaven" (Mt 7:21).

The next section of the *Catechism* explores the petition: "give us this day our daily bread". It says:

> "Give us": The trust of children who look to their Father for everything is beautiful. . . . Jesus teaches us this petition, because it glorifies our Father by acknowledging how good he is, beyond all goodness [2828].

When the widow of Naim, represented by these widows and widowers here, was mourning over the death of her only son, Christ came and said, "Do not weep." And Christ raised her son from the dead. In saying "Give us this day our daily bread", we ask for whatever it is that we need. The *Catechism* continues:

> "*Our bread*": The Father who gives us life cannot but give us the nourishment life requires—all appropriate goods and blessings, both material and spiritual.
> "To those who seek the kingdom of God and his righteousness, he has promised to give all else besides. Since everything indeed belongs to God, he who possesses God wants for nothing, if he himself is not found wanting before God" [2830].

But the presence of those who hunger because they lack bread opens up another profound meaning of this petition. The drama of hunger in the world calls Christians who pray sincerely to exercise responsibility toward their brethren, both in their personal behavior and in their solidarity with the human family. This petition of the Lord's Prayer cannot be isolated from the parables of the poor man Lazarus and of the Last Judgment [2831].

"Our" bread is the "one" loaf for the "many." In the Beatitudes "poverty" is the virtue of sharing: it calls us to communicate and share both material and spiritual goods, not by coercion but out of love, so that the abundance of some may remedy the needs of others [2833].

When we pray for bread and nourishment for ourselves, that is, for the material elements of this world, we must be prepared to share this bread with others. But then the *Catechism* makes an important point. It says:

This petition, with the responsibility it involves, also applies to another hunger from which [we] are perishing: "Man does not live by bread alone, but . . . by every word that proceeds from the mouth of God" (Dt 8:3), that is, by the Word he speaks and the Spirit he breathes forth. Christians must make every effort to "to proclaim the good news to the poor." There is a famine on earth, "not a famine of bread, nor a thirst for water, but of hearing the words of the LORD" (Amos 8:11). For this reason the specifically Christian sense of this fourth petition concerns the Bread of Life: The Word of God accepted in faith, the Body of Christ received in the Eucharist [2835].

The social gospel is absolutely imperative; it is indispensable for true Christianity. We must feed the hungry, and house the homeless, and clothe the naked, and do everything we can for everyone. But there came a point in recent years at which it seemed the entire emphasis was on the social gospel. What you did was one thing, what you believed was another. But we have to accept the totality of Christ's message. The Church came, of course, to teach us the works of mercy but primarily to *save our souls*.

"Give us this day our daily bread." The *Catechism* reminds us that the word "daily" is not used anywhere else in the New Testament but here. St. Augustine says: "The Eucharist is our daily bread. . . . This also is our daily bread: the readings you hear each day in church and the hymns you hear and sing. All these are necessities for our pilgrimage" [2837].

The *Catechism* moves on with the passage: "forgive us our trespasses, as we forgive those who trespass against us."

Our petition looks to the future, but our response must come first, for the two parts are joined by the single word "as" [2838].

This is tremendously important. For this we need the sacraments. For this we need the grace particularly of the sacrament of Penance. This is what is supposed to be the case when we receive Holy Communion. St. Peter Chrysologus said:

> "The Father in heaven urges us, as children of heaven, to ask for the bread of heaven. [Christ] Himself is the bread who, sown in the Virgin, raised up in the flesh, kneaded in the Passion, naked in the oven of the tomb, reserved in churches, brought to altars, furnishes the faithful each day with food from heaven" [2837].

Most of us will receive that food from this altar, Christ Himself. We have to have forgiveness in our hearts—forgiveness for everyone. It is not simply a matter of luxury. By implication we are told our sins will be forgiven to the degree that we forgive those who trespass against us. You recall that on the Cross Christ used those beautiful words, "Father, forgive them for they know not what they do" (Lk 23:34). Stephen, the first martyr, as he was being stoned to death, used the same words, "Father, forgive them, for they know not what they do." We must forgive as we hope to be forgiven.

"And lead us not into temptation" is the next petition discussed. The *Catechism* says:

> The petition goes to the root of the preceding one, for our sins result from our consenting to temptation; we therefore ask our Father not to "lead" us into temptation. It is difficult to translate the Greek verb used by a single English word: the Greek means both "do not allow us to enter into temptation," and "do not let us yield to temptation." . . . We are engaged in the battle "between flesh and spirit"; this petition implores the Spirit of discernment and strength [2846].
>
> We must . . . discern between being tempted, and consenting to temptation [2847].
>
> "Lead us not into temptation" implies a *decision of the heart*: "For where your treasure is, there will your heart be also. . . . No one can serve two masters" (Mt 6:21, 24) [2848].

Some of us forget to distinguish between temptation and sin. Some of us get very scrupulous. If you fall in a mud puddle by accident, you get wet and covered with mud. But that is very different from running along and jumping into a mud puddle and getting covered with mud. The effect is the same. This is the difference between temptation and sin. You can have all sorts of temptations in your mind and in your heart. They may make you feel dirty. But that is a lot different from deliberately reaching out to sin. We must make that distinction.

We ask God to *"lead us not into temptation and to deliver us from all evil."* The *Catechism* makes very clear that evil is a person in the world. We get ridiculed for saying this. We get ridiculed for talking about the devil, about Satan, prowling the world seeking whom he will devour. We get ridiculed for believing there is a hell. The *Catechism* reminds us this is a basic teaching of the Church and that we must be on our guard constantly.

The *Catechism* includes in this section the text from the Roman Missal prayed in the Mass after the Our Father:

"Deliver us, Lord, we beseech you, from every evil and grant us peace in our day, so that aided by your mercy we might be ever free from sin and protected from all anxiety, as we await the blessed hope and the coming of our Savior, Jesus Christ" [2854].

The *Catechism* ends this chapter on the Our Father with the "Final Doxology":

The final doxology, "For the kingdom, the power and the glory are yours, now and forever," takes up again, by inclusion, the first three petitions to our Father: the glorification of his name, the coming of his reign, and the power of his saving will [2855].

"Then, after the prayer is over you say 'Amen,' which means 'So be it,' thus ratifying with our 'Amen' what is contained in the prayer that God has taught us" [2856].

Thus we end our one-year series of homilies on the new *Catechism*. In recent months I have commented more than quoting the text, because the *Catechism* has been published in English. It would be most unfortunate if anyone who has been here for this series contented himself with my poor stumbling words when you can read it for yourself in its freshness, in its fullness. I would urge you to do that. You will find that my humble commentaries have not begun to do it justice, and I do not say that out of false humility.

Nonetheless, I hope that, during this year that began on the First Sunday of Advent in 1993, your appetite has been whetted for the *Catechism* itself. I hope I have not done any harm in that sense. I hope that all of you will be encouraged now to read the *Catechism* for yourselves. If nothing else should come out of this entire year-long series except that you will procure and at least leaf through a *Catechism*, that would be a wonderful outcome indeed. If, in addition to this, a single soul has come just a little bit closer to Jesus in Whom we live, and move and have our being, then, indeed, I will be infinitely grateful. Other than that, I can only thank you for your patience, those of you who have come here Sunday after Sunday. I have marveled at your patience and your kindness, and for this, too, I am deeply grateful.

CONCORDANCE
TO THE *CATECHISM*
OF THE CATHOLIC CHURCH

This list is provided for readers who might wish to read the relevant sections of the
Catechism *along with the chapters in this book.*

CHAPTER	CCC NUMBERS
1	1–25
2	26–73
3	74–141
4	142–184
5	185–267
6	268–324
7	325–421
8	422–511
9	2197–2257
10	512–570
11	571–623
12	624–682
13	683–747
14	748–870
15	871–975
16	976–1065
17	1066–1209
18	1210–1284
19	1322–1419
20	1420–1535
21	1536–1600
22	1601–1666
23	1877–1948
24	1691–1802
25	1803–1845
26	1285–1321
27	1846–1986